# UNDERSTANDING THE BIBLE AS A SCRIPTURE IN HISTORY, CULTURE, AND RELIGION

# UNDERSTANDING THE BIBLE AS A SCRIPTURE IN HISTORY, CULTURE, AND RELIGION

James W. Watts

**WILEY** Blackwell

This edition first published 2021




The right of James W. Watts to be identified as the author of this work has been asserted in accordance with law.

*Registered Offices*
John Wiley & Sons, Inc., 111 River Street, Hoboken, NJ 07030, USA
John Wiley & Sons Ltd, The Atrium, Southern Gate, Chichester, West Sussex, PO19 8SQ, UK

*Editorial Office*
The Atrium, Southern Gate, Chichester, West Sussex, PO19 8SQ, UK

For details of our global editorial offices, customer services, and more information about Wiley products visit us at www.wiley.com.

Wiley also publishes its books in a variety of electronic formats and by print-on-demand. Some content that appears in standard print versions of this book may not be available in other formats.



*Library of Congress Cataloging-in-Publication Data*
Names: Watts, James W. (James Washington), 1960– author.
Title: Understanding the Bible as a scripture in history, culture, and
  religion / by James W. Watts.
Description: [Hoboken, New Jersey]: Wiley-Blackwell, [2021] | Includes
  bibliographical references and index.
Identifiers: LCCN 2020025374 (print) | LCCN 2020025375 (ebook) | ISBN
  9781119730378 (paperback) | ISBN 9781119730385 (adobe pdf) | ISBN
  9781119730354 (epub)
Subjects: LCSH: Bible–Use. | Bible–Comparative studies. |
  Bible–Socio-rhetorical criticism. | Bible–Study and teaching.
Classification: LCC BS538.3 .W38 2021 (print) | LCC BS538.3 (ebook) | DDC
  220.1–dc23
LC record available at https://lccn.loc.gov/2020025374
LC ebook record available at https://lccn.loc.gov/2020025375

Cover Design: Wiley
Cover Images: Crucifix (1997) by Juvenal Kaliki and Jeffrey Brosk in the Mother of Africa Chapel, Roman Catholic National Shrine, Washington, DC., Full-size reproduction of the Tabernacle in Timna Park, Israel, 2014, Photo by J. W. Watts, Samaritan Torah Scroll, photo by Zeer Elitzur 2007, used by permission, Incipit of Luke's Gospel in a Byzantine Lectionary, ca. 1100 CE, Metropolitan Museum of Art, New York (CCO), Saint Catherine of Alexandria, wooden figurine, 15th century, Germany, Metropolitan Museum of Art, New York (CCO), Book of Psalms © MCCAIG/E+/Getty Images

Set in 10.5/13pt STIXTwoText by SPi Global, Pondicherry, India

10  9  8  7  6  5  4  3  2  1

# Contents

# List of Boxes

# List of Figures

# Preface

Biblical studies is an ancient and flourishing field. Scholars put great effort into explaining the language, meaning, and history of biblical books down to their tiniest detail. They have done so for more than 2000 years and continue to do so today. The published literature on the Bible is vast, and keeps growing.

Yet little of this research focuses on how the Bible functions as a scripture. Biblical scholarship remains focused on *interpretation*, that is, on how people have understood the meaning of the Bible's words and utilized them in various ways. Much less research focuses on how people express those words in religious and secular contexts, and even less on how they make use of the physical books of Jewish and Christian scriptures: Torah scrolls, tanaks, gospels, and bibles.[1]

I think biblical scholars should give more attention to the Bible's function as Jewish and Christian scripture, because that is what attracts people's attention in the first place. Were it not for the Bible's contemporary prestige and influence, the field of biblical studies would be a minor part of the study of ancient Middle Eastern literature rather than a subject of popular and scholarly interest around the world.

Comparing the Bible's scriptural function with the scriptures of other religions reveals similar strategies for using sacred texts across cultures, even when the literary contents and theological meaning of the books differ dramatically. This book therefore positions biblical studies within research on religions generally, rather than just within the study of Judaism and Christianity.[2] It illustrates the insights that come from studying the Bible as a scripture in comparison with other religious scriptures, such as the Qur'an, the Vedas, the Bhagavad Gita, the Buddhist sutras, and the Sikhs' Guru Granth Sahib.

This book takes a comparative approach to show that the Bible functions culturally and socially in many ways like scriptures in other religious traditions. I do not discount the importance of theological interpretation of the Bible for Jewish and Christian audiences.[3] I simply think that a comparative analysis allows us to understand its influence and function in ways that theological interpretation does not.

This book also demonstrates how research on the Bible's scriptural function can integrate studies of its origins with its cultural history. The results illuminate its contemporary interpretation and ritual function in the academy, in synagogues, in churches, and in the wider culture, as well as its origins in ancient Israel and early Christianity.

This book's innovative approach to teaching about the Bible therefore presents an unusual sequence of topics for an introduction to biblical studies. It introduces readers to the contents of the Bible and also to its material forms and uses. It summarizes the history of liturgical recitations and manipulations of the Bible, as well as the history of its interpretation.

This book is organized around those parts of the Bible that have played the most central roles in the rituals, liturgies, art, and interpretations of Jewish and Christian congregations, namely, the Torah, the Gospels, and the modern pandect Bible. The fact that the nouns, "Torah" and "Gospel," and the adjective, "biblical," still get used not only for books, but also to describe a faithful way of life, points to the centrality of these scriptures in Jewish and Christian religious experience.

My discussion of the iconic, expressive, and semantic dimensions of the Torah and the Gospels starts with their use since becoming scripture before addressing questions about their origins in ancient Israel and in ancient Christianity. This sequence grounds discussion of the Bible's different dimensions in better attested periods of its history. It has the pedagogical advantage of showing readers how congregations have socialized people to focus on the original meaning of the Bible's text, before turning to discussions of those origins.

The arrangement – Torah, Gospels, Bible – includes other biblical literature as well, so this book introduces the entirety of the Jewish and Christian canons. Like the religious traditions but unlike most other surveys of biblical literature, this book describes other biblical literature within the ritual and interpretive contexts of the Torah and the Gospels. So I also discuss the historical (Sections 2.2 and 3.3), prophetic (Sections 5.4 and 6.4.2), wisdom (Sections 6.1, and 6.4.4), and poetic literature (Sections 5.3 and 6.4.3) of the Hebrew Bible and Apocrypha. I survey apocalyptic literature in the context of earlier and later religious projections of the future (Section 6.3), and I also include a brief introduction to Rabbinic Judaism (Section 6.5.2).

The Torah Part is therefore the longest in the book because it includes the entire Hebrew Bible and surveys the history of ancient Israel. Many of these topics are necessary background for the discussion of early Christianity in the next Part as well. Part 2 on the Gospels begins by summarizing the story of Jesus and introduces Paul's letters (Section 7.2) before turning to the rhetoric and ritualization of the Gospels themselves. It includes a brief history of Christian doctrines of the atonement (Section 11.1), and introduces the non-canonical gospels about Jesus (Section 11.2). This book lists the different contents of various biblical canons near the beginning (Section 1.3) and closes with a discussion of canonization and scripturalization.

The arrangement – Torah, Gospels, Bible – also has the pedagogical advantage of saving discussion of many of the Bible's "hot-button" issues to the end. Only after readers have been exposed to the scope of the Bible's contents and its cultural history do they reach modern debates over creation and evolution around Genesis 1–2, race and gender around Genesis 3 and 9, and the influence of biblical law (Chapter 14).

Further discussion of this distinctive approach to teaching biblical studies can be found in my other textbook, *Understanding the Pentateuch as a Scripture*.[4] Both books introduce innovative ways of thinking about biblical literature as well as surveying established conclusions in the field. That combination might seem strange for introductory textbooks. In the field of biblical studies, however, an "introduction" has long served to provide a critical evaluation of the state of the field. It shows how biblical studies should go forward as well as summarizing where the field has been. This book follows in that tradition by demonstrating how the study of the Bible can be re-envisioned from a religious studies perspective on comparative scriptures. It demonstrates that research on the Bible's scriptural function can integrate investigations of its origins with its cultural history and ritual use up to the present day.

I hope this book will be read with interest by people in many different settings. It has, however, been organized with classroom instruction in mind, as a textbook in courses about Jewish and Christian scriptures. I have included many images and quotations of ancient texts for illustration. Key names, phrases, and technical terms are <u>underlined</u> where they are defined or described. Quotations from ancient texts appear in *italics* to distinguish them from modern commentary. A list of abbreviations for the names of biblical books appears on pp. 21-22. Text boxes define key ideas and give examples referred to in the immediate context. The Table of Contents therefore provides detailed lists of boxes and figures as well as chapter subheadings to aid in constructing a course syllabus. A sample syllabus can be found at https://surface.syr.edu/rel/106/.

The literature on the Bible that this book presupposes is vast. The endnotes cite sources of direct quotations. I have also included references in the endnotes to a very small number of English-language publications where instructors can find more detailed discussions of particular issues and fuller bibliographies. Some of these texts could serve as further reading assignments to supplement the summaries in this book.

## CITED WORKS AND FURTHER READING

1 In this book, the terms Torah, Tanak, Gospels, and Bible are capitalized when they are used as titles of specific collections of scriptures or to refer to the idealized ideas of scripture in Jewish and Christian communities. Plural nouns that refer to physical books are lower case – torahs, tanaks, gospels, bibles – because they refer to multiple manifestations of scriptures and, in the case of gospels and bibles, may refer to several different collections (see Box 1.4, Sections 10.1, 10.7, 14.2.7, 14.2.8).

2 This approach was advocated years ago by Wilfred Cantwell Smith, "The Study of Religion and the Study of the Bible," *Journal of the American Academy of Religion* 39 (1971): 131–140, reprinted in *Rethinking Scripture: Essays from a Comparative Perspective* (ed. Miriam Levering, Albany, NY: SUNY Press, 1989), 18–28. See also his essay, "Scripture as Form and Concept: Their Emergence for the Western World," in *Rethinking Scripture*, 29–57; and William A. Graham, *Beyond the Written Word: Oral Aspects of Scripture in the History of Religion* (Cambridge: Cambridge University Press, 1987).

3 As exemplified, for example, by the canonical approach of Brevard S. Childs. See his *Introduction to the Old Testament as Scripture* (Minneapolis: Fortress, 1979); and *The New Testament as Canon: An Introduction* (Minneapolis: Fortress, 1984).

4 For my discussion contextualizing this approach within broader trends in biblical studies, see James W. Watts, *Understanding the Pentateuch as a Scripture* (Oxford: Wiley Blackwell, 2017), xvii–xx.

# Acknowledgments

Many people have generously supported my work on this book and the research projects that contribute to it. I am very grateful to all those scholars who have joined me in the Iconic Books Project and in the Society for Comparative Research on Iconic and Performative Texts (SCRIPT). My colleagues in the Department of Religion at Syracuse University have been generous with their support. The College of Arts and Sciences of Syracuse University contributed materially to bringing this project about, as did the Käte Hamburger Kolleg in the Center for Religious Studies at Ruhr University Bochum, which granted me a fellowship for the 2015–2016 academic year.

I am most grateful to the Syracuse University students who took my course, REL/JSP 114 The Bible in History, Culture, and Religion, from 2016 to 2020. They read this textbook, notified me of errors, and gently suggested ways in which it could be improved. This book is much better because of their efforts, which I appreciate very much. Four reviewers for Wiley Blackwell also made helpful suggestions that have improved the final product. I am grateful to them, and its remaining flaws are my responsibility alone.

This book culminates and summarizes much of my previous research on iconic books, comparative scriptures, and the Bible. It therefore includes many ideas and arguments that I have published previously in articles and books. References to those works appear where appropriate in the list of "Cited Works and Further Readings" at the end of each chapter. Many paragraphs of this book have been reproduced from my other textbook, *Understanding the Pentateuch as a Scripture*.

English quotations of biblical verses are my own translations unless labelled NRSV (New Revised Standard Version) or CEB (Common English Bible). Photographs are my own unless otherwise noted.

# CHAPTER 1

# Scripture and Ritual

Scholars of religions struggle to define the word <u>scripture</u>. Religious communities tend to describe their scriptures as holy or sacred, as inspired by God, and as authoritative for their beliefs and practices. They also tend to describe their own scriptures as unique, unlike any other books or texts on earth. Religious communities therefore often resist classifying their sacred texts as belonging to the same category as the scriptures of other religions.

Those who study multiple religions notice, however, that many traditions venerate some texts as sacred and distinguish them from all other texts. Scholars of religion have therefore filled the category <u>scripture</u> with books from many religions. They often distinguish "book religions" from traditions that do not venerate sacred texts. Already in the Middle Ages, Muslim theologians described Judaism, Christianity, and Islam as "religions of the book." In the nineteenth century, Oxford University Press published 50 volumes of English translations of *The Sacred Books of the East.* The editor, Max Müller, wanted to expose Westerners to the scriptures of Hinduism, Buddhism, Islam, Zoroastrianism, Taoism, and Confucianism. Now textbook anthologies, such as Robert Van Voorst's *Anthology of World Scriptures*, make excerpts available from the scriptures of all these religions.

However, reading these various scriptures together shows that their contents have little in common. They contain stories, laws, oracles, moral

*Understanding the Bible as a Scripture in History, Culture, and Religion*, First Edition. James W. Watts.
© 2021 John Wiley & Sons Ltd. Published 2021 by John Wiley & Sons Ltd.

## Box 1.1  The nature of scriptures

William Graham observed: "A text becomes 'scripture' in living, subjective relationship to persons and to historical tradition. No text, written, oral, or both, is sacred or authoritative in isolation from a community. A text is only 'scripture' insofar as a group of persons perceives it to be sacred or holy, powerful and meaningful, possessed of an exalted authority, and in some fashion transcendent of, and hence distinct from, other speech and writing. . . . The 'scriptural' characteristics of a text belong not to the text itself but to its role in a community. 'Scripture' is not a literary genre but a religio-historical one."

principles, philosophical speculation, practical advice, prayers, hymns, spells, and much more. No one genre of literature describes them all. <u>Scripture</u>, then, is not a literary category. Instead, what these texts have in common is that religious communities venerate them (Box 1.1).[1]

Veneration of scriptures takes the form of public and private rituals of various kinds. <u>Rituals</u> draw people's attention to specific practices and ideas. They focus attention on the ritual activity itself in order to make participants more aware of their own relationship to what it represents. Studies of ritual (see Box 1.2) have revealed the central role that rituals play in human societies at every level.

Rituals, however, have a bad reputation. People associate ritual with unreality, with superstition, and with magic, which they contrast with rational, practical, and effective actions. Though this attitude feels modern, it is actually rooted in ancient religious polemics. Christians contrasted "empty rituals" and superstition with knowledge and "true faith." Protestants used the term "ritual" to attack Catholic ceremonies during the Reformation, medieval Christians used it to disparage Jews, and ancient Christians used it to criticize and suppress pagan sacrifices.

In contrast to the reputation of rituals, scriptures have been venerated as containers of knowledge and truth. Reading has been cast as the opposite of ritualizing. It can therefore sound very odd to hear reading and writing described as rituals in some circumstances. The concept of ritualized books is so strange that scholars have done little research on this phenomenon, in contrast to the massive amount of scholarship on the interpretation of books and religions.

Nevertheless, the display, reading, and interpretation of scriptures play obvious roles in the worship services – the rituals – of Jews and Christians, as well as of Muslims, Sikhs, Buddhists, Hindus, Jains, and many other religious groups. In fact, <u>ritualizing scriptures</u> clearly encourages people to

## Box 1.2   Ritual theories

Throughout the twentieth century, many anthropologists and scholars of religion have studied rituals and how they work. They have increasingly focused not on distinguishing rituals from non-rituals, which can be hard to do, but rather on the activity of performing rituals or ritualizing, which can take place at almost any time and place.

"Ritualization is a way of acting that specifically establishes a privileged contrast, differentiating itself as more important or powerful." (Catherine Bell)

Ritualizing requires participants and audience to pay attention to what is being done, how it is being done, and who is doing it. Ritualizing involves doing ordinary activities, such as eating, entering a room, or reading a book, in a formal and regulated way.

"Ritual relies for its power on the fact that it is concerned with quite ordinary activities placed within an extraordinary setting, that what it describes and displays is, in principle, possible for every occurrence of these acts." (Jonathan Z. Smith)

By performing rituals and witnessing them, people identify themselves with the values represented in the rituals.

"By performing a [ritual] the participants accept, and indicate to themselves and to others that they accept whatever is encoded in the canon of that order." (Roy Rappaport)

So rituals identify (index) participants with the institutions and traditions that promote and perform those rituals.[2]

believe that these books are authoritative and inspired texts that establish the truth and legitimacy of the religious tradition. By setting aside the polemical history of debates over ritual, we can better understand how ritualizing books promotes religious ideas and practices, and secular ones too.

Rituals make participants pay attention to people, objects, and actions that they otherwise take for granted. Ritualized meals, for example, draw attention to the food itself, how it is prepared, and what it means: the unleavened bread of a Passover seder, the bread and wine of Communion, the tea of a tea ceremony. Ritual processions require attention to the manner and order in which people enter and leave a room. Ceremonies that mark life transitions focus attention on particular people: the bride and groom at a wedding, the graduates at a college commencement, or the recently deceased at a funeral.

Ritualizing scriptures therefore draws attention to the books themselves – their verbal contents, and also the sound of their words and their physical form and appearance. Scriptures get ritualized in three distinct ways that correspond to the three dimensions of texts.

## 1.1  THE THREE DIMENSIONS OF WRITTEN TEXTS

Every written text consists of three aspects or dimensions (see Figure 1.1). We usually focus on its meaning, the significance of its words and what they tell us. This interpretive act engages a text's semantic dimension.

Before we can understand the meaning of writing, we must turn the visual signs into words. The text must be read aloud or enunciated in our heads. This oral or mental presentation engages a text's expressive dimension.

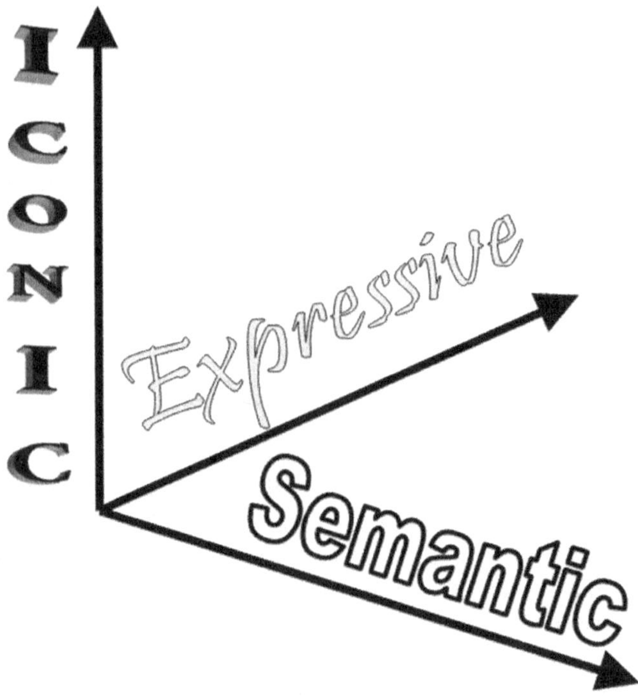


**FIGURE 1.1**  The three dimensions of texts.

But before we can even present a text orally, we must recognize it as a written text. We have to interpret visual marks as written language (letters or signs), not as art or natural patterns, or we must recognize the shape of an object as likely to contain writing (an envelope, a scroll, or a book, for example). This act of recognition engages a text's <u>iconic dimension</u>.

We usually do not pay attention to the three different dimensions of texts. Consider this book that you are now reading. You instantly recognize its shape as a book that probably contains written text. You recognize its Roman letters and (if you are reading this) you turn them into English words without thinking much about what you are doing. I hope that you also understand the meaning of these sentences without too much difficulty.

We pay attention to the individual dimensions of texts only if we have difficulty – if we have trouble figuring out their meaning (the semantic dimension), if we cannot read smudged type or illegible handwriting (the expressive dimension), or if we cannot decide whether marks on paper represent written words or art or random patterns (the iconic dimension). Otherwise, the three dimensions of texts are trivial features of the experience of reading and we usually ignore them.

When texts get ritualized, however, the three dimensions become important, because texts can be ritualized in each of the dimensions.

The <u>semantic dimension</u> of interpretation can be <u>ritualized</u> by delivering lectures and sermons, by staging debates, and by writing interpretive commentaries on texts. For example, laws and national constitutions get ritualized regularly in the semantic dimension by oral and written interpretations that multiply and grow more elaborate over time. They serve the ritual function of drawing attention to the laws and they index the readers' and listeners' responsibilities under those laws.

The <u>expressive dimension</u> of texts can be <u>ritualized</u> by private and public readings and recitations. Religious worship services often focus on reading selections of sacred texts. People may memorize the text. Oral performances may be standardized as chants or set to music as songs. Theatrical scripts, for example, are designed for public presentations in ritual spaces (theaters). They expect audiences and actors to behave in conventional ways that call attention to the play being performed.

The <u>iconic dimension</u> of texts can be <u>ritualized</u> by changing how a book looks and by handling it in special ways. The text can be written in distinctive scripts or printed in unusual fonts. Its pages can be decorated and illustrated. Its binding or container can be embellished with art and valuable materials. For example, publishers produce collector's editions in leather bindings and gilt edges so buyers can show visually that they find a particular book valuable. Texts can also be displayed prominently on shelves or tables, held up for people to see, and carried in elaborate processions. Rare books frequently get displayed in museums, in libraries, and even in private homes.

Only written texts can be ritualized in these three dimensions. A <u>visual symbol</u> such as a cross or a flag can be ritualized in the iconic dimension: it can be displayed, elaborated in art, and paraded in processions. Visual symbols can also be ritualized in the semantic dimension: their meanings can be explained and debated, sometimes at great length. But crosses and flags cannot be ritualized in the expressive dimension: they contain no written words that can be presented as mental or oral language. On the other hand, an <u>oral epic</u> can be ritualized by retelling it or even staging it. Its interpretation can also be explained and debated at length. But there is no physical object to display or decorate. Therefore, oral epics and other oral traditions can be ritualized in the expressive and semantic dimensions, but not in the iconic dimension, while visual symbols can be ritualized in the iconic and semantic dimensions, but not in the expressive dimension. Only written texts can be ritualized in all three dimensions.

## 1.2   RITUALIZING SCRIPTURES IN THREE DIMENSIONS

Most texts do not get ritualized much in any dimension, and those that do usually get ritualized in only one or two dimensions. A distinctive feature of religious <u>scriptures</u> is that they get <u>ritualized in all three dimensions</u>.

Religious traditions that emphasize scriptures give prominent attention to their semantic interpretation. They include Muslims, Sikhs, Buddhists, Taoists, Hindus, and Jains, as well as Jews, Samaritans, and Christians. All of them sponsor speakers and literature that interpret their scriptures, and give their best interpreters positions of respect and influence. Most of them encourage all their followers to study the scriptures and their interpretations. <u>Ritualizing the semantic dimension</u> tends to increase the <u>authority</u> of scriptures and the authority of people who can interpret them convincingly. These religions therefore give respect and influence to scholars, priests, preachers, rabbis, imams, or sages who are learned in the scriptures and their interpretation.

These traditions also highlight the oral presentation of scriptures, to the point that reading or reciting scripture is a key component of their worship services. They often require that scriptures be presented orally in distinctive ways, with particular pronunciations or with prescribed chants. Verses of scriptures frequently get sung to melodies, with or without instrumental accompaniments. Some scriptures that contain vivid stories get performed theatrically. Traditions of enacting scriptural stories are thousands of years old in Europe and India. Now they frequently appear on television and in films. There is even older evidence for artistic traditions of illustrating scriptural stories and calligraphy that elaborates the written texts artistically. All these media can be used to present the words and contents of scriptures. Ritualizing their expressive dimension in these ways draws people's attention to the scriptures and inspires those who hear and see the performances. They often regard inspiration as characteristic of scripture.

Religious traditions that emphasize scripture also ritualize the physical form of their scriptures. The script or type-face may take distinctive forms and be arranged in unusual ways. The pages may be decorated and their contents may be illustrated. The cover or binding of the book may take a stereotypical form so that people easily recognize it as that scripture, or it may be bound in expensive materials. People display scriptures in their congregations, sanctuaries, and homes. They carry them in the form of complete books or as miniature amulets. They wave them in rituals of worship or preaching, of celebration or protest. In all these ways, the visual appearance of scriptures distinguishes them from other books and emphasizes their importance. Ritualizing their iconic dimension in these ways draws attention and legitimizes the religious tradition that venerates them and the people who possess and handle them.

Ritualization plays an important role in making some texts seem more authoritative than others. Regular and repeated interpretation of the same book makes its contents seem more important for how to think and act. But the reverse is also true: displaying a book of instructions makes rituals seem more legitimate. The visible presence of authoritative books counters doubts about the competence or honesty of the person leading the rituals (Box 1.3).[3]

In fact, people in the ancient Middle East first began regarding some texts as normative, that is, as authoritative for how to behave, when those texts described how to conduct rituals. Kings and priests and magicians from Babylon to Egypt consulted ritual texts to tell them, for example, where to build temples, when to make offerings to the gods, and how to cast curses. But the famous law code of Hammurabi and other royal law codes were not consulted for how to conduct criminal trials, which were based on custom instead. Textual authority developed first around ritual texts.

The same pattern can be observed in the developing authority of biblical books. Many claim inspiration from God, most obviously books like Isaiah and Jeremiah that state that God gave the prophets these messages. The first Jewish scripture did not consist of prophetic books, however, but of the Torah/Pentateuch. Genesis 1 does not begin with any explicit claim of inspiration or even of authorship. The Pentateuch does contain laws spoken by God to Moses. But what differentiates it most from other biblical books is that ritual instructions lie at its center in Exodus 25–40, Leviticus, and

---

## Box 1.3   The rhetorical effects of ritualizing scriptures

Ritualizing each of a scripture's three dimensions makes the book's message more persuasive to those who venerate it. Theories of <u>rhetoric</u>, that is, of persuasion, help us understand how this works. The ancient Greek philosopher Aristotle (384–322 BCE) described three factors necessary to make a speech persuasive. The words (*logos*) of the speech must, of course, make a convincing argument. The speech, however, must also appeal to the audience's assumptions and feelings (*pathos*). And the speaker must project an attractive and trustworthy character (*ethos*).

Scriptures are not speeches, but ritualizing their three dimensions increases their persuasive appeal in these same ways: interpreting them increases the <u>authority</u> (*logos*) of their contents and their interpreters, expressing their words and contents <u>inspires</u> audiences (*pathos*), and displaying and decorating them <u>legitimizes</u> (*ethos*) the communities and traditions that venerate them.[4]

---

parts of Numbers. Stories of the Torah's growing authority in the Second Temple period emphasize that it first dictated ritual behavior, especially how to celebrate the annual festivals of Passover and *Sukkot* (Booths). Only centuries later did its laws begin to apply in criminal courts and civil society.

As Jewish and Christian communities increasingly focused on ritualizing their scriptures, the Torah or the Gospels or later the one-volume Bible began to represent the religions. The scrolls and books of scripture became visual symbols of each religion. The sounds of scriptural verses inspired devotion to the religious tradition. And interpreting their significance for directing people's personal and communal lives led people to try to embody their scriptures in themselves. The centrality of scripture to Jewish and Christian religious experience continues to be expressed by associating the words, "Torah" or "Gospel" or "biblical," with the religions' essential teachings. These words describe not just books, but also living faithfully as Jews or Christians. In these communities, Torah, Gospel, or Bible symbolizes the ideal way of life. So the three parts of this book are organized around the parts of scriptures that, to Jews and Christians, represent the highest religious ideals.

## 1.3   JEWISH AND CHRISTIAN SCRIPTURES

Jews and Christians share parts of their scriptures. The Jewish scriptures consist of 24 books divided into 3 parts: the 5 books of the *Torah* "instructions or laws," the 8 books of the *Nebi'im* "prophets," and the 11 books of the

*Kethubim* "writings." A common name for this collection, the _Tanak_, is an acronym from the first letter of each section.

Protestant Christians accept exactly the same literary material as part of their scripture and call it the <u>Old Testament</u>. But the Old Testament books appear in a different order and some are divided into two or more books. So the Protestant Old Testament consists of 39 books. Yet its contents are the same as the Jewish Tanak. (For a neutral designation of the collection of books that Jews and Christians both regard as scripture, scholars now usually call it the <u>Hebrew Bible</u>.)

Ancient Christians, however, accepted more Jewish books in their Old Testament than did Jewish rabbis. These books and additions to biblical books written by Jews in the Second Temple period were segregated into a third section of the Bible, the <u>Apocrypha</u>, by Protestant Reformers in the sixteenth century. Roman Catholic and Eastern Orthodox Christians continue to reproduce them as part of their Old Testament, but sometimes call these additional materials the <u>Deuterocanon</u>.

Christians of all kinds also accept into their scripture 27 uniquely Christian books, which they call the <u>New Testament</u>. The list of books accepted by each tradition is called a <u>canon</u>, which is traditional Christian terminology for the contents of scripture (see Box 1.4).

Another religious tradition accepts some of this material as their scripture. The <u>Samaritans</u> now number fewer than 1000 people, but 2000 years ago they were a large and vibrant community. They accept only the five books of the Torah as their scripture.

For ancient and medieval Jews and Christians, "scripture" was not a single book but a collection of books. Therefore, they did not standardize the sequence of scriptural books until the invention of printing made single-volume, <u>pandect</u> bibles affordable, starting in the fifteenth century.[5]

## 1.4   MANUSCRIPTS AND PRINTING

From the invention of writing more than 5000 years ago to the invention of printing with movable type more than 500 years ago, all written texts were written by hand. Scribes copied and re-copied texts to publish them and preserve them. We can still read ancient literature because of their efforts.

Scribes have used a wide variety of materials to write with and write on. In ancient Mesopotamia in the Middle East, scribes wrote mostly in wet clay with a pointed reed. The clay was then dried in the sun or fired in a kiln to produce <u>cuneiform tablets</u>. Because fired clay is a very durable material, more routine texts have survived from Mesopotamia than from any other ancient civilization.

## Box 1.4  Canons of biblical scriptures

| Samaritan | Jewish | Catholic/ Orthodox Christian | Protestant Christian | Abbreviations of biblical books |
|---|---|---|---|---|
|  | *Tanak* | *Old Testament* | *Old Testament* |  |
| *Torah* | *Torah* | *Pentateuch* | *Pentateuch* |  |
| Genesis | Genesis | Genesis | Genesis | Gen. |
| Exodus | Exodus | Exodus | Exodus | Exod. |
| Leviticus | Leviticus | Leviticus | Leviticus | Lev. |
| Numbers | Numbers | Numbers | Numbers | Num. |
| Deuteronomy | Deuteronomy | Deuteronomy | Deuteronomy | Deut. |
|  |  |  |  |  |
|  | *Nevi'im* | *Histories* | *Histories* |  |
|  | (Prophets) | Joshua | Joshua | Josh. |
|  | Joshua | Judges | Judges | Judg. |
|  | Judges | Ruth | Ruth | Ruth |
|  | Samuel | 1 & 2 Samuel | 1 & 2 Samuel | Sam. |
|  | Kings | 1 & 2 Kings | 1 & 2 Kings | Kgs. |
|  | Isaiah | 1 & 2 Chronicles | 1 & 2 Chronicles | Chr. |
|  | Jeremiah | Ezra | Ezra | Ezra |
|  | Ezekiel | Nehemiah | Nehemiah | Neh. |
|  | The Twelve | Tobit | Esther | Esth. |
|  | Prophets | Judith |  |  |
|  |  | Esther | *Poetry* |  |
|  | *Ketubim* | 1 & 2 | Job | Job |
|  | (Writings) | Maccabees | Psalms | Pss. |
|  | Psalms |  | Proverbs | Prov. |
|  | Proverbs | *Poetry* | Ecclesiastes | Eccl. |
|  | Job | Job | Song of Songs/ | Cant. |
|  | Song of Songs | Psalms | Canticles |  |
|  | Ruth | Proverbs |  |  |
|  | Lamentations | Ecclesiastes | *Prophets* |  |
|  | Ecclesiastes | Song of Songs | Isaiah | Isa. |
|  | Esther | Wisdom of | Jeremiah | Jer. |
|  | Daniel | Solomon | Lamentations | Lam. |
|  | Ezra- | Sirach/ | Ezekiel | Ezek. |
|  | Nehemiah | Ecclesiasticus | Daniel | Dan. |
|  | Chronicles |  | Hosea | Hos. |
|  |  | *Prophets* | Joel | Joel |
|  |  | Isaiah | Amos | Amos |
|  |  | Jeremiah | Micah | Mic. |
|  |  | Lamentations | Nahum | Nah. |
|  |  | Baruch | Habakkuk | Hab. |
|  |  | Ezekiel | Zephaniah | Zeph. |
|  |  | Daniel | Haggai | Hag. |
|  |  | Hosea |  |  |
|  |  | Joel |  |  |

<table>
<tr><td>Amos</td><td>Zechariah</td><td>Zech.</td></tr>
<tr><td>Micah</td><td>Malachi</td><td>Mal.</td></tr>
<tr><td>Nahum</td><td></td><td></td></tr>
<tr><td>Habakkuk</td><td>Apocrypha</td><td></td></tr>
<tr><td>Zephaniah</td><td>1 & 2 Esdras</td><td>1/2 Esdr.</td></tr>
<tr><td>Haggai</td><td>Tobit</td><td>Tob.</td></tr>
<tr><td>Zechariah</td><td>Judith</td><td>Jud.</td></tr>
<tr><td>Malachi</td><td>Additions to Esther</td><td>Add. Est.</td></tr>
<tr><td></td><td>Wisdom of Solomon</td><td>Wis. Sol.</td></tr>
<tr><td>Orthodox canons</td><td>Ecclesiasticus</td><td>Sir.</td></tr>
<tr><td>usually include:</td><td>(Sirach)</td><td></td></tr>
<tr><td>1 & 2 Esdras</td><td>Baruch</td><td>Bar.</td></tr>
<tr><td>Prayer of</td><td>Letter of Jeremiah</td><td>Let. Jer.</td></tr>
<tr><td>Manasseh</td><td>Additions to Daniel</td><td>Add. Dan.</td></tr>
<tr><td>3 Maccabees</td><td>Prayer of Manasseh</td><td>Pr. Man.</td></tr>
<tr><td>4 Maccabees</td><td>1 & 2 Maccabees</td><td>Macc.</td></tr>
<tr><td></td><td></td><td></td></tr>
<tr><td>New Testament</td><td>New Testament</td><td></td></tr>
<tr><td>Gospels & Acts</td><td>Gospels & Acts</td><td></td></tr>
<tr><td>Matthew</td><td>Matthew</td><td>Matt.</td></tr>
<tr><td>Mark</td><td>Mark</td><td>Mark</td></tr>
<tr><td>Luke</td><td>Luke</td><td>Luke</td></tr>
<tr><td>John</td><td>John</td><td>John</td></tr>
<tr><td>Acts of the</td><td>Acts of the Apostles</td><td>Acts</td></tr>
<tr><td>Apostles</td><td></td><td></td></tr>
<tr><td></td><td></td><td></td></tr>
<tr><td>Letters</td><td>Letters</td><td></td></tr>
<tr><td>Romans</td><td>Romans</td><td>Rom.</td></tr>
<tr><td>1 & 2 Corinthians</td><td>1 & 2 Corinthians</td><td>Cor.</td></tr>
<tr><td>Galatians</td><td>Galatians</td><td>Gal.</td></tr>
<tr><td>Ephesians</td><td>Ephesians</td><td>Eph.</td></tr>
<tr><td>Philippians</td><td>Philippians</td><td>Phil.</td></tr>
<tr><td>Colossians</td><td>Colossians</td><td>Col.</td></tr>
<tr><td>1 & 2</td><td>1 & 2 Thessalonians</td><td>Thess.</td></tr>
<tr><td>Thessalonians</td><td>1 & 2 Timothy</td><td>Tim.</td></tr>
<tr><td>1 & 2 Timothy</td><td>Titus</td><td>Tit.</td></tr>
<tr><td>Titus</td><td>Philemon</td><td>Philem.</td></tr>
<tr><td>Philemon</td><td>Hebrews</td><td>Heb.</td></tr>
<tr><td>Hebrews</td><td>James</td><td>Jam.</td></tr>
<tr><td>James</td><td>1 & 2 Peter</td><td>Pet.</td></tr>
<tr><td>1 & 2 Peter</td><td>1, 2, 3 John</td><td>123 John</td></tr>
<tr><td>1, 2, 3 John</td><td>Jude</td><td>Jude</td></tr>
<tr><td>Jude</td><td></td><td></td></tr>
<tr><td></td><td></td><td></td></tr>
<tr><td>Apocalypse</td><td>Apocalypse</td><td></td></tr>
<tr><td>Revelation of</td><td>Revelation of John</td><td>Rev.</td></tr>
<tr><td>John</td><td></td><td></td></tr>
</table>

In ancient Egypt, scribes wrote in ink using reed pens mostly on <u>papyrus</u>. The papyrus plant grows in the delta of the Nile River. Egyptians produced a medium for writing by splitting papyrus reeds, soaking them, and then pressing them together at right angles. Papyrus is much less durable than clay, so what has survived comes mostly from sealed containers in tombs.

The scribes of ancient Israel, like those writing alphabetical scripts in Phoenicia and Syria, wrote in ink mostly on specially prepared leather called <u>parchment</u>. Parchment scrolls are somewhat more durable than papyrus, which they also used. But the oldest surviving texts of the Hebrew Bible date only from the third-to-second centuries BCE.

<u>Paper</u>, which is made from rags or wood pulp, was invented in China by 105 CE. It did not reach the Middle East until the eighth century and Europe only in the twelfth century. The introduction of paper provided a cheaper material medium that enabled written documents to become increasingly common.

That was especially the case after the invention of <u>printing</u>. Buddhists in Korea, Japan, and Tibet printed sutras (Buddhist scriptures) from the eighth century CE on. They carved mirror images of entire pages into wood blocks (see Figure 1.2). Dipped in ink, wood blocks could produce many copies of a page before wearing out. Chinese and Korean printers experimented with movable type as early as the eleventh century.

Wood-block printing came to Europe in the early fifteenth century. By 1456 in Mainz, Germany, Johannes Gutenberg had invented a printing press with movable metal type. His first commercial product was a printed Latin Bible. By the end of the fifteenth century, printing presses were found throughout Europe. They printed books of all kinds on paper, including many copies of Jewish and Christian scriptures.

Printing technology not only made copies of the Bible cheaper and more common. It also made it easier to reproduce elaborate page formats. In Italy in the early sixteenth century, a printer produced a Jewish Tanak that included the

**FIGURE 1.2**   Korean wood block and a page printed with it of a Chinese Buddhist sutra. In the Korean National Museum.

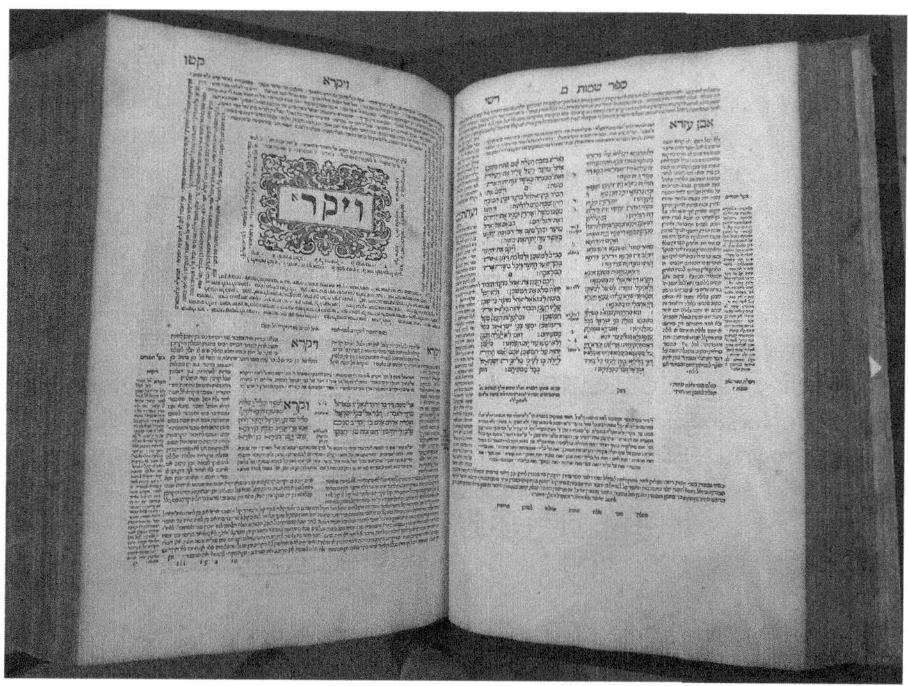

**FIGURE 1.3**    Bomberg's Third Rabbinic Bible, 1547, open to Exodus 40 and Leviticus 1, in the Special Collections Research Center, Syracuse University Libraries.

Hebrew text, its Aramaic translation (targum), and the commentary of medieval experts on every page. This format, known as a <u>rabbinic bible</u> (see Figures 1.3, 12.3), became the most popular way to print Jewish scriptures for many centuries. At the same time in Spain, printers produced multilingual bibles (the Complutensian Polyglot, see Figure 12.4) whose pages included Hebrew, Greek, Latin, and more – each in their appropriate fonts. When the Protestant Reformation broke out in northern Europe, the Reformers printed bibles in vernacular translations and distributed them as widely as possible. Religious groups of all kinds embraced the new technology to distribute their scriptures and teachings.

Jews and Christians continued to adopt new media technologies quickly. Whether stereotype and linotype printing in the nineteenth century, radio and television in the twentieth, or digital media in the twenty-first, religious groups have often been the first to use new inventions to reproduce and publish their scriptures, sermons, and other texts. At the same time, such rapid technological innovations have not impeded the iconic and expressive ritualization of scriptures, often in very old-fashioned forms. It remains to be seen whether or not that combination of rapid adaptation of new media technologies together with conservative maintenance of older ritual forms continues in the digital age.

## CITED WORKS AND FURTHER READING

1   On scriptures, see William A. Graham, "Scripture," in *The Encyclopedia of Religion*, Volume 12 (2nd ed.; ed. L. Jones, M. Eliade, and C. J. Adams; Detroit: Macmillan Reference, 2005), 8194–8205, quotation from 8195; F. E. Peters, *The Voice, the Word, the Books: The Sacred Scripture of the Jews, Christians, and Muslims* (Princeton: Princeton University Press, 2007); Gerald T. Sheppard, "Canon," in *The Encyclopedia of Religion*, Volume 3 (ed. M. Eliade; New York: Macmillan, 1987), 62–69; and Robert E. van Voorst, ed., *Anthology of World Scriptures* (Belmont: Wadsworth, 1997).

2   On ritual, see Jonathan Z. Smith, *To Take Place: Toward Theory in Ritual* (Chicago: University of Chicago Press, 1987), 90; Catherine Bell, *Ritual Theory, Ritual Practice* (Oxford: Oxford University Press, 1992), 109; Roy Rappaport, *Ritual and Religion in the Making of Humanity* (Cambridge: Cambridge University Press, 1999), 119; and Philippe Buc, *The Dangers of Ritual: Between Early Medieval Texts and Social Scientific Theory* (Princeton: Princeton University Press, 2001).

3   On ritualized texts, see James W. Watts, "The Three Dimensions of Scriptures," in *How and Why Books Matter: Essays on the Social Function of Iconic Texts* (Sheffield: Equinox, 2019), 7–29.

4   Aristotle, *Rhetoric* II.1.1–3. in John Henry Freese, *Aristotle with an English Translation: The Art of Rhetoric*, Loeb Classical Library (New York: Putnam, 1921).

5   See Frederick E. Greenspahn, "Canon, Codex, and the Printing Press," in *Le-maʿan Ziony: Essays in Honor of Ziony Zevit* (ed. F. E. Greenspahn and G. A. Rendsburg; Eugene, OR: Cascade, 2017), 203–212.

# PART 1

# THE TORAH AS A SCRIPTURE

The <u>Pentateuch</u> consists of five books: Genesis, Exodus, Leviticus, Numbers, and Deuteronomy. The most obvious fact about these books is that they are <u>scripture</u>. In fact, three different religious traditions revere them as scripture.

Jewish tradition names these five books the <u>Torah</u>, which in Hebrew means "law" or "instruction." The Torah is the first part of the Jewish Bible, the <u>Tanak</u>, and has always been the most important of the three parts. Its five books have shaped Jewish thought and life far more than the other books of Jewish scripture.

Christian tradition preserves the Jewish Bible in the first part, the <u>Old Testament</u>, of the Christian Bible. So the bibles of different churches all start with the Pentateuch just like the Jewish Bible does. However, Christians emphasize the <u>New Testament</u> that consists of uniquely Christian books more than the Old Testament. They focus especially on the four Gospels that contain stories about Jesus's life and teachings, and on the letters of Paul.

Since antiquity, the <u>Samaritans</u> have used the Torah as their only scripture. So Samaritans venerate the Torah as their only scripture. Jews venerate the Torah as the most important part of scripture, but the Tanak also contains 19 other books. Christians do not usually distinguish the

Pentateuch from the rest of the Bible. They venerate it only as the first five books of their Old Testament, which is overshadowed in Christian thought and liturgy by the New Testament and, especially, by the four Gospels. All three religious traditions define the scope of their scriptures differently from one another and by different names.

# CHAPTER 2

# Torah and Pentateuch

The word *torah* appears in the Hebrew Bible frequently to refer to specific instructions (e.g., Lev. 6:9, 14, etc.). It may also refer to sets of instructions (Lev. 7:37) and, together with *mishpatim* and *huqim*, to all the stipulations of God's covenant with Israel (Gen. 26:5; Exod. 24:12; Lev. 26:46). The word, *torah*, by itself often refers specifically to priestly instructions or "teachings" (Deut. 33:10; Mal. 2:4–9). It typifies one of the priests' major responsibilities (Deut. 17:11, 18; Ezek. 22:26).[1]

Torah has traditionally been translated as "law." The first to do so were the ancient translators of the Septuagint who used the Greek word *nomos*. Many interpreters now find this translation too restrictive, because *torah* connotes instruction in the form of advice and direction as much as legal mandate. Furthermore, ancient Middle Eastern law collections do not seem to have functioned as normative legislation. Actually, the Greek word *nomos* described correct performance of temple rituals just as priestly *torah* does in the Hebrew Bible. In fact, written ritual instructions seem to have functioned as normative texts long before written legislation did, and may have been the stimulus for the gradual development of normative written law.

Deuteronomy uses *torah* most often to refer to itself as containing all the stipulations of the covenant (e.g., Deut. 1:5) in the form of a written scroll, *sefer hatorah* "the book of the Torah" (e.g., Deut. 28:61; cf. 2 Kgs. 22:8, 11).

Other books of the Hebrew Bible connect this book with Moses, *sefer torat Moshe* "the book of the Torah of Moses" (e.g., Josh. 8:31; 1 Kgs. 2:3; Ezra 7:6; Neh. 8:1). By the early Second Temple period, "the Torah" had come to refer to the Pentateuch in more or less the form we have it today.

Early Christian writers referred to the collection as *ho nomos* "the Law," often together with "the prophets" to describe all the scriptures. The Greek name *pentateuchos* "Pentateuch" means "five cases" and refers to the five books of the Torah. It appeared first in second- and third-century CE Christian authors such as Origen and Tertullian, and probably reflected Hebrew or Aramaic phrases used by the ancient rabbis, such as "the five books of the Torah" (*y. Sotah* 5:6) or "the five fifths of the Torah" (*b. Meg.* 15a).[2] However, the Torah's division into five books was already reflected in the first century CE by Philo (*De Abrahamo* 1) and Josephus (*Apion* 1.8), and perhaps by a fragment among the Dead Sea Scrolls (*1Q30*).

For Jews and Samaritans, "the Torah" remains the name of the five books of the Pentateuch. It evokes not just the literature but the entire tradition of interpreting and living according to its teachings. Thus "Torah" names how the Pentateuch functions as scripture in Jewish and Samaritan communities.

## 2.1   THE PENTATEUCH IN THREE DIMENSIONS

Understanding how a book functions as scripture involves analyzing how it gets ritualized in each of three dimensions and the social effects of these rituals (see Chapter 1). The specifics vary from one religious tradition to another and from time to time and place to place.

For example, Jews and Samaritans use scrolls of the Torah in synagogue services. This physical form of the book therefore distinguishes it as sacred scripture. Torah scrolls also receive distinctive covers and get housed in cabinets, Torah arks, that emphasize the sanctity of the text. Christians, by contrast, use a different book form for their scriptures, a codex that binds folded pages together on one edge. Because of Christian influence, the codex became the standard shape for almost all books in Western cultures. But Christians continue to distinguish their bibles from other books by decorative bindings and distinctive typography. Jews, Samaritans, and Christians have reproduced quotations from their scriptures in monumental form on walls, plaques, and gravestones. All three religions tend to display their books of scripture prominently and parade them publicly. So they all ritualize the iconic dimension of their scriptures, even though the specific forms and methods vary.

Jews, Samaritans, and Christians also give prominent attention to reading scriptures. <u>Reading</u> selected texts <u>aloud</u> is so common in their worship services that it is a defining characteristic of what makes them worship services. The services of Jewish and Samaritan synagogues highlight the Pentateuch by reading the entire Torah through sequentially over the course of a year. Christian churches focus on other parts of their bibles and usually read only selected parts of the Pentateuch aloud, mostly from Genesis, Exodus, and Deuteronomy. The readings often take musical form as chants. Scriptural texts are also set to music and sung by congregations and choirs. Biblical stories are a major source of themes for artistic illustration and theatrical productions, now including television and film. Though the methods and forms vary, all three religions <u>ritualize</u> the Pentateuch's <u>expressive dimension</u> to a high degree.

The three religions that venerate the Pentateuch as scripture also give attention to <u>interpreting</u> its meaning. Worship services feature sermons based on scriptural texts. Congregations promote group study of scripture by children and adults. To support these activities, scholars write commentaries explaining the texts. The published literature about the Torah, Tanak, and Bible is therefore vast and grows every year. Most scholars would distinguish their activities from the rituals of congregational worship. But their repetitive focus on religious texts bears all the hallmarks of ritualizing activity, and has the same effect: it draws attention to the scriptures and publicly enhances their value. So, again, though the methods vary over time and by tradition, Jews, Samaritans, and Christians have all <u>ritualized</u> the Pentateuch's <u>semantic dimension</u> from antiquity to today.

The tendency to ritualize the Pentateuch can partly be explained by the fact that the Pentateuch itself commands its ritualization in all three textual dimensions. Deuteronomy 31:10–13 requires that the Torah be read aloud to all the Israelites every seven years (Box 2.1). The expressive dimension of this activity is clearly marked by scheduling the reading every seven years, by its setting during *Sukkot*, the Festival of Booths, and by requiring that everyone participate, including men, women, and children. The ritual aims explicitly for instructional goals, "so that they may hear and learn," thus implicitly ritualizing its semantic dimension. Later, the same chapter commands its iconic ritualization. The physical scroll must be placed beside the ark in the holiest part of Israel's sanctuary as an icon of Israel's covenant with God. The ark itself contains the tablets of the commandments (Deut. 10:1–5) that God spoke aloud to Israel, according to Deuteronomy 5:22 (and also Exod. 20:1–19, 25:16). The Ark, then, served as a <u>reliquary</u>, a container for a sacred relic. In this case, that relic is a text, stone tablets of the commandments that were written by God.

> ## Box 2.1   Deuteronomy commands Torah's ritualization
>
> ("YHWH" is the name of God in the Hebrew Bible; see p. 69).
>
> *YHWH spoke these words to your whole congregation on the mountain in a loud voice out of fire, cloud and darkness, and added nothing more. Then God wrote them on two stone tablets and gave them to me.* (Deut. 5:22)
>
> *Have the words that I am commanding you today in your heart. Repeat them to your children and talk about them when you sit at home and when you walk down the road, when you lie down and when you get up. Bind them as a sign on your hand and let them serve as a symbol on your forehead. Inscribe them on the doorposts of your house and on your gates.* (Deut. 6:6–9)
>
> *YHWH said to me, "Carve two stone tablets…and make a wooden ark. I will write the words on the tablets…and you must put them in the ark."* (Deut. 10:1–2)
>
> *Moses wrote down this law and gave it to the Levitical priests, who carry the Ark of the Covenant, and to all the Israelite elders. He commanded them, "Every seventh year…you shall read this Torah in the presence of all Israel. Gather the people, men, women, children and foreigners among you, so that they may hear and learn to be in awe of YHWH your God and to be careful to do all the words of this Torah."* (Deut. 31:10–12)
>
> *Moses commanded the Levites who carry the Ark of the Covenant of YHWH, "Take this Torah scroll and put it beside the Ark of the Covenant of YHWH your God, where it will serve as a witness against you."* (Deut. 31:25–26)

Deuteronomy also requires that at least parts of the Torah be ritualized by Israelites at home. It emphasizes meditating regularly on its words "in your hearts," that is, by memorizing them, and teaching them to children. Such expressive and semantic ritualization should be joined with iconic ritualization by wearing its words on arm and forehead and writing them on gates (Deut. 6:6–9).

So the writers of Deuteronomy anticipated that the Torah would be ritualized as scripture in all three of its textual dimensions. And, in fact, the Torah's three dimensions did get ritualized when it first began to function as a scripture, in the time of the priest and scribe Ezra.

## 2.2   SCRIPTURALIZING THE TORAH IN THE TIME OF EZRA

The biblical books of Ezra and Nehemiah describe Ezra as a Jewish priest and scribe from Babylon. The Persian emperor commissioned him to appoint judges. Ezra also devoted himself to religious reform based on "the Torah of

Moses that YHWH the God of Israel gave to him" (Ezra 7:6). He focused especially on two issues. He led the Jerusalem community to prohibit marriage to foreign women and to dissolve such marriages that had already taken place (Ezra 10). This ban on intermarriage was more comprehensive than what the Pentateuch actually requires. That discrepancy has led some historians to think that Ezra's Torah was not exactly the same as the Pentateuch that we now possess. Others argue that Ezra simply interpreted the Pentateuch more strictly than necessary. At any rate, the story implies that Ezra used the Torah's authority to regulate marriages.

Ezra also led the Jerusalem community in a public reading of the Torah scroll (Neh. 8; Box 2.2). He was visibly supported by community leaders standing on either side of him. When he displayed the scroll, the people responded with ritual words ("Amen") and bows of reverence. They stood at attention while Ezra read aloud for the whole morning. Levites interpreted or translated the meaning of what Ezra read. (The Levites were related to the Aaronide priests and were supposed to assist them in the Temple: Num. 18:21–32.) Readings and study continued on the following days. They culminated in celebrating the annual festival of *Sukkot* on the basis of the Torah's instructions (Neh. 8:14–17). Later, the whole community renewed the covenant with God and committed themselves to funding the temple in Jerusalem (Neh. 10).

This scripture reading ceremony illustrates a typical feature of rituals. Simply by participating and being seen to participate in this ritual, the people of Jerusalem accepted the legitimacy of the Torah and of Ezra as its authoritative interpreter. Whatever their private misgivings may have been, they

## Box 2.2  Ezra's Torah reading

*All the people joined as one… and asked Ezra to bring the book of the Torah of Moses which YHWH had commanded Israel.… He read from it…from dawn to noon to the men and women and children old enough to understand, and the people listened closely to the Torah. The scribe Ezra stood on a wooden speaker's platform, and [the priests and elders] stood next to him. Ezra opened the book where all the people could see, because he was standing higher than the people. When he opened it, all the people stood up. Then Ezra blessed YHWH, the great God, and all the people raised their hands and responded, "Amen, amen." Then they bowed down before YHWH with their faces to the ground.… The Levites helped the people in their places understand the Torah. Thus they read from the book of the Torah of God with interpretation to explain the meaning, so they could understand the reading. (Neh. 8:1–8)* publicly committed themselves to obey the commandments of the Torah. That meant, to begin with, celebrating *Sukkot* correctly.

To later Jews and by the standards of the Torah itself (Deut. 6:1–9; 31:9–13), the description of Ezra and his actions in Nehemiah 8 exemplifies what a rabbi (a Jewish religious leader) should be and do. He leads the people to read and study the Torah, and to observe the laws of God that it contains. Ezra establishes the model of scholarly religious leadership that has predominated in Judaism for 2000 years, and in Christianity and Islam as well.

So it is surprising to notice that Ezra is almost the first person that the Bible shows acting this way. Moses, of course, exemplifies this kind of leadership in the Pentateuch, and his successor, Joshua, also read and inscribed the Torah for Israel (Josh. 8:30–35). However, from the time of Moses and Joshua until the time of Ezra more than 800 years later, there is only one story about Israel's political or religious leaders behaving in this way. In fact, the stories of events during these centuries contain almost no references to the book of Torah, except three times in commentary by characters or narrators (1 Kgs. 2:3; 2 Kgs. 14:5–6; 17:34–40). Only one story features a Torah scroll as a key element. That is the story of the Torah found in the late seventh century and its ritualized reading by King Josiah (2 Kgs. 22–23) see Box 4.7. But the resulting religious reform seems to have had no lasting impact. The stories of the following kings and of Judah's exile from its land do not feature a book of the Torah. In the Bible after the Pentateuch and apart from 2 Kings 22–23, the Torah appears as a prominent feature of the plot only in the books of Ezra and Nehemiah and in the books of Chronicles, which is a history of the kingdoms written after the time of Ezra. The Bible suggests that from the generation of Moses to the post-exilic generation of Ezra, the religious practices of Israel and Judah were not based on a written book of scripture.

It was only in the time of Ezra and afterwards, that is, in the Persian period (539–ca. 330 BCE), that the Torah began to function regularly as scripture for many Jews. We will examine the evidence for this claim later. For now, it is important to notice that, according to Nehemiah 8, Ezra ritualized all three dimensions of scripture. He displayed the physical scroll to the people, who rose to their feet at the sight and then bowed down (iconic dimension vv. 5–6). He read it aloud on each day of the festival (expressive dimension vv. 3, 18). And the Levites interpreted its meaning to the people, while the leaders studied it for guidance (semantic dimension vv. 7–8, 13). Here we find the three-dimensional ritualization that distinguishes later scriptures like the Torah scroll, the Bible, and the Qur'an from secular texts.

Historical arguments about the accuracy of the biblical depiction of Ezra and his Torah in the context of Persian imperial policies (see Boxes 2.3

## Box 2.3   The Persian Empire and Torah

The Babylonian Empire conquered the Kingdom of Judah in 587 BCE. Many Judeans, especially upper-class priests, scribes, and royalty, were exiled to Mesopotamia. Less than 50 years later, the Babylonians themselves were conquered by the Persians. The Persian conqueror, Cyrus, issued a decree allowing exiles to return to their native lands and rebuild their homes and temples. Descendants of the Judean exiles began to slowly make their way back to Jerusalem. They rebuilt their villages and their temple (Ezra 2–6), but restoring the city and its economy took hundreds of years.

Sometime in the next century (historians give dates ranging from 450 to 399 BCE), the Persian emperor sent Ezra to the province containing Judea. Some historians argue that Ezra's story shows that the Persian Empire played a role in turning the Pentateuch into official Jewish law. At least, the biblical writers claimed there was imperial support for scripturalizing the Torah in the Persian period.

Whatever the historical facts may have been, Nehemiah 8 shows that its authors thought the Torah should be ritualized just as Deuteronomy requires. From the time of Ezra in the Persian period on, the Pentateuch was in fact increasingly ritualized in all three dimensions as a scripture. So the story of Ezra's Torah illustrates a turning point in the history of the Pentateuch's scripturalization, whatever the role of the Persian empire may have been.

and 2.4) do not affect the claim that the Pentateuch began to be ritualized as scripture, as Torah, during this time. The story of the priest and scribe Ezra – who brought the Torah from Babylon and read it to the people of Jerusalem so that they renewed their commitment to God and the temple – shows how the writers of Ezra and Nehemiah thought the Pentateuch should be ritualized. From the time of Ezra on, Jews and Samaritans did increasingly ritualize the Torah. There is no sign that this was the case before this time. It is only from the time of Ezra on, that is, from the middle or late Persian period or, more broadly, from the early Second Temple period, that the Torah began to function regularly as scripture.

The story of Ezra therefore serves to mark a turning point in religious history and in the history of scripturalization.[3] It provides information about the political, social, and religious reasons Jews began to ritualize the

## Box 2.4 Ezra in history and tradition

The Persian emperor sent Ezra "to appoint judges," according to Ezra 7:25. He apparently carried with him a Torah scroll (7:14). Ezra, besides being a Persian official, was also a Jewish priest and "a scribe skilled in the law (torah) of Moses" who "had set his heart to study the law of YHWH, and to do it, and to teach the statutes and ordinances in Israel" (Ezra 7:6, 10). The biblical books of Ezra and Nehemiah depict Ezra as entirely concerned with the people's religious faithfulness. Once he reached Jerusalem, Ezra reformed the community's marriage laws (Ezra 10) and ritual calendar (Neh. 8) according to his interpretation of the Torah. He even required Judean men to divorce and send away their foreign wives for fear that the foreigners would introduce their gods to the Judeans.

Many historians suspect that the biblical writers changed Ezra from being a Persian official who oversaw the appointment of judges to being a religious reformer. They think that the biblical writers reinterpreted the commission of Ezra as a Persian bureaucrat (Ezra 7:12–26) and turned him into a Torah scribe and religious reformer. In that case, Nehemiah 8's depiction of Ezra reading the Torah scroll may not be historically accurate. Other historians defend the story as a plausible account of how the Persians sponsored the development of local ethnic laws (see Box 2.3).

What is clear is that the biblical writers presented Ezra as a model of Torah observance. They were not interested in Persian bureaucracy. Instead, they used the story of Ezra to show how the Torah *should* be ritualized and what its effects *should* be.

Within a century after the books of Ezra and Nehemiah were written, someone revised them to emphasize this theme even more. The author of the book of *1 Esdras* omitted the governor Nehemiah as well as the criticisms of the priests' marriages. This rearrangement turns Ezra's ritual of Torah reading into the climax and conclusion of the work. *1 Esdras* thus presents Torah observance as the ultimate solution to the problem of sin and divine punishment.[4]

Torah in all three dimensions. It shows us how they imagined doing it properly, and this model of ritual behavior corresponds more or less with how later congregations ritualize their scriptures. The story illustrates the social effects of ritualizing Torah: in the iconic dimension by legitimizing Ezra's leadership, in the expressive dimension by inspiring the whole community to devote themselves to following Torah, and in the semantic dimension by empowering the authority of Torah's interpreters, in this case Ezra and the Levites who assisted him. This book therefore organizes its discussion of the scripturalization of the Pentateuch around this turning point in the time of Ezra.

## CITED WORKS AND FURTHER READING

1 On Torah, see H. Kleinknecht, "νόμος," *TDNT* 4 (1967), 1024–1035; and James W. Watts, "Torah," in *The New Interpreter's Dictionary of the Bible* (Nashville: Abingdon, 2009), 5:629–630.

2 In citations of rabbinic literature, a prefixed "m." indicates a tractate in the Mishnah, "y." the Jerusalem Talmud, "b." the Babylonian Talmud, and "t." the Tosefta. For a brief description of rabbinic literature, see Section 6.5.2.

3 See further in James W. Watts, "Using Ezra's Time as a Methodological Pivot for Understanding the Rhetoric and Functions of the Pentateuch," in *The Pentateuch: International Perspectives on Current Research* (ed. T. B. Dozeman, K. Schmid, and B. J. Schwarz; Tübingen: Mohr Siebeck, 2011), 489–506.

4 On Ezra, Persia, and the books of Ezra, Nehemiah, and 1 Esdras, see Lisbeth S. Fried, *Ezra and the Law in History and Tradition* (Columbia, SC: University of South Carolina Press, 2014); Konrad Schmid, "The Persian Imperial Authorization as an Historical Problem and as a Biblical Construct: A Plea for Distinctions in the Current Debate," in *The Pentateuch as Torah: New Models for Understanding Its Promulgation and Acceptance* (ed. G. N. Knoppers and B. M. Levinson; Winona Lake: Eisenbrauns, 2007), 22–38; James W. Watts, ed., *Persia and Torah: The Theory of Imperial Authorization of the Pentateuch* (Atlanta: Society of Biblical Literature, 2001); and Jacob L. Wright, "Writing the Restoration: Compositional Agenda and the Role of Ezra in Nehemiah 8," *Journal of Hebrew Scriptures* 7 (2007), online at http://www.jhsonline.org/cocoon/JHS/a071.html#3.

# The Torah's Rhetoric

Rhetoric is the discipline that studies forms of persuasion (Box 1.3). Rhetoric asks: How do people persuade each other to do or believe something? Why are some people more persuasive than others? What kinds of speeches and actions are more persuasive than others?

When applied to written texts, rhetoric studies the literary forms of persuasion: What literary forms are persuasive? Do different kinds of literature have different persuasive effects?

For any given text, rhetorical analysis asks: Who is trying to persuade whom of what

   …by writing this text?
   …by reading this text?
   …by copying or printing or publishing this text?
   …by interpreting this text?
   …by decorating this text?
   …by dramatizing this text?

Rhetoric provides a useful way of studying the Bible because Jews and Christians have found that scriptures can be persuasive for how they conduct themselves individually and as communities. This has been true ever since the Pentateuch first began to function as scripture, even though different people have understood its teachings in very different ways. So rhetorical analysis highlights one of the characteristic features of normative texts.

Rhetoric also provides a methodological framework within which the results of other kinds of analysis (literary, historical, legal, theological, sociological, etc.) can be related to each other. It provides a convenient way to search for the overall effect of a particular passage or book. Rhetoric pays attention both to a text's literary form and to its social function. So it asks why the text is written in a particular way and it also asks what effect the text has had on readers from the time it was first written until now.

Of course, we frequently do not know how readers responded to what they read or heard read. Nor do we know exactly whom writers were addressing. We have to try to figure that out inductively from what the text says. So, rhetoric combines literary analysis of the biblical text with historical research into its production and use in various situations and cultures from antiquity to the present.

## 3.1   THE TORAH'S RHETORIC OF ORIGINS

The Pentateuch's stories take the form of a rhetoric of origins. The stories of Genesis took place in the distant past even for the Israelites who were led by Moses out of Egypt in the book of Exodus. All the stories of the Pentateuch took place in the distant past for the Judeans and Samaritans who began to use the Torah as scripture in the Persian period, and even more so for every generation since then. The stories tell of obligations incurred and commitments made by ancestors long ago. They do so to explain why their descendants and followers should obey the commandments and instructions contained in the Torah (see Box 3.1).

The Pentateuch's stories tell the origins of things in order to explain why its readers and hearers are obliged to do what God says. The stories of world creation and destruction (Gen. 1–11) establish human obligations to God as the provider of life, environment, food, and family. The stories of Israel's ancestors (Gen. 12–50) document a divine plan for Israel long before the people existed. Exodus tells about the origins of Israel as a people when God rescued them from Egypt (Exod. 1–18), before narrating their willing acceptance of a covenant obliging them and their descendants to obey God's rules (Exod. 19–20, 24). This contract between God and Israel included the plans for constructing the tent sanctuary, the Tabernacle (Exod. 25–40), and for inaugurating its priests (Lev. 8–9). So the Pentateuch's rhetoric of origins credits God with creating Israel as a people and their religious institutions.

> **Box 3.1   Law and narrative**
>
> The legal theorist Robert Cover argued that laws necessarily imply their story of origins, even when they do not state it: "No set of legal institutions or prescriptions exists apart from the narratives that locate it and give it meaning. For every constitution there is an epic, for each decalogue a scripture. Once understood in the context of the narratives that give it meaning, law becomes not merely a system of rules to be observed, but a world in which we live. In this normative world, law and narrative are inseparably related. Every prescription is insistent in its demand to be located in discourse – to be supplied with history and destiny, beginning and end, explanation and purpose. And every narrative is insistent in its demand for its prescriptive point, its moral."[1]

As good stories always do, the Pentateuch's stories establish convincing main characters. Besides all the individuals like Abraham, Sarah, Jacob, Joseph, Moses, and Miriam, the Pentateuch's plot depends on the interaction of two main characters, God and Israel. God's creation of Israel and Israel's relationship with God form the fundamental theme and plot of the Pentateuch, and of the rest of the Hebrew Bible. We will discuss the stories about world creation in Genesis 1–11 later (Section 14.2). Here I summarize the plots and themes of the Pentateuch's stories about the origins of Israel, and I also point out how they characterize God and Israel.

## 3.1.1   Ancestral Origins: Genesis 12–50

The contents of Genesis 12–50 are united and structured by a concern with ancestry and descent. God's promises to Israel's ancestors punctuate the stories about them. The stories about Abraham begin with the three-part promise of a land, of descendants ("a great nation"), and that "you will be a blessing" (12:1–3). Genesis does not define this blessing much beyond its initial description (similarly 22:17–18). It specifies the land grant as stretching "from the river of Egypt to the Euphrates" (15:18) or simply as "Canaan" (17:8). Most of its stories focus on the promise of descendants to Abraham.

Family sets the common theme for Genesis 12–50 and also its literary structure. Genealogies (Hebrew *toledot* "descendants" or "generations") introduce the stories by listing the families that do not inherit God's promises before listing those who do (see Box 3.2). The stories of three

**Box 3.2  Genealogies in Genesis**

| *Other descendants* | *Divinely favored descendants* |
| --- | --- |
| Cain's 4:17–24 | Seth's 5:1–32 |
| Ham's and Japhet's 10:1–32 | Shem's 10:21–31; 11:10–30 |
| Ishmael's 25:12–18 | Isaac's 25:19–26 |
| Esau's 36:1–43 | Jacob's 37:2; also 35:22–26 |

generations follow these genealogical introductions. These stories therefore fall into collections focused on Abraham (Gen. 12–25), his grandson Jacob (Gen. 25–35), and his great-grandson Joseph (Gen. 36–50).

Outlining Genesis by the names of major male characters accurately reflects the patriarchal emphasis of these stories. Genealogical structure reinforces patriarchy by emphasizing descent from fathers to sons. But it obscures the fact that many of these stories, especially in the Abraham and Jacob cycles, give significant roles to female characters (as do Genesis 3, Exodus 1–2, and Numbers 12). Genesis tells more stories about women than most other biblical books. Nevertheless, the stories of Sarah (Gen. 16–18, 20–21), Hagar (Gen. 16, 21), Rebekah (Gen. 24–27), and Tamar (Gen. 38) revolve around children or their lack of children, specifically male heirs. Feminist critics have rightly seen the need to imaginatively "counter-read" these women's stories as they might have told them themselves, rather than to meet the patriarchal needs of patrilineal descent.

Almost unique in this regard is the story of the first woman, Eve. Her words and actions drive the plot of Genesis 3 and do not involve motherhood or children, which are mentioned only once near the end as part of her punishment (Gen. 3:16). Only then does the man name her Eve, "the mother of all living" (3:20). However, the patriarchal pattern structures the next chapter, which begins with the birth of her sons, Cain and Abel (4:1–2), and concludes with genealogies of the descendants of her third son, Seth (4:17–5:32), but mentions no daughters of Eve.

The Pentateuch depicts the ancestral period as a golden age marked by close, even intimate, relationships between God and some humans. The ancestral stories take place in a world without religious conflicts. Abraham can invite YHWH (or YHWH's angels – the difference is not very clear) to dinner and argue with God over how to punish those who offend God (Gen. 18:23–33). Jacob can literally wrestle with God and limp as a result (Gen. 32:22–32). Both

Abraham's family and neighboring peoples interact with the same God, who even speaks to Egyptian and Philistine kings in dreams (Gen. 20:6–7; 41:16). Occasional notices of polytheistic practices (31:34–35; 35:2–4) pass with little comment and no controversy. This religious setting stands in sharp contrast to the other books of the Hebrew Bible in which conflicts over the status of gods and over rituals feature heavily.

Many cultures around the eastern Mediterranean and Middle East in the first millennium BCE remembered the preceding (second) millennium as a golden age better than their own. Their stories featured larger-than-life Bronze Age heroes – Gilgamesh in Babylon, Ptah-hotep in Egypt, and Achilles, Odysseus, and Theseus in Greece. Their kings sometimes chose the names of legendary third- and second-millennium kings as their own throne names, such as Sargon and Nebuchadnezzar (Figure 3.1). In Egypt and Mesopotamia, they sometimes tried to revive and preserve ancient patterns of architecture and literature – as exemplified by the activities of kings Nebuchadnezzar and Nabonidus in Babylon and by the kings of the Egyptian Twenty-Sixth Dynasty.

Genesis similarly portrays a time that it marks off as religiously different from the time of the exodus as well as of its readers. It is a time when Israel's ancestors enjoyed special relationships with God. These relationships

**FIGURE 3.1**    Barrel cylinder with a cuneiform inscription of Nebuchadnezzar II, King of Babylon from 605 to 562 BCE, to celebrate the discovery of a temple foundation inscription of Naram-Sin, King of Akkad, 1700 years earlier. In the Israel Museum, Jerusalem.

characterize YHWH as "the God of Abraham, Isaac, and Jacob" (Exod. 3:6, 15–16; 6:3). Invoking their memory can persuade YHWH to help their descendants (Exod. 2:24; 6:8; 32:13; Lev. 26:42; Deut. 1:8; 34:4).[2]

Apart from this religious setting and periodic mention of the divine promises, the cycles of stories in Genesis differ from one another (and sometimes even within cycles) in theme, in narrative style, and in their portrayal of the major characters, including God.

The Abraham stories (Gen. 12–25) are a loosely connected cycle of independent episodes. Many of them revolve around the issue of Abraham's heir, or rather his lack of one. Despite YHWH's promise right at the start of the cycle that Abraham will have many descendants (12:2), Abraham and Sarah grow old and still have no son. They attempt to arrange for other heirs, such as Abraham's slave Eliezer (15:2–3) or Ishmael, the son of their slave, Hagar (16:1–16; 17:18). But God insists that only a son of Sarah will inherit the divine promises to Abraham (15:4; 17:19). After Genesis finally narrates the birth of that son, Isaac (21:1–8), God commands Abraham to sacrifice Isaac and Abraham tries to do so (22:1–19). The theme of Abraham's missing or endangered heir provides these varied stories with a narrative trajectory.

The Abraham stories present an anthropomorphic characterization of God. Whether called by the divine designation, God (Hebrew 'Elohim), or the personal name, YHWH (replaced by "the LORD" in Jewish reading tradition and in English bibles; see p. 69), the deity is an active character in these stories. God intervenes in the plot to punish misbehaving kings (12:17; 20:3–18) and cities (19:24–29). God talks directly and frequently with Abraham, visits him for dinner, and tolerates Abraham's negotiations on behalf of the cities of Sodom and Gomorrah (18:1–33). Other texts remark on this extraordinary relationship by calling Abraham God's "friend" (Isa. 41:8; 2 Chr. 20:7). The Abraham stories portray God with many human qualities, though of course also possessing superhuman knowledge and power. The other cycles of ancestral stories portray God quite differently.

Abraham's son, Isaac, does not feature in many stories of his own, but rather in stories about his father or his son. Even the story of how his marriage was arranged (Gen. 24) features Abraham's slave and Rebekah, Isaac's future wife, as main characters rather than Isaac himself.

The cycle of stories that revolve around Jacob (Gen. 25–35) form a more cohesive plot. Now there are too many heirs claiming the divine promises. The story begins with several conflicts between the twin brothers, Esau and Jacob (Gen. 25–28), then continues with Jacob's life story as he competes also with his uncle, Laban (Gen. 29–31), and finally with a man who turns out to be God (32:24–32). This last episode results in Jacob's name being changed to Israel, which is interpreted in the text as meaning "one who fights with God and humans, and wins" (32:28). These stories characterize Jacob as a competitive trickster. Their rhetoric of ancestral origins does not necessarily recommend the ancestors as models of morality. Nevertheless, the Hebrew Bible uses Jacob's new name for all of his descendants, "the children of Israel."

The stories about Jacob characterize God more mysteriously than did the Abraham stories. God appears in dreams (28:11–17) and night visions (32:24–32) rather than speaking directly to Jacob. These experiences cast God in the role of Jacob's protector and also his adversary. In return, Jacob places conditions on his loyalty to God (28:20–22). Though Jacob received the honor of being the eponymous ancestor of Israel (see Box 3.3), his relationship with God is not as friendly as Abraham's.

The stories about Joseph (Gen. 36–37, 39–50) form a single narrative with a tight plot – a contrast in style and composition with earlier parts of Genesis. With the single exception of Genesis 38's focus on Judah, these chapters follow Joseph from his boyhood as Jacob's favorite and pampered son through his brothers' betrayal of him to slave traders and his up-and-down career in Egypt until he rises to the very top of the Egyptian bureaucracy. His wisdom in managing Egypt's agricultural economy leads to a reunion with his brothers and, eventually, with his father when a famine drives them to Egypt in search of grain. The issue of who will inherit the divine promises that provided the theme to the Abraham and Jacob stories does not reappear in the Joseph cycle: these stories presuppose that all 12 brothers will inherit equally. The position of the Joseph stories at the end of Genesis seems to be motivated by the need to explain why the Israelites moved to Egypt, where the beginning of Exodus finds them.

Apart from this contribution to the geographic route of the Pentateuch's plot from Mesopotamia to Canaan, then to Egypt and back again to Canaan,

## Box 3.3  Eponymous ancestry in Genesis

Eponymous ancestry describes the practice of naming a group of people by the name of a common ancestor. Jacob is not the only character in Genesis to lend his name to his descendants. Moab and Ben-Ammi, the sons of Lot, become eponymous ancestors to Israel's eastern neighbors, the Moabites and the Ammonites (Gen. 19:37–38). The sons of Jacob and two of his grandsons lend their names to the tribes of Israelites: Reuben, Simeon, Levi, Judah, Issachar, Zebulun, Dan, Naphtali, Gad, Asher, Benjamin, and the two tribes descended from Joseph's sons, Ephraim and Manasseh.

the Joseph story is driven by its own internal logic and themes. Central among them is the theme of God's control over the course of events. Unlike other parts of Genesis, the Joseph stories do not show God talking with Joseph or intervening personally in events. All the action seems motivated by human behavior and intentions. Joseph, however, interprets dreams and his own life story as governed by divine intention. He tells his brothers that "it was not you who sent me here, but God" (Gen 45:8). So rather than the anthropomorphic supernatural friend of Abraham, Joseph's God is transcendent, like a director who controls the action behind the scenes without ever stepping on stage.

To summarize: the rhetoric of ancestral origins in Genesis provides the background for understanding the following books. It justifies Israel's claim to a promised land on the basis of a divine grant to Israel's ancestors (Gen. 12, 15, 35), but it qualifies that grant by requiring obedience to divine commandments (Gen. 15, 17, 22). Though it defines the Israelites as descendants of Jacob/Israel, it broadens Israel's ethnic identity by including in Abraham's family tree the Arameans (28:5), the Moabites (19:37), the Ammonites (19:38), the Edomites (36:1), and desert tribes later identified as Arabs (17:20; 25:12–18), and by marriage to the Canaanites (38:2) and Egyptians (41:45, 50–52; 46:20).

Nevertheless, Genesis depicts Israel as something new, an ethnic identity defined by loyalty to covenants with God. This covenant identity must be accepted anew by future generations (Exod. 24; Deuteronomy). So Genesis maintains that both possession of the land and ethnic identity depend on the people's relationship with God. And it shows God interacting with them in a wide variety of ways, ranging from Abraham's friendly relationship through Jacob's struggles to Joseph's intellectual interpretation of God's control over his life. It foreshadows the stories of tumultuous divine–human relationships in the following books by telling stories about the challenging life of Jacob/Israel, the eponymous ancestor of the Israelites.

## 3.1.2  Israel's Origins: Exodus 1–18

The story of the Israelites' exodus (departure) from Egypt is *the* defining story for the identity of Israel and for Judaism. It tells how God established Israel as a people by rescuing their ancestors from oppression. That rescue gives their descendants reason to accept the obligations of the covenant with God. It also establishes a major new aspect of God's character.

Exodus begins in the same place that Genesis ends, the land of Egypt. For ancient readers and listeners just like moderns, the name "Egypt" evoked images of great wealth, god-like kings, and great antiquity. The pyramids at Giza were already 1000 years old by the time this story took place.

However, the golden age of Genesis is over. Exodus portrays religious conflicts between Israel and the Egyptians and within the Israelite community. Moses presents demands from a new god, or at least God using a new name, YHWH (see p. 69). The Egyptian king, Pharaoh, does not recognize this god and refuses Moses' demands (5:2). The Israelites question whether Moses speaks for God (5:21; 6:9) and whether either God or Moses can take care of them (14:11–12; chaps. 16–17). The story of God's plagues on the Egyptians that enable Israel to escape into the wilderness establishes YHWH's ability and willingness to fight for the Israelites against their wealthy and powerful enemies.[3]

Knowledge of YHWH and of YHWH's power is a central theme in the exodus story. God reveals a new name to Moses: YHWH (3:14–15; 6:3). The cryptic explanation of its meaning, "I am who I am," does not diminish Moses' concern that the Israelites will doubt that he brings messages from God. He is right: they do not believe him and neither does Pharaoh. Establishing the reputation of YHWH as the God who rescued Israel from Egypt then becomes a major motive for God bringing 10 plagues on the Egyptians (see Box 3.4).

The story begins with Egypt subjecting the Israelites to forced labor (Exod. 1). Their dramatic change of circumstances since the end of Genesis is explained by the rise of "a new king" and the Israelites' rapidly growing population (1:7–10). The story of Moses' amazing rescue as a baby (2:1–10) uses ancient literary conventions to emphasize his future importance. Exodus raises expectations for Moses' future further by narrating his encounter with God in the burning bush (Exod. 3–4). This dialogue uses the conventions of prophetic call narratives (cf. Jer. 1 and Isa. 6) to establish Moses' identity as a true prophet.

The story of God's plagues on the Egyptians in Exodus 7–12 takes an unusual amount of space. Hebrew stories tend to be short and cryptic. For example, Exodus 2 narrates the stories of Moses' birth, rescue from the river, adoption by an Egyptian princess, growth to adulthood, murder of a slave driver, and flight into the wilderness all in 22 verses or sentences. By contrast, the narrator lingers over the 10 plagues, describing the negotiations before and after each one and detailing the enormous suffering of the Egyptians. So it is not just the Egyptians and Israelites who need to recognize the power of YHWH: this repetitive story wants readers and listeners to feel God's overwhelming power and control. As the story progresses, even the king of Egypt is changed from a dangerous opponent into a puppet in God's hands: YHWH makes Pharaoh stubborn ("hardens

## Box 3.4    YHWH's reputation in Exodus

*"I will take you as my people and I will be your God. You will know that I am YHWH your God who rescued you from forced labor in Egypt." (6:7)*

*"The Egyptians will know that I am YHWH when I stretch out my hand against Egypt and rescue the Israelites from among them." (7:5)*

*"...so that you (Pharaoh) will know that I, YHWH, am in the land." (8:22)*

*". . . so that you (Pharaoh) will see my power and so that my fame will echo through the earth." (9:16)*

*"I have hardened Pharaoh's heart and his officials' hearts so that I can do these signs among them, in order that you can tell your children and grandchildren how I tricked the Egyptians and what signs I did among them so that you will know that I am YHWH." (10:1–2)*

*"You shall tell your children (when you eat unleavened bread at Passover) 'It is because of what YHWH did for me when I came out of Egypt'...for with a strong hand YHWH rescued you from Egypt." (13:8–9; see also vv. 14–16)*

*"I will harden Pharaoh's heart so he will pursue them. Then I will magnify myself at the expense of Pharaoh and his entire army, so the Egyptians will know that I am YHWH." (14:4; see also vv. 17–18)*

*Then Israel saw the mighty hand that YHWH used against the Egyptians. They were in awe of YHWH and they believed in YHWH and his servant Moses. (14:31)*

Pharaoh's heart") to make sure that all 10 plagues occur (Exod. 9:12; 10:20; 14:4, 8). The land, the people, and the king of Egypt are under the control of the God of Israel.

The purpose of this demonstration of divine power becomes clear once the Israelites reach Mount Sinai. God tells them through Moses:

*You yourselves have seen what I did to the Egyptians and how I carried you on eagles' wings and brought you to myself. Now, if you listen to my voice and keep my covenant, you will be my treasured possession out of all the peoples. The whole world is mine, but you will be a kingdom of priests for me and a holy nation. (19:4–6)*

God claims "possession" of Israel by right of conquest. Though the whole world and all its inhabitants belong to God from creation (Gen. 1), YHWH takes Israel away from Egypt like a king claiming territory by military force.

And like a conquering king, YHWH now offers Israel a covenant of protection in return for their loyalty.

The <u>covenant at Mount Sinai</u> is modeled on ancient political treaties between emperors and the rulers of cities or small territories. The local rulers became vassals of the emperor and promised to remain loyal to him and his successors, to pay taxes, and to supply the imperial army with troops. The emperor promised protection to the vassal from other enemies, and from himself: these treaties were usually negotiated when the imperial army had either already conquered or was threatening to conquer the city (see Box 6.4).

In the exodus story, it is not territory but a people that God takes away from Egypt by force. Now, having witnessed YHWH's power over a foreign enemy, God asks the Israelites to become YHWH's vassals. They must remain loyal ("no other gods before me" Exod. 20:3) and they must obey God's commandments, including making regular offerings at the sanctuary. In return, YHWH promises economic prosperity and protection from their enemies. Through the covenant, God becomes Israel's king (see Box 3.5).

The story of Israel's exodus from Egypt mixes together characterizations of God that are distinct in different parts of Genesis. In the plague stories, Exodus depicts YHWH as miraculous and mysterious, both transcendent and immediately responsive to Moses and the other human actors. YHWH speaks directly and intimately with Moses, as with Abraham. At Moses' death, Deuteronomy 34:10 celebrates Moses' relationship to God as uniquely close: "Never again was there a prophet in Israel like Moses, whom YHWH knew face to face." But the Israelites fight with God like Jacob did, to the point that the generation who participated in the Exodus fails to believe that YHWH could conquer Canaan for them. They die in the wilderness as punishment for their lack of loyalty to their divine king. God in this story, as in the Joseph story, completely controls the course of events, including the Egyptian king. But unlike the Joseph story, here God acts directly and decisively. Like earlier parts of Genesis, God is the protagonist who propels the exodus story's plot.

### 3.1.3   The Story-List-Sanction Rhetorical Strategy

Many ancient Near Eastern texts combine different kinds (genres) of literature to make a more persuasive argument. One typical combination employed a distinctive <u>story-list-sanction</u> pattern that starts with stories about the past that establish obligations between different people or groups of people. Then lists of rules or instructions direct the audience's behavior. The pattern concludes with sanctions that promise blessings on those who obey and threaten curses

## Box 3.5  The Pentateuch's unstated premise

If Exodus portrays God as a conquering king, why does it never call YHWH a "king"? Aristotle pointed out that rhetorical arguments usually presuppose common beliefs which they leave unstated. In such an *enthymeme*, the unstated premise unites speaker and audience in an implicit understanding. It makes the speech more persuasive without drawing attention to any problems with the premise.

The Torah's most general enthymeme presupposes the imperial ideology of ancient Middle Eastern kingship:

*Stated premises:* YHWH saved Israel from Egypt and Israel accepted the covenant with YHWH at Sinai.

*Unstated premise:* Military rescue and subsequent covenant/treaty establish royal authority over vassals and their descendants.

*Conclusion:* Israel owes YHWH loyalty (stated), because YHWH is Israel's king (unstated except in poetry).

That explains why Pentateuchal stories and instructions do not call God "king." Only some inset poems do (Num. 23:21; Deut. 33:5; cf. Exod. 15:18) just as the psalms often do (Pss. 44:4, 93:1–4, 95:3, etc.). 1 Samuel 8 shows Israelites later arguing over whether God's kingship allows for a human king or not. This story illustrates the conflicts that can arise from exposing the premise of God's kingship to explicit discussion. The Pentateuch leaves God's kingship unstated while showing God performing royal duties by defending Israel against enemy armies, giving laws, and establishing the Tabernacle and its rituals. This unstated premise motivates the Pentateuch's argument that Israel owes God obedience without engaging the political consequences of having a divine ruler.[4]

on those who do not.[5] The story-list-sanction pattern is effective because it combines past, present, and future to persuade people to obey its instructions. First it tells a story to explain what led to the present circumstances. Then it lists a series of actions that must or must not be taken. Finally, it promises good results if its instructions are followed or disaster if they are ignored.

This story-list-sanction structure of persuasion appears, for example, in the law code of King Hammurabi, which precedes the laws with stories of the king's military victories and gifts to temples, and concludes with curses on anyone who might modify or destroy his inscription.

The Pentateuch uses this rhetorical strategy too, though on a much larger scale (see Box 3.6). In Deuteronomy, Moses recounts the story of Israel's

## Box 3.6     Outline of the Pentateuch's rhetoric

At a very general level, the whole Pentateuch takes the shape of the story-list-sanction pattern:

1. Stories (Genesis 1 – Exodus 19)
2. Lists (Exodus 20 – Numbers)
3. Sanctions (Deuteronomy)

A closer look shows that the rhetoric moves back and forth between stories, lists, and sanctions even as the preponderance of stories at the beginning shifts to lists of laws and instructions, and finally to sanctions as the Pentateuch progresses:

1. Stories of origins, including
   - Where the world and nations came from (Genesis 1–11)
   - Where Israel's ancestors came from (Genesis 12–50)
   - Where Israel came from (Exodus 1–18, parts of Numbers)
   - Where Torah came from (Exodus 19–20, Deuteronomy 1–11, 31, 34)
   - Where Israel's Tabernacle came from (Exodus 32–40)
   - Where Israel's priests and rituals came from (Leviticus 8–10, parts of Numbers)
2. Lists of laws and instructions for the present (Exodus 20–23, 25–31, Leviticus, parts of Numbers, Deuteronomy 12–26)
3. Future sanctions for obedience or disobedience (Leviticus 26, Deuteronomy 27–30, 32–33)

journeys in the wilderness (Deut. 1–11) before repeating the lists of laws and instructions given by God on Mount Sinai (Deut. 12–26). He concludes by promising God's blessings if the Israelites obey the covenant and divine punishments if they do not (Deut. 27–30, 32–33).

A more complicated variation on this pattern shapes the entire Pentateuch (see Box 3.6). Genesis and the first half of Exodus tell the story of Israel's origins by God's actions starting from the creation of the world. The rest of Exodus, all of Leviticus, and much of Numbers present instructions for building the Tabernacle and for worshipping God in it, as well as moral, civil, and criminal rules for conducting Israel's community life. Deuteronomy as a whole can be viewed as delivering, in the voice of God's prophet, exhortations predicting future blessings or punishments depending on Israel's behavior.

Another way of summarizing the Pentateuch's story-list-sanction rhetoric is to say that it uses the *rhetoric of origins*, the *rhetoric of law*, and *the rhetoric of promise and threat* to persuade its hearers and readers to accept their identity as a people in covenant with God. The Pentateuch uses past, present, and future to urge readers and hearers to accept their identity as Israel.

## 3.2  AUTHORITY, SANCTIONS, AND READERS

Aristotle pointed out that effective persuasion depends not only on making rational arguments (*logos*), but also on exhibiting a trustworthy character (*ethos*), and appealing to the audience's feelings and values (*pathos*). The speaker and audience often bring a certain ethos and pathos to the situation. We have already observed that a book of scripture's physical appearance and oral presentation invoke ethos and pathos to establish its legitimacy and inspiration (see Box 1.3). But Aristotle also observed that the contents of a speech establish or reinforce ethos and pathos. On the one hand, a speech can characterize the speaker explicitly by describing her or his education or experience and implicitly by using language skillfully to elicit the audience's admiration and respect. On the other hand, a speech can lead the audience to think of themselves and their values in certain ways and not in others.

So, in addition to paying attention to the persuasive argument advanced by a text, rhetoric makes us consider how it characterizes its speaker/author and audience/readers. In the case of the Pentateuch, the relationship between author and audience works on several levels. Three voices reinforce each other's messages. God and Moses both speak major portions of the text, and are themselves characters within the story voiced by an anonymous third-person narrator. God gives commands but never tells stories, the narrator tells stories but does not command, while Moses does both in Deuteronomy by repeating, and modifying, the stories and laws of Exodus, Leviticus, and Numbers. The resulting Pentateuch combines divine, prophetic, and story-telling voices into one authoritative, and so very persuasive, discourse.

The multiple speakers create multiple audiences. God and Moses address the Israelites in the wilderness. More accurately, God mostly addresses Moses who is expected to repeat the speeches to the Israelites. The narrator addresses the readers and hearers of the Pentateuch. Much of the Pentateuch's rhetoric works to identify readers with the wilderness Israelites. Moses says so explicitly to the new generation 40 years after the revelation of the Torah at Mount Sinai/Horeb:

> *YHWH our God made a covenant with us at Mount Horeb. YHWH did not make this covenant only with our ancestors but with us who are alive today. YHWH spoke with you face to face out of the fire on the mountain.* (Deut. 5:2–4)

But the Pentateuch also blames the people of the exodus generation for their lack of faith in God's promises and their disobedience to Moses' commands. They are punished by dying in the wilderness. This persuasive lesson wishes readers and hearers to distinguish themselves as obedient to the Torah's teachings in contrast to the generations of Israelites who were not. In this way, the speeches of God and Moses break out of story time and address readers and hearers in their own time. The Pentateuch tries to convince its readers and hearers to understand themselves as directly addressed by God's commandments and Moses' interpretation of them.

### 3.2.1   The Rhetoric of Omniscient Narration

Prophetic books often name and describe prophets to legitimize their claim to present revelations from God. For example, the book of Jeremiah begins,

> *The words of Jeremiah, son of Hilkiah, of the priests of Anathoth in Benjamin, to whom the word of YHWH came in the days of King Josiah of Judah, from the thirteenth year of his reign … until the captivity of Jerusalem in the fifth month.* (Jer. 1:1–3)

The Pentateuch never introduces its narrator. The narrative books of the Hebrew Bible make no attempt to identify and legitimize their authors. Genesis begins without introducing either its author or its sources:

> *When God started to create the heavens and the earth …* (Gen. 1:1)

Despite the lack of claims to prophetic inspiration, the Pentateuch's narrator knows everything necessary to tell stories of world creation and 1000 years of human history. The narrator can even tell us what God is thinking:

> *God said, "Let us make humans in our image."* (Gen. 1:26)

*YHWH regretted making humans on the earth, and it disturbed God's heart.* (Gen. 6:6)

*The Israelites groaned under their forced labor and their cry rose up to God. God remembered the covenant with Abraham, Isaac and Jacob, so God looked at the Israelites and paid attention to them.* (Exod. 2:23–25)

This is a typical <u>third-person omniscient narrator</u>. Such anonymous, all-knowing narrators appear frequently in both ancient and modern literature. Calling the narrator "omniscient" does not make a theological claim in the same way as calling God "omniscient" does. The narrator should not be confused with the writer who composed the story. Omniscient narrators are simply a literary device for telling stories. Authors create narrators who know everything about the story. Omniscient narrators appear so commonly that few writers find it necessary to explain how the narrator knows all the details of this story.

The Pentateuch nevertheless restricts its narrator to relating only the story. This narrator does not comment very much about the characters in the story and their behavior. The narrator never voices laws or instructions, and does not pronounce blessings or curses. The narrator is restricted to telling stories about the past and introducing the speeches of characters. It is the characters, YHWH and Moses, who pronounce normative teachings and make predictions about the future.

## 3.2.2   The Rhetoric of Divine Speech

The divine character, alternately called "God" or "YHWH" or sometimes both together (e.g., Gen. 2–3), dominates the Pentateuch from beginning to end. God can therefore be considered the Pentateuch's protagonist, the character who drives the plot both with narrated actions and by quoted direct speech. God's character as revealed in actions shows considerable variation in Genesis, as we have seen. In Exodus, Leviticus, and Numbers, the divine character is both miraculous and mysterious, transcendently in control of nature and history, even of foreign kings like Pharaoh, yet immediately responsive to Moses and the people. God is notably unable or unwilling, however, to control the minds of the people of Israel. More than Abraham or Moses or Pharaoh, therefore, it is Israel who emerges as the true antagonist to the divine protagonist. It is the interaction between YHWH and Israel that drives the plot of the later books of the Pentateuch, and also of the future that the Pentateuch's sanctions anticipate.

The Pentateuch's depiction of God's character, however, does not depend entirely or even primarily on narrated action. Readers also gain an impression of a character by what that character says. The narrator quotes God speaking throughout the Pentateuch, from the very first chapter to the very last. From Exodus 19 through the book of Numbers, God's speeches take up most of the text, and Moses spends much of Deuteronomy paraphrasing what God said. The laws (see Box 3.7), instructions, and sanctions characterize God as much as the stories do.[6]

Laws try to characterize their authors as just, fair, and merciful. This may have been the original function of written law codes. Ancient law collections did not govern the legal practices of their law courts, so far as we can tell. Instead, they depicted the kings who promulgated them, such as Hammurabi (Figure 3.2), as ruling justly. That characterization helped legitimize their rule, especially if they ruled violently.

The Pentateuch differs from most other ancient legal collections by placing the laws in the mouth of a deity, rather than a king. By doing so, it reinforces the impression that YHWH is Israel's king. The contents of the laws and instructions then reveal this character's interests. Cataloging their topics provides a summary of God's main concerns:

1. YHWH is very interested in gaining and preserving Israel's loyalty. That is expressed by banning the worship of other gods and the use of images in worship (Exod. 20:3–5; Deut. 5:7–9), and by restricting ritual worship to the Tabernacle or centralized sanctuary (Lev. 17:1–8; Deut. 12:2–7), among other things.

2. The detailed ritual instructions in Exodus 25 through Leviticus 16 express a concern to preserve holiness and purity so that YHWH can live in Israel's midst.

3. God is also concerned about how the Israelites behave toward each other. This concern gets expressed through moral instructions regarding right behavior and attitudes (Exod. 20:12–17; Deut. 5:16–21), criminal legislation for the punishment of murderers and thieves (Exod. 21:12–14; Lev. 6:1–7; 24:17–22), and exhortations against sexual relations regarded as immoral or impure (Lev. 18). God's concern for human relationships extends to immigrants who live in Israelite territory, and to slaves: while the Pentateuch does not ban slavery, it does require that owners allow slaves to rest on the Sabbath (Exod. 20:10; Deut. 5:14) and to release Israelite slaves after six years of service (Deut. 15:12–18).

God's concerns include many more issues, as the detailed stipulations of the Pentateuch make very clear.

## Box 3.7   Law collections in the Pentateuch

Interpreters typically identify three separate collections of laws in the Pentateuch. These collections cover many of the same subjects but often differ in how they treat them. They are:

- the Covenant Code (Exodus 20:22–23:33)
- the Holiness Code (Leviticus 17–27)
- the Deuteronomic Code (Deuteronomy 12–26).

Another collection of instructions containing rules for offerings and impurities appears in:

- Leviticus 1–7, 11–16 with parallels and additions scattered through Numbers.

The Ten Commandments appear separately from these collections and twice in nearly identical form in:

- Exodus 20:2–17
- Deuteronomy 5:6–21

and once with very different contents that have earned it the name "the Ritual Decalogue," in:

- Exodus 34:14–28.

Other laws and instructions on specific topics appear in various stories, such as:

- the rule against eating blood in Genesis 9:2–6
- instructions for circumcising male descendants of Abraham in Genesis 17:9–14
- instructions for celebrating Passover in Exodus 12–13.

God does not just ask Israel to obey the covenant. YHWH promises rewards for obedience and threatens dire punishments for disobedience. In this way, God assumes the role of judge and enforcer, traditional roles of ancient kings. In fact, the Pentateuch emphasizes this role as the epitome

**FIGURE 3.2**   Diorite stela of Hammurabi's Laws, from Babylon, ca. 1700 BCE. Relief at top shows King Hammurabi standing before the god Shamash. The cuneiform text of the laws covers the front, back, and sides of the stela. In the Louvre Museum, Paris.

of divine self-expression. When Moses sees God on Mount Sinai, he hears YHWH proclaim:

> *YHWH, YHWH, a merciful and gracious God, slow to anger and great in steadfast love and faithfulness, who keeps steadfast love to the thousandth generation, who forgives guilt and transgression and sin, but who certainly does not acquit but rather punishes children for the parent's guilt and the children's children to the third and fourth generation.* (Exod. 34:6–7)

This self-description appears also in the introduction to the Ten Commandments in Exod-us 20:5–6. Moses quotes it in Numbers 14:18 and Deuteronomy 7:9–10. The promises and threats of the Pentateuch's sanctions therefore express a fundamental aspect of its characterization of God.

Just as Mesopotamian law codes served to establish the justice and legitimacy of the kings who issued them, the Pentateuch's lists of laws and sanctions characterize the king of Israel, YHWH. The rhetoric makes it clear that God wants the Israelites to do as the laws say. But the laws and sanctions also aim to get the Israelites, and later readers and hearers, to recognize the justice of these laws and, therefore, that their promulgator, YHWH, is a just and merciful king. The laws' reputation should be a credit to Israel:

> *See, I have taught you mandates and regulations...You must keep them and do them, because this is your wisdom and your understanding in the sight of the nations who will say when they hear of all these mandates, "This great nation is surely a wise and understanding people." For what nation is so great that God comes near to them like YHWH our God whenever we call on him? For what nation is so great that it has such righteous mandates and regulations as all this Torah that I have set before you today?* (Deut. 4:5–8)

The effect of these stories on readers' impressions of the divine character can be judged from the history of liturgy. Jewish and Christian prayers and hymns emphasize God's character as ruler and judge and the qualities that go with these roles: <u>justice</u>, <u>mercy</u>, and <u>steadfast love</u>. Despite modern readers' tendency to focus on the stories and ignore the laws, liturgical characterizations of God show that Pentateuchal law has exerted greater power in shaping later estimations of God's character.

## 3.2.3   The Rhetoric of Moses' Speech

Another major character in Exodus, Leviticus, Numbers, and Deuteronomy is Moses. He plays a central role in every story. He hears all of God's laws and instructions, and carries many of them out, such as building the Tabernacle and consecrating the priests. He repeats and interprets the laws to Israel. John van Seters therefore described the literary form of the Pentateuch, or actually one of its major sources, as a biography of Moses, with Genesis as prologue.[7]

Moses, however, rarely instigates the action. That role falls to YHWH or, occasionally, to the Israelites, who therefore function as the protagonist and antagonist of the story. Moses stands in between them as messenger and mediator, a position to which both God and Israel commission him (God's commission appears first in Exod. 3–4 and 6, and gets repeated throughout; Israel's commission of Moses to act as intermediary appears in Exod. 20:18–20). Most of what he does is at the command or request of YHWH or Israel.

Moses shows the most independence when he argues with one or the other. That happens frequently, and Moses wields great influence with YHWH as well as with the people. For example, his arguments limit divine punishment of the Israelites after they worship the golden calf (Exod. 32:11–14; 33:12–17), though he then punishes them himself. It is his words that sum up and conclude the Pentateuch in the book of Deuteronomy.

In all these ways, the Pentateuch presents Moses as the model mediator between God and humans. He sets an example for later mediators, who in biblical traditions appear usually as priests and prophets, and later as scribes. The job of the <u>priests</u> is to make offerings according to Moses' instructions to intercede with YHWH on behalf of the Israelites (Lev. 4, 16). The Pentateuch presents true <u>prophets</u> as those who urge Israel to learn and obey Torah, and who announce God's judgment on those who do not keep the covenant. Deuteronomy compares their role explicitly with that of Moses (18:15). By repeating and interpreting the laws of God, Moses also models the behavior of <u>scribes</u>, who read and copy the Torah's text and explain it to the people. The Pentateuch's Moses therefore sets the pattern that the priest and scribe Ezra emulates in scripturalizing the Pentateuch as Torah.

In fact, the Pentateuch's depiction of Moses models how to ritualize the three dimensions of Torah and of later scriptures. He both copies the Torah and he ritualizes its semantic dimension by interpreting and applying the Torah to the lives of hearers and readers. Moses thus models the authority of scribes/rabbis/scholars. He also ritualizes the expressive dimension by reading the text aloud and requiring the people to do so. Moses therefore models the devotional presentation of scriptures. And he commands veneration of the text in the form of tablets and scroll along with the reliquary Ark of the Covenant. Moses' story provides Torah with a foundation myth: he meets God "face to face" (Exod. 34; Deut. 34:10), he brings heavenly tablets to earth, and he installs both tablets and written Torah scroll in a holy sanctuary. Moses thereby models the legitimizing power of iconic texts.

The Pentateuch thus uses a complicated <u>strategy of authority</u>. It deploys three authoritative voices, that of an omniscient narrator, an omniscient God, and a divinely inspired prophet, to legitimize its message. The voices play distinct roles and reinforce each other's authority and messages. The narrator's voice encompasses those of God and Moses, since they speak only as direct quotations within the narrative. Yet the narrator restricts its voice to stories of the past, while the voices of YHWH and Moses address readers and hearers directly. Readers who accept this direct address will feel the force of their commands in the present moment and worry about their predictions of the readers' possible futures. The authority of the divine and prophetic voices therefore tends to dominate the Pentateuch's rhetoric.

## 3.2.4   The Rhetoric of Identity

The Pentateuch's rhetorical force depends, however, on hearers and readers accepting it as addressed to themselves. To this end, the Pentateuch works very hard to construct a particular vision of who Israel is, in hopes that hearers and readers will claim that identity for themselves.

The origin stories of ancestors and of divine covenants provide the essential elements for understanding Israel's identity and obligations to God. Israel does not appear among the peoples of the earth listed in Genesis 10. The Pentateuch describes Israel as a late-comer on the stage of history, a new creation by God. Unlike the boundless optimism that calls the creation of the world unequivocally good (Gen. 1), the much longer story of the creation of Israel consists of struggles. Conflicts between God and the people of Israel, individually and corporately, dominate the plot of Genesis 12 through Deuteronomy, and beyond. Jacob/Israel's tortuous life journey and conflicts with humans and with God typify the history of his namesake descendants, "the children of Israel" (often translated as Israelites), as told in the Pentateuch and in the larger Bible.

The Pentateuch wants readers and hearers to see their own experience in the trials of Jacob and of exodus Israel. But more than that, it wants readers to adopt the identity of Israel, of this new people created by God in the wilderness. This identity requires hearers and readers to take Israel's covenant obligations as their own. That means, first of all, understanding what those obligations are. Like ancient vassals bound to their imperial overlord by suzerainty treaties, Israel owes God loyalty, taxes (offerings and tithes), and nonaggression against other Israelites. The overall quality of the Israelites' relationship to God and to each other is marked by *chesed* "steadfast love," which was a conventional ideal in ancient treaties. The laws and instructions play the dominant role in shaping the behaviors that the Torah exhorts its hearers and readers to adopt.

However, readers and hearers must also feel dependent on God, just as the Israelites of the exodus were dependent on YHWH. To do that, the Pentateuch works to get readers and hearers to place themselves inside the story of the exodus. Celebrating Passover by eating unleavened bread while standing in traveling clothes (Exod. 12:11) lets later generations take their place among those whom YHWH rescued from Egypt. They will accept Moses' claim that God made the covenant at Sinai "not with our ancestors but with us" (Deut. 5:3). Then they will accept for themselves the obligation to observe Torah.

The Pentateuch's rhetoric also distinguishes readers and hearers from the exodus and wilderness generation. First of all, the narrator speaks only to them. Readers and hearers are therefore in a *better* position to understand God's covenant with Israel than was the exodus generation, because they hear the entire story as well as the laws and sanctions. Furthermore, many of these stories present the Israelites behaving badly and suffering the consequences. The Pentateuch asks readers and hearers to learn from their example. Therefore, this rhetoric aims to turn its audience into a better Israel than the people described in the text. The Pentateuch's rhetoric tries to convince communities of readers and listeners to find the true Israel in themselves.

### 3.2.5   The Rhetoric of Promise and Threat

Promises and threats lead readers and hearers to imagine their own futures as the consequences of their obedience or disobedience to the laws. This rhetoric of <u>sanctions</u> forecasts two possible futures. It gives a sense of urgency to the implications of the stories and lists of laws.[8]

The Pentateuch leaves no doubt that Israel's future depends on observing Torah. Promises structure its plot. God promises Abraham land, descendants, and blessing and repeats these promises to his son and grandson (Gen. 12:1–3; 15:1–21). But the promises are conditional on obedience, as is made clear by requiring male <u>circumcision</u> (cut off the penis's foreskin) as the sign of God's covenant with Abraham (Gen. 17:14). Obedience is also the explicit moral of the surprising story of God ordering Abraham to sacrifice Isaac, only to call it off at the last minute (Gen. 22:16–18). The exodus story is driven by YHWH's promise to rescue Israel from Egypt and settle the people in Canaan (Exod. 3:7–8). Israel only watches while YHWH plagues the Egyptians, but taking possession of Canaan requires their willing obedience. When they prove unwilling (Num. 13–14), an entire generation is doomed to live and die in the wilderness. It is their children who will finally settle the land (Num. 26:63–65).

The Pentateuch's stories demonstrate YHWH's power and willingness to destroy those who act contrary to the divine will. This point appears early in Genesis in the stories of Noah's flood (Gen. 6), the tower of Babel (Gen. 11), and Sodom and Gomorrah (Gen. 18:16–19:29). The story of the plagues on the Egyptians (Exod. 7–12) provides the most thorough illustration of YHWH's power and willingness to use it against wrongdoers. Moses recalls this story as a warning to the Israelites of what YHWH can do (Deut. 28:27, 60).

In ancient cultures, divine promises and threats frequently took the verbal form of blessings and curses. People invoked the name of a god to promise good or threaten evil to others. Thus, Noah cursed his grandson Canaan while blessing two of his sons (Gen. 9:25–27) and Jacob blessed his grandson Ephraim over his older brother Manasseh (Gen. 48:8–20). The Pentateuch's ritual instructions incorporate curses and blessings as well. The trial by ordeal of a suspected adulteress employs a written curse that must be drunk in water (Num. 5:23–24). On the other hand, the priests must pronounce blessings on the people after concluding their offerings (Lev. 9:22–23). The Pentateuch mandates what words the priests must say:

> *You must bless the people of Israel in this way, by saying:*
> *May YHWH bless you and keep you,*
> *May YHWH's face shine on you and favor you,*
> *May YHWH smile on you and give you peace.* (Num. 6:23–26)

The words of this priestly blessing continue to be repeated by priests, rabbis, and ministers in Jewish and Christian congregations to this day (see below, pp. 89-90, 109).

The story of Balaam provides an extended narrative illustration of how blessings and curses should work (Num. 22). Balaam is a foreign prophet hired by an enemy king to curse the Israelites. An angel intervenes and forces Balaam to proclaim God's blessings on Israel instead. Balaam himself explains the power of his words as coming from God: "Do I have the power to say just anything? I must say what God puts in my mouth" (Num. 22:38). His blessings take the form of extended poems that anticipate Israel's military victories over its neighbors (Num. 23–24).

The Pentateuch's rhetoric of sanctions reaches its fullest expression in the long lists of blessings and curses that conclude the major law collections (Box 3.7). This pattern reflects the ancient convention of concluding treaties by invoking the gods' blessings on those who fulfill the treaty and cursing those who do not. Lists of sanctions in the names of many gods also appear in the conclusions of royal inscriptions of many types, including Hammurabi's Law Code (Fig. 3.2).

The Covenant Code concludes with positive promises of good for Israel if they obey YHWH's laws. They will be victorious in war, have plenty of food, and suffer no diseases or difficulties in bearing children (Exod. 23:20–31). The only negative sanction appears in the vague threat, "Do not rebel against (my angel), for he will not take away your guilt" (v. 21).

The <u>Holiness Code</u> concludes with an entire chapter of promises and threats (Lev. 26; chap. 27 seems to be an appendix to the main collection of laws). First comes the condition, "if you follow my mandates and keep my commandments" (26:3), then the blessings: agricultural abundance, peace, victory in war, and large families. They culminate in the promise of God's continuing presence with Israel: "I will walk among you and be your God" (26:12). But if the people disobey (26:14), punishments will follow. God threatens famine, plague, war, and defeat. If they continue to be disobedient to the covenant, they will be conquered by foreign armies that will devastate their cities and exile the survivors away from the land. The language is vivid and horrifying: "You will eat the bodies of your sons and your daughters....I will pile your carcasses on the carcasses of your idols" (26:29–30). Leviticus describes the coming exile as a "sabbath for the land," a vivid image of the land as suffering while inhabited by the rebellious Israelites (26:34–35). In exile, Israel will continue to be punished by oppression. In the end, however, Leviticus offers a glimpse of hope: if the exiled people confess their sins, YHWH will remember Abraham, Isaac, Jacob, and the covenant (26:45).

<u>Deuteronomy</u> deploys the rhetoric of blessing and curse most fully and elaborately. Already by chapter 4, Moses anticipates Israel rebelling and suffering exile as punishment:

> *I call on heaven and earth to witness today that you will soon die out from the land...YHWH will scatter you among the peoples.* (Deut. 4:26–27)

Near the end of the book, he summarizes all his speeches in the form of sanctions:

> *I have set before you life and death, blessing and curse. Choose life, so that you and your descendants may live.* (Deut. 30:19)

At a very generalized level, then, the whole book of Deuteronomy can be viewed as the sanctions that complete the Pentateuch's rhetoric of stories (roughly Genesis through Exodus 19) and lists (Exodus 20 through Numbers). But as we have seen, sanctions and even long lists of sanctions show up within the stories and laws throughout the Pentateuch. Deuteronomy mixes them together as well, though the book has clearly been organized by the rhetoric of story (Deut. 1–11) followed by lists (Deut. 12–26) concluding with sanctions (Deut. 27–30, 32–33). The book's narrative setting provides only a very short framework at the beginning and end (1:1–5; 34:1–12) and a somewhat longer account of how Moses transmitted the Torah and leadership to his successors (Deut. 31).

Lists of sanctions bring the Pentateuch to a climactic finale in Deuteronomy 27–33. Chapter 27 actually takes the form of instructions for performing blessings and curses after the people enter the land. The Levites must recite the curses and the people accept them by responding "Amen." In Deuteronomy 28, Moses recites promises and threats himself. Deuteronomy 29–30 take the form of a ritual renewal of the covenant with the new generation of Israelites who are about to enter the land. After some brief references to events in Egypt and the wilderness, Moses warns the Israelites of future catastrophe and exile for abandoning the covenant. But he promises that, if the people repent, God will restore them to the land. Moses then recites two poems whose evocative language intensifies the rhetoric of threat (Deut. 32) and promise (Deut. 33) even more.

Both Leviticus and Deuteronomy anticipate Israel's future history. Not only will Israel conquer the land, Israel will then be exiled from the land. Both also promise, however, that God will continue to remember the covenant and remain Israel's God in exile (Lev. 26:45) or restore the people to the land once again (Deut. 30:3–5). But the Pentateuch does not predict sanctions in the afterlife (see Box 3.8).

## Box 3.8   Eternal sanctions

Readers often expect the Pentateuch, like many later Jewish and Christian texts, to include eternal sanctions in the afterlife, such as a blessed life in heaven and eternal punishment in hell. However, the Pentateuch contains no trace of such ideas. At most, it grants the possibility of some lingering pollution of people and land due to violent deaths (Gen. 4:10; Num. 35:33).

Instead, the Torah projects future blessings and punishments only in the course of normal human life. Peace, long life, and prosperous circumstances are all signs of divine blessing. The Pentateuch distinguishes its heroes by these attributes. Abraham gathered wealth throughout his life and lived to be 175 years old, according to Gen. 25:7–8. Moses lived 120 years and was strong and keen-eyed to the end, according to Deuteronomy 34:7. But God promised neither of them a heavenly afterlife.

Afterlife beliefs varied in other ancient Middle Eastern cultures. Egyptian religion and ritual aimed at achieving a good afterlife, as shown by its elaborate tombs and the Egyptian *Book of the Dead*. Mesopotamian religions, on the other hand, nurtured more skepticism of that possibility, as in the *Epic of Gilgamesh*. The Hebrew Bible resembled the latter (see Eccl. 3:1–21; 9:5–6), until the growing popularity of apocalyptic in the later Second Temple period raised expectations of reward or punishment in the afterlife (Dan. 12:1–4). See Sections 6.3.2–3.

## 3.3   THE RHETORIC OF THE DEUTERONOMISTIC HISTORY

The books of Joshua, Judges, Samuel, and Kings tell the history of Israel from the people's settlement in the land of Canaan to their exile from the land 600 years later. They tell the story from the perspective of Deuteronomy, so biblical scholars call these books the Deuteronomistic History. In Deuteronomy, Moses predicts that Israel will prosper if the people obey the Torah and they will suffer if they do not. The Deuteronomistic History shows how both predictions came true.[9]

**Joshua** tells the story of Israel's conquest of Canaan. After Moses' death, Joshua led the Israelites across the Jordan River (Josh. 1–4). The stories of three battles then set the paradigm for the rest of the history. First, YHWH ordered the people to attack Jericho, a large and well-fortified city, by walking around the city for seven days and seven times on the seventh day. After they followed these bizarre instructions, the walls fell down and they took the city (Josh. 6). The second story tells of Israel's attack on Ai, a small unfortified town whose residents nevertheless defeated the attack. An investigation by drawing lots revealed that one Israelite man had stolen loot from Jericho that should have been donated to YHWH's sanctuary (6:19). Once he was punished, the Israelites successfully conquered Ai (Josh. 7–8). The stories of Jericho and Ai illustrate Moses' teachings in a nutshell: obey God and win, or disobey God and lose.

The third story complicates this simple moral. The people of Gibeon tricked Joshua into making a peace treaty with them by acting like they lived far outside the land, when in fact their city was nearby. Their neighbors attacked to prevent them from becoming Israel's allies, so the Gibeonites appealed to Joshua for help. The Israelites marched through the night to rescue the Gibeonites, who were then incorporated into Israel as a lower class (Josh. 9–10). Despite their deception, YHWH supported rescuing and adding the Gibeonites to Israel. This story shows more flexibility than you would expect from Deuteronomy's laws against making peace treaties with people in the land (Deut. 20:10–18). It acknowledges the fact that Israel's population would become an ethnic mix of invaders and Canaanites.

The book of Joshua narrates Israel's conquest of the rest of the land simply by listing the conquered kings and territory (Josh. 10–12). It gives more details about how the land was divided among the Israelite tribes (Josh. 13–22). The book concludes with the story of how Joshua led the people to renew the covenant with YHWH, now that God had fulfilled the promise to Abraham to give Israel the land (Josh. 23–24; cf. Gen. 15:18–21).

**Judges:** After Joshua's triumphant conclusion, you may be surprised to read in the book of Judges that the Israelite tribes were still fighting Canaanites after Joshua died. Furthermore, they had not conquered many major cities (Judg. 1). While the book of Joshua celebrates Israel's religious faithfulness and military success, Judges records Israel's apostasy and failures. Judges 2 summarizes the book's plot concisely:

> *The Israelites did wrong in the eyes of YHWH and worshiped the Baals.…So YHWH became angry with Israel and handed them over to pillagers.…YHWH then raised judges who saved them from the pillagers.…But when the judge died, they would relapse…to worship other gods.* (Judg. 2:11, 14, 16, 19)

Judges 3–16 then tells the stories of military heroes called "saviors" (3:9) and "judges" (2:16–19). They were, in fact, not judges but warlords like Ehud (3:15–30), Barak (4:6–15), and Gideon (6:11–8:32), who rallied Israel's militia to fight against neighboring peoples. Only one, Deborah, did any judging (4:4–5). She also led Israel to war because Barak was afraid to fight without her (4:8–9).

Israel's condition, however, worsened over time, according to the book of Judges. The early judges mobilized several tribes of Israel, though not all (3:27; 5:14–18; 6:35; 8:24; 12:1). One of Gideon's sons tried to make himself king and ruled for three years (Judg. 9). Jephthah led Israel's armies to victory, but sacrificed his own daughter because of a stupid promise (Judg. 11). Finally, stories about Samson (Judg. 13–16) describe him as a hero with super-human strength who can be defeated only through trickery and his own failures. These themes are still familiar from super-hero comics and movies today. But in the larger scope of Judges, the Samson stories illustrate how bad Israel's condition had become.

The book's final chapters (Judg. 17–21) deepen that dark theme with stories of idolatry (17:4), theft (18:14–26), rape (19:25), murder and dismemberment (19:29), and civil war (chap. 20). The civil war ended in nearly wiping out one Israelite tribe, Benjamin. The tribe's future was saved only by the mass abduction and forced marriage of 600 young women (chap. 21). The narrator explains these events by repeating a political observation: "There was no king in Israel" (18:1; 19:1; 21:25). That explanation anticipates stories about the rise of Israelite kings in the following books.

**1 and 2 Samuel:** The people of Israel asked for a king to defend them against their enemies, especially against the five Philistine cities along the Mediterranean coast. The story in 1 Samuel tells how God sent the prophet Samuel to anoint Israel's kings, Saul and David.

Saul led Israel's militia army successfully (1 Sam. 14:47–48), but struggled to fulfill the rules of holy war (1 Sam. 15). Because of that failure, he was condemned by YHWH through the prophet Samuel, who anointed David as king instead (1 Sam. 16:1–13). When Saul and his son, Jonathan, died in battle (1 Sam. 31), the Israelite tribes were defeated and divided. The lesson drawn by the writers of 1 Samuel is that God rejected Saul for his sins.

Even during Saul's life, the books of Samuel really focus on David, whose descendants ruled Judah for 400 years. David began as a famous warrior and general in Saul's army (1 Sam. 17; 18:7). When Saul grew suspicious of David's ambitions, David embarked on a career as a warlord in his native Judah, where he led a private army (1 Sam. 22–23). After Saul's death, the tribe of Judah asked David to be their king because of his military successes (2 Sam. 2:4). Seven years later, the other tribes of Israel accepted him as king as well (2 Sam. 5:1–5).

David's military victories continued: he never lost a battle. After consolidating control of Israel and defeating its enemies, his army conquered Jerusalem from the Jebusites (2 Sam. 5:6–10). The city became his capital, "the city of David." There he built his palace and relocated the Tabernacle with its Ark of the Covenant (2 Sam. 6). Through the prophet Nathan, YHWH promised David that his kingdom and his dynasty would last "forever" (2 Sam. 7:16).

David's story then takes a darker turn. Because he forced a married woman, Bathsheba, to have sex with him and murdered her husband to cover it up (2 Sam. 11), the prophet Nathan predicted that David's dynasty would never avoid violence. That prediction came true when David's oldest son, Amnon, was murdered by his half-brother for raping his sister, Tamar (2 Sam. 13). That brother, Absalom, then fomented rebellion and led a militia army that included most of Israel's tribes to seize the kingdom for himself (2 Sam. 15–17). David defeated him (2 Sam. 18), probably because the Israelite tribesmen were no match for his professional mercenaries, many of them non-Israelites (15:18).

Nevertheless, the books of Samuel insist that God supported David to the end. The books conclude with two songs sung by David, who insisted that

*YHWH rewarded my righteousness, repaid me for my clean hands,*
*because I kept YHWH's ways and did not abandon my God*
*(2 Sam. 22:21–22)*

and

> *He has made an eternal covenant with me, completely in order and secure, won't he support my every victory and desire?* (2 Sam. 23:5)

The books of Kings evaluate subsequent kings of Israel and Judah against the standard set by David. They conclude that all but three failed to "completely follow YHWH as his father David had done" (1 Kgs. 11:6; cf. 2 Kgs. 22:2).

**1 and 2 Kings:** One of David's younger sons, <u>Solomon</u>, whose mother was Bathsheba, defeated his brothers to take the kingdom for himself (1 Kgs. 2). The Hebrew Bible celebrates Solomon's wisdom (1 Kgs. 3:3–14; 4:29–34; Prov. 1:1; 10:1), which he demonstrated by making international alliances sealed with marriages (1 Kgs. 11:1–3) and by reorganizing Israel's internal territories (4:7–20). His most famous accomplishment was building the <u>Temple</u> to YHWH in Jerusalem (1 Kgs. 5–7). The Deuteronomistic writer of 1 Kings, however, condemns him for <u>apostasy</u>, that is, for worshipping other gods besides YHWH (11:5–8). As a result, external and internal enemies fought wars against Solomon (11:14–40).

After Solomon's death, these conflicts caused his kingdom to come apart. His son, Rehoboam, could not keep control of the northern tribes of Israel, but remained king only of Judah and Benjamin (12:16–19). The northern tribes made Jeroboam king, who was one of Solomon's generals who had rebelled against him (11:26; 12:20). For the next 200 years, the tribes of Israel were <u>divided between two kingdoms</u>. In the north was the larger and richer <u>kingdom of Israel</u>, also called "Ephraim" after its largest tribe or "Samaria" after its capital city. In the south was the smaller and poorer <u>kingdom of Judah</u>, still ruled by David's dynasty in Jerusalem.

As time went on, the history of the kingdoms of Israel and Judah was increasingly shaped by the power of Mesopotamian empires (see Box 3.9). While four kings of the dynasty of Omri ruled Israel independently and prosperously in the ninth century (1 Kgs 16:21–34), Israel and Judah fell under Assyrian domination in the eighth and seventh centuries. Rebellions led to conquest and then destruction, which Israel suffered in 722 BCE (2 Kgs. 17:1–6). At best, little kingdoms barely survived Assyrian attack with reduced territories, as Judah did in 701 BCE (2 Kgs. 18–19). When Assyria's empire fell apart in 609 BCE, King <u>Josiah</u> of Judah tried to reassert independent control of much of Israel's traditional territory. But he soon died in battle and his kingdom was reabsorbed by the empires. Rebellions by his successors led Judah to follow Israel's fate in destruction and exile in 587 BCE (2 Kgs. 24–25).

The books of 1 and 2 Kings tell this catastrophic history, but draw a religious moral from it. The heroes of its story are prophets like Samuel, Nathan

## Box 3.9   The beginning of the age of empires

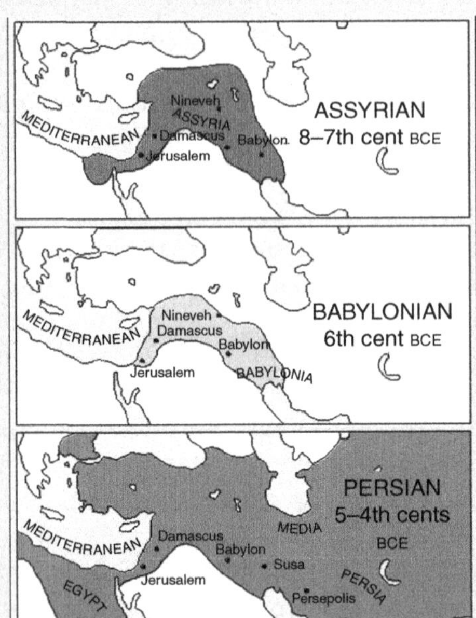


**FIGURE 3.3**   The beginning of the age of empires.

Israel emerged in the Middle East during a time when empires were in eclipse. The beginning of the Iron Age, from around 1200–900 BCE, experienced a decline in international trade and large-scale political organizations. That changed in the ninth and eighth centuries, when <u>Assyria</u> reorganized its army and began to take over territory to its south in Mesopotamia and its west on the Mediterranean coast. In 853 BCE, King Ahab of Israel led a coalition of western kingdoms in the battle of Qarqar, which stopped the Assyrians for several generations. A century later, they could not be stopped. Assyria conquered the kingdom of Israel and deported many of its people in 722 BCE. In the following century, it also conquered Egypt.

In 609 BCE, the Assyrian empire fell apart and was partly replaced by the <u>Babylonians</u>. Their king, Nebuchadnezzar, seized control of Judah in 605. When Judean kings rebelled against him, he conquered Jerusalem in 597 and again in 587 BCE. He then destroyed the city and its temple, and exiled the royal family and upper classes to Mesopotamia (see Box 5.2).

However, Babylon was already in the shadow of the Medes and Persians to its north-east. In 539 BCE, the Persian king, Cyrus, took control of Babylon and all its territories, including Judea. Cyrus allowed exiles to return home, thus ending the <u>Babylonian Exile</u> of the Jews. The Persians used policies like this to gain the loyalty of native upper classes all over the Middle East. They succeeded in ruling the Middle East for 200 years.

Even after the Persian Empire fell to <u>Alexander</u>'s army in 333–330 BCE, the age of empires continued through the Hellenistic kingdoms, the Romans, the Parthians, and so on. Small nations like Israel and Judah, who found themselves on the crossroads between Africa, Asia, and Europe, were rarely left in peace by ambitious empires.

(2 Kgs. 12), <u>Elijah</u> (1 Kgs. 17–21; 2 Kgs. 1–2), and <u>Isaiah</u> (2 Kgs. 19–20). They challenged the kings of Israel and Judah to depend on YHWH, the God of Israel, rather than on military power and alliances. The Deuteronomistic History concludes that Israel and Judah were destroyed because of the religious failures of their kings and people (2 Kgs. 17:7–20; 23:26–27). According to these books, history is not determined by politics and military force, but rather by God's support or punishment. So the books of Samuel show that Israel was successful because YHWH supported David, while the books of Kings show that Israel and Judah failed because YHWH punished them for their sins.

## 3.3.1   The Theme of the Deuteronomistic History

The Deuteronomistic History is remarkably self-critical in comparison with other national histories in the ancient Middle East, or in modern times for that matter. Whereas most other ancient accounts of the past are propaganda celebrating a king or city, the Deuteronomistic History uses ritual rhetoric to criticize the Israelites and their kings for unfaithfulness to YHWH. In a similar way, a Babylonian history (the Weidner Chronicle from the sixth century BCE) explained the successes and failures of Babylon's kings by whether they supported the city's temple of Marduk or not. The Deuteronomistic History also evaluates Israel's leaders by their loyalty to Israel's national god, YHWH, but reaches a more negative conclusion. It judges all the kings of the northern kingdom and all but a handful of the kings of Judah as unfaithful failures.

This history, however, also expresses other themes that sit uncomfortably with Deuteronomy's theology. Stories about Samson (Judg. 13–16), Saul (1 Sam. 9–15), and David (1 Sam. 16–2 Sam. 24) depict these characters as tragic heroes. Their fates raise questions about YHWH's retributive justice. Even the more mechanical evaluations of the narrator of Kings have difficulty explaining the fates of Judah's seventh-century rulers. King <u>Manasseh</u>'s outrageous sins are judged to have caused Judah's exile as punishment (2 Kgs. 21), yet he reigned for 55 years and died of old age. On the other hand, King Josiah, whose religious reforms brought Judah back to Torah observance (2 Kgs. 22–23), died in battle at a young age.

Despite these occasional failures of the retributive principle, the Deuteronomistic History provided Judeans with a convincing explanation for the destruction of their country. The Babylonians defeated and exiled Judah because its people were not faithful to YHWH. This history illustrated the threats in Leviticus 26 and Deuteronomy 27–30 that also appear in the Hebrew Bible's prophetic books. So Torah and Prophets unite in claiming that Israel's and Judah's fates were their own fault for abandoning YHWH.

Modern readers might call this "blaming the victims." After all, the Assyrian and Babylonian empires were far larger and more powerful than Israel and Judah. They had geo-political interests in controlling the roads to Egypt that ran through Israel and Judah. They would have conquered this land no matter who lived there.

The Hebrew Bible insists, however, that God controls the empires. They come when YHWH calls and they retreat when YHWH sends them away (2 Kgs. 19:25–28). It is Israel's and Judah's relationship to their God that determines their fate. This judgment may seem harsh, but for ancient readers it held the seeds of hope. By changing their behavior, the people of YHWH could gain God's support once again. This hope fueled their efforts to return to the land and rebuild their country after the Babylonian Exile.


## CITED WORKS AND FURTHER READING

1  Robert M. Cover, "Foreword: Nomos and Narrative," *Harvard Law Review* 97/1 (1983), 4–68, quotation from pp. 4–5.

2  On the ancestors' origins in Genesis 12–50, see R. W. L. Moberly, *The Old Testament of the Old Testament: Patriarchal Narratives and Mosaic Yahwism* (Minneapolis: Fortress Press, 1992).

3  On Exodus 1–18, see David M. Gunn, "The 'Hardening of Pharaoh's Heart'? Plot, Character and Theology in Exodus 1–14," in *Art and Meaning: Rhetoric in Biblical Literature* (ed. A. J. Hauser, D. J. A. Clines, and D. M. Gunn; Sheffield: JSOT Press, 1982), 72–96; and William H. Propp, *Exodus 1–18, Anchor Bible* (New Haven: Yale University Press, 1999).

4  For more on the Pentateuch's enthymeme, see James W. Watts, "The Unstated Premise of the Prose Pentateuch: YHWH is King," *Journal of Hebrew Scriptures* 18/2 (2018), online at http://jhsonline.org/Articles/article_238.pdf.

5 For ancient Near Eastern examples of the story–list–sanction rhetoric, see James W. Watts, "Story, List, Sanction: A Cross-Cultural Strategy of Ancient Persuasion," in *Rhetoric Before and Beyond the Greeks* (ed. Carol Lipson and Roberta Binkley, Albany: SUNY Press, 2004), 197–212.

6 On God's character in the Pentateuch, see Jack Miles, *God: A Biography* (New York: Knopf, 1995); and James W. Watts, "The Legal Characterization of God in the Pentateuch," *Hebrew Union College Annual* 67 (1996), 1–14.

7 On Moses' character in the Pentateuch, see John Van Seters, *The Life of Moses: The Yahwist as Historian in Exodus-Numbers* (Leuven: Peeters, 1994); and James W. Watts, "The Legal Characterization of Moses in the Rhetoric of the Pentateuch," *Journal of Biblical Literature* 117 (1998), 415–426.

8 On the rhetoric of promise and threat, see Timothy G. Crawford, *Blessing and Curse in Syro-Palestinian Inscriptions of the Iron Age* (New York: Peter Lang, 1992); John G. Gager, ed., *Curse Tablets and Binding Spells from the Ancient World* (New York: Oxford University Press, 1992); and Timothy A. Lenchak, *Choose Life! A Rhetorical-Critical Investigation of Deuteronomy 28,69–30,20,* (Rome: Pontifical Biblical Institute, 1993).

9 The Deuteronomistic History was first named and described in 1943 by the German scholar Martin Noth. See the English translation: Martin Noth, *The Deuteronomistic History*, 2nd ed., JSOTSup 15 (Sheffield: Sheffield Academic Press, 1991). For a review and evaluation of research since Noth, see Thomas Römer, *The So-Called Deuteronomistic History: A Sociological, Historical, and Literary Introduction* (London: T&T Clark, 2005); for a broader overview of the historical books, see Mark A. Leuchter and David T. Lamb, *The Historical Writings: Introducing Israel's Historical Literature* (Minneapolis: Fortress Press, 2016).

# CHAPTER 4

# The Torah's Iconic Dimension

Written texts are physical artifacts. Books are most commonly constructed of paper and ink and bound in cardboard covers. In the 5000-year history of writing, books have also been made of parchment, papyrus, palm leaves, and bark. They have taken the form of a continuous <u>scroll</u> as well as a <u>codex</u>, which is made of folded pages bound together between wooden or cardboard covers – what we think of as a book today. Written texts may also be inscribed on stone or pressed into clay. They may be wrapped in envelopes. Texts and books may be displayed publicly for all to see, stored in libraries, or buried in the ground. Texts have frequently been written for all these purposes. Now, many written texts take digital form, but e-books are also material objects made of computer processors, internet servers, memory chips, and screens.

The material form and visual appearance of a book or other written text allow it to be manipulated and displayed like any other physical object. Most texts appear in a form that we instantly recognize as a text by its script or fonts, and by its shape as a scroll or codex or screen. These forms allow their appearance to function symbolically. Carrying or displaying a book can represent the owner's education or wealth. If the book's contents are well-known, it may also show that the owner subscribes to the ideas contained in the book. The material form and visual appearance of a book make up its <u>iconic dimension</u>.

## 4.1   RITUALIZING THE ICONIC DIMENSION OF SCRIPTURES

Ritualizing a book's iconic dimension pays careful and repeated attention to the form and material of a book. It may involve manipulating the physical book or displaying it or portraying it in art. The comparative study of religions illustrates the many ways in which religious scriptures can be ritualized in the iconic dimension.

Sacred texts often take the first or central position in religious processions during worship services or on holy days (see Figure 4.1). This is the position in

**FIGURE 4.1**   A Sikh carrying Guru Granth Sahib, the Sikh scripture.

a procession that, in other traditions or on other occasions, might be occupied by an image of a god or a saint. Scriptures also get touched and handled during oath ceremonies, especially at inaugurations to religious or government offices. People display scripture verses in their homes and carry them with them as protective amulets (see Figure 4.2). Some copies of scriptures are richly decorated and covered in expensive materials to distinguish them from ordinary books (Figure 4.3).

Ritualizing the iconic dimension of texts has the effect of <u>legitimizing</u> the tradition, institutions, communities, and individuals to whom the texts belong. Clergy and theologians pose for portraits holding a book of scripture to show their scholarship, piety, and orthodoxy. Museums and libraries display the oldest copies of treasured books for the prestige of owning such rarities and to establish the reliability of more recent copies.

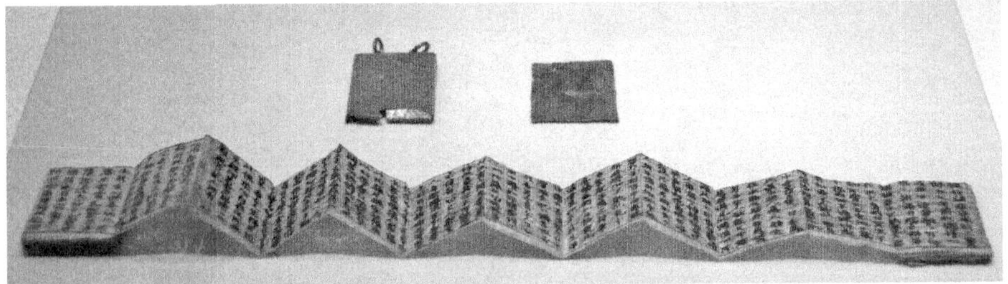

**FIGURE 4.2**   Miniature sutra, in the Korean National Museum, Seoul.

**FIGURE 4.3**   Qur'an from India, ca. 1851. In the library of the University of Saint Andrews, Scotland.

Anyone who possesses a scripture can manipulate and display it. People without any expert training or position of authority can ritualize a scripture's iconic dimension more easily than its other dimensions. Pious lay people (non-clergy) are therefore especially likely to take offense when someone desecrates a copy of their scripture. Attacks on a tradition try to undermine it by mutilating or destroying its books. Book burnings aim to wound and outrage the sensibilities of opponents. Ritualizing the iconic dimension of scriptures includes scripture desecration as well as scripture veneration.[1]

## 4.2  THE PENTATEUCH'S ICONIC DIMENSION AFTER EZRA

The Pentateuch first began to be ritualized regularly as a scripture in the time of Ezra, during the fifth or fourth centuries BCE when the Persian Empire ruled Judea. Scripturalizing a book by ritualizing it in all three dimensions tends to result in more historical evidence for that book's use because more copies get created and distributed. Other texts are also more likely to refer to scriptures. Information about a book's use therefore increases after its scripturalization. There is much less evidence for the Pentateuch's form and uses before it began to function as scripture. We therefore start our study of ritualizing the Pentateuch's iconic dimension with the periods for which we have increasing amounts of evidence, beginning with the time of Ezra.

### 4.2.1  Ezra's Scroll

The Book of Ezra describes Ezra as a scribe and a priest who led a group of priests and Levites from Babylon to immigrate to Jerusalem in the late fifth century BCE (Ezra 7–8). The Persian king commissioned him to act "according to the law of your God, which is in your hand" (Ezra 7:14). The contents of Ezra's Torah seems to have been the Pentateuch more or less as we have it today.

Ezra ritualized the Torah's iconic dimension deliberately and effectively by gathering the people in Jerusalem's main plaza and carrying the scroll to a raised platform where prominent members of the community stood alongside him (Neh. 8:1–8). This arrangement visually associated the book with its reader, Ezra, and with his supporters. Before one word of the Torah was read, the act of physically unrolling the scroll prompted a ritual response from the audience. They stood up and then, after Ezra blessed them, they bowed down to the ground.

The sight of the physical scroll validated Ezra's claim to be reading the words of God to Moses. Reading the Torah publicly legitimized Ezra's leadership and everything that he proposed to do. It also legitimized the people's identity as Israel. One outcome of the Torah reading was that they celebrated the annual festival of *Sukkot* (Booths) out of obedience to Torah (Neh. 8:13–20). Another outcome was that the people committed themselves to obeying Torah generally and to paying for the temple services (Neh. 9:38–10:39). They also agreed to "separate from the people of the land for the sake of God's Torah" (10:28). In Ezra and Nehemiah, then, the Pentateuch defines and legitimizes the people as God's people. The Torah has become a fundamental element in defining Jewish identity.

Modern commentators have questioned whether a Persian official would really act in the way that Ezra does. The books of Ezra and Nehemiah have been modified by many editors, as is clear from the many irregularities in the narrative. The most obvious irregularity is the change in languages from Hebrew to Aramaic and back again (Ezra 4:8–6:18 and 7:12–26 are written in Aramaic). Nevertheless, it is clear that the writers and editors of the books of Ezra and Nehemiah portray Ezra as a model of how they thought a scribe and priest should behave with a Torah scroll. This narrative also shows how people should respond to seeing it and hearing it read. Nehemiah 8–10 therefore present a model for ritualizing the Torah's iconic dimension. It is a pattern of behavior that became increasingly common as the Second Temple period progressed.

## 4.2.2  Torah Scrolls in the Late Second Temple Period

In the middle of the Pentateuch in Leviticus 1–17 lie instructions for conducting temple rituals. Temples therefore seem like the Torah's natural home. Torah scrolls were probably kept in the temples of Judea and Samaria in the Persian period. Yet the stories of religious apostasy in Israel's earlier history suggest that the Torah did not govern temple rituals in the monarchic period (so, explicitly, 2 Kgs. 23:21–23). The books of Ezra and Nehemiah indicate much more concern for following the teachings of Torah in the Persian period, even before Ezra's reform (see Ezra 3:4). Presumably, priests stored Torah scrolls in the post-exilic temples and read them regularly in public ceremonies. However, there is no evidence for Torah scrolls and public Torah readings outside the books of Ezra and Nehemiah until after the Persian period. Historians therefore debate exactly when the Pentateuch began functioning as the law book of the Jerusalem and Samaritan temples.

The next clear reference to the Pentateuch being ritualized in all three dimensions appears in the *Letter of Aristeas*, written in the second century BCE. This document tells of the translation of the Torah into Greek in the third century, a translation called the Septuagint. *Aristeas* lavishes attention on its iconic dimension. It describes beautiful Hebrew Torah scrolls written in gold ink being sent by the high priest in Jerusalem to Egypt for the translators. There, the king bowed down at their sight (Box 4.1). Once the work was complete, the Jewish community in Egypt received the Greek translation with more bows (*Aristeas* 317). The Greek Torah probably symbolized the Egyptian Jews' status as upper-class Greek speakers within the Hellenistic culture of Ptolemaic Egypt. Historians think that *Aristeas* exaggerated both the expense of the scrolls and their reception by the non-Jewish king. (We have no examples of ancient manuscripts written in gold ink, though Jewish, Christian, and Muslim scriptures written in gold have survived from the Middle Ages.) Nevertheless, the letter provides evidence for how Jews in the second century BCE thought temple scrolls *should* look and how they *should* be treated ritually.

The only surviving Torah scrolls from the Second Temple period were found among the Dead Sea Scrolls. These fragments of more than 800 ancient Jewish manuscripts were discovered in caves near the north end of the Dead Sea in the middle of the twentieth century. The scrolls were written between the third century BCE and the first century CE. They seem to have been brought to the caves for safekeeping from a local settlement, Qumran (see also Section 5.2.2), when Roman armies invaded Judea in 68 CE. Around one-quarter of these scrolls contain biblical texts. They are the oldest surviving biblical manuscripts and provide valuable evidence about the state of biblical literature at the end of the Second Temple period in the last two centuries BCE.

## Box 4.1   The Letter of Aristeas 177

*So they arrived with the gifts which had been sent at their hands and with the fine skins on which the Law had been written in letters of gold in Jewish characters; the parchment had been excellently worked, and the joining together of the letters was imperceptible. When the king saw the delegates, he proceeded to ask questions about the books, and when they had shown what had been covered and unrolled the parchments, he paused for a long time, did obeisance about seven times, and said, "I offer to you my thanks, gentlemen, and to him who sent you even more, and most of all to the God whose oracles these are."[2]*

The manuscripts show how Qumran scribes ritualized the iconic dimension of the Torah by distinguishing the books of the Pentateuch. Each of the Pentateuch's books appears among the Dead Sea Scrolls in more than a dozen copies. Only the book of Psalms appears more often (see Box 6.13). Qumran scribes produced especially deluxe manuscripts of pentateuchal books in a large format with wide margins (though they were not so large as later Torah scrolls – in the first century, it was not yet possible to produce a scroll containing all five books of the Pentateuch). And they sometimes used old-fashioned <u>Paleo-Hebrew</u> letters for the books of Moses, instead of the standard Aramaic square letters that they used for almost all other books. These practices show greater reverence for the books of Torah than for other books.[3]

Several sources tell us that by the second and first centuries BCE, Torah scrolls had become emblems of Jewish identity not only to Jews, but to Greeks and Romans as well. When Roman armies destroyed Jerusalem and its temple, they took a Torah scroll from the temple and paraded it in Titus's victory procession after the golden table and candlestick. <u>Josephus</u> (*War* 7.121–157, 162), who witnessed many of these events himself, wrote:

> *Last of all the spoils was carried the Law of the Jews.*

Josephus thought it was kept in the imperial palace in Rome. But no Torah scroll appears among the loot from the Jerusalem temple depicted on Titus's arch in Rome. We are left to wonder if the Jewish historian, Josephus, placed more value on the temple's Torah scrolls than did the Romans or, at least, the Roman artists who designed the reliefs for the victory arch.

More than a century later, the Mishnah remembered that a Torah scroll was brought forward in the temple for the high priest to read on the Day of Atonement (<u>Yom Kippur</u>):

> *The official of the congregation took the book of the Torah and gave it to the head of the congregation, and the head of the congregation gave it to the assistant [high priest], and the assistant [gave it] to the high priest. The high priest stood and received it and read. (m. Yoma 7:1; m. Sotah 7:7)[4]*

The scrolls were handled by these same officials when a king read Torah in the temple. The Talmud understood the requirement to stand when reading Torah as more than a sign of respect. Ruth Langer pointed out that:

> As the Talmud recognizes (BYoma 69a; BSotah 40b, 41b), there is a symbolic message encoded in this movement....Rabbinic law

required that every reader stand. In the hierarchy of symbols, Torah reigns supreme over all human beings, including kings.... By standing, the reader emulates, not Moses who stood to receive the Torah, but God who revealed it. The ritual reading of the Torah, then, is not simply an act of study, but a reenactment of Sinai itself.[5]

The Mishnah reflected the synagogue practices of its own time when describing these older temple rituals. Standing to read the Torah aloud and to hear it read reenacts God giving the law to Israel. By revering the Pentateuch in this way, readers and congregations identify themselves with the Israelites who agreed to the divine covenant at Mount Sinai.

## 4.2.3  Textual Amulets

People often ritualize the iconic dimension of a scripture by manipulating or carrying small parts of it as an amulet. Scriptural amulets may depict books of scripture or contain scripture verses. People in many cultures and religious traditions wear them constantly or hold them while praying. They often keep them in their homes to bless their families and to protect them from danger. Amulets easily cross religious boundaries. People frequently use scripture amulets because they believe in their power even though they do not identify themselves with the religion that venerates that particular scripture. For example, amulets containing Qur'anic verses are valued from Africa to South Asia by many people who are not Muslims. Amulets also stir controversy between advocates of traditional practices and critics of "superstition." Many people take a mediating position: they deny that amulets exert any physical effects, yet defend their symbolic value.

The use of certain kinds of amulets has been widespread in Jewish practice since antiquity. It is grounded in the commands of the Torah itself. Jewish families typically install small boxes (*mezuzahs*) containing texts from the Pentateuch on the doorposts of their homes (see Figure 4.4). People traditionally touch the mezuzah when entering or leaving the room or house. When praying, Jewish men have traditionally tied small boxes (*tefillin*) on their arm and forehead. Both practices fulfill the commandment to

> *Tie [these words] as a sign on your hand, make them a symbol between your eyes. Write them on the door jams of your house and on your gates.* (Deut. 6:8–9)

*Mezuzahs* and *tefillin* contain parchments on which Exod. 13:1–10, 11–16 and Deut. 6:4–9, 11:13–21 are written in tiny script.

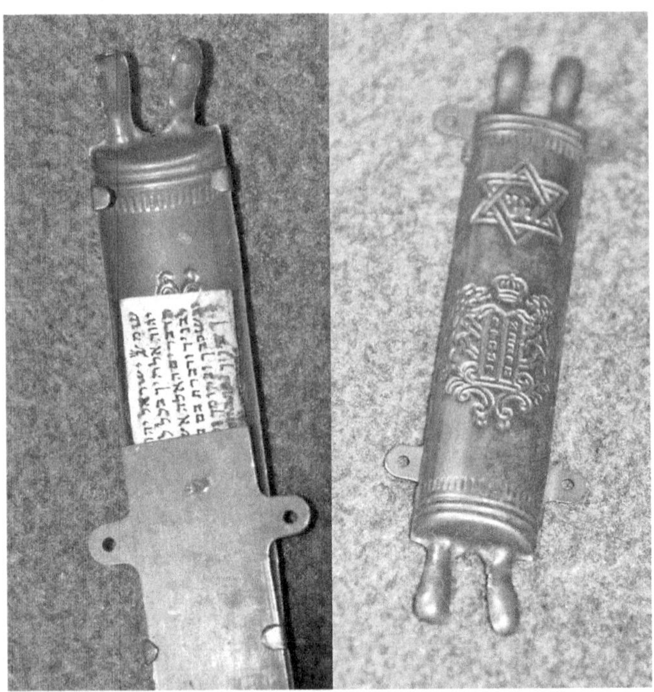

**FIGURE 4.4** A modern *mezuzah*.

Archeologists found *tefillin* boxes and their slips of parchment at Qumran, near where the Dead Sea Scrolls were discovered. So amulets incorporating pentateuchal texts were already in common use by the second or at least the first century BCE. Some of the slips seem to have actually come from *mezuzot* and so are evidence that Jews were already putting them on doorposts as well. These discoveries provide our earliest physical evidence for the iconic manipulation of Torah texts.[6]

The Karaites, a Jewish sect that rejects the rabbinic lore of the Talmuds, do not use *mezuzahs* and *tefillin*. They understand the commandments of Deut. 6:8–9 as metaphors that require people to internalize the commands of Torah and let them direct their actions. The Samaritans, a religious community that traces its origins to the northern tribes of Israel, also interpret the commands metaphorically and do not use *tefillin*. Samaritan *mezuzahs* consist of scriptural blessings written in archaic Hebrew script and displayed on parchment or stone tablets.

These differences show that controversies over the proper use of scriptural amulets extend back in time to the ancient divisions between these groups. Even more controversial has been the use of amulets to bring about particular results, such as personal protection or healing. Archeologists have discovered many Samaritan amulets from the Middle Ages. They often arrange scripture texts in numerological sequences. Modern Samaritans deny that they wear amulets, so these medieval amulets may have been produced for sale to other people.

Belief in the power of textual amulets often grows from belief in the power of the <u>names of God</u>. The Hebrew name of God is written with the letters *yod-heh-vav-heh*, יהוה <u>YHWH</u>, and appears very often in the Hebrew Bible. During the Second Temple period, the tradition developed that only the Jewish high priest should pronounce that name, and only in the Temple. Otherwise, Jews should not pronounce the divine name. This tradition continues today: when reading biblical texts aloud, readers substitute other Hebrew words, such as *Adonai* "Lord" or *haShem* "the Name." The <u>Septuagint</u>, the translation of the Pentateuch into Greek in the third century BCE, already rendered God's name with the Greek title, κύριος *kurios* "<u>Lord</u>," rather than transliterating the name YHWH. Many Dead Sea Scrolls written in standard Aramaic letters wrote the divine name in Paleo-Hebrew letters to distinguish it and, perhaps, to warn readers not to pronounce it. Rabbinic traditions insisted that any text containing the divine name in Hebrew is, by virtue of this fact alone, a sacred text. Medieval Jewish mystics claimed that all the letters of the Torah are really code for the name of God, written over and over again.

These traditions stimulated the belief that the Hebrew name of God is very powerful. Its use in prayer and incantations became popular across the Mediterranean world in Late Antiquity. Amulets reproduced IAΩ, the Greek equivalent of Hebrew יהוה YHWH, in combination with the names of Greek gods. <u>Greek magical papyri</u> utilized IAΩ more than any other divine name. Far from avoiding its pronunciation, they encouraged chants of its vowels or of all the vowels of the alphabet:

> *I call thy name that is hidden within me: a o ee o ee o eee ooo iii oooo ooooo ooooo uuuuuuu oooooooooooooo.*

<u>Christian amulet scrolls</u> also combined biblical verses and the names of God with the name and titles of Jesus and esoteric symbols.[7]

Ancient Christian biblical manuscripts followed the practice of the Septuagint by rendering the divine name with the Greek word κύριος "Lord." That word appears frequently in the New Testament to refer to Christ. Christian scribes distinguished this and other holy names, such as "Jesus" and "Christ," by abbreviating them. Such *nomina sacra* marked Christian scripture as sacred. In the Middle Ages, they became frequent subjects for artistic illumination.

Biblical texts then functioned as scripture in cultures that saw divine power in their graphic symbols, especially those that represent the name of God. Of course, the sound of the words and the meaning of the text were also sacred. But in writing, the divine text and name took physical forms that could be manipulated in amulets by Jews, Samaritans, and Christians, and by people of many other religious traditions as well.

### 4.2.4   Torah Arks

Jewish synagogues keep Torah scrolls and other scrolls of scripture in a cabinet called *Aron ha-Qodesh* "the holy ark." Arks have been used to protect and enshrine Torah scrolls in synagogues for almost two thousand years. Already at the end of the second century CE, the Mishnah required that scripture scrolls be treated as more holy than any other objects or the synagogue itself (*m. Meg.* 3.1). Some second- and third-century synagogues excavated by archeologists contain niches for scrolls or platforms for placing portable Torah arks. The ark could be carried into the synagogue in procession, or wheeled on a cart (see Figure 4.5).

By the fourth to sixth centuries CE, many synagogues had permanently installed arks. Art from the period shows their typical form. The doors were

**FIGURE 4.5**   Relief of wheeled ark, ca. third century CE. In the ruins of the synagogue at Kefer-Nahum/Capernaum, Israel. Neculaes Teodor-Ion/Shutterstock.com.

flanked by two columns, like those that stood in Jerusalem's temple (1 Kgs. 7:15–22). Inside, the scrolls were laid horizontally on shelves (see Figure 4.6). A curtain hung in front. The gable of the peaked roof contained a sculpted conch shell, often flanked by lions. The ark itself was flanked by lamp stands (*menorahs*) like the one in the Tabernacle (Exod. 25:31–38). No ancient Torah arks have survived, but archeologists found the burned remains of a Torah ark in the seventh-century synagogue at Ein Gedi that contained pieces of a Leviticus scroll.[8]

Jewish architecture and art from the Middle Ages have been poorly preserved, due to persecution that frequently expelled Jewish communities from one place to another. But prayer books dating from the tenth century and later show the emergence of a standard liturgy for taking Torah scrolls from the ark, reading them, and then returning them to the ark (see below). Synagogue architecture of the last 500 years is better preserved. Most modern synagogues have wooden Torah arks permanently installed on the wall towards Jerusalem. The ark serves as the focal point of the room. In front of the ark or in the middle of the room is a platform (*bimah*) and table where the scrolls are unrolled and read. When they are not being used, the scrolls get placed in the ark behind closed doors. A curtain (*paroket*) hangs in front of the ark like the curtain that hung in front of the Tabernacle's Ark

**FIGURE 4.6**    Golden glass bowl from Rome, ca. 300–350 CE, showing an open Torah ark with scrolls on its shelves. In the Metropolitan Museum of Art, New York.

of the Covenant that contained the tablets of the Ten Commandments (Exod. 26:31–33). Images of those tablets usually appear above the Torah ark's doors (see Figure 4.7). The name, *aron* "ark," the curtain, and the image of the tablets all associate Torah scrolls with the tablets that Moses received from God at Sinai. They also link synagogue arks with the Ark of the Covenant that represented God in the holiest part of the Tabernacle.

Many Jews consider synagogues <u>holy</u> because they contain Torah scrolls. The place becomes <u>sacred</u> because of the sacred books housed there. This

**FIGURE 4.7**  Torah scrolls in the ark of the Vilna Shul (synagogue) in Boston, Massachusetts, built in 1919.

attitude marks a dramatic shift in how people think about sacred space. Temples in ancient Mediterranean and Middle Eastern cultures, including ancient Israel, occupied specific locations sanctified by stories of divine activity or revelation in those places. Synagogues, by contrast, can be located wherever Jews gather to pray together. They are sacred spaces whenever they house a Torah scroll. Since antiquity, Jewish religious architecture has featured such assembly halls for praying and listening to scripture read aloud. This assembly-hall model has been imitated by Christian churches and Muslim mosques. These worship places sanctified by sacred books or relics function very differently from ancient temples.

## 4.2.5 Synagogue Scrolls

Rules for creating, handling, and storing Torah scrolls emphasize their sanctity and value.

The Talmud records precise rules for creating a Torah scroll (*b. Meg.* 18b–19a, 29b; *b. Men.* 29b) (Figure 4.8). The scroll must be made from the skin of a pure animal (Lev. 11). The parchment must be ruled with lines and must be written in a consistent square Aramaic script with large margins on all sides. The scribe cannot add vowels to the consonantal Hebrew text, but seven letters must always be decorated with small crowns (*tagin*) wherever

**FIGURE 4.8**  A scribe copying a new Torah scroll. Image "Writing a Torah" from Wikimedia Commons under a Creative Commons Attribution-Share Alike 3.0 Unported license.

they occur. Up to three copying mistakes can be corrected on a page, but four or more require that the page be buried and recopied on new parchment. The scroll must have two wooden staves, one at each end. Scrolls of scriptures copied by heretics must be burned. Later legal codes add that <u>scribes</u> must purify themselves before copying a Torah. They must pray before and after their work, and every time they write the divine name.

Talmudic references show that Torah scrolls were already being wrapped in covers in antiquity. Later Jewish cultures developed distinctive traditions of "clothing" the Torah when it is not being read (Figure 4.9). <u>Ashkenazi Jews</u> from Central and Eastern Europe usually wrap the scroll in a mantle. Crowns with bells get placed on its staves and a metal shield hangs over the front of the mantle. Modern synagogues associate these clothes with the ceremonial clothes of Israel's <u>high priest</u>, who wore a mantle, bells, crown, and breastplate (Exod. 28). Art historians doubt, however, that these customs developed in conscious

**FIGURE 4.9**    Clothed Torah scroll in the Portuguese Synagogue in Amsterdam, the Netherlands.

imitation of the high priest's clothing. <u>Sephardic Jews</u> from Mediterranean countries instead keep Torah scrolls in cylindrical cases that open in two halves (Figure 4.10). <u>Samaritans</u> place their Torah scrolls in three-part cylinders.

A synagogue congregation interacts with Torah scrolls through a sequence of ritual actions and oral responses, which have become a standardized liturgy since the Middle Ages. The congregation stands throughout the Torah reading and the rituals that surround it. When a Torah scroll is taken from the ark, it is processed around the room while the congregation sings a psalm. Then it is laid on a table on a platform (*bimah*) to be unrolled and read. Blessings precede and follow its reading. Any member

**FIGURE 4.10**    Torah case in the Yosef Caro synagogue in Tzfat/Safed, Israel.

of the congregation may have the privilege of being "called to the Torah" to recite a blessing. The Torah is rolled up and returned to the ark, or placed on a special stand or chair, when it is not being read. Ruth Langer summarized the ritual effect:

> The emergence of the Torah scroll from its ark, its presence in the midst of the congregation before, during and after its reading, forms the ritual highpoint of the service. Far from being a routine reading of the book, these liturgies have emerged as expressions of the deep symbolic significance of the ritual.[9]

More prolonged Torah processions take place on special occasions and particularly on the annual holiday celebrating the Torah, *Simhat Torah*, when Torah scrolls may be paraded through the streets. It is a privilege to carry the Torah. Sometimes, a scroll within its mantle may be handed around the congregation.

All of this – mantles or cases decorated with ornaments containing two-stave scrolls of hand-written parchment that are taken from and returned to synagogue arks in processions accompanied by singing and blessings – serves to mark <u>Torah scrolls</u> as the <u>holiest objects</u> in Judaism. The containers and ornaments mark the Torah visually as different from and superior to all other books. They also mediate materially between the book and the person handling it, so that you never need to touch the Torah's pages with a bare hand. When the Torah is carried through the congregation, people touch it with their prayer shawls or prayer books and then kiss the shawl or book as a form of blessing. In some medieval communities, arks were left open after a service so that women, who otherwise stayed in the gallery, could approach and pray close to the Torah scrolls. Donations of expensive ornaments, clothing, and cases are believed to earn merit. Donors often specify the blessings they seek in dedicatory plaques (Box 4.2).

---

### Box 4.2　Dedicatory Torah plaque

*El Shaddai, this takhshit (ornament) was dedicated by the honored Mrs. Esther, wife of Meyuhas Moses Mazza, to heal her. May God cure her entirely when he enters the Holy Place in the New Holy Congregation on the New Moon of First Adar, in the year 5641 [= 31 January 1881], in Ioannina. May the Supreme One Protect her, Amen.*

Thus, the shape, materials, ornaments, and containers of a Torah scroll all draw attention to its uniquely <u>holy</u> status whenever people see and handle it. William Scott Green observed:

> Whatever else it may have been, the writing we would call "Scripture" was conceived by Rabbinic culture as a holy object, a thing to be venerated.... In the absence of the Temple and its Holy of Holies, the scroll and its writing became for ancient rabbis primary repositories and conveyers of social legitimacy, cultural authenticity, and religious meaning.

These ways of ritualizing the Torah's iconic dimension also make it available to those who do not have the education or status to ritualize its expressive or semantic dimensions. The scroll and its accouterments make its holiness accessible to people who otherwise have little opportunity or ability to read and study Torah.[10]

## 4.2.6   Scroll and Codex

Today, the Torah is visually distinctive because it takes the form of a manuscript <u>scroll</u>. Pages of parchment containing three or four columns of hand-written text are stitched together edge to edge. Synagogues today commission new scrolls from highly trained torah scribes at a cost of $20,000 or more.

Almost all other modern books take the form of a codex. A <u>codex</u> ties folded pages together on only one edge. This allows scribes and printers to put writing on both sides of the page and allows readers to skip quickly back-and-forth in the book.

The ancient Greeks and Romans used codices as notebooks. They preferred to keep literary and religious works in scrolls. Christians, however, quickly adopted the codex for their religious books. By the early Middle Ages, the codex had become the most common form of book due to Christian influence. Jews, perhaps in deliberate contrast to Christians, have preserved the scroll form for the Torah up to the present day (Figure 4.11). The physical forms of the scriptures – scroll or codex – therefore function as <u>symbols</u> that distinguish the religions from each other.

Ritualizing the iconic dimension of a scripture can interfere with reading it. Torah scrolls must be unrolled carefully. Their lack of vowel marks makes

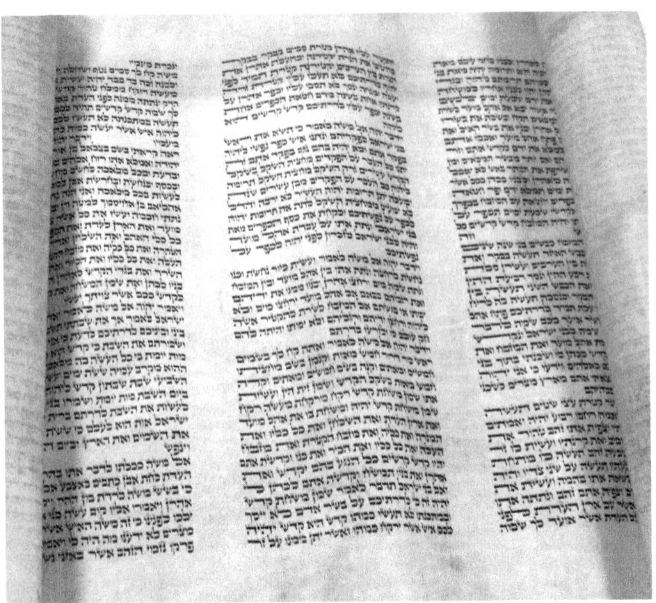

**FIGURE 4.11**   A Torah scroll open to Exodus 30.

their pronunciation difficult. They should be kept only in synagogue arks. The rules for making and using Torah scrolls thus restrict access to them and make them hard to read. Jewish culture addresses this problem by also producing scriptures in the form of codices that are less restricted and easier to read.

Jewish scribes began to make torahs and tanaks in codex form starting in the eighth century CE (Figure 4.12). They supplied <u>vowel points</u> to indicate how to vocalize the ancient Hebrew text. They added marginal comments about rare words or variant readings. The <u>Tiberian Masoretes</u> perfected these systems of notation to produce the most authoritative manuscripts of the Jewish Bible to this day: the <u>Aleppo Codex</u> (ninth century) and the <u>Leningrad Codex</u> (tenth century). Since the invention of printing using movable metal type in the fifteenth century, printers have published many codices of Jewish scriptures. The Pentateuch often gets printed and bound as a codex (a *chumash*) for individuals to read and study.

As a printed and bound codex, the Pentateuch and Tanak do not carry the unique sanctity that Torah scrolls do for Jews. They therefore make the text of the Torah accessible for private study and devotion. Modern advances in printing technology and distribution have made such books inexpensive and readily available. Nevertheless, because the name of God

**FIGURE 4.12**    The end of Job with masorah and micrography in a codex manuscript of the Tanak from Castile, Spain, 1300–1350 CE. In the Cloisters of the Metropolitan Museum of Art, New York.

appears in printed pentateuchs, tanaks, and prayer books, many Jews try to avoid desecrating them. They will not leave them open unattended or place other books on top of them. If they drop accidentally, it is customary to pick them up immediately and kiss them.

Unlike Jews, <u>Samaritans</u> use Torah scrolls only for ritual processions and display. They read the Torah from a codex, even when reading aloud to the congregation.

## 4.2.7   Torah Myths

Many people believe that the most important relic texts are in heaven. Books in heaven were a common motif already in ancient literature. Sumerian texts from the third millennium BCE describe the scribal goddess, Nisaba, writing down the decisions of the gods in the stars of the sky. Mesopotamian traditions conceived of this book of fate as written on supernatural tablets that gave the king of the gods power to rule on heaven and on earth. These "Tablets of Destiny" remained in heaven, but humans could learn to read their contents in omens, in the stars, and in the entrails of butchered animals. In Egyptian traditions, the scribal deities Seshet and Thoth wrote the decrees and judgments of the gods, including ritual instructions for the living and the dead. Over time, ritual texts originally credited to human "reading priests" were credited to Thoth instead (Figure 4.13). By the first millennium BCE, the restricted libraries of Egyptian temples were the subject of legends about their divine texts that convey magical powers. Stories of the revelation of divine texts became a common feature of mystical traditions in the Hellenistic and Roman periods.

The Pentateuch's story of Moses receiving tablets written by God fits this broader cultural context well. In fact, it seems modest in comparison

**FIGURE 4.13**   This first-millennium BCE version of the Egyptian Book of the Dead shows, at right, the ibis-headed scribal god, Thoth, recording human worship of the gods.

## Box 4.3    The heavenly Torah

*Wisdom praises herself, and tells of her glory in the midst of her people.... "My Creator chose the place for my tent. He said, 'Make your dwelling in Jacob, and in Israel receive your inheritance'. Before the ages, in the beginning, he created me, and for all the ages I shall not cease to be."...All this is the book of the covenant of the Most High God, the law that Moses commanded us as an inheritance for the congregations of Jacob. (Sir. 24:1, 8–9, 23 NRSV)*

*God found the whole way to knowledge, and gave her to his servant Jacob and to Israel, whom he loved. Afterward she appeared on earth and lived with humankind. She is the book of the commandments of God, the law that endures forever. All who hold her fast will live, and those who forsake her will die. (Baruch 3:35–4:1 NRSV; cf. Acts 7:53)*

with the claims about heavenly texts in other traditions. So, by the third century BCE, Jews began to assert that the Torah too has existed in heaven since before the creation of the world. Writers adapted a wisdom hymn from Proverbs 8 to apply it to the Torah (Box 4.3). The idea of an eternal Torah in heaven soon prompted speculation that it could have been revealed to others before Moses. So, Enoch sees heavenly tablets according to *1 Enoch* 106:19. The book of *Jubilees* claims that the heavenly Torah was revealed to Enoch, Noah, Abraham, Jacob, Levi, and Amram, as well as to Moses.[11]

Belief in an eternal heavenly Torah had become widespread by the end of the first century CE when Christians drew an analogy between the heavenly scripture and the pre-existent Christ. John's Gospel adapted the heavenly book motif to apply it to a living person, Jesus (John 1:1–17). A century or two later, a Valentinian Gnostic writer made the connection even more explicit by speaking of a "living book" and of Jesus as "putting on the book" (*Gospel of Truth* 19–20).

When rabbinic literature began to emerge at the end of the second century CE (see Section 6.5.2), it reflected the belief that God wrote the Torah on the evening of the first Sabbath after creation (*'Abot* 5:6), or even before. Rabbi Akiva is quoted as saying that God consulted the Torah while creating the world (*'Abot* 3:14). John Sawyer summarized later rabbinic elaborations of this theme:

There is in fact a whole series of traditions to the effect that the Torah was written in heaven by God before creation. According to one, when Moses went up to heaven to receive the Torah, he found God sitting weaving crowns for the letters (BT Men. 29b; RA: 168). The pre-existent Torah was written with black fire on white fire (Midrash Psalm 90, para. 12)....When God was about to give the Torah to Moses, the angels at first complained: "The beautiful Torah which you have hidden away since creation...do you now propose to give to a mere mortal?" (BT Shab. 88b). When God gave the Torah to Israel, the earth rejoiced and the heavens wept (Pes. R. 95a).

Mystical traditions in Hellenistic (Greek) culture also celebrated this theme. They adapted Jewish as well as Egyptian and Mesopotamian legends about heavenly tablets, as Stephanie Dalley observed:

> The emerald tablet of Hermes Trismegistos contained the secrets of the gods, and was sometimes said to have been sealed with the seal of Hermes. Hermes was called Trismegistos "thrice great" because he was thought to embody the wisdom of three ancient sages: the Greek Hermes, the Mesopotamian-Jewish Enoch, and the Egyptian god of wisdom and writing Thoth.

In the seventh century CE, the Qur'an picked up the theme of heavenly tablets. Sura 85:21–22 refers to the Qur'an as a "guarded tablet" and Suras 43:4 and 13:39 envision scripture as a heavenly "Mother Book." Dalley noted that a collection of tenth-century Muslim stories described the guarded tablet as "made of pearl and the pen made of a gigantic gemstone as the first things created by God."

Belief in a heavenly scripture ritualizes the iconic dimension of earthly scriptures by basing their legitimacy on a heavenly original. Books regularly fall victim to human incompetence and neglect, as well as to natural disasters and violent persecution. Scriptures suffer these problems as well, though now their millions of copies protect their contents more than most books.

## Box 4.4   The eternal word of God in Jewish, Christian, and Muslim scriptures

*The word of our God will remain forever.* (Isaiah 40:8)
*Heaven and earth will pass away, but my word will not pass away.* (Mark 15:31 NRSV)
*We have, without doubt, sent down the Message; and We will assuredly guard it.* (Qur'an 15:9 Yusufali)

Promises in scriptures that their message is eternal reinforce beliefs that God must preserve the scripture in heaven (see Box 4.4). That supernatural book then becomes the eternal relic text that legitimizes all its earthly copies.[12]

## 4.3   THE PENTATEUCH'S ICONIC DIMENSION BEFORE EZRA

The story of Ezra displaying the Torah scroll to a crowd of people in a Jerusalem plaza is one of the earliest examples of its ritualization in all three textual dimensions – iconic, expressive, and semantic. You might think that the iconic ritualization of Torah followed from its semantic dimension's growing authority over Jewish worship and conduct. But there is reason to believe that the iconic ritualization of Torah and of parts of the Pentateuch began much earlier in Israel's history. In fact, the text of the Pentateuch models and demands its own iconic ritualization.

The evidence for Ezra's ceremony and for earlier iconic texts in Israel comes only from references within the Hebrew Bible itself. This fact makes it difficult to understand the history of Israel's iconic text rituals because (i) the writing of many biblical texts cannot be dated accurately, especially the contents of the Pentateuch, and (ii) they were edited many times in antiquity. Historians do not recognize the survival of any pentateuchal manuscripts older than the Dead Sea Scrolls that date from the third century BCE and later. The Hebrew Bible provides evidence that ancient Israelites treated Decalogue tablets and Torah scrolls iconically, but we do not know when they did so or how such practices evolved. Nor can we be sure of the contents of these Decalogue tablets and Torah scrolls. However, material and literary evidence from other ancient Middle Eastern cultures provides contexts that can help us understand the Bible's references to iconic texts in ancient Israel.

### 4.3.1   The Tablets of the Commandments

According to Exodus and Deuteronomy, Moses received stone tablets from God on Mount Sinai. The tablets of the commandments are the most obviously iconic texts mentioned in the Bible (Box 4.5).

The descriptions do not say much about the tablets, but their stone material indicates their purpose. <u>Stone</u> is the most permanent writing surface. It is difficult to carve, which makes stone inscriptions expensive. Therefore, texts inscribed on stone look permanent and extravagant. These qualities

## Box 4.5   The tablets of the commandments

*I will give you the stone tablets and the torah and the commandment that I have written for their instruction.* (Exod. 24:12)

*God gave Moses two tablets of the covenant, stone tablets written by the finger of God.... written on both sides, front, and back. The tablets were the work of God and the writing was the writing of God engraved on the tablets.* (Exod. 31:18, 32:15–16)

*YHWH spoke these words in a loud voice out of the deep dark fiery cloud on the mountain to your whole assembly, and added no more, and wrote them on two stone tablets and gave them to me.* (Deut. 5:22)

*YHWH said to me: Carve two stone tablets like the first ones. Bring them up the mountain to me and make a wooden ark.... YHWH wrote on the tablets what was written on the first ones, the ten words that YHWH your God spoke out of the fire on the mountain on the day of the assembly. YHWH gave them to me and I put the tablets in the ark that I had made, and there they are, just as YHWH commanded.* (Deut. 10:1, 4–5)

have made stone a favorite medium for displaying the propaganda of kings and governments for 5000 years. Archeologists have found royal inscriptions on stone from most ancient literate cultures (though so far not from the kings of Israel and Judah). Ancient kings also deposited tablets of stone or metal out of sight in the foundations of palaces and temples. Their durable media was intended to remind the gods of the king's architectural accomplishments and worshipful donations forever.

Though the prominent display of Decalogue tablets in Jewish and Christian art resembles ancient displays of royal inscriptions, the Pentateuch's description of the tablets evokes the tradition of <u>deposit texts</u> instead. Moses does not read the tablets aloud or even display them to the Israelites. He deposits them in the Ark of the Covenant. This story also evokes the ancient practice of placing the texts of treaties and laws in temples so that the gods act as witnesses to binding commitments. Stone inscription and temple deposit ratified the contents of the texts and put their legal provisions into force.

The Pentateuch tells a complicated story about the tablets. After Moses repeats God's instructions to Israel and writes them on a scroll (Exod. 24:3–4), YHWH promises to write them down on stone tablets (24:12). Moses receives the tablets 40 days later (31:18) and then immediately smashes them in fury because the Israelites were worshipping the golden calf (32:19). His actions vividly depict the breaking of the covenant. Moses then rewrites the commandments on a second pair of tablets at God's command (34:27). It is not clear, however, whether the mention here of writing the "ten words" refers to the commandments in this chapter (vv. 12–26, often called the Ritual Decalogue) or to God's speech to the Israelites in Exod. 20:2–17, which is known as the Ten Commandments or the Decalogue. Deuteronomy insists that "the ten words" refers to the speech to the Israelites. It also says that God wrote both sets of tablets personally (Deut. 5:22; 10:1–5).

Exodus and Deuteronomy report that Moses also wrote the whole Torah on a scroll (Exod. 24:4–7; Deut. 31:9). Deuteronomy goes on to say that he gave it for safe keeping to "the levitical priests who carry the Ark of the Covenant of YHWH and to all the Israelite elders." This indicates that the Torah scroll, too, was ritually deposited in the sanctuary (Deut. 31:26). Unlike the tablets of the commandments, however, the Torah scroll circulated publicly both orally and in writing (Deut. 31:12–13, 22; cf. 17:18–19).

So the Pentateuch depicts God speaking aloud to the Israelites and writing the words on stone tablets. It also shows Moses writing down God's words on a scroll and reading it aloud to the Israelites. Furthermore, it requires that the tablets and the scroll be preserved in the sanctuary. Later Jewish and Christian ritualization of iconic Decalogues and Torah scrolls grew from these precedents in the Pentateuch itself.

These stories and commandments tie writing and oral presentation closely together. Writing down the commandments ratifies the covenant between God and Israel. The command to preserve them in the sanctuary and to read them aloud aims to remind the Israelites regularly of their obligations under the covenant. The written texts provide physical evidence to legitimize the claims of priests and prophets who called on Israel to keep the covenant with YHWH.

## 4.3.2   The Ark of the Covenant as Torah Shrine

Exodus and Deuteronomy say that Moses deposited the Decalogue tablets in the Ark of the Covenant (Box 4.6). This ark gets more attention from biblical writers than do the tablets themselves. Joshua describes it being carried into battle during the conquest of Canaan (Josh. 6:4–6; 1 Sam. 4:3–11). Wherever it settled in its tent shrine automatically became the central sanctuary of the Israelite tribes. 1 Samuel narrates how God's anger at the priests of Shiloh led to the Philistines capturing the ark. They installed it in their own temple next to the image of their god. But plague devastated their cities until they sent it back to Israel (1 Sam. 4–6). King David brought the ark to Jerusalem, but even this proved dangerous. On the first attempt, a man

## Box 4.6   The Ark of the Covenant

*YHWH said to Moses: ... Have them also make an ark of acacia wood. ... Cover the ark with pure gold. ... Make poles of acacia wood ... and use them to carry the ark. ... Then make a mitigation center of pure gold. ... Make two winged sphinxes of hammered gold, one at each end of the mitigation center. ... Put the mitigation center on top of the ark. Put the stone tablets of the covenant that I will give you inside the ark. There I will meet with you, there above the mitigation center between the two sphinxes that are on top of the Ark of the Covenant. (Exod. 25:1, 10–11, 13–14, 17–18, 21–22)*

who accidentally touched the ark died instantly (2 Sam. 6). The ark then stayed for three months with a family who miraculously became rich. David was more successful at claiming the ark on his second attempt, and Solomon installed it in the newly built temple in Jerusalem (1 Kgs. 8:4–9; 2 Chr. 35:3). No story tells of the ark emerging from the temple after this time.[13]

Only Exodus 25 and 37 describe the ark in detail. This gilded wooden box measured approximately 4 feet long, 2 feet wide, and 2 feet high (ca. $120 \times 60 \times 60$ cm). Its solid gold lid, the "mitigation center," was surmounted by two winged <u>sphinxes</u> (<u>*cherubim*</u> in Hebrew) whose wings stretched out toward each other. The ark was carried by two poles attached to its sides.

The ark was built to contain the tablets of the commandments (Exod. 25:21; 40:20; Deut. 10:5). The Pentateuch portrays it essentially as a book box, and 1 Kings 8:9 insists that it contained nothing else. But the Pentateuch claims that other objects of great religious significance were also deposited inside or beside it: a jar of miraculous food, <u>manna</u> (Exod. 16:33–34), Aaron's flowering rod (Num. 17:10), and scrolls containing the Torah and Moses' indictment of Israel (Deut. 31:9, 24–26).

The ancient objects that most resemble this description of the Ark of the Covenant are Egyptian <u>Anubis chests</u>. A spectacular example was found in the tomb of King Tutankhamen (Figure 4.14), who died around 1323 BCE. This gold-plated wooden box with carrying poles is surmounted by a statue of a jackal that represents Anubis, the Egyptian god of burial and embalming. The chest contained several amulets in the form of figurines, a papyrus-shaped scepter, jewels, and embalming chemicals. The chest's gold carvings include speeches by Anubis about embalming. Another, less-elaborate Anubis chest was found with papyrus scrolls inside, mostly texts of funeral rituals.[14]

The appearance and contents of Israel's Ark of the Covenant, then, derived from the broader religious culture of the ancient Middle East, or at least Egypt. Its iconography, of course, differs from that of Anubis who

**FIGURE 4.14**    Anubis chest in the treasury of Tutankhamun's tomb in the Valley of the Kings, Egypt. Photo by Harry Burton, 1926. Image distributed under a Creative Commons CC BY-NC-SA 2.0 license.

presided over Egyptian graveyards. The Hebrew Bible describes YHWH as a sky god who, like many ancient sky gods, was represented by winged mythological creatures. Phoenician iconography frequently depicted gods sitting on <u>sphinx thrones</u>. But because they believed their gods to be invisible, the Phoenicians installed empty sphinx thrones in their temples, sometimes with steles on the seat (Figure 4.15). In the same way in Israel, the ark's cover surmounted by two sphinxes functions as the throne of an invisible god:

*The Ark of the Covenant of YHWH of hosts who sits enthroned upon the sphinxes.* (1 Sam. 4:4)

**FIGURE 4.15**   Stone sphinx throne supporting carved stelae; Phoenician, first millennium BCE. In the Louvre Museum, Paris.

The ark could also be thought of as God's footstool (Lam. 2:1), especially since other ancient cultures frequently deposited important texts "at the feet" of gods in temples.

Exodus says the ark occupied the inner-most room of Israel's tent sanctuary, the Tabernacle, and Kings tells us that it later occupied the inner sanctum of Solomon's temple. The ark took the place of the statue of the god in temples of other ancient cultures.[15] The Ark of the Covenant, then, represented the presence of God in ancient Israel more than any other material object. Its presence inside the Tabernacle and First Temple made these sanctuaries "the house of YHWH." But the Pentateuch portrays the ark itself as the container of even more sacred objects, tablets written personally by YHWH.

It is surprising, therefore, that the priests who rebuilt the temple after the Babylonian Exile apparently did not build another ark for its inner sanctum. Jeremiah predicted that the Ark of the Covenant would not be remade:

*They will no longer announce, "The Ark of the Covenant of YHWH!" It will not come to mind, they will not remember it or look for it, and they will not make another one. In that time, they will call Jerusalem "The throne of YHWH!"* (Jer. 3:16–17)

Texts from the end of the Second Temple period agree that the "holy of holies" in the Jerusalem Temple was empty (so explicitly Josephus and Tacitus; implicitly 1 Macc. 4:49–51). Perhaps the builders of the Second Temple believed they could follow the instructions in Exodus for building the Tabernacle and its furnishings, but they could not recreate tablets written by God. Since the ark served as a reliquary for the tablets, there was no point in rebuilding the ark for it to stay empty. They apparently could tolerate an empty Holy of Holies, since they believed God is invisible anyway, better than an ark without tablets inside.[16]

## 4.3.3   The Priestly Blessing Amulets

In 1979, an archeologist found two, 1-inch-wide silver scrolls in a burial cave above the Hinnom valley in Jerusalem (Figure 4.16). Once unrolled, they proved to contain words closely resembling the priestly blessing found in Numbers 6:23–26 (see p. 49 above). The writing on the tiny scrolls and other discoveries in the same cave show that they may be as much as 2600 years old, dating from the last decades of the Kingdom of Judah before the Babylonian Exile or, possibly, shortly after the Exile.

Many have called the Ketef Hinnom amulets the oldest physical evidence for the text of any part of the Pentateuch. It is more likely that both the Pentateuch and the amulets quote the oral blessings pronounced by priests in Jerusalem's temple and circulating orally in Judean society. Many historians do not think the Pentateuch existed yet when the amulets were made. Even if it did, nothing suggests that its priestly texts were widely published at this time. The regular temple liturgy or popular religious practices are more plausible sources for the similar language in the amulets and the Pentateuch. The amulets prove that some Judeans in the seventh to fifth centuries considered the blessing very important, just as its quotation as the only verbal liturgy in the books of Leviticus and Numbers indicates.[17]

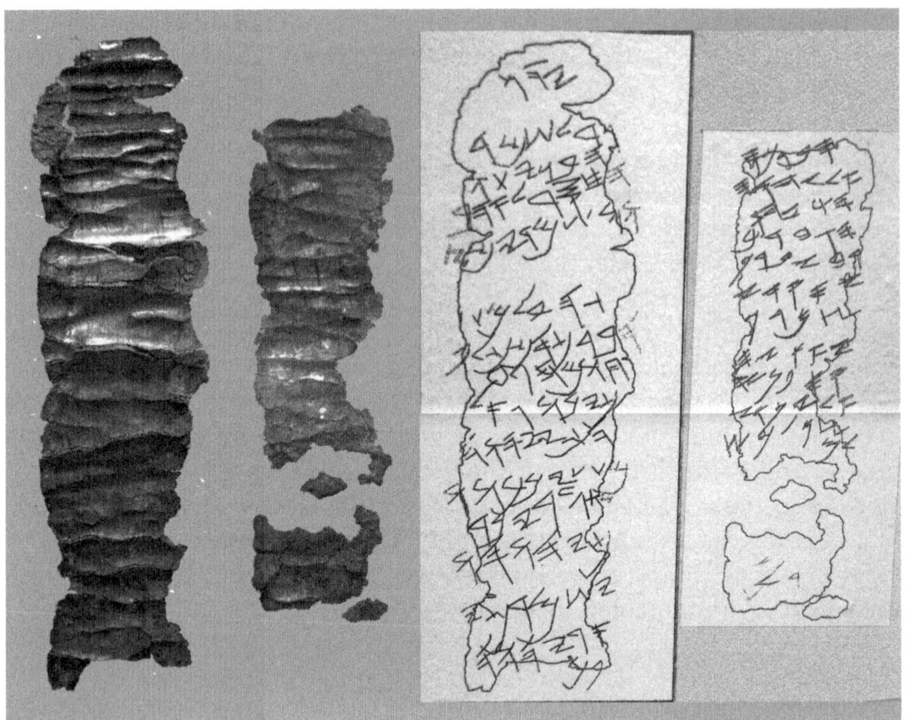

**FIGURE 4.16**    Silver amulet scrolls from Ketef Hinnom; seventh to fifth century BCE. In the Israel Museum, Jerusalem.

The silver scrolls were, of course, never intended to be unrolled. Their silver material and tiny size show that they were created to be carried as an amulet, not to be read, and were probably worn on a string around the neck. Amulets are a common feature of human religious practice world-wide. Textual amulets were common in the ancient Middle East. Tiny papyrus scrolls containing spells for protection have been found in first-millennium BCE metal containers in Egypt, and scroll amulets proliferated in Hellenistic and Roman cultures, including among Jews and Christians. That is not surprising, since Deuteronomy seems to require ritualization of the Torah's iconic dimension in the form of amulets and inscriptions:

> *Tie [these words] as a sign on your hand, make them a symbol between your eyes.* (Deut. 6:8)

The priestly blessing invokes YHWH's protection and favor and so is perfectly suited to iconic ritualization in the form of amulets.

## 4.4  ANCIENT LOST-AND-FOUND BOOKS

According to 2 Kings 22–23, a Torah scroll was found in the Jerusalem temple during renovations in the late seventh century BCE. The priests read it to King Josiah, who as a result launched far-reaching reforms of Judah's religious practices (see Box 4.7 and Section 5.5.2).

---

**Box 4.7   Finding a Torah scroll in the Temple**

*Hilkiah, the high priest, said to Shaphan the scribe: "I have found a Torah scroll in the temple of YHWH." Hilkiah gave the scroll to Shaphan and he read it….Shaphan the scribe informed the king: "Hilkiah has given me a scroll." He then read it to the king. When the king heard the words of the Torah scroll, he tore his clothes.* (2 Kgs. 22:8, 10–11) [The prophet Huldah then authenticated the scroll as representing YHWH's will (22:12–20).] *The king went up to the temple of YHWH and with him all the men of Judah, the inhabitants of Jerusalem, the priests, the prophets, and all the insignificant as well as significant people. He read in their hearing all the words of the covenant scroll that was found in the temple of YHWH. The king stood beside the pillar and made a covenant before YHWH to follow YHWH and to observe all the commandments, the testimonies, and the statutes with all his mind and will and to keep the words of this covenant written in this scroll. All the people joined in this covenant.* (23:2–3) [Josiah then removed illegitimate cult objects from the Jerusalem temples and destroyed worship sites ("high places") in the villages of Judah as well as in the old northern kingdom around Samaria (23:4–20).] *The king commanded all the people: "Keep the Passover to YHWH your God as it is written in this covenant book."…Josiah also did away with all the nauseating things that were found in the land of Judah and in Jerusalem, so that he kept the words of the Torah that were written in the scroll that Hilkiah the priest found in the temple.* (23:21–24)

---

Stories of lost-and-found ritual books were a staple feature of ancient literate cultures from the Babylonians, Hittites, and Egyptians to the Greeks and the Romans.[18] Already around 2100 BCE, Sumerian king Shulgi boasted about his own scribal and linguistic skills and his zeal in preserving ancient hymns and ritual texts:

*I am no fool…when I have discovered tigi and zamzam hymns from past days, old ones from ancient times, I have never declared them to*

*be false, and have never contradicted their contents. I have conserved
these antiquities, never abandoning them to oblivion....So that they
should never fall into disuse, I have added them to the singers' repertoire, and thereby I have set the heart of the land on fire and aflame.*[19]

In the second millennium BCE, an Ugaritic omen text specified the need to
eat the meat offering "in accordance with the documents." Around the same
time, Hittite kings cited their examination of old written documents as proof
of their ritual fidelity:

*And whatever I, My Majesty, discover now in the written records, I will
carry out.*

During a long-drawn-out plague, searches of Hittite archives turned up old
ritual and treaty texts. When prophets confirmed that failure to follow these
texts had brought the plague on Hatti (just like the prophet Huldah confirmed
the threats in Josiah's law book, 2 Kgs. 22:13–20), the rituals were reinstated
and offerings were made to compensate for the violations.[20]

An example contemporary with 2 Kings can be found in a fragmentary
inscription of King Nabonidus of Babylon (539 BCE), which depicts him con-
sulting various kinds of texts about temples and rituals:

*A stela of Nebuchadnezzar, king of Babylon, son of Ninurta-nādin-
šumi, on which appeared the representation of an ēntu-priestess and
were described the rites, rules, and ceremonies relating to her office, was
brought with other tablets from Ur to Babylon, in ignorance of what
Sîn, lord of kings, wished . . .. He (Nabonidus) took a good look at the
tablets and was afraid. He was attentive to Sîn's great commandment.*[21]

Later, during the Roman Empire, the geographer Pausanias (ca. 115–180 CE)
described how the Messenian culture survived defeat and banishment by
the miraculous preservation of their rituals on a tin scroll in a bronze urn.
The Messenians discovered it after returning to their homeland in 369 BCE,
which allowed them to revive their traditions. The scroll and urn became
venerated icons.[22] So there was much interest in various periods and cultures
in the ritual requirements of old texts.

Ancient art and artifacts, especially from Egypt, reinforce this impression. Egyptian art regularly depicts priests holding scrolls aloft in public
processions and funerary rituals (Figure 4.17). Their temple libraries were
called "Houses of Life" and were off-limits except to some priests. From at

**FIGURE 4.17**    Scribe holding scroll over sarcophagus in a model of a funerary boat from the tomb of Djehuty, ca. 1962–1786 BCE. In the Metropolitan Museum of Art, New York.

least the early second millennium BCE on, Egyptians used portable chests topped by statues or images of the god Anubis to keep ritual texts as well as cultic implements. This artistic evidence combines with literary references to show that, throughout their literate histories, ancient Middle Eastern and Mediterranean cultures manipulated scrolls, tablets, and the boxes that contained them for ritual purposes.

The story of the discovery of Josiah's scroll in 2 Kings uses this widespread motif. Modern historians often doubt that Josiah's scroll was as old as he claimed. They think it may have been a "pious fraud" created by the temple priests (see Section 14.2.3). Some scholars argue that the entire scene in 2 Kings is fictional and never happened. There can be no doubt that many ancient stories of lost-and-found ritual books describe forgeries that were created to justify religious and political claims. On the other hand, many ancient kings and priests were really worried about the negative consequences of failing to follow the instructions of ancient rituals. That made them vulnerable to being deceived by forgeries, but it also raised their interest in discovering genuinely old books.

So, claiming to have found an ancient ritual book may well be a fictional device used by priests when conducting rituals and by authors when writing about them. The appearance of this theme nevertheless attests to the *existence* of the scroll of Torah at the time that 2 Kings was written in the sixth century BCE, since there would be no point in validating the authority of a non-existent book. The story of the scroll's discovery in the temple was plausible to ancient readers, and King Josiah's reaction resembles stories about pious kings in many literatures of the ancient world. So, the story of the book's discovery glorifies Josiah's piety. It also used his good reputation to establish the authority of written Torah.

The contents of Josiah's book are not so obvious. Many historians have associated it with the book of Deuteronomy because of the nature of Josiah's religious reforms. In 1805, Wilhelm de Wette argued that Deuteronomy was written early in Josiah's reign to justify the reforms, and that view has dominated biblical studies for two centuries. However, Deuteronomy's restricted view of kingship and its emphasis on legal issues do not fit the Josiah story very well. Some scholars have suggested that the role of the high priest and the emphasis on purifying religious practices resemble the Holiness Code of Leviticus more than Deuteronomy.

Neither 2 Kings nor other biblical texts provide any reason to think that Josiah's reforms had a lasting effect. After he died in battle in 609 BCE, his successors reversed his religious reforms. Twenty-two years later, the Babylonians destroyed Judea and Jerusalem and exiled its king and upper classes. 2 Kings and many other biblical books maintain that this event was divine punishment for failing to keep the covenant with God. There is therefore no reason to think that a Torah scroll was ritualized regularly after Josiah's death, until priests who returned from exile did so to legitimize the rituals of Jerusalem's Second Temple.

The story of Ezra's Torah reading provides our first account of the Torah's ritualization after Josiah, which is our first account of the Torah's ritualization after Joshua. So, the Hebrew Bible's story of the written Torah consists of four episodes widely separated in time:

- Moses writes down the Torah in the wilderness.
- Shortly thereafter, Joshua reads and ratifies the Torah in the land.
- 600 years later, Josiah discovers and reads the Torah in the temple and renews the covenant.
- 200 years after that, Ezra reads and teaches Torah and renews the covenant.

In between these Torah readings, biblical books tell a story of widespread religious infidelity in Israel and Judah that led to the kingdoms' destruction. Their account aims to persuade readers and listeners not to repeat the mistakes of their ancestors. They should instead follow the examples of Moses, Joshua, Josiah, and Ezra by venerating the Torah scroll and obeying its commandments.

## CITED WORKS AND FURTHER READING

1 On iconic books, see the essays in *Iconic Books and Texts* (ed. J. W. Watts; London: Equinox, 2013), especially Dorina Miller Parmenter, "The Iconic Book: The Image of the Bible in Early Christian Rituals," pp. 63–92; and James W. Watts, *How and Why Books Matter* (Sheffield: Equinox, 2019), 7–69.

2 Quotation of the letter of Aristeas is from the translation by R. J. H. Schutt in *The Old Testament Pseudepigrapha* (ed. J. H. Charlesworth; Garden City, NY: Doubleday, 1985), 2: 24.

3 On Pentateuch manuscripts among the Dead Sea Scrolls, see Emanuel Tov, "The Scribal and Textual Transmission of the Torah Analyzed in Light of its Sanctity," in *Pentateuchal Traditions in the Late Second Temple Period* (ed. Akio Moriya and Gohei Hata; Leiden: Brill, 2012), 57–72 [64–65].

4 Translation of *m. Yoma* 7:1 and *m. Sotah* 7:7 by Lawrence H. Schiffman, "The Early History of Public Reading of the Torah," in *Jews, Christians, and Polytheists in the Ancient Synagogue: Cultural Interaction during the Greco-Roman Period* (ed. Steven Fine; New York: Routledge, 1999), 48.

5  Ruth Langer, "From Study of Scripture to a Reenactment of Sinai: The Emergence of the Synagogue Torah Service," *Worship* 72/1 (1998), 43–67.

6 On mezuzahs and *tefillin,* see Yehudah B. Cohn, *Tangled Up in Text: Tefillin and the Ancient World,* BJS 351, Providence: Brown University, 2008; and Robert T. Anderson and Terry Giles, *Tradition Kept: The Literature of the Samaritans* (Peabody, MA: Hendrickson, 2005), 408–409.

7 On divine names in Jewish and Christian texts, see John Barton, *Holy Writings, Sacred Text: the Canon in Early Christianity* (Louisville: Westminster John Knox, 1997), 106–130; and Patricia Cox Miller, "In Praise of Nonsense," in *Classical Mediterranean Spirituality* (ed. A. H. Armstrong; New York: Crossroad, 1986), 481–505; repr. in P. C. Miller, *The Poetry of Thought in Late Antiquity* (Burlington: Ashgate, 2001), 221–245, who provides (1986, p. 224) the translated quotation from *The Discourse on the Eighth and the Ninth*, Nag Hammadi Codex VI, 6, p. 296.

8  On Torah arks in ancient synagogues, see Eric M. Meyers, "The Torah Shrine in the Ancient Synagogue," in *Jews, Christians, and Polytheists in the Ancient Synagogue: Cultural Interaction during the Greco-Roman Period* (ed. Steven Fine; New York: Routledge, 1999), 201–223, who provides on pp. 206–207 the translation of John Chrysostom's polemic in *Adversus Judaeos*, 6:7; PG 48, col. 913. See also Rachel Hachlili, *Ancient Jewish Art and Archaeology in the Land of Israel* (Leiden: Brill, 1988), 273–280.

9  Ruth Langer, "From Study of Scripture to a Reenactment of Sinai: The Emergence of the Synagogue Torah Service," *Worship* 72/1 (1998), 43–67; see also Katrin Kogman-Appel, *A Mahzor from Worms: Art and Religion in a Medieval Jewish Community* (Cambridge, MA: Harvard University Press, 2011).

10  On synagogue scrolls as sacred objects, see William Scott Green, "Scripture in Classical Judaism," in *The Encyclopedia of Judaism* (ed. J. Neusner, S. Peck, and W. S. Green; New York: Continuum/Leiden: Brill, 1999), 1302–1309, quotation from 1305; Marianne Schleicher, "Artifactual and Hermeneutical Use of Scripture in Jewish Tradition," in *Jewish and Christian Scripture as Artifact and Canon* (ed. C. A. Evans and H. D. Zacharias; London: T. & T. Clark, 2009), 48–65; Marianne Schleicher, "Accounts of a Dying Scroll: On Jewish Handling of Sacred Texts in Need of Restoration or Disposal," in *The Death of Sacred Texts* (ed. K. Myrvold; London: Ashgate, 2010), 11–30; and Shalom Sabar, "Torah and Magic: The Torah Scroll and Its Appurtenances as Magical Objects in Traditional Jewish Culture," *European Journal of Jewish Studies* 3 (2009), 135–170, who on p. 154 supplies the translation of the dedicatory plaque from Ionnia.

11  On heavenly tablets in Jubilees, see Hindy Najman, "Interpretation as Primordial Writing: Jubilees and Its Authority Conferring Strategies," *Journal for the Study of Judaism* 30 (1999), 379–410; and Florentino García Martínez, "The Heavenly Tablets in the Book of Jubilees," in *Studies in the Book of Jubilees* (ed. M. Albani, J. Frey, and A. Lange; Tübingen: Mohr Siebeck, 1997), 243–260.

12  On myths of heavenly books, see Stephanie Dalley, *The Legacy of Mesopotamia* (Oxford: Oxford University Press, 1998), quotations from p. 166; John F. A. Sawyer, *Sacred Languages and Sacred Texts* (London: Routledge, 1999), quotation from p. 105; and Dorina Miller Parmenter, "The Bible as Icon: Myths of the Divine Origins of Scripture," in *Jewish and Christian Scripture as Artifact and Canon* (ed. Craig A. Evans and H. Daniel Zacharias; London: T. & T. Clark, 2009), 298–310.

13  On the Ark of the Covenant, see C. L. Seow, "Ark of the Covenant," *Anchor Bible Dictionary* (New York: Doubleday, 1992), 1:386–393; and John Day, "Whatever Happened to the Ark of the Covenant?" in *Temple and Worship in Biblical Israel* (ed. J. Day; London: T.&T. Clark, 2007), 250–270.

14 On Egyptian Anubis chests, see Harco Willems, *The Coffin of Heqata (Cairo JdE 36418): A Case Study of Egyptian Funerary Culture of the Early Middle Kingdom* (OLA 70; Leuven: Peeters, 1996), 142–145.

15 On comparing the ritual use of Torah scrolls and of statues of gods, see Martin Goodman, "Sacred Scripture and 'Defiling the Hands'," *Journal of Theological Studies* 41 (1990), 99–107; and Karel van der Toorn, "The Iconic Book: Analogies Between the Babylonian Cult of Images and the Veneration of the Torah," in *The Image and the Book: Iconic Cults, Aniconism and the Rise of Book Religion in Israel and the Ancient Near East* (ed. K. van der Toorn; Leuven: Peeters, 1997), 229–248.

16 For more on the relationship between the ark, the tablets, and Torah scrolls, see James W. Watts, "From Ark of the Covenant to Torah Scroll: Ritualizing Israel's Iconic Texts," in *Ritual Innovation in the Hebrew Bible and Early Judaism* (ed. Nathan MacDonald; BZAW 468; Berlin: De Gruyter, 2016), 21–34.

17 On the Ketef Hinnom amulets and the priestly blessing, see Brian B. Schmidt, "The Social Matrix of Early Judean Magic and Divination: From 'Top Down' or 'Bottom Up'?" in *Beyond Hatti: A Tribute to Gary Beckman* (ed. B. J. Collins and P. Michalowski; Atlanta: Lockwood, 2013), 279–294; and Jeremy Daniel Smoak, *The Priestly Blessing in Inscription and Scripture: The Early History of Numbers 6: 24–26* (Oxford: Oxford University Press, 2015).

18 On lost-and-found ritual texts in antiquity, compare Katherine Stott, "Finding the Lost Book of the Law: Re-reading the Story of 'The Book of the Law' (Deuteronomy-2 Kings) in Light of Classical Literature," *Journal for the Study of the Old Testament* 30 (2005), 153–169, who provides examples from Greco-Roman literature, with the response by Nadav Na'aman, "The 'Discovered Book' and the Legitimation of Josiah's Reform," *Journal of Biblical Literature* 130 (2011), 47–62, who provides many ancient Middle Eastern examples of the theme.

19 Shulgi's boast is a quotation from lines 270–280 of Shulgi B, translated in the *The Electronic Text Corpus of Sumerian Literature* (ETCSL) online project of the Faculty of Oriental Studies, University of Oxford, http://etcsl.orinst. ox.ac.uk/section2/tr24202.htm.

20 The Hittite examples are translated by Itamar Singer, *Hittite Prayers* (WAW 11; Atlanta: SBL, 2002), 58–59, 83.

21 The quotation from a Nabonidus inscription is translated by Jean-Jacques Glassner, *Mesopotamian Chronicles* (WAW 19; Atlanta: SBL, 2005), 315.

22 For Pausanius on the Messenian text, see W. H. S. Jones, *Pausanius' Description of Greece* (Loeb edition; London: Heinemann, 1917–1935), 4.20.2–8, 4.26.7–8, 4.27.5, 4.33.5.

# CHAPTER 5

# The Torah's Expressive Dimension

The first step in reading written texts is to turn their visual signs into language. The fonts and layout of most modern texts have been optimized to make this as quick and easy as possible. People who are literate in the text's language usually read silently to themselves – as I assume you, the reader of this book, are doing right now.

Ancient texts were not so easy to scan. They lacked many of the visual aids that we now take for granted, such as punctuation, lower-case and capital letters, and paragraph divisions. Some writing systems, such as the Hebrew alphabet, omitted most of the vowels. Greek texts contained vowels but usually did not mark word divisions. And, of course, all ancient texts were written by hand.

Readers in ancient times therefore customarily <u>read</u> texts <u>aloud</u>. If they planned to read to other people, they would usually practice in advance, studying the written text and perhaps even <u>memorizing</u> it in order to read fluently. Public readings and recitations were the common way of <u>publishing</u> a text. Traditions of recitation developed that dictated how to vocalize a given text in order to standardize performances. They often included instructions for reading melodically by <u>chanting</u> or <u>singing</u>. Sometimes texts were presented <u>dramatically</u> by multiple actors or accompanied by <u>artistic illustrations</u> to increase audience interest. All these ways of transforming written signs into oral language and visual illustration constitute the <u>expressive dimension</u> of a text.

## 5.1   THE EXPRESSIVE DIMENSION OF SCRIPTURES

Paying careful and repeated attention to oral, dramatic, and artistic presentations of a text <u>ritualizes</u> its expressive dimension. The comparative study of religions illustrates the many ways in which religious scriptures can be ritualized in the expressive dimension. Religious communities throughout the world place importance on the oral reading and recitation of their scriptures. That is naturally the case in communities that pass on their tradition primarily in oral form, such as the Brahmins of India who memorize and recite the Vedas and other Hindu sacred texts. But it is also the case in traditions that revere written scriptures. The oral reading or recitation of scriptures is a characteristic feature of the worship services of Jews, Zoroastrians, Buddhists, Jains, Christians, and Muslims. Devotional scripture reading by individuals, silently or aloud, is also typical in many traditions (see Figure 5.1).

Ritualizing the expressive dimension of scripture conveys a feeling of <u>inspiration</u>. Of course, religious communities regularly claim that divine inspiration directed the writing of their scriptures. However, it is in their expressive presentation that scriptures have inspiring effects on congregations and, often, on the presenters themselves.

Communities frequently invite their members to participate in scripture reading and recitation. For example, many Christian services feature lay readers. Jewish coming-of-age ceremonies (*bar* and *bat mitzvahs*) focus on the child reading a passage from the Hebrew Torah aloud. All Muslims are expected to be able to recite the first *surah* (chapter) of the Arabic Qur'an from memory. In these ways, congregations broaden participation in worship by inviting people to join in ritualizing the expressive dimension of their scriptures.

Experts with interpretive authority often express the texts, too. They may lace their preaching with scriptural quotations and allusions. Thus preaching, though based in semantic interpretation and its authority, becomes <u>inspiring</u> to the degree that it also presents the text. But <u>artists</u> and <u>actors</u> frequently express the contents of scriptures in ways that inspire audiences quite apart from, or even in conflict with, religiously authorized interpreters.

The inspiring power of oral reading and recitation has not only strengthened belief in the divine inspiration of scriptures. It has also fueled mystical speculation about supernatural words and about <u>sound</u> itself (Box 5.1).

**FIGURE 5.1**   Buddhist monks chanting sutras at Bodh Gaya, India. Photo by Lyn Watts 2014, used by permission.

## Box 5.1   The power of sound, word, and scripture

William Graham observed: "In many of the major, literate traditions of history, the idea of the primordial word of power is linked to the power of scripture itself. This is most explicitly evident in theological formulations such as we find in Rabbinic Judaism and medieval Islam concerning the preexistence of the divine word of scripture. Ideas of the eternality of the Buddha-word, the Qur'ān, or the sounds of the Veda also reflect the identification of the preserved scriptural texts with the primal power of the original word of truth."[1]

Beliefs in a heavenly scripture draw even more attention to the language of that scripture (see Section 4.2.7 above).

Most religious traditions that venerate written scriptures employ the <u>original language</u> or, at least, an ancient language of those scriptures for their ritual presentations. A few traditions, most notably strands of Christianity and Mahayana Buddhism, employ <u>translations</u> in most ritual situations. This difference between traditions does not revolve around the decision to translate scripture or not, because almost everybody translates for religious education. It instead has to do with what <u>language</u> to use when expressing scriptures orally in ritual settings. Rival religious traditions originating in both India (Hinduism and Buddhism) and the Middle East (Christianity and Islam) have developed opposite ritual practices regarding the languages of their scriptures. Hindus and Muslims insist on the importance of expressing the Vedas and the Qur'an in the original Sanskrit and Arabic languages. By contrast, Buddhists and Christians have ritualized their scriptures in translations since the origins of their religions.[2]

Many paintings and sculptures depict scenes from scriptural stories. <u>Art</u> in a religious context, such as in a temple or a church, can therefore function as a ritualized expression of scripture. Art, however, usually presents the contents rather than the words of scripture, and mostly focuses on narratives. Like oral performance, religious art has an inspiring effect on devout viewers. <u>Theater</u> has also been used frequently to present the stories of scriptures both orally and visually. Some famous works of art and <u>films</u> on scriptural themes have shaped the religious imaginations of very many people.

By its nature, oral expression does not leave direct evidence behind for historians to examine. We can only look for written references to ritualizing the expressive dimension of scripture. This evidence is not as plentiful as it is for the iconic and semantic dimensions in any period of history. Nevertheless, there are indications that the Pentateuch was increasingly being read aloud ritually after it was first ritualized as a scripture in the time of Ezra, during the fifth or early fourth centuries BCE (see Box 5.2).

## 5.2  READING TORAH AFTER EZRA

The history of ritualizing the Torah's expressive dimension as a scripture begins with stories about Ezra reading it aloud himself and extends to the common practices of Jewish and Christian congregations today.

### 5.2.1  Ezra's Torah Reading

Nehemiah 8 tells the story of Ezra's Torah reading. Ezra stood on a platform in the open plaza before a main gate of the walled city of Jerusalem. He was flanked on either side by other leaders of the community. The crowd consisted

## Box 5.2   Judah's exile and restoration

The Kingdom of Judah fell under the control of Babylon in 605 BCE. Twice its kings tried to rebel against Babylonian rule, and twice they were defeated and reconquered (2 Kings 24–25). In 597 BCE, Nebuchadnezzar, the king of Babylon, conquered Jerusalem, looted its temple, and exiled King Jehoiakin to Babylon along with many officials, priests, and other members of Judah's upper class. He placed another member of the royal family, Zedekiah, on the throne. Ten years later, Nebuchadnezzar again put down Judah's rebellion. This time the Babylonians killed Zedekiah's sons and blinded the king before taking him to Babylon. They destroyed the temple in Jerusalem and exiled many more Judeans, leaving the city and territory in ruins.

Fifty years later, Babylon itself was conquered by Cyrus, king of Persia, who established an empire that would rule the Middle East for 200 years. Unlike the empires before them, the Persians gave careful thought to how they could gain and retain the loyalty of the people that they ruled. So, as soon as he conquered Babylon in 538 BCE, Cyrus allowed people who had been exiled by the Assyrians and Babylonians to return to their native homelands. Judeans who had lived for two generations in Mesopotamia were now allowed to return to Jerusalem (Ezra 1).

Over the next two decades, several return parties were organized by the royal princes, Sheshbazzar and Zerubbabel (Ezra 1–2). It took some time for the returnees to settle themselves in Judean territory. Finally, in 520 BCE, Jeshua the high priest and Zerubbabel the prince led the effort to rebuild Jerusalem's temple, which was finished five years later (Ezra 3–6). So historians date the beginning of Judea's Second Temple period to 515 BCE when the new temple began to function.

Life in Judah remained difficult for many years. More exiles returned to Judah in the fifth century BCE. They were led by Persian imperial officials of Judean heritage: the governor Nehemiah (Nehemiah 1–7, 11–13) and the scribe Ezra (Ezra 7–10, Nehemiah 8–9). Jerusalem's defensive walls were only completed by Nehemiah almost 100 years after the first exiles returned.

The traumatic memory of the destruction and exile of Judah shapes much of the Hebrew Bible. The Pentateuch anticipates it with its warnings and threats (Leviticus 26, Deuteronomy 27–30). The prophetic books warn that God will destroy Israel and Judah for breaking the covenant. The history books document the kingdoms' destruction in detail (2 Kings 17, 24–25;

2 Chronicles 36) and the difficulties of the restoration (Ezra, Nehemiah). Lament poems mourn the slaughter of their populations and the ruin of their towns and cities (Lamentations, Psalm 137). The literature and religion of the Hebrew Bible have been shaped deeply by this experience of catastrophe. Many Jews and Christians have therefore found it to be a profound resource for dealing with their own traumatic experiences.[3]

of "men and women and everyone who could listen and understand." Ezra read from dawn until noon. He accompanied the reading with a <u>blessing</u> and the audience responded "Amen, amen" and bowed to the ground. Ezra declared the day of the reading holy. Public readings continued on every day of the seven-day festival of *Sukkot* (Booths). So, the story depicts Ezra ritualizing the Pentateuch's expressive dimension by the arrangement and posture of the audience, by verbal cues and responses, and by the length and repetition of the readings.

This story appears in a literary context, the books of Ezra and Nehemiah, that describes considerable <u>conflict</u> within the Jerusalem community. The leaders, Ezra the priest and Nehemiah the governor, had both come from Babylon as appointees of the Persian emperor. Ezra required the men of Jerusalem to divorce their foreign wives and send them away in order to keep the religious community pure (Ezra 9–10). Nehemiah excluded neighboring rulers from Jerusalem and feared their military attack (Nehemiah 4, 6). So, the social situation was very conflictual both internally and externally.

The immediate consequence of Ezra's Torah reading was that the people learned how to observe <u>*Sukkot* (Booths)</u>, which they proceeded to celebrate. (Instructions for celebrating *Sukkot* appear in Lev. 23:33–43.) The story claims that the feast of *Sukkot* had not been celebrated properly since the days of Joshua, some eight centuries earlier (Neh. 8:17, though Ezra 3:4 claims that the returning exiles celebrated *Sukkot*). So, a public presentation of the old book led to the revival and performance of an old pilgrimage festival. Reading the Torah inspired the people's desire to celebrate *Sukkot* in the ways required by the old book.

The story of Ezra's Torah reading tells of temple officials, the Levites, standing among the people to interpret the text to them:

*The Levites made the people understand the Torah.... They read from the book of the Torah of God with interpretation to give insight, so the people understood the reading.* (Neh. 8:7–8)

Many commentators think this refers to oral translation into Aramaic. The Pentateuch is written in Hebrew, the vernacular language of people living in the kingdoms of Israel and Judea in the eighth to sixth centuries BCE. Nehemiah 13:23–24 says that, in Ezra's time, many people in Jerusalem could not understand Hebrew. Apparently, Aramaic was already replacing Hebrew as the vernacular by the end of the fifth century. That means, then, that when the Torah was first being regularly ritualized as a scripture, its audience already spoke a vernacular different than the language of the text.[4] The scripture's archaic language distinguished it as an old text and as authoritative for ritual practice.

The book of Nehemiah records a meeting later in the same month when the people gathered wearing sackcloth, ashes, and fasting – all symbols of mourning and repentance:

> *They stood and confessed their sins and their ancestors' liabilities. They arose where they stood and read in the Torah scroll of YHWH their God for one quarter of the day, and for another quarter they confessed and bowed down to YHWH their God.* (Neh. 9:2–3)

Again, the Levites played a leading role, this time by voicing the people's prayer of repentance that summarizes the biblical story line from Genesis through Kings (Neh. 9:4–37). Here, reading Torah and reciting Israel's history have been incorporated into the people's communal worship. Torah reading now plays an important role in regular religious experiences.

## 5.2.2   Reading Torah in Later Second Temple Judaism

Our next evidence for ritualizing the Torah's expressive dimension also involves translation, this time written translation. The Pentateuch was translated into Greek sometime in the third century BCE. We have a highly embellished account of how this Septuagint translation was made in the Letter of Aristeas, written one century later. *Aristeas* credits the translation to the desire of the Hellenistic (Greek-speaking) king of Egypt to include the Torah in his library at Alexandria. It is much more likely that this translation was motivated by the desire of Greek-speaking Jews to hear the Torah read in their vernacular language.

*Aristeas*' account of how the new translation was received (see Box 5.3) is probably fictional. It nevertheless tells us how this second-century Jewish writer thought the translated Torah *should* be received: by bowing to the ground and a public reading of the entire document, followed by curses on anyone who would dare change this new text. Three centuries after the Septuagint translation of the Pentateuch, Philo reported that the

## Box 5.3   Reading the Greek Torah

*Demetrius [the royal librarian] assembled the company of the Jews in the place where the task of translation had been finished and read it to all, in the presence of the translators, who received a great ovation from the crowded audience for being responsible for great blessings. . . . [The Jewish priests and elders] commanded that a curse should be laid as was their custom, on anyone who should alter the version by any addition or change to any part of the written text, or any deletion either. This was a good step taken to ensure that the words were preserved completely and permanently in perpetuity. (Letter of Aristeas 308–312)*

translators' accomplishment was still celebrated by an annual festival near Alexandria. Rabbinic literature from the second through sixth centuries CE (see Section 6.5.2) also attests to the practice of reading Torah aloud in synagogue services in vernacular translations. Though the rabbis preferred synagogue readings in Hebrew or at least interlacing vernacular translations with verses in Hebrew, they admitted that many synagogues were reading the Torah only in Greek.[5]

References to reading Torah or scripture aloud began to proliferate in sources from the first centuries BCE and CE. Second Maccabees claims that the armies of Judah Maccabee marched into battle to the sound of Torah being read aloud:

*He appointed Eleazar to read aloud from the holy book, and gave the watchword, "The help of God"; then, leading the first division himself, he joined battle with Nicanor. (2 Macc. 8:23 NRSV)*

Many first-century CE sources indicate that Torah reading had become institutionalized in synagogues. The Theodotus Inscription (Box 5.4 and Figure 5.2) summarizes the characteristic activities of such institutions as public readings and study of the Torah. The New Testament, Philo, and Josephus all portray such synagogues as central institutions in Jewish life. The New Testament book of Acts describes the role of scripture reading in a synagogue service:

*And on the sabbath day they went into the synagogue and sat down. After the reading of the law and the prophets, the officials of the synagogue sent them a message, saying, "Brothers, if you have any word of exhortation for the people, give it." (Acts 13:14–15 NRSV)*

## Box 5.4  The Theodotus inscription

*Theodotos, son of Vettenos, priest and head of the synagogue, son of the head of the synagogue, who was also the son of the head of the synagogue, built the synagogue for the reading of the Law and for the study of the precepts, as well as the hospice and the chambers and the bathing-establishment, for lodging those who need them, from abroad; it (the synagogue) was founded by his ancestors and the elders and Simonidas.[6]*

**FIGURE 5.2**   The Theodotus Inscription, Jerusalem, mid-first century CE. In the Israel Museum.

This story already exhibits the standard synagogue ritual sequence of reading a portion of Torah followed by a passage from a prophetic book and then an interpretive sermon.

Multiple references in the <u>Dead Sea Scrolls</u> (Section 4.2.2) show that public readings of scripture were routine in the Qumran religious community. In fact, they were required:

*The assembly shall be assiduous to read the book as a community one-third of each night of the year, and to expound the Torah and recite benedictions as a community.*

Other Qumran texts emphasize readings on the Sabbath and also expect scripture readings to be prominent in the afterlife. The community seems to have reenacted every year the blessings and curses of the covenant ceremony in Deuteronomy 27–28.[7] Priests read aloud constantly to the members of the community, and one document prohibits anyone from doing so

> *whose speech is too soft or speaks with a staccato voice not dividing his words so that his voice may be heard, none of these shall read from the book of the Torah, lest he cause error in a capital manner.*

As this sentence from the *Damascus Document* makes clear, the members of the Qumran community dictated how to read aloud because reading scripture publicly carried ultimate stakes. They had exiled themselves from the religious establishment in Jerusalem because of disagreements about ritual practice. They organized their communal life around their ideal of how the Jerusalem temple and community should function. Their rituals of scripture reading probably reflect how scripture was being read in the Jerusalem Temple or, at least, how they thought it should be read there.[8]

Unfortunately, we do not have any direct evidence for how scripture was in fact read in the Temple. Later rabbinic literature described how the rabbis remembered the high priest reading Torah in the Second Temple:

> *The high priest stood and received it and read [the portions] Ahare Mot* [After the death … – Lev. 16:1–34] *and Akh Be-'Asor* [But on the Tenth … – Lev. 23:26–32]. *He rolled up the Torah and placed it on his breast and said, "More than what I have read before you is written here." Uve-'Asor* [And on the Tenth …] *in the book of Numbers* [29:7–11] *he recited by heart, and he blessed upon it [the reading] eight benedictions. (m. Yoma 7:1; m. Sot. 7:7,8)*[9]

The priest probably recited the Numbers passage from memory because he could not quickly roll a scroll to that passage. The rabbis prohibited reciting Torah from memory in synagogue services and recommended using a second scroll instead. The same Mishnaic passage also reports that King Agrippa read aloud portions of Deuteronomy, including the rule of the king (Deut. 17:14–20), in the Temple during a festival.

## 5.2.3  Reading Torah in Synagogues

Synagogue rituals of reading scripture began to be reflected in the design of synagogue buildings in the second century CE and later. The ruins of many ancient synagogues built in Late Antiquity show clear evidence of reading platforms (*bemot*) as well as Torah arks.

Rabbinic literature (Section 6.5.2) from the same centuries reveals how ritual readings were being developed in synagogue liturgies. The Mishnah (circa 200 CE) shows concern for who may read, the posture of the readers, how often Torah should be read, and what other readings and blessings should accompany the reading. It also recognizes considerable variations between the reading practices of different communities, which suggests that their reading customs were already entrenched from long practice by this time (Box 5.5).

Reading Torah aloud explicitly indexes levels of social prestige and honor within the congregation. The Mishnah lists three Torah readers that reflect the continuing prestige of priestly families in rabbinic Judaism: first a priest should read if one is present, second a Levite, then another knowledgeable Jewish man. Today, it continues to be regarded as a great honor to "be called to the Torah," that is, to be asked to read the Torah in a synagogue service. Synagogues traditionally grant this honor especially to bridegrooms, to boys celebrating their *bar mitzvahs* (coming of age), to a new father, and to a man mourning his parent or ending his mourning period. Many Reformed and Conservative synagogues call on women as well as men for Torah readings. They also encourage girls to celebrate their coming of age with a *bat mitzvah*. These rituals thus chart disagreements over social issues between Jewish denominations. They also reflect the relative obscurity of Biblical Hebrew for many Jews. Those "called to the Torah" often only recite the blessings (Box 5.6) before and after a Torah portion that is read by the rabbi or cantor, because it is important that the Hebrew text be read and chanted accurately.[10]

In antiquity, synagogue liturgy settled on reading portions of Torah sequentially over time. That way, the congregation eventually reads the whole Pentateuch aloud. Some synagogues read it over a period of more than three years. Mesopotamian Jews used a one-year cycle of Torah readings that later became the standard practice in most synagogues.

## Box 5.5   The Mishnah on reading rituals

*The Megilla (scroll of Esther) may be read either sitting or standing, by one person only, or by two persons at the same time. They alike fulfil their duty. In places where it is usual to say a blessing (after reading it) it is obligatory to say it, but not when it is not customary. Three men are called to read in the Holy Scrolls on Mondays and Thursdays; and in the afternoon of the Sabbath neither more nor less than that number may be called, nor shall any section from the Prophets then be read. He who commences the reading of the Holy Scrolls shall pronounce the first benediction before reading it, and he who concludes the reading shall pronounce the last benediction after reading it. (m. Megilla 3)*

> **Box 5.6   Torah blessings in synagogue liturgy**
>
> *Blessing before the Torah reading:*
> Bless you, Adonai (the LORD) our God, king of the universe,
> who chose us from all the peoples to give us his Torah.
> Bless you, Adonai, you give the Torah.
>
> *Blessing after the Torah reading:*
> Bless you, Adonai our God, king of the universe,
> who gave us a true Torah and planted eternal life within us.
> Bless you, Adonai, you give the Torah.[11]

Synagogue liturgies use texts from other parts of the Tanak mostly piece-meal. Thematically related passages (haftorah) from the prophetic books are paired with Torah readings and read after them. Individual psalms are sung at appropriate points in regular and special services. The reading of some other books, such as the five festival scrolls (Ruth, Esther, Lamentations, Ecclesiastes, and Song of Songs), became traditional on special occasions and annual festivals. Some books of the Tanak find no place in the synagogue's services at all. The Torah, then, is ritually elevated above all other books by being read aloud sequentially in its entirety in the course of regular synagogue worship services.

Particular passages in the Pentateuch also get recited separately because of their contents and importance. For example, the *Shema* and the Priestly Blessing feature prominently in Jewish worship. The *Shema* consists of Deuteronomy 6:4–9, 11:13–21, and Numbers 15:37–41. Everyone should recite the *Shema* during morning and evening prayers, and before sleeping. The Priestly Blessing, on the other hand, is traditionally recited only by men who claim descent from the first priest, Aaron. It consists of Numbers 6:24–26. The priests (*kohenim*) should recite it over the congregation at the end of a synagogue worship service. This hierarchical restriction has proven controversial in Jewish cultures. The blessing has been modified for congregational recitation in some synagogue services and has also been used privately within families.

## 5.2.4   The Languages of Jewish Public Readings

Language is a prominent feature of any oral performance. Listeners' responses will be determined by whether they recognize and understand the language they hear. However, recognition and understanding are not the same thing. Many people recognize the sound and cadence of familiar recitations even if they do not understand the language. For example, experienced travelers recognize the sound of the call to prayer echoing through cities and villages of Muslim countries even if they do not understand Arabic.

A synagogue service can be recognized by the sound of the Hebrew Torah and of Hebrew and Aramaic prayers as much as by any visual symbol or architecture. The sound of scripture being read aloud in a synagogue service distinguishes itself in two ways: by its ancient Hebrew language and by its prescribed melodic chant (<u>cantillation</u>). For more than 2000 years, Jews spoke vernacular languages other than Hebrew, from Aramaic and Greek in antiquity to German, Yiddish, Polish, Spanish, Arabic, English, and many other languages in modern times. The language of the scriptures and the prayer book is <u>Hebrew</u>, though a few parts of the Tanak and more of the prayer book are in the related language, <u>Aramaic</u>. Hebrew and Aramaic distinguish the sounds of worship services from the sounds of everyday life.

Now that Hebrew has been revived as the national language of the State of Israel, Israeli Jews may not find the sound of biblical Hebrew as distinctive as do Jews living in other countries. Nevertheless, <u>chanting</u> still distinguishes prayer and public readings of Torah and other books of scripture. The sound of the Hebrew Torah being chanted provides Jews a common experience of worship across different denominations, cultures, and time periods.

Jewish scholars have also translated their scriptures into other languages for more than 2000 years. <u>Translation</u> may have already been part of Ezra's Torah reading, as we have seen. Oral Aramaic translation was probably the rule rather than the exception from the time of Ezra on. The ancient rabbis argued that if synagogues use translations, they should always precede an oral translation with reading the Hebrew text. Free translation into Aramaic was interspersed between readings of Hebrew verses. Written Aramaic translations appeared after the end of the Second Temple period. These Aramaic <u>targums</u> crystalized into three traditions of manuscripts: the Palestinian targums, Targum Onqelos, and Targum Pseudo-Jonathan.[12]

Centuries earlier, the <u>Septuagint Greek translation</u> of the Pentateuch had been extended to the rest of Jewish scriptures. Greek-speaking Jews read them in that language. That is most obvious in the pages of the New Testament, whose Greek-speaking Jewish authors quoted the scriptures from the Septuagint translation in the first century CE. Aquila, Symmachus, and Theodotion created more literal Greek translations in the following centuries.

Attempts to restrict Jewish scripture to only Hebrew texts gained strength in two periods of ancient Jewish history. In the second and early first centuries BCE, the <u>Hasmonean</u> dynasty of high priests and kings sponsored a collection of Hebrew literature consisting of historical and prophetic books as well as the Pentateuch (Box 5.7). The textual evidence for this development is

> ## Box 5.7  A Hasmonean curriculum
>
> David Carr has argued that the Hasmoneans broadened the Jerusalem temple's scribal traditions in an effort to enculturate a wider elite through Hebrew literature: "The Jewish Hebrew Scriptures were defined and functioned within the regional empire of the Hasmoneans as part of a project of specifically Hebrew (and non-Greek) education-enculturation to create a 'Jewish' identity. This identity was analogous yet opposed to the emergent, transnational 'Hellenistic' identity of the Hellenistic educational system."[13]

very limited: one sentence in a dynastic history from the beginning of the first century refers to Judah Maccabee collecting books in Jerusalem just like Nehemiah, who collected

> *books about the kings and prophets, and the writings of David, and letters of kings about votive offerings.* (2 Macc. 2:13)

This verse seems to describe the historical and prophetic books of the Hebrew Bible and the Psalms ("the writings of David"). Some first-century CE texts refer to Jewish scriptures as "the Torah and the Prophets," and sometimes also the Psalms, indicating that this innovation dates to the Hasmonean period. The fleeting reference to Judah Maccabee's library may therefore hint at a broader cultural transformation. By the turn of the era, the vernacular languages spoken by Jews were mostly Aramaic and Greek. Yet the Torah, Prophets, and Psalms consist entirely of texts originally written in Hebrew. The Hebrew language had become a defining characteristic of Jewish scriptures.

Rabbinic literature from the following centuries debated the scriptural status of Torah in translation. The rabbis labeled Hebrew "the sacred language" (*leshon haqodesh*, maybe meaning "the temple language") and wrote down their own traditions in Hebrew and Aramaic, but never in Greek. The rabbis also accepted as scripture two books, Daniel and Ezra, that contain chapters written in Aramaic, but no part of the Tanak contains texts originally written in Greek. Some of the ancient rabbis treated translations as if they are sacred texts, while others did not. For example, the Mishnah maintains at one point that worn-out scrolls of translated scriptures must be stored in *genizas*, just like Hebrew scrolls of scriptures (*m. Shab.* 16.1), while at another point saying that translated scrolls are not sacred like Hebrew scriptures (*m. Yad.* 4.5). This debate reflects the conflict between the desire to see scriptures used in their original Hebrew language and the reality that many synagogue members did not understand that language. It probably also reflects the ancient rabbis' efforts to distinguish and insulate Jewish identity from the growing numbers of Greek-speaking Christians.[14]

The earlier rabbinic texts seem more open to reading Torah in Greek if no one in the congregation can read Hebrew. Later texts from the third through fifth centuries restrict the practice. This debate was waged through the Middle Ages and continues in modernity. The use or avoidance of vernacular languages in worship became a distinguishing feature of some Jewish denominations as they evolved in the nineteenth and twentieth centuries. It continues to be debated in congregations today.[15]

In traditional Jewish synagogues, Torah reading and recitation are reserved for men. Women listen and observe, but do not read the Torah aloud to the congregation and were usually not taught Hebrew. At home, however, Jewish women have played an active role in reading scripture and teaching it to their children. While Jewish men may have studied Torah and Talmud with their sons in Hebrew and Aramaic, women traditionally read biblical texts in translation together with explanatory stories (*midrash*). Literacy in Hebrew, the language of the Torah, marked status at home as well as in the synagogue. However, as Penny Shine Gold observed:

> *The irony is that in many homes, the mother, reading the text in the (low prestige) current vernacular and with commentary pitched to an unlearned audience, would have a greater chance of understanding what was being read than the father and son, reading the text in Hebrew and Aramaic.*[16]

## 5.2.5  Recitation, Cantillation, and Song

Since antiquity, the Torah and other scriptures have been chanted to specific tonal patterns. Synagogue readers now follow rules of <u>cantillation</u> developed in the Middle Ages. The words must be chanted to a melody prescribed by a system of accents. The accents, however, do not appear in Torah scrolls.[17]

The ancient rabbis wrote the rules for reading Torah aloud that many synagogues still follow today. The Torah should not be recited from memory during a synagogue service. It must be read aloud from an undecorated and <u>unpointed</u> Torah scroll. "Unpointed" refers to the absence of small marks above and below the Hebrew letters that indicate how to pronounce the <u>vowels</u> and how to <u>accent</u> and <u>chant</u> the sentences. Medieval Jewish

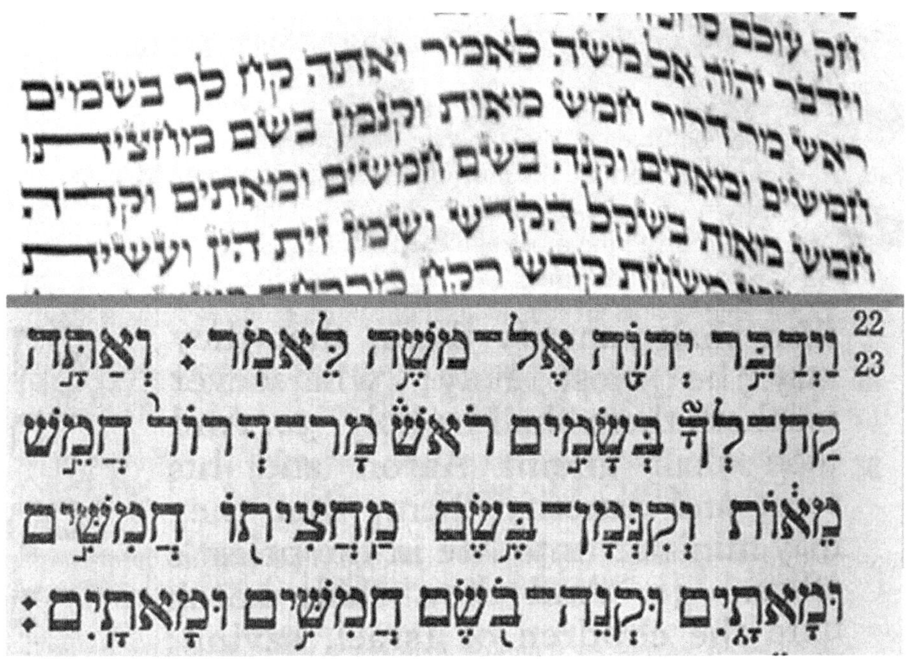

**FIGURE 5.3**  Exodus 30:22–23 in a manuscript scroll (top) and a printed *chumash* (bottom).

scholars developed a system of "points" to record how the scriptures should be pronounced. These signs do not appear in the scrolls used for synagogue worship (Figure 5.3), but are recorded in codices of the Pentateuch (a *chumash*) and of the whole Jewish Bible (a *tanak*).

Readers study the proper vocalization and cantillation of the text from a *chumash* or *tanak* before they read scripture aloud from an unpointed scroll in public (Box 5.8). Many synagogues employ a trained cantor who both reads to the congregation and trains others to read scripture aloud, as well as leading the congregation in prayers and psalms. Penny Shine Gold remarked:

*The special production of and reverence toward the Torah scroll and the repetition, blessing, and chanting of the text when read – all this marks out the text not as studied but as performed, not learned but experienced, not understood but absorbed. In this way the Torah, the embodiment of Judaism, is passed from one generation to the next, a quasi-procreative act, insuring the ongoing life of the Jewish community.*[18]

> **Box 5.8   Why do Jews, Christians, and Muslims chant scripture?**
>
> Alan Gampel observed: "The practice of cantillation has historically served to guide and remind the reader of this accurate pronunciation and of the hierarchy of word importance within sentences. Clerical leaders have generally viewed the musical element of cantillation to be ancillary to the grammatical and syntactical contributions that help to accurately transmit the word of God. This insistence on the primacy of the text and on a clear understanding of each word led to the imposition of restrictive musical guidelines, which in turn resulted in limited melodic freedom in the traditional cantillation of all three religions."[19]

Chanting scripture according to prescribed melodies distinguishes reading aloud within synagogue and church rituals from reading scripture aloud in group and personal study. This difference encourages a tendency to distinguish liturgical from didactic reading. In practice, however, recitation for study frequently becomes almost as ritualized as the liturgies of synagogues and churches.

## 5.3   SONGS AND POETRY IN THE HEBREW BIBLE

Oral presentations are by their nature ephemeral, and no art depicting biblical stories has survived from ancient Israel and Judah in the centuries BCE. Evidence for the ritualization of the expressive dimension of Israel's religious texts before Ezra appears only in references to oral readings in the Bible itself. The artistic and literary remains of other ancient Middle Eastern cultures, however, show how the peoples around Israel ritualized the expressive dimension of their texts. This cultural context allows us to understand better the traditions and innovations reflected in the Hebrew Bible.

Of course, telling stories and singing songs are common features of every human culture. Oral presentations have left their mark on ancient texts, not just in stories, but also in collections of songs and hymns. The music can no longer be reconstructed, but song lyrics that sing the praises of various gods appear among the texts of most ancient cultures. They also appear in the Hebrew Bible.

Song lyrics usually take poetic form, but what counts as poetry differs from one language to another. Poetry in biblical Hebrew, like in ancient languages such as Ugaritic, Akkadian, and Egyptian, was distinguished from prose mainly by word plays and parallelism.

Word plays (paronomasia or puns) take advantage of the fact that many words and phrases sound alike or almost alike. They play on different meanings of the same sounds. For example, a joke asks, "How does Moses make his coffee?" Answer: "Hebrews it."[20] This pun works only in English, of course. For the same reason, Hebrew word plays in the Bible cannot be translated, only explained. Unlike in English, however, biblical poetry uses word plays not to be funny (though it can be ironic or sarcastic), but rather to make its message forceful and memorable. For example, the prophet Amos sees a basket of "summer fruit" (Hebrew: *qayits*), which means that Israel is about to experience a destructive "end" (Hebrew: *qets*; Amos 8:2).

Parallelism is the repetition of the same idea in different words in two, three, or more lines. For example, Amos sarcastically calls people to worship wrongly at Israel's shrines and temples:

*Come to Bethel and do wrong,*
*to Gilgal and multiply wrongdoing,*
*bring your slaughtered offerings in the morning,*
*and your tithes on the third day.* (Amos 4:4)

Here the second and fourth lines express the same general idea as the first and third lines, but with different words and examples. Hebrew poetry can employ three parallel lines and even more complicated patterns of parallels in larger compositions. Later lines can not only repeat an idea but also extend it in one way or another.[21] Unlike word plays, poetic parallelism does appear in translations because it depends on meaning rather than sounds. As a result, biblical poetry often gives readers the impression that it repeats everything two or three times in a row.

Many books of the Hebrew Bible contain poems. Occasional hymns appear in the Pentateuch and history books (Exod. 15; Deut. 32–33; Judg. 5; 1 Sam. 2; 2 Sam. 22–23). Prophetic books contain more poetry, because the prophets' oracles frequently take the form of poems. Poetry makes up significant parts of Jeremiah and Ezekiel, and dominates Isaiah, Hosea, Amos, and most other prophetic books.

The Hebrew Bible also contains several books that are collections of songs. Their contents seem to be intended as scripts for individual and group singing. They are the books of Psalms, Lamentations, and Song of Songs.

**Psalms**: The Book of Psalms is often called "the hymnbook of the Second Temple." Some of its hymns are older and reflect the theology of the Judean kingdom. Its chapters consist of 150 separate poems. The Dead Sea Scrolls show that the number and order of hymns had not been standardized in the late Second Temple period. Later Christian manuscripts often added hymns that appear elsewhere in the Bible to the end of the book.

The psalms were composed for <u>oral expression</u> by individuals or groups of people in worship settings. <u>Superscriptions</u> to many of the psalms refer to instruments, song tunes, and several different choirs of Levites (e.g., Ps. 46). Some refer to well-known biblical characters, such as Hezekiah, Moses and, especially, David. It is not clear if these references claim that the psalm was written "by" these people, or was "for" them, or dedicated "to" them. Some bibles count the superscriptions as the first verse of the psalm, while others do not.

Many psalms reflect their oral composition by taking the standard form typical of their contents. <u>Form Criticism</u> studies the oral composition of written texts and has proven particularly useful for categorizing and analyzing the structure of the psalms. The categories called "hymns" and "thanksgivings" praise God. <u>Hymns</u> celebrate God's general gifts to humans in nature, in Israel's history, and in the Torah (Pss. 1, 8, 106):

*YHWH, our Lord,*
*how great is your name in the whole world,*
*you make it majestic throughout the heavens.* (Ps. 8:1)

<u>Thanksgivings</u> give thanks for particular things that God has done for individuals (Ps. 9) or for Israel as a whole (Ps. 124). <u>Royal hymns</u> celebrate YHWH's support for the Davidic king in Jerusalem (e.g., Pss. 2, 110). <u>Zion psalms</u> focus on God's presence in the Jerusalem temple (Pss. 46, 48).

The largest category of psalms, however, contains <u>lament</u> psalms. They complain about the desperate situations that an individual (Ps. 3) or the community (Ps. 44) find themselves in, and appeal for God's help. Lament psalms follow a standard outline, though not all of them include every element:

1. Address to God (3:1a)
2. Complaint, often vague (3:1b–2)
3. Confession of trust that God can help (3:3–6)
4. Petition for God's help (3:7)
5. Assurance of God's help, maybe spoken by a priest or prophet (3:8)
6. Vow of praise (absent in Ps. 3; cf. 7:17)

The complaint is often vague in order to fit the different problems that worshippers might have, ranging from sickness to conflicts with enemies:

*My God, my God, why have you abandoned me?* (Ps. 22:1)

The concluding vow promises to return to the temple to give thanks and make offerings after the worshippers have been relieved of their problems. Lament psalms, then, match thanksgiving psalms: laments appeal for God's rescue in the future, while thanksgivings celebrate God's help in the past.[22]

**Lamentations**: The book of Lamentations is a collection of lament psalms. They all focus on the experience of the people of Jerusalem when the city was conquered and destroyed by the Babylonians in 587 BCE. The book admits the people's guilt for having sinned against God, but also complains about how extreme their punishment was.

The structures of both books, Psalms and Lamentations, have been shaped to guide readers through the changing experiences of prayer and worship. Psalms begins by celebrating Torah study (1:2), groups its contents in five books reminiscent of the Pentateuch, and ends with five hymns of praise to YHWH (Pss. 146–150). Older collections can be recognized in superscriptions that associate them with David or with the Levitical families of Korah and Asaph. Some psalms seem to respond to psalms on either side of them (e.g., Pss. 106–107). Three chapters of Lamentations are organized alphabetically, with each line or stanza beginning with the next letter. Such poems are called alphabetical acrostics and clearly depend on readers (not listeners) to recognize their structure.

Biblical poems and songs express strong emotions, both good and bad, in vivid language. They provide models for how to express gratitude and joy to God, and also fear and anger. The poetry and imagery of these books carve out space in the Bible, and in the religious experience of the Bible's readers, to complain about how God treats people, individually and as communities. They urge readers to express their fears and complaints in order to transform them into hope and trust in God's salvation

**The Song of Songs (or Song of Solomon or Canticles)**: Not all biblical songs are obviously intended for singing in religious worship. The book called either the Song of Songs or the Song of Solomon contains a collection of love songs. Two solo voices express the feelings of the female and male lovers, while a chorus of her friends frequently comments on them and their relationship. The Song stands out in the patriarchal literature of the Hebrew Bible by depicting the woman on equal terms with the man. Her voice sings first (1:2–7) and their songs alternate. She frequently takes the initiative in their relationship (e.g., 1:7; 3:1–4).

The Song of Songs is similar to love poetry from other ancient cultures, especially from Egypt. Originally its songs were probably performed at weddings. The imagery is frequently erotic (e.g., 2:2–6; 4:1–16; 5:10–16; 7:2–10). The book does not mention God or Israel. Only Solomon's name (3:7–11) alludes to any aspect of Israel's history, though the songs are saturated with references to Israel's geography and natural environment (e.g., 8:4–5, 11, 14).

Many interpreters, ancient and modern, have therefore wondered why the Song of Songs is in the Bible. They have resorted to <u>allegory</u> to make it compatible with biblical religion. Jewish interpreters have read the Song as an allegory of God's love for Israel and the covenant between them as a marriage (as explicitly in Hosea 1–3). Christian readers have understood it to portray the marriage between Jesus and the Church (so explicitly Ephesians 5:25–27, 32). The Song, however, does not make any such allegory explicit.

In Jewish tradition, the Song of Songs is one of the five festival scrolls. It is read in its entirety at <u>Passover</u> by many communities. Perhaps it was the popularity of the Song and its association with festivals and weddings that guaranteed it a place in scripture.[23]

## 5.4  EXPRESSING THE COVENANT: THE PROPHETS

The section of the Tanak called "the Prophets" consists of the four books of the Deuteronomistic History and four books of prophetic oracles. The historical books of Joshua, Judges, Samuel, and Kings may have been classified as "prophets" because their stories often feature prophets like Samuel, Nathan, Elijah, and Elishah. But in terms of literary genre, we classify these books as stories and histories, rather than as oracular (prophetic) texts.

The other four books are quite different in genre and contents. Isaiah, Jeremiah, Ezekiel, and the Book of the Twelve Prophets consist largely of prophets' speeches. They are <u>oracular speeches</u> because the prophets speak for Israel's God. They often quote YHWH's words. So in contrast to the history books, these prophetic books consist largely of divine speeches, often cast as poetry. They also include speeches and prayers by the prophets themselves, quotations of their opponents, and prose stories about the prophets. The interaction between poetic voices in, especially, Isaiah and the Twelve Prophets gives the impression of theatrical <u>drama</u>. Aside from God, however, the books do not explicitly label many of the voices, which leaves their identification and interpretation ambiguous.

These four prophetic books of the Tanak each begin with oracles condemning Israel and Judah for their sins. They predict the destruction and exile of both kingdoms. After the fulfillment of those predictions in exile, however, they emphasize messages of hope and restoration. In between, they call down God's judgment on other nations. This common three-part structure to each prophetic book presents the prophets as interpreters of Torah, even though they hardly quote or even reference Torah. Instead, they express the demands of Israel's <u>covenant</u> with God. Like Moses, they warn that breaking the covenant will lead to destruction, but they also insist that God will preserve the covenant with Israel in and beyond the Babylonian Exile.

**<u>Isaiah</u>**: The book of Isaiah is credited to the prophet Isaiah, who worked with kings Ahab and Hezekiah in the late eighth century BCE (2 Kgs. 19–20; Isa. 7, 36–39). Most of the oracles in the first part of the book reflect this pre-exilic setting, though very few feature Isaiah himself. They are followed, however, by oracles that directly address the exiles and urge them to hope for the restoration of Jerusalem (Isa. 40). Here the sixth-century Persian emperor Cyrus is twice referenced by name (44:28; 45:1). Then the book's last 11 chapters address the community that returned to Jerusalem after the exile. Critical scholars therefore customarily divide the book into three and refer to <u>first Isaiah</u> (chaps. 1–39), <u>second Isaiah</u> (chaps. 40–55), and <u>third Isaiah</u> (chaps. 56–66). The book of Isaiah also shows many signs of having been edited to form a unified book. For example, its beginning and end (chaps. 1–2, 65–66) echo each other.

**<u>Jeremiah</u>**: The book of Jeremiah prominently features the seventh-to-sixth century prophet Jeremiah (1:1–3). He lived during the last years of the kingdom of Judah and survived in the ruins of Jerusalem after the Babylonian attacks, until he was kidnapped and taken to Egypt by Judean refugees (Jer. 39–44). The book vividly portrays Jeremiah's conflicts with kings and other prophets in pre-exilic Jerusalem (Jer. 28, 36). His opponents called him a traitor because he urged them not to resist the Babylonians (Jer. 26). The persecution he suffered led Jeremiah to complain bitterly about his situation in poems using Israel's poetic tradition of <u>laments</u> (Jer. 20:7–18).

**<u>Ezekiel</u>**: The book of Ezekiel contains the oracles of Ezekiel, a priest and prophet who was taken into exile in Babylon in 597 BCE (Ezek. 1:1–3). From there, he predicted the destruction of Judah 10 years later (Ezek. 10). He encouraged the exiles by telling them that YHWH goes with them into exile and will protect them there. The book ends with an elaborate <u>vision</u> of how the <u>Jerusalem Temple</u> and the land of Israel will be restored in the future (Ezek. 40–48).

**The Twelve Prophets**: The <u>book of the Twelve Prophets</u> is divided into 12 books in Christian bibles. However, treating it as one book with the Tanak reveals how it mirrors the structure of the other three prophetic books. First come pre-exilic prophets predicting mostly the destruction of Israel and Judah (Hosea, Joel, Amos, Micah), then prophetic oracles against foreign nations (Obadiah, Nahum, Habakkuk, Zephaniah), completed by prophets addressing the Jerusalem community after the exile (Haggai, Zechariah, Malachi). Also included here is a short story (Jonah) that meditates on the theme of divine justice and mercy.[24]


## 5.5   EXPRESSING TORAH BEFORE EZRA

Ancient texts were written with the expectation that they would be read aloud. Sometimes they specified when they should be read and what effects reading them will bring about. *Enuma Elish*, the Babylonian creation epic from the later second millennium BCE, concludes with a list of the 50 names of the god Marduk. It then admonishes that the names

> *must be grasped: the first one should reveal them, the wise and knowledgeable should ponder them together, the master should repeat, and make the pupil understand. The shepherd, the herdsman should pay attention.*[25]

Ancient treaties explicitly required regular readings of the treaty documents.

There is evidence from cultures across the ancient Middle East and eastern Mediterranean that ritual texts were particularly likely to mandate that their stipulations be followed exactly as written. It is also clear that many priests and kings did so (see Section 4.4), to the point that reading and manipulating ritual texts became part of the ritual itself.

A number of Egyptian texts require verbatim repetition of their contents. For example, the stele in Pahery's tomb from the fourteenth century BCE asks readers to make offerings and recite the prayer for the deceased that is also recorded on the stele:

> *Say, "An offering, given by the king," in the form in which it is written, "An invocation offering," as said by the fathers, and as it comes from the mouth of god.*

Other Egyptian texts link exact repetition of spells and prayers with detailed ritual instructions. For example, an Osiris ritual from the last three centuries BCE records an elaborate liturgy and then ritual instructions that begin:

> *Now when this is recited the place is to be completely secluded, not seen and not heard by anyone except the chief lector-priest and the setem-priest.*[26]

The Egyptian ritual for vivifying the dead, called "Opening the Mouth," shows how ritual texts could be used. One of the priests at this rite was the lector priest, literally "the one who holds the ritual," that is, who holds the papyrus scroll on which the words of the ritual are written. Many tomb paintings, models, and papyri illustrate this official presiding over the ceremony, open scroll in hand (see Figure 4.17).[27]

Such priests were, of course, <u>literate</u>, which means they were also <u>scribes</u>. Reading aloud the ritual texts demonstrated their scribal skills. Their responsibilities included preserving the ancient scrolls, which required recopying them when they wore out. Egyptian scribes thus <u>embodied</u> their texts: their hands copied the scrolls and their voices read the scrolls aloud. In so far as the ritual texts were believed to have been dictated by gods, the scribes embodied a divine tradition. Portraits portraying Egyptians posing as scribes marked them as both learned and pious. Over the 3000 years of ancient Egyptian culture, the scribal god, Thoth, was increasingly credited as the author of ritual texts. Sometimes, statues of scribes show them in the company of baboons, one of Thoth's representative animals. In one case, the baboon seems fused to the back of the scribe's head in a striking visual claim to divine <u>inspiration</u> (Figure 5.4).

Around the time of Ezra, old books were being read aloud in other cultures to revive customs and festivals in much the same way as described in Nehemiah 8. The first-century Roman historian Livy described a Samnite ritual that was performed around 300 BCE (Box 5.9). Livy emphasized the antiquity of the ceremony that was revived for this occasion. A priest read an old linen scroll aloud to ensure that the correct words were recited and to show that he was performing the ritual accurately. The rite required an oath of service in the Samnite army. Refusal meant execution as an offering to Jupiter, a threat actually carried out, according to Livy. So the ritual was performed in the face of considerable conflict, and reading the old book aloud helped the priest and his supporters keep the upper hand.

Israel's textual culture was, of course, not the same as that of its neighbors. For example, archeologists have found no royal inscriptions by Israelite or Judean kings, though such inscriptions are common in surrounding territories. Nor is there any reason to think that Israelite scribes ever illustrated their manuscripts, though Egyptian scribes produced elaborately illustrated scrolls to accompany the dead into the afterlife. However, the Hebrew Bible preserves direct evidence of oral presentation, both in its descriptions of public readings and in the way in which its text is written. Israelite scribes therefore utilized and developed practices of oral presentation that were common in other ancient Middle Eastern and Mediterranean cultures.

**FIGURE 5.4**   Statue of a scribe with a baboon representing the scribal god, Thoth, sitting on or fused to his head. Egyptian, ca. 1275–1085 BCE, in the Metropolitan Museum of Art, New York.

## Box 5.9   A Samnite reading ritual

*A space, about 200 feet square, almost in the centre of their camp, was boarded off and covered all over with linen cloth. In this enclosure a sacrificial service was conducted, the words being read from an old linen book by an aged priest, Ovius Paccius, who announced that he was taking that form of service from the old ritual of the Samnite religion. It was the form which their ancestors used when they formed their secret design of wresting Capua from the Etruscans. (Livy, History of Rome 10.38)*[28]

## 5.5.1  The Pentateuch's Instructions for Ritual Readings

The Pentateuch explicitly requires its own publication through oral presentation. In Deuteronomy, Moses commands the priests to <u>read</u> written Torah <u>aloud</u> at *Sukkot* (Booths) to the entire people of Israel:

> *Moses wrote down this Torah and gave it to the levitical priests who carry the ark of the covenant and to all the Israelite elders. He commanded them: "Every seventh year…during the festival of Sukkot,…you must read this Torah in the hearing of all Israel. Gather the people—men, women, children and foreigners who live in your cities—so that they will hear it and learn it and revere YHWH your God and do all the words of this Torah obediently, so their descendants who do not know it will hear it and learn it and revere YHWH your God."* (Deut. 31:9–13)

He also requires every Israelite to <u>recite</u> the Torah's commandments at home:

> *Repeat them to your children and say them when you sit at home and when you walk on the road, when you lie down and when you rise.* (Deut. 6:7)

When they were first written, these texts probably referred to the book of Deuteronomy or just to the lists of laws in Deuteronomy. When Deuteronomy became attached to Exodus and Leviticus, however, the meaning of "this Torah" expanded to include all the laws of the Pentateuch, and eventually the Pentateuch as a whole. As a result, the Pentateuch concludes with instructions for its reading and recitation, just like many other ancient ritual texts.

Public reading served to instruct and inspire listeners, but it also aimed for other effects. Throughout the ancient world, people believed that public reading *activated* the power of texts. Public reading and inscription put <u>new laws</u> into effect. Reading and ritual manipulation activated blessings and curses. <u>Blessings</u> were recited by priests over worshippers (Num. 6:22–27). <u>Curses</u> were recited and then written in order to break the texts or for their ink to be washed into drinking water to make them take effect (Num. 5:23–28).

The Hebrew Bible contains several stories of ritualizing texts this way. Deuteronomy requires that the Torah be activated inside Canaan by being written on a <u>monument</u> on Mount Ebal. Then the Levites must proclaim the book's threats against disobedience over all the people of Israel while facing each other on two mountains, and the people must acknowledge the threatened punishments by answering "Amen" (Deut. 27–28). Joshua 8 tells us that Joshua led the people in following these instructions. Similarly, near the end of the book of Jeremiah, the prophet orders the expressive and iconic <u>actualization</u> of his threats against Babylon:

> *Jeremiah wrote on one scroll all the disasters coming against Babylon …. Jeremiah said to Seraiah, "When you come to Babylon, make sure you read all these words. Then you must say, 'YHWH, you yourself pronounced the destruction and elimination of this place, so that neither humans nor animals will ever live here again.' When you finish reading this scroll, tie a rock to it and throw it into the Euphrates river and say, 'Thus will Babylon sink and rise no more because of the disasters I am bringing against her.'" (Jer. 51:60–64)*

## 5.5.2   Biblical Stories of Torah Readings

Moses sets the example with public Torah readings early in the story of Israel at Mount Sinai. After meeting God on the mountain, he reports to the Israelites what YHWH said to him (Exod. 24:3, referring to Exod. 20–23). After they agree to the covenant with YHWH, Moses writes down what he has already reported. Again, the Israelites hear the provisions of the covenant, this time <u>read aloud</u> by Moses from the newly written "covenant book" (Box 5.10) Again they agree, and Moses ritually seals the covenant by splashing them with the blood of offerings.

### Box 5.10   Moses reads the covenant book

*Moses came and reported to the people all the words of YHWH and all the commandments. All the people responded with one voice: "We will do everything that YHWH said." Then Moses wrote down all the words of YHWH. The next morning, he built an altar below the mountain and set up twelve standing stones to represent the twelve tribes of Israel. He sent young Israelites to raise rising offerings and to slaughter amity slaughter offerings of oxen to YHWH. Moses put half the blood in basins and splashed the other half against the altar. Then he took the book of the covenant and read it in the people's hearing. They said, "We will do and observe everything YHWH said." Then Moses took the blood and splashed it on the people, saying "This is the blood of the covenant that YHWH made with you through all these words." (Exod. 24:3–8)*

More than anywhere else in the Hebrew Bible, this story places Torah reading in the middle of a ritual performance, complete with burned offerings and a short unison liturgy of commitment. All three ritual elements together – the offerings, the unison commitment, and the reading of the covenant book – serve to ratify the covenant between Israel and YHWH. Public reading of Torah plays a central role in sealing the relationship between Israel and God.

The Hebrew Bible tells us that Deuteronomy's instructions were followed later by a few of Israel's leaders. Moses' successor, Joshua, did so after Israel's initial victories in Canaan. Joshua built an altar on Mount Ebal and wrote the "law of Moses" on it.

> *Afterwards, he read all the words of the Torah, the blessings and the curses, according to everything written in the book of the Torah. There was not one word that Moses commanded that Joshua did not read to the whole congregation of Israel and the women and the children and the foreigners among them.* (Josh. 8:34–35)

Joshua 8 combines the ceremony of blessings and curses from Deuteronomy 27 with the reading ritual of Deuteronomy 31.

After this point in the story, however, the written Torah disappears from much of the history of Israel and Judah. The books of Judges, Samuel, and Kings rarely mention the Torah, and the books of Chronicles only slightly more often. This silence draws special attention to those scenes in which the Torah is read aloud.

Around 600 years after Joshua, near the end of the history of the kingdom of Judah, King Josiah again read the Torah aloud to the people of Jerusalem, according to 2 Kings 22–23 and 2 Chronicles 34. This story accounts for the Torah's absence from the preceding history by saying that a Torah scroll was found in the Temple during renovations. It implies that the "book of the Torah" had been forgotten until then. When Josiah heard the book read aloud, he asked for confirmation of its authenticity from the prophet Huldah. She warned that YHWH would carry out the book's threats (2 Kgs. 22:14–20). Then Josiah assembled

> *all the people of Judah and all the inhabitants of Jerusalem, the priests, the prophets and all the people small and large. He read aloud to them all the words of the book of the covenant that had been found in the temple of YHWH.* (2 Kgs. 23:2)

According to 2 Kings, reading the Torah led Josiah to renew the covenant, purify Jerusalem's Temple of illegitimate objects, destroy religious sites in the other towns of Judah, and depose their priests. According to 2 Chronicles, these reforms preceded the discovery of the book. Both agree that, after finding the book, Josiah ordered the people to observe <u>Passover</u>. 2 Kings emphasizes that they should do

> *as is written in this book of the covenant. For no Passover had been observed like this since the days of the Judges.* (2 Kgs. 23:21–22)

The biblical histories also narrate, however, that after Josiah died, his successors reversed his religious policies. There is no record of any other public readings of Torah until the time of Ezra, some 200 years later.

The story of the written Torah that emerges from the whole Hebrew Bible starts with Moses, who wrote it down and read it aloud and commanded Israel to do so regularly. His successor, Joshua, did so, but no one did it again for 600 years until Josiah. Then another two centuries passed until Ezra read the Torah aloud in Jerusalem.[29]

Modern biblical scholars wonder whether these stories of law readings are really historical. They also wonder about the contents of the books of Torah described in these stories. We have already discussed the historical plausibility of Josiah's law book and concluded that the writer of 2 Kings must at least have known of such a book (Section 4.4). This writer uses Deuteronomic themes and vocabulary, so his idea of the Torah probably corresponded more or less with the book of Deuteronomy that we have today. We therefore know that Judeans in the time of the Babylonian Exile knew the tradition that the Torah commands its own oral presentation and believed that such a presentation had taken place at least once in the last years of the kingdom of Judah.

Did the writers of Deuteronomy invent the tradition of public Torah reading? The stories and instructions for public readings in Exodus, Deuteronomy, Joshua, and 2 Kings bear a family resemblance that suggests a common literary model. They all emphasize reading the whole book, "all the words of the Torah." They also focus on the physical Torah being written, rewritten, or discovered. The instructions in Deuteronomy and Josiah's fulfillment of them in 2 Kings may therefore have been written at nearly the same time. If that was the case, the stories in Joshua and Exodus project a practice of later times back into Israel's early history.

The story of Ezra's reading in Nehemiah 8 presupposes this same literary tradition, but also emphasizes translation and interpretation of the Torah and the length of time devoted to the reading over several days. It seems to be a later development of the literary theme of public law readings. It presupposes a larger Torah containing much, if not all, of the Pentateuch.

Many commentators on Exodus suspect that the <u>Covenant Code</u> (Exod. 21–23) was originally an independent document that may have concluded with the covenant reading ceremony in 24:3–8.[30] If that is the case, Exodus preserves a story about reading the law that could be older than Deuteronomy's requirements to do so. It may be the model from which the Deuteronomic tradition of law reading developed. Nevertheless, the <u>language</u> of the Pentateuch is the <u>Hebrew</u> that was spoken by Judeans in the eighth to the sixth centuries BCE. There is no evidence of Hebrew literature older than this, though some poetry may have been passed down orally from earlier times. Written stories of reading Torah scrolls aloud therefore all come from these centuries of Israel's history, long after the events narrated in the Pentateuch.

So the writers of the Pentateuch not only expected their work to be read aloud, like all other ancient literature. They expected it to be read aloud in imitation of Moses' readings and his instructions for readings. The Pentateuch contains indications that it was composed to be read aloud by scribes to mixed audiences of listeners.

## CITED WORKS AND FURTHER READING


1 On the oral performance of scriptures in different religions, see William A. Graham, *Beyond the Written Word: Oral Aspects of Scripture in the History of Religion* (Cambridge: Cambridge University Press, 1987), quotation from p. 65.

2 On the role of language and translation in ancient religions, see John F. A. Sawyer, *Sacred Languages and Sacred Texts* (London: Routledge, 1999).

3 See David M. Carr, *Holy Resilience: The Bible's Traumatic Origins* (New Haven: Yale University Press, 2014).

4 On the vernacular language in Ezra's Jerusalem, see Ingo Kottsieper, "'And They Did Not Care to Speak Yehudit': On Linguistic Change in Judah During the Late Persian Period," in *Judah and the Judeans in the Fourth Century B.C.E.* (ed. Oded Lipschitz, Gary N. Knoppers, and Rainer Albertz; Winona Lake, IN: Eisenbrauns, 2007), 95–124.

5. On the evidence for reading scriptures in late Second Temple Judaism, see Philo, *On Dreams* 2:127; Hypothetica 7:12–13; *Omnus probus* 81–82; Josephus, *Antiquities* 16:43; *Apion* 2:175; Luke 4:16–17; Acts 13:13–15. Quotation of the letter of Aristeas is from the translation by R. J. H. Schutt in *The Old Testament Pseudepigrapha* (ed. J. H. Charlesworth; Garden City, NY: Doubleday, 1985), 2:33.

6 Translation of the Theodotus Inscription by the Israel Museum in Jerusalem.

7 On enacting blessings and curses at Qumran, see *1QS* 1.16–2.18, and Steven D. Fraade, "Rhetoric and Hermeneutics in *Miqsat Ma'ase ha-Torah* (*4QMMT*): The Case of Blessings and Curses," *Dead Sea Discoveries* 10/1 (2003), 150–161.

8 On public scripture reading at Qumran, see Lawrence H. Schiffman, "The Early History of Public Reading of the Torah," in *Jews, Christians, and Polytheists in the Ancient Synagogue: Cultural Interaction during the Greco-Roman Period* (ed. Steven Fine; New York: Routledge, 1999), 44–56. The two quoted texts are Schiffman's translations (p. 45) from the Rule of the Community, *1QS* 6.7–8, *4Q266* 5.ii.1–3 and parallels, and from the Zadokite fragment/ Damascus Document, *4Q266* 5 ii.1–3 = *4Q267* 5 iii:3–5 = *4Q273* 2 1.

9 The translations of the parallel passages from *m. Yoma* 7:1 and *m. Sot.* 7:7,8 are by Schiffman, "Early History of Public Reading of the Torah," 48.

10 On reading Torah and other scripture in the synagogue liturgy, see Ruth Langer, "From Study of Scripture to a Reenactment of Sinai: The Emergence of the Synagogue Torah Service," *Worship* 72:1 (1998): 43–67; Elsie R. Stern, "What Is Jewish Scripture?" *Biblical Theology Bulletin* 43 (2013): 191–199; Louis Jacobs, "Torah, Reading of," *Encyclopaedia Judaica* (ed. M. Berenbaum and F. Skolnik; 2nd ed.; Detroit: Macmillan Reference, 2007), 20: 46–50; and Schiffman, "Early History of Public Reading of the Torah." See also Daniella Talmon-Heller, "Reciting the Qur'an and Reading the Torah: Muslim and Jewish Attitudes and Practices in a Comparative Historical Perspective," *Religion Compass* 6/8 (2012): 369–380.

11. For text, transliteration, and translation, see Nosson Sherman, *The Rabbinical Council of America Edition of the Artscroll Siddur* (Brooklyn, NY: Mesorah Publications, 1984), 440, 444. Translation of *m. Megilla* 3 in Box 5.5 by Michael L. Rodkinson, *The Babylonian Talmud* (2nd ed.; Boston: New Talmud Publishing Co., 1918), vol. 4.

12 On the Aramaic Targums, see Willem F. Smelik, "The Translation as a Bilingual Text: The Curious Case of the Targum," *AJS Perspectives* (Fall, 2015), online; and Paul V. M. Flesher and Bruce Chilton, *The Targums: A Critical Introduction* (Waco, TX: Baylor University Press, 2011), esp. 71–89.

13 On the Hasmoneans' advocacy of Hebrew literature, see David M. Carr, *Writing on the Tablet of the Heart: Origins of Scripture and Literature* (Oxford: Oxford University Press, 2005), quotation from p. 262.

14 On the ancient rabbis' advocacy of reading Torah in Hebrew, see Seth Schwartz, "Language, Power and Identity in Ancient Palestine," *Past and Present* 148 (1995), 3–47 [33]; Philip Alexander, "The Rabbis, the Greek Bible and Hellenism," in *The Jewish-Greek Tradition in Antiquity and the Byzantine Empire* (ed. J. K. Aitken and J. C. Paget; Cambridge: Cambridge University Press, 2014),

229–246; and Irven M. Resnick, "The Codex in Early Jewish and Christian Communities," *The Journal of Religious History* 17/1 (1992): 1–17 [6].

15   On reading the Torah in Greek, see the *Letter of Aristeas* 308–312, translated by R. J. H. Shutt in *Old Testament Pseudepigrapha* (ed. J. H. Charlesworth; 2 vols.; New York: Doubleday, 1983), 7–34; Philo, *Vita Mosis* 2. 41–42; in ancient rabbinic literature: *m. Meg.* 2.1, *t. Meg. 3:13*, *y. Meg.* 4.3, 75a; and see Willem F. Smelik, "Code-Switching: The Public Reading of the Bible," in *Was ist ein Text? Alttestamentliche, agyptologische und altorientalische Perspektiven* (ed. L. Morenz and S. Schorch; BZAW 362; Berlin: de Gruyter, 2007), 123–151 [134–137].

16   Penny Shine Gold, *Making the Bible Modern: Children's Bibles and Jewish Education in Twentieth-Century America* (Ithaca, NY: Cornell University Press, 2004), quotation from p. 13.

17   On chanting scripture in contemporary synagogues, see Jeffrey A. Summit, *Singing God's Words: The Performance of Biblical Chant in Contemporary Judaism* (Oxford: Oxford University Press, 2016).

18   Gold, *Making* the *Bible Modern*, 12.

19   Alan Gampel, "The Origins of Musical Notation in the Abrahamic Religious Traditions," in *Age of Transition: Byzantine Culture in the Islamic World* (ed. H. C. Evans; New York: Metropolitan Museum of Art, 2015), 144–154, quotation from p. 144.

20   From "27 Delightfully Terrible Christian Puns to Annoy the Heck Out of Your Friends With," ChurchPop online at https://churchpop.com/2014/09/10/18-delightfully-terrible-christian-puns-annoy-friends/ (accessed November 28, 2017).

21   On parallelism and other features of Hebrew poetry, see David L. Petersen and Kent Harold Richards, *Interpreting Hebrew Poetry,* Minneapolis: Fortress, 1992; and, for more detail, Wilfred G. E. Watson, *Classical Hebrew Poetry: A Guide to Its Techniques,* rev. ed. (London: T.&T. Clark, 2005).

22   See further in Nancy L. deClaissé-Walford, *Introduction to the Psalms: A Song from Ancient Israel* (St. Louis: Chalice, 2004); Harold W. Attridge and Margot E. Fassler, eds., *Psalms in Community: Jewish and Christian Textual, Liturgical, and Artistic Traditions* (Atlanta: SBL, 2003); Susan Gillingham, *Psalms Through the Centuries* (London: Wiley Blackwell, 2008).

23   For more about the Song of Songs, see Athalya Brenner and Carole Fontaine, eds., *A Feminist Companion to* Song of Songs (Sheffield: Sheffield Academic Press, 2000; David M. Carr, *The Erotic Word: Sexuality, Spirituality, and the Bible* (Oxford: Oxford University Press, 2003).

24   For more on the prophets, see Jack R. Lundbom, *The Hebrew Prophets: An Introduction,* (Minneapolis: Fortress, 2010); Mark McEntire, *A Chorus of Prophetic Voices: Introducing the Prophetic Literature of Ancient Israel* (Louisville:

Westminster John Knox Press, 2015); James D. Nogalski, *Interpreting Prophetic Literature: Historical and Exegetical Tools for Reading the Prophets* (Louisville: Westminster John Knox, 2015); Carolyn J. Sharp, ed., *The Oxford Handbook of the Prophets* (Oxford: Oxford University Press, 2016).

25 Translated by Benjamin Foster, *Before the Muses: An Anthology of Akkadian Literature* (2 vols.; Bethesda, MD: CDL Press, 1993), 400.

26 Both quotations translated by Miriam Lichtheim, *Ancient Egyptian Literature: A Book of Readings* (3 vols.; Berkeley: University of California Press, 1973, 1976, 1980), 2: 20; 3: 116–121.

27 On Egyptian lector priests, see David Lorton, "The Theology of the Cult Statues in Ancient Egypt," in *Born in Heaven, Made on Earth: The Making of the Cult Image in the Ancient Near East* (ed. Michael Dick; Winona Lake, IN: Eisenbrauns, 1999), 149.

28 For the Samnite ritual, see Livy, *History of Rome* (ed. Ernest Rhys; trans. Rev. Canon Roberts; Everyman's Library; New York: E. P. Dutton, 1912), 10: 38.

29 On stories of reading Torah in the Hebrew Bible, see James W. Watts, *Reading Law: The Rhetorical Shaping of the Pentateuch* (Sheffield: Sheffield Academic Press, 1999), 15–31.

30 On Exodus 24:3–8 as the conclusion to the Covenant Code, see Thomas B. Dozeman, *Exodus* (Grand Rapids: Eerdmans, 2009), 562–563.

# CHAPTER 6

# The Torah's Semantic Dimension

Written texts frequently require interpretation. What do they really mean? But then life requires interpretation, too. We often wonder about the significance of things we see, or hear, or experience. People often look to religious traditions for guidance about how to interpret their own lives and the course of events around them. In that sense, religions are in the business of interpretation (sometimes named by the technical term, <u>hermeneutics</u>). The comparative study of religions illustrates the many ways in which religious scriptures can be ritualized in the semantic dimension. In addition to ritualizing the interpretation of scriptures through teaching, preaching, and commentary, religious communities that venerate a book of scripture often use its interpretation as a model for how to interpret life. In fact, interpreting scripture can become a way of interpreting not only one's own life, but also the world around us and the course of history.

The Hebrew Bible actually says less about interpreting its semantic dimension than its other two dimensions. But every page interprets life, frequently through the lens of ancient Israel's history. However, it also addresses broader issues of how to live wisely and well. The ancient genre that gives advice about such topics is called <u>wisdom literature</u>.

## 6.1   INTERPRETING LIFE: WISDOM LITERATURE

Though professional scribes wrote almost all ancient texts, they wrote some texts particularly for themselves and their students. This "wisdom literature" emphasizes the importance of diligent study for learning scribal skills. It claims that the same studious work ethic is needed to comprehend how the world works. Wisdom literature depicts the wise scribe as understanding nature, human behavior, and even the gods. It encourages belief in meritocracy: the smartest and most diligent scribes rise to the positions of greatest power and prestige in royal courts.

There was also a tradition of wisdom literature in ancient Egypt, Mesopotamia, and Israel that took a more skeptical view. This literature observed the limits on what humans can know and understand. It raised questions about people's ability to know divine plans and about people's hopes for an afterlife. Even in Egypt, which is famous for its elaborate tombs to preserve the dead for the afterlife, "harper's songs" appear on the walls of some tombs. Many convey conventional hopes for life after death, but some of them express doubts about it:

> *Lo, none is allowed to take his goods with him,*
> *Lo, none who departs comes back again!*[1]

Ancient Middle Eastern cultures seem to have tolerated both points of view. So did Israel.

The Hebrew Bible contains some wisdom psalms (e.g., Pss. 1, 37, 49) and several wisdom books (Proverbs, Ecclesiastes, and Job). The Apocrypha/Deuterocanon contains two more (Sirach/Ecclesiasticus and the Wisdom of Solomon). The three wisdom books in the Hebrew Bible give voice to both the positive and the skeptical wisdom traditions of the wider Middle East.

**Proverbs:** Proverbs expresses the positive wisdom tradition (see Box 6.1). It advises "my son" (so the Hebrew; some translate "my child") to listen to his mother's and father's advice (1:8). He should study hard, be good, and expect to be rewarded for it. Failing to do so inevitably leads to ruin:

> *The righteousness of the innocent makes their path straight,*
> *but offenders are tripped up by their offenses.* (11:5)

Proverbs thus reinforces the retributive theology typical of the Pentateuch and the Prophets, but without referring to Israel's history or covenant with

> ### Box 6.1  Outline of Proverbs
>
> The book of Proverbs begins with poetic speeches that urge studying wisdom, and then continues with collections of proverbial sayings (aphorisms):
> - Chapters 1–9: Recommending wisdom and warning of folly
> - Chapters 10–31: Collections of aphorisms

God. Here, as in wisdom texts from other ancient cultures, the principle of retribution has become a natural feature of the world itself. Wisdom appears as a personified female figure who calls students to learn from her (1:20–33) and boasts of her knowledge of how the world works:

> *When [God] decreed the foundations of the world,*
> *I was beside him like an artisan.* (8:29–30)

The book ends with a poetic portrait of a wise woman who works hard to manage her household's business. Since business in ancient times was mostly a household activity, her range of activities includes manufacturing cloth, marketing and exporting products, and buying and selling real estate (31:10–18). Nevertheless, the book's intended audience is clearly male. Some sayings verge on misogyny (25:24) and others betray a clear fear of women's sexuality (5:1–6; 7:10–27). Proverbs fits the setting of a school for male scribes who are being socialized into a meritocracy while they learn to read and write.

**Ecclesiastes:** The book of Ecclesiastes expresses the skeptical wisdom tradition. It announces its skeptical theme at the beginning and end of the book:

> *Worthless worthlessness, everything is worthless!* (1:2; 12:8)[2]

The book collects sayings and examples to show that "time and chance happen to all" (9:11). It presents the example of a wealthy king who finds that achievements, pleasure, and even wisdom itself provide no enduring value (chapter 2). The success of every endeavor depends on timing (3:1–8). Ecclesiastes does offer some advice. It recommends finding pleasure in the common goods of life: food, productive work, companionship, and love (2:24; 3:12–13; 4:9–12; 5:18). The book argues that since God has provided these good things, it would be wrong to reject them. But beyond that, humans cannot understand God's plans for themselves in this world or in the afterlife, if there is one (3:17–22; 4:2–3; 6:12).

**Job:** The book of Job expresses both the positive and skeptical traditions in the voices of different speakers (Box 6.2). But the book clearly sides with the skeptical tradition by, in the end, having God demonstrate that humans cannot understand how the world works (chaps. 38–41).

The story of Job, whom God declares to be "innocent and upright" (1:8) but who nevertheless suffers terribly (1:13–2:8), is therefore a case study in the problem of innocent suffering. Job's friends represent the positive wisdom tradition. They reverse the retributive principle to argue that Job's sufferings prove that he has done something terrible. Job defends his own innocence, and accuses God of attacking him without reason. He asks only for God to explain why this has happened. God finally does appear to Job in the form of a tornado, but instead of explaining what has happened, God asks Job to explain how the universe works (38:1–3). Job, of course, cannot answer. The book ends with Job's health, family, and fortune being restored, but God also repudiates the friends' reasoning, saying "you did not tell the truth about me, like Job did" (42:7). So, like Ecclesiastes, the book of Job teaches that humans cannot understand why some people suffer and others do not.

The wisdom books therefore hold up a major theme of the Hebrew Bible to critical examination. The retributive principle (reward for obedience and punishment for disobedience) justified by God's covenant with Israel in the Pentateuch, preached by the prophets, and illustrated by the Deuteronomistic History gets extended into a universal principle by Proverbs. But the other two wisdom books observe that random chance (so Ecclesiastes) and innocent suffering (so Job) raise questions about whether God is really rewarding good and punishing evil in this world. They both conclude that humans cannot understand how God is running the world.

## Box 6.2   Outline of Job

The book of Job consists of a short prose story that surrounds long cycles of poetic speeches by Job, by his friends, and eventually by God:

- Chapters 1–2: Beginning of Job's story
- Chapters 3–31: Debate between Job and his friends
- Chapters 32–37: Speeches of Elihu
- Chapters 38–41: Speeches of YHWH from a tornado
- Chapter 42: End of Job's story

In the later Second Temple period, the Wisdom of Jesus ben Sirach (Ecclesiasticus) and the Wisdom of Solomon reconciled wisdom literature with the Torah tradition. Both teach that Torah is compatible with wisdom, while Sirach actually identifies them as one and the same thing (Sir. 24:23–29). This had the effect of reinforcing the positive wisdom tradition once again.[3] The problem of retribution and innocent suffering was addressed instead in the later Second Temple period by apocalyptic literature.

## 6.2  THE TANAK AS A SCRIPTURE

The Jewish Bible is called the Tanak, an acronym made up of the first letters of the names for its three parts: the *Torah* "Law" (Pentateuch), the *Nevi'im* "Prophets," and the *Ketuvim* "Writings." So far as we know, the books of the Tanak apart from the Pentateuch were not ritualized as scripture prior to the second century BCE. But several centuries later, by at least the end of the Second Temple period, prophetic books were being read aloud in synagogue services (Luke 4:16–17) and psalms were being sung outside the Temple as well as inside (Matt. 26:30). This growth of Jewish scriptures may have been stimulated by political events in the later Second Temple period.

In the second century BCE, King Antiochus IV Epiphanes tried to unify the Seleucid Empire by forcing Hellenistic (Greek) cultural institutions onto Judea. According to the books of 1 and 2 Maccabees, many Judeans embraced Greek sports and educational institutions. But the Seleucids also suppressed traditional Jewish religious practices and required offerings to Greek gods in Judean villages and in the Jerusalem temple (1 Macc. 1). That provoked violent resistance from a country priest and his sons, who were nicknamed the Maccabees "hammers." From 167 to 164 BCE, this family led an armed revolt against the Seleucid Empire (1 Macc. 2–4).

As a result of the Maccabean Revolt, Judea became semi-autonomous and, eventually, independent. War continued for two more decades, during which the Maccabean brothers, Judah, Jonathan, and Simon, established themselves as the dynastic rulers of Judea. This family is usually called the Hasmoneans after one of their ancestors. Starting with Jonathan, the Hasmoneans took the title and functions of high priest for themselves. Simon's grandsons also took the title "king." For the first time in 500 years, Jewish kings ruled an independent Judea. The Hasmonean kingdom lasted for a century until Rome conquered it in 63 BCE.

The sources do not give us much information about the Hasmoneans' influence over Judean literature. One brief story tells of Judah Maccabee

> ## Box 6.3   The libraries of Nehemiah and Judah Maccabee
>
> *Reported in the records and in the memoirs of Nehemiah … that he founded a library and collected the books about the kings and prophets, and the writings of David, and letters of kings about votive offerings. In the same way Judah also collected all the books that had been lost on account of the war that had come upon us, and they are in our possession. So if you have need of them, send people to get them for you. (2 Macc. 2:13–15 NRSV)*

collecting books in Jerusalem that had been scattered in the war (2 Macc. 2:13–15; see Box 6.3). As Aaronide priests, the Hasmoneans benefited from the Torah's rhetoric authorizing their priesthood and control of the Jerusalem temple. The Hasmonean period, however, also seems to coincide with the growing influence of many of the books classified as "prophets" and "writings" in the Tanak. David Carr has argued that, as kings of a wider territory around Jerusalem, they needed to counter the influence of Hellenistic literature among upper-class lay people (non-priests). To that end, they seem to have authorized a larger and more diverse collection of Hebrew texts to define classical Jewish culture and education in contrast to the Hellenistic model.[4]

The reference in 2 Maccabees 2:13–15 mentions books about kings and prophets, which describes rather well the histories and oracular collections of the Prophets, the second division of the Tanak. "The writings of David" refers to Psalms. The contents of the Tanak show that the Hasmoneans also distinguished these books by language and age. Only books apparently written before the fourth century and mostly in <u>Hebrew</u> were counted as among the Prophets. (The division into "Prophets and Writings" probably developed later.) Hebrew was no longer the vernacular language of Judea, so Hebrew now became a distinguishing mark of "classical" Jewish literature. The books' antiquity associated them with the age of prophecy, which was believed to have ended several centuries before the Maccabean Revolt.

The Hasmoneans fought wars to defend Judea's independence and tried to extend its territory into the lands of the old northern kingdom of Israel. This political context gave new importance to the books of Joshua, Samuel, and Kings. These histories demonstrated the antiquity of Judean territorial claims and political independence. Prophetic books showed Jewish oracular authority, poetic books demonstrated literary genius, and wisdom literature paraded Jewish scholarship. The books now divided between the Prophets and the Writings thus provided examples of classical Jewish learning to compete with Greek history, philosophy, and literature.

Starting in the Hasmonean period in the second and first centuries, learning Torah and Prophets became the Jewish educational ideal for priests and non-priests alike. Though only elite families had the resources to master these texts, this ideal became a hallmark of Jewish identity and of resistance to Hellenistic culture. Jews now had a national literature to show the antiquity and legitimacy of their religious and political claims.

The <u>Samaritans</u> frequently found themselves at odds with the Jerusalem community during the Second Temple period, according to Jewish books recounting this history (Ezra, Nehemiah, 1 Maccabees, and Josephus' *Antiquities of the Jews*). Their conflicts became violent during the second century BCE. The Hasmonean high priest, John Hyrcanus, conquered the Samaritan cities of Samaria and Shechem. He demolished the Samaritans' temple on <u>Mount Gerizim</u>. It is therefore not surprising that Samaritan scriptures never included the books of the Deuteronomistic History and the prophets that advanced Judean policies. To this day, the Samaritan scripture consists only of the Torah/Pentateuch. The scripturalizing choices of the Hasmoneans are highlighted by the different choices of the Samaritans.

## 6.3   PROMISES, THREATS, AND APOCALYPTIC

The tumultuous history of Second Temple Judaism shaped religious ideas in ways that would be decisive for later Judaism and Christianity. As we have seen, it led to expanding scripture toward the Hebrew Bible we have today. It also led to changing ideas about how God fulfills the promise to reward the good and punish wrongdoers.

### 6.3.1   Biblical Promises and Threats

Many books in the Hebrew Bible predict a good or bad future for Israel depending on whether people obey the covenant with God. Their threats and promises reflect the political rhetoric of the ancient Middle East. Royal inscriptions concluded with promises of divine blessing on those who follow their instructions and threats of divine punishment on those who do not. The rhetoric of sanctions became very violent in suzerainty treaties that powerful kings dictated to their vassals (see Box 6.4). Their threats often parallel the detailed threats of the Pentateuch and Prophets against disobedient Israelites.

## Box 6.4   Sanctions in ancient suzerainty treaties

The Pentateuch's sanctions lists (Lev. 26; Deut. 27–30) are similar to the sanctions in treaties from the Hittite Empire (fourteenth to thirteenth centuries BCE) and the Neo-Assyrian Empire (eighth to seventh centuries BCE). The Pentateuch makes promises as well as threats, like the Hittite treaties, but its threats are long and detailed, like the Neo-Assyrian treaties. For example, King Esarhaddon required his subjects to swear a loyalty oath (*adê*) to his son, Assurbanipal. The copy of this succession treaty found at Tell Tayinat in 2009 included the entire local community:

*The adê of Esarhaddon, king of Assyria, son of Sennacherib, king of Assyria, with the governor of Kunalia, with the deputy, the majordomo, the scribes, the chariot drivers, the third men, the village managers, the information officers, the prefects, the cohort commanders, the charioteers, the cavalrymen, the exempt, the outriders, the specialists, the shi[eld bearers (?)], the craftsmen, (and) with [all] the men [of his hands], great and small, as many as there are—[wi]th them and with the men who are born after the adê in the [f]uture, from the east [...] to the west, all those over whom Esarhaddon, king of Assyria, exercises kingship and lordship, concerning Assurbanipal, the great crown prince designate, the son of Esarhaddon, king of Assyria.*

The treaty concludes with divine threats against anyone who breaks this loyalty oath:

*May Aramiš, lord of the city and land of Qarnê (and) lord of the city and land of Aza'i, fill you with green water.*
*May Adad (and) Šāla of Kurba'il create piercing pain and ill health everywhere in your land.*
*May Šarrat-Ekron make a worm fall from your insides.*
*May they strike down you, your sons, and your daughters like a spring lamb or kid.*[5]

Some scholars have used the resemblance between the Pentateuch's sanctions and the Hittite treaties to date the Pentateuch's composition to the second millennium BCE, that is, to the time of Moses. But other features of the Pentateuch's sanctions, especially their long and detailed threats and their address to the whole people, more closely resemble the first-millennium Neo-Assyrian treaties. For example, like Deuteronomy 6:1–9, King Esarhaddon bound his subjects to teach their children about the treaty:

*You shall speak to your sons and grandsons, your seed and your seed's seed which shall be born in the future, and give them orders as follows.*

Though good examples have survived only from the Hittite and Neo-Assyrian periods, it is likely that treaties like these were widely used in ancient politics. In that case, the Pentateuch's use of treaty rhetoric cannot help date its composition.

The Pentateuch's lists of sanctions (Lev. 26; Deut. 27–30) show how imperial ideology and imperial politics shaped Israel's ideas about its covenant with God. The relationship is imperial, because YHWH demonstrates complete mastery of the world and its nations, most obviously by rescuing Israel from Egypt. Like a conquering king, God demands loyalty from vassals.[6]

These relationships are usually with individual vassals, but some Neo-Assyrian treaties demand the loyalty of a city's inhabitants or of entire tribes (see Box 6.4). In the same way, God's covenant with the Israelites at Mount Sinai is not with Moses, their leader, but with the people as a whole (unlike the covenants that God makes individually with Abraham and David, which nevertheless have consequences for the people of Israel; see Gen. 15 and 2 Sam. 7). YHWH's laws and instructions from Mount Sinai address all the people (Exod. 19:3–6; 24:3; Deut. 31:11–13) and expect their obedience, both individually and as a group.

The Pentateuch, then, depicts God in the role of Assyrian and Persian rulers who claimed to rule the world and demanded loyalty from their subjects. It describes YHWH as the world's creator and ruler who chose Israel for a special relationship defined by treaty/covenant:

*If you listen to my voice and keep my covenant, you will be my treasured possession out of all the peoples. The whole world is mine, but you will be a kingdom of priests for me and a holy nation.* (Exod. 19:5–6)

This relationship depends on Israel's obedience, as the lists of sanctions in Leviticus 26 and Deuteronomy 27–30 make explicitly clear.

Many other books of the Hebrew Bible share the view that God rewards and punishes Israel according to how well it keeps the covenant (see Box 6.5). The books of Hosea, Micah, and Isaiah in oracles they date to the eighth century BCE, predict the destruction of the kingdoms of Israel and Judah because of the people's infidelity to YHWH. After the Babylonians' conquest of Judah in 597 BCE, the books of Jeremiah and Ezekiel show these prophets warning Judeans that the punishment is not yet over. They predict another, more destructive conquest and the exile of many more people, which in fact occurred in 587 BCE. The books of Kings narrate the kingdoms' history up to and including their utter destruction by the Assyrians and Babylonians to

## Box 6.5   Sanctions in the Hebrew Bible outside the Pentateuch

The rhetoric of divine sanctions is prominent in the prophets, in history books, and in the psalms. For example:

*Hear the word of YHWH, people of Israel;*
*for YHWH indicts those living in the land.*
*There is no faithfulness or loving kindness*
*or knowledge of God in the land....*
*My people are destroyed for lack of knowledge.*
*Because you have rejected knowledge,*
*I reject you as my priest.*
*Because you have forgotten your God's Torah,*
*I will forget your children, I will!* (Hos. 4:1, 6)

*YHWH sent bands of the Chaldeans, Arameans, Moabites, and Ammonites against Judah to destroy it, according to YHWH's word spoken through his servants, the prophets. It was certainly by YHWH's command that this happened to Judah to take them away, because of the sins of Manasseh and everything he did, for the innocent blood that he shed ..., which YHWH was not willing to forgive.* (2 Kgs. 24:2–4)

*They polluted themselves by their actions,*
*and prostituted themselves by their deeds.*
*Then YHWH's anger burned against his people,*
*and he abhorred his inheritance;*
*YHWH handed them over to the nations,*
*so that their enemies ruled over them.* (Ps. 106:39–41)

show that the threats of the prophets came true. The Psalter contains hymns that confess this history and ask for God's mercy. Much of the Hebrew Bible explains the catastrophic history of the kingdoms of Israel and Judah as God's punishment of Israel because they broke the covenant by worshipping other gods and by oppressing their own people.

Other ancient Middle Eastern texts share the Hebrew Bible's tendency to explain historical events as reward or punishment from the gods. They depict the successes or failures of kings as due to their piety or impiety, usually as measured by their gifts to temples. For example, the sixth-century Weidner Chronicle explains the fortunes of a long list of Babylonian kings by their treatment of the temple of Marduk and concludes:

*Whosoever offends the gods of this city, his star will not stand in the sky.*[7]

Within the biblical storyline, the Pentateuch provides the first warnings that Israel's history as YHWH's "treasured possession" may not turn out well. Both Leviticus and Deuteronomy explicitly threaten expulsion from the land God has given Israel (Lev. 26:32–39; Deut. 28:64–68). The warnings of later prophets then become repetitions of threats already voiced by Moses. The Deuteronomistic History's narration of the kingdom's destruction demonstrates that these predictions came true. All this literature shows how, in the middle of the first millennium BCE, some Judeans accepted and internalized responsibility for their catastrophic history. They were already committing themselves to observe the covenant with God better than their ancestors (Neh. 9–10) when they began to ritualize the Torah as scripture in the time of Ezra (Neh. 8).

## 6.3.2   The Rhetoric of Promise and Threat after Ezra

As we have seen, the rhetoric of sanctions in the Pentateuch and prophetic books was internalized by the post-exilic community depicted in Ezra, Nehemiah, and Chronicles. They accepted the defeat of the kingdoms of Israel and Judah as God's punishment for abandoning the covenant, thus fulfilling the threats of Leviticus 26:27–39 and Deuteronomy 28:25–68 as well as of the prophets. They committed themselves to keeping the covenant in hopes of receiving the promises offered by the Torah and prophets. The books of the Hebrew Bible portray human decisions as shaping the future for individuals and for the community.

However, the history of the Second Temple period did not bear out the Pentateuch's promises of rewards for observing Torah. Though Jews became progressively more Torah-observant, foreign empires continued to rule them. Then the Jews' reputation for Torah observance led to outright religious <u>persecution</u> in the early second century BCE. According to 1 Maccabees 1, the Seleucid king Antiochus Epiphanes tried to replace worship of YHWH with the worship of Zeus in the Jerusalem temple and in Jewish villages. Relief from persecution came through 80 years of independence under the Jewish priest-kings of the Hasmonean dynasty, but their achievement was blemished by internal conflicts between Jewish sects (see Box 7.3). Independence ended with the Roman conquest of Judea in 63 BCE. Attempts to regain it led to frequent conflicts and then two catastrophic wars, in 66–73 CE and in 132–135 CE. These wars left the Temple in ruins and Judea inhabited mostly by non-Jewish people.

Religious persecution increasingly shaped Jewish world views in this later Second Temple period, as well as those of Christians and Jews in the following centuries. Contrary to the Torah's promises that fidelity to the covenant would bring protection and reward individually and as a community (Lev. 26:3–13; Deut. 28:1–14), they discovered that righteous living often led to being singled out for persecution. While they believed that the kingdoms of Israel and Judah had been punished for their lack of faith in God, they found that they themselves were punished for their faithfulness. Evil seemed to rule the world instead of God.

This experience of persecution expressed itself religiously in apocalyptic literature. Apocalyptic thinking provided a powerful sense of hope to many Jews and Christians who felt like they had no control over their circumstances. Apocalyptic literature depicts history as decided by God in advance. God allows evil, often personified as Satan or the devil, to control the world and persecute the people of God for a limited period of time. Then God's armies will defeat evil in battle and bring an end to history or, in some versions, destroy the whole world. Both the living and the dead will then be judged for their deeds and rewarded or punished accordingly in the afterlife (see Box 6.6).

Apocalyptic depicts the course of history as predestined. Human decisions can at most determine our individual fates, and mostly in the next life rather than in this one. Apocalyptic reflects the experience of communal persecution under the rule of foreign empires. It describes a divine plan for

## Box 6.6   Apocalyptic eschatology

*At that time Michael, the great prince, the one who stands by your people, will stand up. It will be a time of anguish, such as has never occurred since nations first came into existence. But at that time your people will be delivered, everyone who is found written in the book. Many of those who sleep in the dust of the earth will awake, some to everlasting life, and some to shame and everlasting contempt.... "How long will it be until these wonders end?"...It will be for a time, two times, and half a time, and when the shattering of the power of the holy people comes to an end, all these things will happen. (Daniel 12:1–2, 6–7 NRSV)* all of history that allows evil to rule the world temporarily. But it promises that in the end, righteousness will be rewarded and evil will be punished.[8]

Apocalyptic texts differ in form and content from the Hebrew Bible's prophetic books. Where the prophets reported *hearing* God speak (Isaiah 1) and only occasionally saw visions (Isaiah 6), apocalypses reported *seeing* elaborate visions whose meaning was then interpreted by angels (Daniel 7). Where prophets expected God to save Israel by using historical forces such as kings and empires (Isaiah 45), apocalypses predicted that God would soon bring history to an end (Daniel 7) and even destroy the whole world (Revelation 21).

Apocalyptic used symbolic imagery that was vivid and emotional. It depicted a final judgment on every individual soul that determined whether the afterlife consists of reward in heaven or punishment in hell. Apocalyptic literature described a cosmic battle between good and evil carried on by God's armies of angels against the devil's armies of demons. Angels and demons now gained names and specific responsibilities, such as the angelic soldier and general, Michael (Dan. 12:1), and the angelic messenger, Gabriel (Luke 1:26). And apocalyptic raised expectations for a future king (the Messiah; see Box 7.1) sent by God to bring about the final war between good and evil and the end of history (Dan. 7:13–14).

Apocalyptic literature became very popular in the later part of the Second Temple period. A large number of Jewish apocalypses survive to this day, ranging from Daniel 7–12, *1 Enoch*, and *Jubilees* in the third and second centuries to the Qumran *War Scroll* and *4 Baruch* in the first. The Christian New Testament is full of apocalyptic ideas, and ends with the Apocalypse of John, better known as the Book of Revelation.[9] Because of books like these, apocalyptic thinking changed Jewish and Christian eschatology, that is, their beliefs about the future.

So, the Hebrew Bible presents several different views of how the future will be determined. Deuteronomy's retributive theology — Israel will prosper if they obey God, but suffer illness, invasion, and exile if they disobey – is supported by the other Pentateuchal sources, the history books, the prophetic books, Psalms, and Proverbs. Ecclesiastes, however, wonders if the world really works this way, and the book of Job forces attention to the problem of innocent suffering. Apocalyptic restates the Deuteronomic answer, but with a twist: the righteous may suffer now, but will be rewarded in the afterlife. Some later Second Temple texts even suggest that the suffering of the righteous may serve to redeem other people (4 Macc. 17:21–22), an idea that would become central to Christian thinking. Jewish and Christian apocalyptic books continue to emphasize retribution for wrongdoing, too.

### 6.3.3  Biblical Rhetoric about the Future in Judaism and Christianity

Apocalyptic thinking provided hope to persecuted people and inspired resistance to foreign empires. Its message of powerlessness in this life and consequences in the next also fueled fanaticism. Martyrdom for God's sake became an ideal. At the end of the Second Temple period, the apocalyptic expectation that angels would fight to defend Jerusalem, according to the *War Scroll*, probably encouraged the uncompromising rebellion that led to the Temple's destruction in 70 CE. Sixty years later, another Jewish rebellion gained strength on the belief that its leader, Shimon Bar Kochba, was the Messiah sent by God to save the Jews.

In the catastrophic aftermath of these revolts, Rabbinic Judaism rid itself of the political consequences of apocalyptic fanaticism. The rabbis privatized apocalyptic expectations to focus on the influence of personal piety. In rabbinic literature, world history and imperial politics do not determine the future. Instead, the coming of the Messiah and the restoration of Israel depend only on the prayers, good works, and Torah observance of the Jewish people. So, the Mishnah (ca. 200 CE) expresses confidence that divine justice rules the world. But by the time of the Babylonian Talmud (ca. 550 CE), the rabbis reflect again the full range of biblical views about justice in this life or the next.[10]

The story of Jesus's crucifixion by Roman soldiers established the martyr ideal at the center of Christian theology. Apocalyptic thinking provided a powerful explanation for the persecution of Christians in the second and third centuries CE. When the Roman Empire became Christian in the fourth century, however, history took a turn that no prophet or apocalypse had predicted. Now a religion that had defined itself by suffering martyrdom was wielding political power. Eastern churches of the Byzantine Empire often identified the rule of God with that of the Christian empire. Roman Catholic churches in the west tended to distinguish the "city of God" from "the city of the world," in Augustine's words. Both approaches drove apocalyptic to the fringes of Christian politics.

The Jewish and Christian mainstreams preserve apocalyptic ideas like reward and punishment in the afterlife but downplay their political implications. Yet apocalyptic expectations continue to flourish whenever political discontent creates real or imagined feelings of persecution.

The Christian Bible's presentation of both Deuteronomic and apocalyptic rhetoric about the future still echoes in modern culture. For example, twenty-first-century debates about environmental climate change have, in the United States, pitted environmentalists' warnings and proposals for change against fatalistic defenses of the status quo by, especially, evangelical Christians. The scientists promise benefits from reducing carbon emissions while warning that current human behavior will produce world-wide catastrophe. Like Moses, their threats are longer and more detailed than their promises. Their opponents argue that climate change is not real or is the product of natural processes because they believe in the inevitability of the future. Like Daniel, they believe that our actions influence only our individual afterlives while world history follows a predetermined plan. The Bible's two different visions of the future continue to shape many people's ideas of what is possible and what is not.

## 6.4   SCRIPTURALIZING PROPHETS, PSALMS, AND WISDOM

The books of the Prophets and Writings have been inconsistently ritualized in later Jewish practice. Historical and prophetic books have frequently been ritualized in the semantic dimension to interpret Israel's past and future. They get read aloud in the expressive dimension, but piecemeal to accompany particular Torah readings. Use of the Psalms emphasizes their expressive performance, which is natural for hymns designed to be sung aloud. The five scrolls associated with Jewish festivals, Ruth, Esther, Song of Songs, Ecclesiastes, and Lamentations, also receive regular oral presentations. Esther scrolls frequently get decorated and illustrated to function as iconic symbols of Jewish identity (Figure 6.1). Their illustrations also distinguish them from the more sacred but undecorated Torah scrolls.

So, despite the expansion of Jewish scriptures starting around the time of Judah Maccabee, the books of the Prophets and Writings have not been regularly ritualized in all three dimensions. Some books of the Tanak, such as Chronicles, Ezra, and Nehemiah, have hardly been ritualized at all. Because they contain the <u>name of God</u>, the ancient rabbis insisted that they all must be treated as holy texts. But only the Torah has been regularly ritualized in its iconic, expressive, and semantic dimensions, which has maintained its pre-eminent status among Jewish scriptures.

Nevertheless, the expansion of scripture in the Hasmonean period changed how Jews and Christians interpret the Pentateuch as well as these

**FIGURE 6.1**   A Megillah (Esther scroll) from Italy, ca. 1616. In the National Library of Israel. Image from Wikimedia Commons under a Creative Commons Attribution-Share Alike 3.0 Unported license.

other books. James Kugel observed that, because it is scripture, people read biblical literature as <u>relevant</u>, <u>cryptic</u>, <u>perfect</u>, and <u>divinely inspired</u>. By relevant, Kugel meant that readers think what scripture says must be relevant to themselves in their present circumstances. Readers also think scripture is cryptic: its significance is not limited to the normal meaning of its words, but reflects other, deeper messages. They also expect scripture to be perfectly harmonious: everything about it is significant and any part of scripture may inform the meaning of any other part. Readers assume that scriptures are relevant, cryptic, and perfect because they think scriptures come from God. Therefore, scriptures must contain divinely inspired messages. But Kugel cautioned that claims for divine inspiration do not appear as often or as early in the Second Temple period as the other three assumptions. This sequence suggests that belief in divine inspiration may have been a product of reading scriptures as relevant, cryptic, and perfect, rather than a precondition for doing so. All four assumptions likely grew stronger together.[11]

Kugel found these assumptions about scriptural books in Jewish and Christian literature starting from around 200 BCE, shortly before the Maccabean Revolt. This is several centuries after Ezra, around 400 BCE, but the scripturalization of the Torah in Ezra's time may have participated in this trend, or even caused it. Kugel's observations concisely describe the changes in the semantic meaning of biblical literature because of its ritualization as scripture in all three dimensions. The Bible has for the most part been interpreted like this by Jews and Christians ever since.

The expansion of Jewish scriptures starting in the Hasmonean period may have encouraged these interpretive trends. Scripturalizing the genres of the Prophets, the Psalms, and Wisdom books led to applying the reading conventions of each genre to other books of scripture. Scripturalizing the Pentateuch's lists of ritual rules was already leading to its stories becoming normative.

### 6.4.1    Scripturalizing Ritual Lists

Writing seems to have been invented around 5000 years ago for recording lists in the form of accounts and receipts. The writing and interpretation of lists was the most basic and also the most prestigious scribal activity in Mesopotamian cultures. Comprehensive lists of omens represented the pinnacle of scribal expertise.

The power of lists has not waned since. Lists govern modern bureaucracies in the form of regulations, procedural instructions, and filing systems. Lists play a determinative role in human behavior. J. D. O'Banion, a theorist of rhetoric, remarked:

> Rendered as tallies, recordings of the movements of the stars, word lists, dictionaries, or codified laws, the list is a powerful tool for arranging and disseminating isolated pieces of information. It also comes to arrange and, to a considerable degree, dictate the nature of the lives of those who are affected by lists.

As tools for economic and legal control, lists dictate modes of exchange and social standing. The historian of law, Cornelia Vismann, observed: "Lists do not communicate; they control transfer operations." The original and continuing dominance of lists in literate cultures justifies Jonathan Z. Smith's description of them as "the most archaic and pervasive of genres."[12]

Readers use lists differently from how they use stories or poems. Lists invite readers and listeners to choose items relevant to themselves and ignore the rest. Whether the list contains omens, ritual instructions, or recipes, readers act only on those parts they regard as appropriate to their situation. When a list appears in a scripture, people often assume that all of it must be relevant somehow, but they still pick and choose as their own wishes, time, and circumstances require or allow, leaving the rest for another occasion.

Jewish and Christian interpreters have extended this pick-and-choose characteristic of lists to every verse of Torah and Bible. The common belief that somewhere in the Torah or the Bible, some verse of scripture must be relevant to me, now – that belief extends and develops an inherent feature of lists of laws and instructions. This characteristic way of reading lists for relevance to oneself became a distinguishing feature of how many religious individuals and communities read scriptures.

Other transformations of reading practices came from including prophetic books, the Psalter, and wisdom books in scripture.

## 6.4.2   Scripturalizing Prophecy

Prophets seem, for the most part, to have spoken oracles in response to very particular situations. They addressed specific people at certain times. For example, Isaiah predicted that a young woman would conceive and bear a son as a way of promising King Ahaz rescue from military attack within a few years (Isa. 7). However, collecting prophetic oracles together and editing them into written books implies that they continue to be relevant beyond that original situation. In written form, they can be read again at any time and interpreted to apply to situations faced by readers and their communities. So, the Gospel of Matthew takes Isaiah 7 as predicting Jesus's birth hundreds of years later (Matt. 1:22–23) and the Gospel of Luke depicts Jesus reading Isaiah 61 and applying it to himself (Luke 4:16–21). Similarly, the book of Daniel quotes Jeremiah's prediction of a 70-year exile as meaning "70 weeks" of years, that is, 490 years, to apply the prophecy to the writer's own time in the second century BCE (compare Dan. 9:2, 24 with Jer. 29:10). Written prophecies therefore invite ongoing interpretation and reapplication.

Once prophetic books began to be ritualized as scripture, this way of reading and reapplying oracles to one's own time and situation spread to other parts of scripture. The <u>relevant</u> and <u>cryptic</u> reading tendencies identified by Kugel extended oracular interpretation to non-oracular texts. This trend was accelerated by the popularity of apocalyptic thinking in the late Second Temple period. Apocalyptic increased readers' inclination to find scripture cryptic and relevant to their near future. It led them to search every scriptural text for clues to future events, which also strengthened scripture's reputation for perfect harmony and universal significance. Now psalms were read as oracles predicting Jewish revolts against Rome or the coming of the Christian messiah. Instructions for the Tabernacle were read as oracular visions of heavenly worship. Even stories about the past could be read as forecasting coming events. For example, because of Abraham's attempt to sacrifice him (Gen. 22), Isaac became a prophetic model or "type" that shaped how Jews and Christians think typologically about innocent victims.

Prophetic books introduced an oracular way of reading that was then applied to the rest of the scriptures.

Prophetic books also brought into scripture an oracular emphasis on the identity of the prophet. They name the prophets and date their experiences of revelation to validate the legitimacy of their messages (Jer. 1:1–3; cf. Isa. 1:1; Ezek. 1:1–3; Amos 1:1; etc.). Because they need to validate the prophet's authority, prophetic books give much more attention to their composers and settings than do other genres of biblical literature.

Ritualizing prophetic books as part of scripture and reading the rest of scripture like prophetic oracles raised readers' interest in validating the prophetic authors of other books as well. Now the anonymous writers of stories, psalms, and wisdom collections began to be identified with known heroes of the biblical tradition. The assumption that all scripture must be divinely inspired, that Kugel identified as appearing in later Second Temple literature, extended oracular interpretation to non-oracular texts. The logic soon seemed irrefutable that all scripture must have been written by people whom scripture describes as divinely inspired or motivated. Each book should therefore be credited to known, legitimate prophets or other biblical heroes.

Since the Pentateuch tells of Moses writing down the laws, it was easy to credit him with all five books. Samuel was proclaimed the author of Joshua and Judges, Jeremiah the historian of the books of Samuel and Kings, David of almost all the Psalms, and Solomon of most of the wisdom literature. Historians who cannot agree with the traditional identifications of biblical authors still work hard to identify the writers. The oracular concern to validate scripture's authorship takes new forms in modern historical criticism's reconstructions of the Pentateuch's composition. The presuppositions of oracular reading continue to shape how the Bible is read and interpreted by preachers, scholars, and congregation members alike.

### 6.4.3   Scripturalizing Psalms

Like hymns in many religious communities, psalms provide scripts for congregational and individual singing. They are sung in Jewish synagogue services, festivals, and wedding ceremonies. They are sung in Christian churches, monasteries, and prayer meetings (see Figure 6.2). The Psalms have exerted an overwhelming influence on Western music. They have inspired new hymnic compositions and collections since at least the first century BCE, when Qumran's library included several collections. They continue to feature in

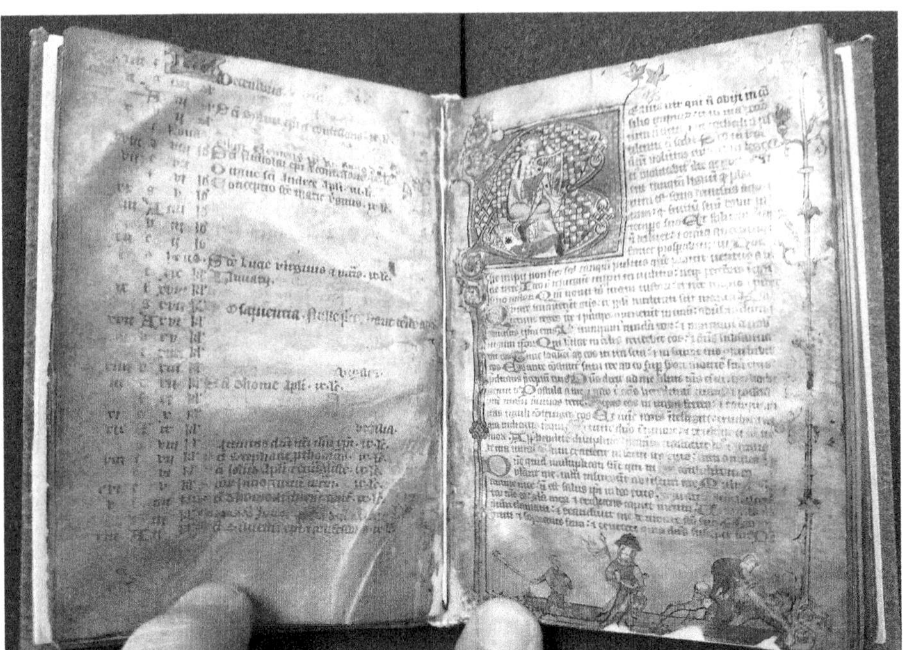

**FIGURE 6.2**   Psalter manuscript with calendar of readings from East Anglia, England, fourteenth century. In the Special Collections Research Center, Syracuse University Libraries.

the ever-expanding corpus of modern religious music for both lay singers and expert performers.

By scripturalizing song in the form of the Psalter, psalms function as a model for <u>singing</u> or <u>chanting</u> the rest of scripture as well. We do not know how early the tradition of singing scripture began, but it is attested by the fourth century CE in both Jewish and Christian sources (see Chapter 5). Because religious and literary texts were designed to be read aloud, ancient public readings tended to use tone and rhythm to project the voice and make the reading more memorable. We cannot be sure that scripturalizing the Psalter began the trend of singing other scriptures. But at the very least, the Psalms encouraged it to develop into the traditions of chant and hymnody that mark Jewish and Christian worship throughout history.

Scripturalizing the Psalter also influenced Jewish and Christian traditions of individual devotion and piety. The Psalms were composed so people can appropriate their words to express their own appeals and praise to God. Their language is frequently ambiguous in order to make it easier for different people to use them. Recent interpreters have also pointed out that the Psalter, as a collection, has been shaped for use in private devotion apart from public worship. For example, it begins by celebrating the pious student of Torah (Ps. 1) and ends with five songs of praise to YHWH (Pss. 146–150), which suggests that it was arranged to be sung through in sequence.[13]

Scriptural texts were modified to model devotional use of psalms. Psalms were inserted into the narratives of biblical heroes to make them models of piety and to provide a theological interpretation of their stories. Thus Psalm 18 has been inserted in 2 Samuel 22 to provide a theological conclusion to David's story. Hannah's song similarly announces God's plan for a king in 2 Samuel 2. Such inset psalms deliberately shape biblical stories to be used as devotional scripture. Other examples include the Song of the Sea in Exodus 15, the psalms and poems concluding the Pentateuch in Deuteronomy 32–33, and Hezekiah's prayer in Isaiah 38 inserted into narratives taken from 2 Kings. Superscriptions to some of the Psalms suggest more applications to specific stories (e.g., Pss. 3, 7, 34).[14]

Psalms, then, model a way of reading and listening that encourages applying their words to the singer's and reader's own circumstances and concerns. Ritualizing the Psalter as part of scripture led to reading the rest of scripture in the same way. The assumption of <u>relevance</u> that Kugel identified as characteristic of scriptural interpretation extended hymnic interpretation and singing practices to non-hymnic texts. Just as psalms can give voice to anyone's hopes and fears, so can scripture's prophetic, narrative, and legal texts.

## 6.4.4  Scripturalizing Wisdom

Including books of wisdom like Proverbs in scripture strengthened the tendency to read scripture as <u>relevant</u> to individual personal circumstances. The ancient Middle Eastern wisdom genre featured moral and practical advice. Wisdom texts explicitly tell readers how to behave for their own good. Of course, the Pentateuch's commandments also call on readers and listeners to follow their instructions, and Deuteronomy incorporates wisdom themes to make this appeal. Scripturalizing wisdom books then strengthened the tendency to read all scriptures as good advice for daily life.

Wisdom was transformed during and after Hasmonean rule. Unlike the Hebrew Bible's wisdom books (Proverbs, Ecclesiastes, Job), literature from the late Second Temple period amalgamates wisdom with Israel's history and its religious institutions (Wis. 10–11). It identifies wisdom with the Torah of Moses (Sir. 24:23; Bar. 4:1). It praises the Jerusalem Temple and its priests (Sir. 45, 50). And it incorporates apocalyptic themes: eternal life as reward for the righteous (Wis. 5:15), the devil as the cause of death (Wis. 2:24), Israel's salvation from foreign empires (Bar. 5), the glorious restoration of Jerusalem (Tob. 13), and wisdom itself in the form of divine light as a messiah figure (Wis. 7:24–8:1; John 1). It combines wisdom with law, prophecy, and apocalyptic to make scripture give advice for this life and the next. These Jewish and Christian texts of the Hellenistic and Roman periods make wisdom more "biblical" than do the wisdom books of the Hebrew Bible itself.

## 6.5  INTERPRETING SCRIPTURE: SCRIBES AND RABBIS

To read a text, any written text, you must first recognize it as a text. That is its iconic dimension. Then you must turn its visual signs into spoken or mental language. That is its expressive dimension. But one more step is required: you must understand the meaning of the text's language. That is its semantic dimension. Literate people normally take all three steps without thinking about them. We pay attention to the expressive and semantic dimensions only when we do not understand what we read – maybe because the text is in a language we do not know or because its contents confuse us. The Bible gets interpreted for both reasons. Its original languages, Hebrew, Aramaic, and Greek, are foreign to most readers and listeners. Even when they understand its language, they find its contents confusing.

Intensive study and interpretation ritualize a scripture's semantic dimension. As a result, study and interpretation become acts of religious devotion. Congregations encourage people to study the scriptures. They honor teachers and scholars who excel at interpreting the scriptures for the community. In many traditions that revere written scriptures, scholars get elevated to positions of religious leadership. The most influential Muslim imams, Buddhist monks, Jewish rabbis, and Christian preachers are famous for their ability to interpret sacred texts. Written commentaries extend the influence of scriptures and, by their large number and widespread use, emphasize the importance of the scriptures. The authors of the most widely read commentaries can influence the teachings of a religion for centuries or even millennia.

So, ritualizing the semantic dimension of scriptures establishes religious authority. Religious communities sponsor training in interpretation not only for personal devotion but also to help the group make decisions. They interpret scriptures in order to direct community behavior and to resolve conflicts.

Because they understand the text to be divine communication, its interpretation becomes a form of divination. It is usually the preferred and sometimes the only legitimate means for determining God's will. Religious leadership in these communities therefore depends to some degree, frequently to a great degree, on mastering interpretation of the semantic meaning of scripture.

The semantic dimension of the Bible always receives most of the attention of scholars, for the very good reason that the Jewish and Christian traditions place great emphasis on scholarly expertise in scriptural interpretation. A concern for interpreting the Pentateuch appears already in the Hebrew Bible itself. The stories of Josiah's and Ezra's Torah readings (2 Kgs. 22–23; Neh. 8) end with the listeners interpreting the laws to know how to perform their rituals or conduct their marriages or celebrate festivals like Passover and *Sukkot*. Historians have used evidence of the Hebrew Bible's interpretation to trace its growing status as scripture in the Second Temple period.

## 6.5.1   Ezra as Expert Scribe

The books of Ezra and Nehemiah celebrate the scribal skills of Ezra and his Levite assistants. Their emphasis on expert interpretation has echoed throughout later Jewish and Christian traditions.

The <u>book of Ezra</u> introduces Ezra as a priest and a scribe, but his priestly standing is hereditary and the story never depicts him officiating at the temple. The book instead celebrates his achievements as a scribe, as a scholar of Torah (see Box 6.7). This does not contradict his priestly identity, since the priests' job included interpreting and teaching Torah (Lev. 10:11). Nevertheless, this depiction of Ezra is unusual in emphasizing his textual scholarship. It describes Ezra's "skill" and devotion to Torah study, his commitment to observing the Torah's commands, and his dedication to teaching Torah (Ezra 7:6, 10). The book of Ezra, for the first time in Jewish literature, celebrates scholarly commitment and textual expertise in the Torah as a religious ideal.

The <u>book of Nehemiah</u> continues the story of Ezra and its emphasis on interpreting the Torah's semantic dimension. Its story of Ezra reading the Torah aloud in Jerusalem describes Levites interpreting Ezra's reading (Neh. 8:7–8). Their activity may have consisted, at least in part, in translating the Hebrew Torah into Aramaic, the colloquial language of the time. The story emphasizes that it was important for the people to understand what they were hearing. Thirteen Levites mixed with the crowd to make sure they did. The story celebrates the Levites' interpretive skill and dedication by listing their names. Though public readings of Torah appear prominently in several earlier

---

## Box 6.7   Interpretive expertise in Ezra–Nehemiah

*Ezra … was a scribe skilled in the Torah of Moses given by YHWH the God of Israel. … For Ezra had committed himself to study the Torah of YHWH and to do it and to teach its mandates and regulations in Israel.* (Ezra 7:6, 10)

*The Levites helped the people understand the Torah … They read the Torah with interpretation to provide insight, so the people would understand the reading.* (Neh 8:7–8)

*On the second day, the clan leaders of all the people came with the priests and Levites to the scribe Ezra to gain insight into the words of the Torah.* (Neh 8:13)

---

episodes in Israel's history (Exod. 24:3–8; Deut. 31:9–13; Josh. 8:34–35; 2 Kgs. 23:2–3), only this story about Ezra describes such interpretation (Box 6.7).

Nehemiah 8's emphasis on interpretation continues in its account of the following days, when the leaders of the people gathered with Ezra, the other priests, and the Levites for that purpose. They discovered the instructions for celebrating *Sukkot*, the festival of Booths, recorded in Lev. 23:39–43 and Num. 29:12–38. All the people then celebrated *Sukkot* "as it is written" and "according to the regulation" (Neh. 8:15, 18). Later in the same month, the people gathered to confess their sins and recommit themselves to YHWH. On this occasion, the Levites recited a prayer that summarized the biblical story line. They emphasized God's deliverance of Israel from Egypt and the people's repeated failures to keep the covenant (Neh. 9). Here their knowledge and interpretation of Torah and of Israel's history shape the people's religious experience and behavior.

Later communities have frequently used the figure of Ezra to mirror their own disputes over scripture and religious identity. One legend about Ezra has been particularly useful for this purpose.

Shortly after Rome destroyed the Second Temple in 70 CE, a Jewish writer wrote a book usually called *4 Ezra* or the *Ezra Apocalypse*. Here Ezra complains how hard it is to avoid God's judgment and punishment in this life. He then sees visions of judgment in the afterlife and reward for those who observe Torah faithfully. Ezra is inspired to rewrite the 24 books of the Tanak that *4 Ezra* claims were lost in the Babylonian Exile. He writes 70 secret books as well, probably including *4 Ezra* itself. Because of Ezra's scribal efforts, people will again have the chance to observe God's Torah and find reward in the afterlife.

This story of Ezra rewriting scripture echoed through the apologetics and polemics of different religious communities in the first millennium CE. Jewish rabbis celebrated Ezra as a second Moses whose inspired and faithful rewriting saved the Torah. But Christian, Samaritan, and Muslim critics claimed that Ezra falsified the scriptures. They reasoned that God's true revelation to Moses must have mentioned Jesus Christ, or the temple on Mount Gerizim, or the Prophet Mohammed. They thought that these omissions of important elements of their own faith must therefore be due to Ezra's negligence or malfeasance. This late and fictional story of Ezra rewriting scripture has therefore shaped the reputation of Ezra in all these traditions, as well as the reputation of their scriptures in each other's eyes.[15]

Unlike the religious traditions that use the figure of Ezra to mark the preservation or corruption of scripture's contents, this book argues that the crucial change brought about in Ezra's time was one of scripturalization. The story of Ezra shows that it was then, in the early Second Temple period, specifically the middle or late Persian period, that the Pentateuch began to be ritualized in all three dimensions as a scripture.

## 6.5.2  Expert Interpreters

The writers of Ezra-Nehemiah and other biblical books from the fourth to second centuries BCE increasingly conformed to Ezra's model of scribal expertise themselves. They not only wrote about the Torah, they also began to cite specific pentateuchal laws and instructions (see Box 6.8).

---

**Box 6.8   Citations of the Pentateuch elsewhere in the Hebrew Bible**

Ezra 3:2 → Lev. 1–7
Ezra 9:10–12 → Deut. 7:1–4; cf. 23:2–8
Neh. 8:15 → Lev. 23:39–43
Neh. 8:18 → Num. 29:12–38
Neh. 13:1–2 → Deut. 23:3–6
2 Chr. 23:18 → Lev. 1–7
2 Chr. 25:4 / 2 Kgs. 14:6 → Deut. 24:16
2 Chr. 30:16 → Lev. 1:5, 3:2
Mal. 1:8, 13–14 → Lev. 1:3, 10
Mal. 3:10 → Lev. 27:30–33; Num. 18:21
Dan. 9:13 → Lev. 26; Deut. 27–28

It is not always clear exactly which text they had in mind or even whether their Pentateuch had exactly the same contents as ours, but the growing trend of citing written Torah is clear enough.

The books of 1 and 2 Chronicles were probably written several decades after Ezra and Nehemiah. They share the belief in the importance of Torah interpretation and instruction. Chronicles repeats much of the history of Israel and Judah from the books of Samuel and Kings, but the writers also added new material not found in those sources. One of these additional stories tells of King Jehoshaphat's efforts to bring Torah instruction to the villages of Judah. He appointed a committee composed of royal officials, Levites, and priests to teach the people from the Torah scroll that they carried with them (2 Chr. 17:7–9). The Chronicler does not specify the contents of the teaching.

The growing authority of the Pentateuch in the later Second Temple period led to its interpretation being projected into the early history of Israel. The books of *Jubilees* and *1 Enoch* claim that, before Moses, the heavenly Torah was revealed to Enoch, Abraham, Jacob, and Levi. The *Testament of Levi* shows Levi being instructed in the priesthood by his grandfather, Isaac.[16] So, even the patriarchs of Genesis are depicted as Torah scholars.

The discovery of the Dead Sea Scrolls from 1947 to 1956 (see Section 4.2.2) gave us a new window onto the culture of Torah interpretation in late Second Temple Judaism. Many of these works discovered near Qumran are devoted to that subject. The *Community Rule* (*1QS*) interprets and extends pentateuchal laws to regulate the conduct of members of the Qumran community. The *Temple Scroll* (*11QT*) rewrites Deuteronomy 12–23 in God's voice, rather than that of Moses. It adds ritual rules from Exodus, Leviticus, and Numbers to present the community's views on how the temple rituals should be performed. That the Qumran scribes did not approve of the conduct of the temple priests is abundantly clear from another text, an open letter to the temple authorities called *Miqṣat Ma'aśeh ha-Torah* "Some Precepts of the Torah" (*4QMMT*). This letter cites regulations from Leviticus and Deuteronomy to argue that they should be carried out differently than was current practice in the Jerusalem temple (see Box 6.9).

Early Christian texts reproduce this Jewish emphasis on authority from scripture interpretation. The Gospel of Luke depicts Jesus as an insightful interpreter of scripture from his childhood (Luke 2:46–47) through his adult ministry (4:16–30) to after his resurrection (24:27). The Gospel of Matthew portrays Jesus citing and intensifying the demands of Torah (Matt. 5:17–48). According to Matthew, his teachings impressed listeners as exceeding the authority of the scribes (7:29). The book of Acts shows the Christian apostles summarizing the history of Israel from Torah and Prophets before

## Box 6.9   Citing and debating Torah in 4QMMT

Multiple manuscripts of the letter *4QMMT* were found among the Dead Sea Scrolls. They are fragmentary, so brackets [] mark gaps and recon-structed letters.

*These are some of our regulations:*

(On Num. 19:2–10) *And also in what pertains to the purity of the red heifer in the sin-offering that whoever slaughters it and whoever burns it and whoever collects the ash and whoever sprinkles the [water of] purification, all these ought to be pure at sunset, so that whoever is pure sprinkles the impure....*

(On Lev. 4:12) *And concerning what is written [...] outside the camp, "a bull, or a [she]ep or a she-goat"...And we think that the temple [...Je]rusalem is the camp, and outside the camp is [outside Jerusalem;] it is the camp of their cities....*

(On Lev. 19:19 and Deut. 22:9, and citing Jer. 2:3, Lev. 19:2, and Lev. 21:7) *And concerning the practice of illegal marriage that exists among the peo-ple, despite their being sons of holy [seed], as is written, Israel is holy. And concerning his (Israel's) [clean] animal it is written that one must not let it mate with another species, and concerning his clothes [it is written that they should not] be of mixed stuff; and he must not sow his field and vineyard with mixed species. Because they (Israel) are holy, and the sons of Aaron are [most holy]. But you know that some of the priests and [the laity mingle with each other.] [And they] unite with each other and pollute the holy seed as well as their own [seed] with women whom they are forbidden to marry....*

(On scripture) *To you we have wr[itten] that you must understand the book of Moses [and the books of the pro]phets and of David....*

(On Deut. 27–30) *And we are aware that part of the blessings and curses have occurred that are written in the b[ook of Mo]ses and this is the end of days, when they go back to Israel for[ever]....*

(On Torah) *We have written to you some of the precepts of the torah which we think are good for you and for your people....*[17]

announcing Jesus as the Messiah (Acts 7:2–53; 8:35; 13:16–41). The apostle Paul emphasizes his education in the Torah (Gal. 1:14; Phil. 3:5; Acts 22:3) and his letters demonstrate it by discussing pentateuchal stories and laws (e.g., Gal. 3; Rom. 7, 9–11) as well as quoting the Psalms and Prophets (e.g., Rom. 3). The New Testament's most detailed exposition of the Hebrew Bible appears in the Letter to the Hebrews. This anonymous book cites scriptures throughout. It analyzes the Pentateuch's laws for rituals and priests to argue that Jesus is the new high priest whose self-sacrifice atones for human sins (Heb. 5–11). So the early Christians used interpretation of scripture to advance their movement. They also celebrated the interpretive abilities of Jesus and his apostles as models of Christian preaching and piety.

By the end of the Second Temple period in 70 CE, ritualization of the semantic dimension of Torah had become characteristic of all Jewish religious movements. After the failed Jewish revolts against Rome in the first and second centuries CE, semantic ritualization of Torah and scripture became even more pervasive and determinative of religious authority.

Rabbinic Judaism traced its authority through a line of Torah experts stretching from Moses and Joshua to the rabbis Hillel and Shammai in the first century CE and to Judah *ha-Nasi* (Box 6.10) and his colleagues at the beginning of the

## Box 6.10   Judah *ha-Nasi*

By the end of the second century CE, rabbis were trying to rebuild Jewish life after two catastrophic wars against Rome. The failure of the Jewish revolts of 66–73 and 132–135 CE had left the temple in ruins and Jerusalem populated mostly by non-Jews. Aaronide priests lost their power base in the temple and its income. The wars also disrupted many of the Jewish sects that competed for religious influence in previous centuries. However, the Pharisees' oral torah survived in schools of rabbis. They developed it further to build religious institutions for the new circumstances faced by Jewish communities.

Judah ben Simeon ben Gamaliel II (135–220 CE) was born into a family descended from the famous first-century rabbi Hillel. Judah succeeded his father as leader of the rabbinic assembly (*bet din*) with authority over Galilee and Judea. Hence his title *ha-Nasi* "the prince" or "the patriarch," though it may also reflect his family's supposed descent from King David. Judah's decisive leadership and diplomacy smoothed relations with Roman rulers. Renowned for his deep scholarship, humility, wealth, and generosity, he was the leading Jewish figure of his day.

Judah's subsequent fame, however, stems from the fact that he edited the <u>Mishnah</u>. Over many generations, the Pharisees had developed traditions of law and interpretation called the "oral torah" to accompany the written Torah of the Pentateuch. After the wars against Rome, the oral torah began to be written down and edited into various collections, and Judah gathered them together. His edition emphasized the teachings of four generations of students of Rabbi Akiva (d. 135 CE), especially the last generation.

Judah's dominant influence established the Mishnah as the authoritative basis for Jewish law and religious practice. All subsequent rabbinic literature shows its normative influence. The Mishnah's paragraphs formed the central text of later <u>Talmuds</u> that surrounded them with commentary. For his role in editing the Mishnah, Judah earned a remarkable honor. Of all the hundreds of rabbis cited in rabbinic literature, the simple title "rabbi," without any name or further qualification, refers specifically to him.[18]

In much of subsequent Judaism, the meaning of the written Torah and the rest of the Tanak became what the Mishnah, and the rabbis who interpreted the Mishnah, said it means. The Torah scroll remained the central icon of Jewish devotion, and the Torah scroll and prayer book together exemplified scripture's expressive dimension. But from the time of Judah *ha-Nasi* on, the Mishnah and, later, the Talmuds dominated the semantic dimension of legal interpretation and textual commentary on the Pentateuch.

third (*m. 'Avot* 1–2). These rabbis claimed that an oral tradition of interpreting Torah accompanied revelation of the written Torah and was passed down along with it. The <u>Pharisees</u> of the late Second Temple period taught this "oral torah" and the rabbis of Late Antiquity wrote it down in the <u>Mishnah</u> (around 200 CE) and in the two <u>Talmuds</u> (around 450 and 550 CE). The Talmuds and other rabbinic literature established an interpretive framework around the Torah that has remained influential, and frequently authoritative, for Jews ever since.

The contents of the Mishnah do not follow the Pentateuch's literary sequence, but are organized around major legal themes, such as agriculture, family laws, and rituals (Box 6.11). Yet the Mishnah also gives a great deal of space to issues, such as temple rituals, that were no longer of practical importance after the Jerusalem Temple was destroyed in 70 CE. So the Mishnah is not just a code of practice. It discusses both practical and theoretical issues that the rabbis thought should be of major concern to Jews.

## Box 6.11   The sections of the Mishnah

*Zeraim* "Seeds" about agriculture and prayer
*Mo'ed* "Festival" about Sabbaths and other holidays
*Nashim* "Women" dealing with marriage and divorce
*Nezikin* "Damages" about civil and criminal laws
*Qodashim* "Holy Things" about temple rituals and diet
*Tohorot* "Purities" about impurities and purification

Even more importantly, it establishes how one should think about issues that arise when trying to observe Torah. The Mishnah reports the rabbis' decisions and also their debates and disagreements to model how to think through issues with legal precedents and reasoning. It shows interpretation taking place through discussion and debate (see Box 6.12). It cites the rabbis by name, who often cast their arguments as representing the views of their teachers. Sometimes the majority decides an issue, but at other times the literature allows different views to remain unreconciled. By this discourse of perpetual debate, the Mishnah displays the ancient rabbis' knowledge of the Torah, both written and oral, and their interpretive and reasoning skills. It celebrates their scholarship and makes them models of Jewish piety.

In this way, rabbinic literature also depicts the ancient rabbis as the pre-eminent authorities for determining the meaning of Torah. It established an "aristocracy of learning" that privileges rabbinic scholars as both spiritual and political leaders. Their debates model the directions in which interpretive reasoning may be pursued, but they also set the boundaries within which such reasoning should be limited. For example, they exclude the views of heretics and Christians as unworthy of consideration.

After the creation of the Mishnah around 200 CE, other rabbinic literature took up the task of harmonizing the Mishnah's regulations with the written Torah. This took the form of legal commentaries and also of collections of stories (*midrashim*) that embellish biblical stories with rabbinic interpretation. The Jerusalem Talmud and the Babylonian Talmud synthesize much of this discussion together.

Rabbinic literature presents the rabbis as having the power to direct Jewish religious and legal life since the destruction of the Temple in 70 CE. Actually, it seems to have taken many centuries for rabbinic teachings to become normative in the synagogues of Late Antiquity. Nevertheless, in the end the rabbis and their literature became authoritative for determining the ideas and practices of Judaism. The hereditary priests who led Jews during

## Box 6.12  Rabbinic interpretation through discussion and debate

*Genesis Rabbah* is a collection of rabbinic interpretations arranged as a sequential commentary on the book of Genesis. It was completed around 400 CE. The following excerpts interpret the end of the first creation story in Gen. 1:31–2:1.

*"And God saw everything that He had made and, behold, it was very good"* (Gen. 1:31). *R. Johanan and R. Simeon b. Lakish each commented thereon. R. Johanan said: "When a mortal king builds a palace, he can only take in the upper stories with one look and the lower stories with another, but the Holy One, blessed be He, casts but a single look at the upper and the lower portions simultaneously." R. Simeon b. Lakish said: "Behold, it was very good" implies this world; and "behold" implies the next world: The Holy One, blessed be He, cast but one look at this world and at the future world [together]. (Genesis Rabbah ix.3, ix.12)*

*All our Rabbis said the following in R. Flanina's name, while R. Phinehas and R. Hilkiah said it in R. Simon's name:* Me'od *is identical with* 'adam *(man), for the letters of both are identical. Thus it is written, "And God saw everything that He had made, and, behold, it was very* (me'od) *good," i.e., and behold,* 'adam *(man) was good. (Genesis Rabbah ix.12)*

*"And the heaven and the earth were finished,"* etc. (Gen. 2:1). *How did the Holy One, blessed be He, create His world? Said R. Johanan: The Lord took two balls, one of fire and the other of snow, and worked them into each other, and from these the world was created. R. Hanina said: [He took] four [balls], for the four corners [of the universe]. R. Hama said: Six: four for the four corners and one for above and one for below. (Genesis Rabbah x.3)*[19]

the Second Temple period were replaced in Late Antiquity by the religious leadership of scholarly rabbis. This Rabbinic Judaism privileged Torah study as the highest form of piety and Torah expertise as the most important qualification for leadership.[20]

In the Middle Ages, many Jewish interpreters found new interest in the "plain meaning" (*pshat*) of biblical texts. This development reflected the influence of the Aristotelian philosophy of Maimonides. It was also motivated by challenges from a Jewish sect, the Karaites, who rejected Talmudic interpretation, and by criticisms of Jewish scripture by Muslims and Christians. The result was a flowering of biblical interpretation by scholars who are still read widely today, including Abraham Ibn Ezra, David Kimchi, and, most famous of all, Shlomo Yitzchaki, better known by the acronym Rashi.

Their focus on plain meaning led them to take literary context into account in interpretation. It also drew their attention to the ambiguities and contradictions in the Pentateuch's text that raise questions about some traditional beliefs. Ibn Ezra, for example, gently questioned how Moses could possibly have written the account of his own death in Deuteronomy 34.[21]

Though scholars have dominated biblical interpretation since Antiquity, Jewish and Christian congregations have encouraged everyone to learn the Bible's stories and abide by its rules. Ritualizing its semantic dimension has therefore had wide cultural influence. I cannot begin to survey here the range of the Bible's influence over the last 25 centuries as well as today, so I will focus on just one theme. In Chapter 2, we saw how the Pentateuch encourages its readers and listeners to identify themselves with Israel. That rhetoric has shaped the identities of many Jews and Christians throughout history.

## 6.6   IDENTIFYING WITH ISRAEL

The Pentateuch's laws and stories have defined Jewish and Samaritan identity ever since the Torah first began to function as a scripture. Demarcating Jewish identity is a major concern of the books of Ezra and Nehemiah. The scribe, Ezra, and the governor, Nehemiah, discriminated by ancestry between those who were members of the covenant community and those who were not. They required those whose families belonged in the community to swear fidelity to the Torah (Neh. 10), and they required everyone else to leave (Ezra 10:6–44; Neh. 13:1–9, 23–30).

In the following centuries and millennia, Jewish identity was not usually policed so harshly as it was by Ezra and Nehemiah. But the Torah became ever more important as a key component of Jewish identity. Jewish prayers in the Second Temple period frequently referred to the stories of the Pentateuch, and sometimes also to stories in Joshua, Judges, Samuel, and Kings. Ezra led the people of Jerusalem to confess their ancestors' sins against YHWH before committing themselves to do better (Ezra 9; Neh. 9; compare Ps. 106). Psalms recounted God's rescue of Israel in the past to plead for divine intervention in the present (Pss. 77, 78, 99, 105, 114). These prayers reproduce the Pentateuch's rhetoric by calling on worshippers to identify themselves as Israel and learn from their predecessors' mistakes.

This use of the Torah and history books to provide positive and negative role models continued in the rhetoric of Chronicles (1 Chr. 16:8–36; 2 Chr. 20:5–12) and of Jesus ben Sira (Sir. 44–49), and became common in later literature. By at least the second century BCE, Jews consciously distinguished themselves from Hellenistic (Greek) culture by living according to the

Pentateuch's regulations, especially by worshipping only the God of Israel, resting on the <u>Sabbath</u>, <u>circumcising</u> their sons, and following the Pentateuch's <u>diet laws</u>. For example, Judith and Daniel and his friends among the Babylonians show their piety by eating only pure food (Judt. 12:1–4; Dan. 1:8–17) and refusing to worship Babylonian gods (Dan. 3:4–12; 6:6–11). We are told that the Maccabees used Torah scrolls for divination in the same way that "the gentiles consult images of their gods" (1 Macc. 3:48). The book of 1 Maccabees judges the Jews who collaborated with the Seleucid Greeks as traitors because they "removed the mark of circumcision and abandoned the sacred covenant" (1 Macc. 1:15).

This growing identification of Jews with the Torah's rules raised concern for how to apply them in changing circumstances. Some Jewish rebels against the Seleucid Empire were defeated because they rested on the Sabbath, a policy that the more successful Maccabees ignored (1 Macc. 2:29–41). The Maccabees also had to decide what to do with the Temple's altar that the Seleucids had defiled. Lacking any clear instructions for this situation in the Pentateuch, they put the altar stones in storage "until a prophet should come to tell them what to do with them" (1 Macc. 4:44–47).

The Torah's validation of <u>Aaronide priests</u> as the only hierarchy in Israel (Lev. 8–10; Num. 16–18) had political consequences in the Hellenistic period. The high priest Jaddua successfully negotiated with Alexander when his armies swept by Judea (Josephus, *Ant.* 11.317–345). With the permission of the Hellenistic empires, <u>high priests</u> of the Oniad family continued to rule Judea until the second century. When Hasmonean warlords led Judea to independence, they buttressed their authority with their Aaronide ancestry to claim the high priesthood for themselves. At the end of the first century CE, Josephus wrote that Jews distinguish themselves by being a nation led by priests, rather than kings. He invented the term "theocracy" for their system of government (*Ap.* 2:16).

Jewish priestly groups opposed to the Hasmoneans also invested time and effort into reading and interpreting the Pentateuch and the Prophets. The <u>Dead Sea Scrolls</u> found near <u>Qumran</u> contain the library of a community led by priests who had split from the hierarchy in Jerusalem. Their library of over 800 manuscripts contained more than a dozen copies of every book of the Pentateuch, as well as of Isaiah and collections of Psalms (Box 6.13). Other Qumran scrolls provide evidence of systematic interpretation of Torah and prophetic texts by strings of citations (in *4QMMT*) and by commentary (in the *Habakkuk Pesher*). The Qumran community's interest in ritual interpretation, as demonstrated by *4QMMT* (see Box 6.9), raised their concern for the accuracy of ritual texts. Russell Hobson pointed out that the texts of books that deal with rituals, that is, the Pentateuch, were standardized at Qumran more than other books that appear there in multiple copies.[22]

## Box 6.13   Books of more than 10 copies among the Dead Sea Scrolls

| | |
|---|---|
| Psalms | 36 |
| Deuteronomy | 30 |
| Isaiah | 21 |
| Genesis | 19 |
| Leviticus | 17 |
| Exodus | 15 |
| *Jubilees* | 14 |
| *Community Rule* | 12 |

(counts of copies are approximate)

The investment of Jewish identity in the Torah and in its interpretation became even greater in Late Antiquity when the Temple disappeared and its priests lost their positions as religious authorities. Without their land or temple, Jews could not follow many of the Pentateuch's laws as written. Rabbinic Judaism provided alternative ways to fulfill Torah. The ancient rabbis taught that prayer and good deeds can take the place of animal offerings in the Temple (*b. Berak.* 26a; *Avot d'Rabbi Natan* 4:21). They maintained that study of the Pentateuch's rules for offerings would earn the same merit as making those offerings (*b. Menaḥ.* 110a; *b. San.* 43b). In this way, the Torah's commandments could be fulfilled in the very different circumstances in which Jews found themselves after 70 CE. Torah study became a ritual practice as well as an intellectual pursuit.

Thus, the Torah continued to define what it means to be Jewish. Indeed, the story of the exodus and wilderness wandering took on new poignancy for Jews living outside the traditional land of Israel. The annual celebration of Passover in obedience to the Torah's directives (Exod. 12–13) became a commemoration of the land's loss and of hopes for its eventual recovery, encapsulated in the concluding refrain, "Next year in Jerusalem!"

The themes of exodus and travel to the promised land played a large role in Zionism, the Jewish movement that led to founding the modern State of Israel in 1948. The leading theorist of early Zionism, Theodor Herzl, depicted his plan as an "exodus to the Promised Land." Jewish settlers in Palestine celebrated the land's agricultural potential with art depicting the spies exploring the land (Num. 13). They often showed the Tabernacle set up in the land to represent Israel's return. But because many Zionists rejected traditional rabbinic religion, they drew on nationalistic themes from the books of Maccabees more than on the exodus and wilderness themes that had characterized Jewish diaspora experience for millennia. Nevertheless, the renaming of a blockade-running immigrant ship as *The Exodus* in 1947 was immortalized as a symbol of the nation's founding by news media, as well as by Leon Uris' novel of the same name and its film adaptation starring Paul Newman (see Figure 6.3). Jewish experience in the nineteenth and twentieth centuries – from emancipation to Shoah/Holocaust to the founding of the

**FIGURE 6.3**  Poster for the film *Exodus*, 1960. Artist: Paul Bass. Public domain image (copyright expired).

state of Israel – has resonated for many with the story of Israel in the Pentateuch and in Joshua.[23]

Among <u>Christians</u>, the Pentateuch's rhetoric of identification with exodus Israel has received a more complicated response. Paul argued that <u>gentiles</u> (non-Jews) can become Christian without adopting Jewish practices and identity (Rom. 9–11; see Section 14.1.2). Because of this New Testament argument, Christians have felt free to distinguish themselves from Jews and to ignore many of the Pentateuch's laws. Paul insisted that God's support for Israel remains unchanged (Rom. 11), but on the basis of other New Testament texts, Christians have claimed for themselves God's promises to Israel in the Pentateuch. They have declared themselves to be the <u>new Israel</u> who replaces the Jews in God's plan for humanity (Matt. 21:33–44; Gal. 3:28–29; Heb. 8:13). This <u>supersessionist</u> logic leaves no room for Israel outside the Church, and has led many Christians to persecute Jews over the centuries. As a result, Christians' message of love for all people has often been contradicted by their anti-Semitism.

The universalism of the Christian message has also not prevented particular groups of Christians from claiming the Pentateuch's description of Israel for themselves (see Box 6.14). As we saw in Chapter 2, the Pentateuch's rhetoric works to get hearers and readers to identify with the Israelites of the exodus. Many different Christian groups as well as Jews have accepted that rhetoric and

## Box 6.14   Identifying with Exodus Israel

Eric Kling described two typical ways in which groups have appropriated the identity of exodus Israel as their own: "Time after time in myriad creative ways, Jews and Christians (even Muslims) envisioned themselves as the Israelites of old, subjected to oppressive conditions but delivered by God's power and rewarded a Promised Land (figuratively or literally) for maintaining their faith.... Historically, exodus movements have been generally expressed in two ways. Some movements, such as those of the New England Puritans, the Mormons, the Afrikaners of South Africa, and the Jews of America, were actual physical migrations, viewed as a kind of exodus to the Promised Land.... Other exodus movements, such as those identified with black liberation theology in North America and liberation theology in Latin America, appropriated the exodus motif theologically, in the sense of liberating one's outlook, raising one's consciousness, and demanding justice on behalf of the poor and oppressed."[24]

applied the exodus story to their own experiences. Some have revived Israelite practices and institutions that most Jews and Christians do not replicate.

Samaritans plausibly trace their ancestry to the northern kingdom of Israel around whose capital, Samaria (now Nablus), they have lived since antiquity. Their traditions of Torah observance may be as old as those preserved in Jewish tradition. They claim the Pentateuch's promises as Israelites and continue to live on part of the land promised to Abraham. The politics of two millennia, however, have not been kind to the Samaritans, who now number fewer than 1000 people.

Other groups also remember ancestral links to ancient Israel. Ethiopia's kings claimed descent from King Solomon through the son of the Queen of Sheba (1 Kgs. 10). Many Ethiopians believe that he brought the Ark of the Covenant to Ethiopia. They claim to still keep it in a church in Aksum, where it is hidden from view. Ethiopian Christians remember their Jewish heritage by following the Pentateuch's diet laws and by circumcising infant boys. The last ruler of their Solomonic dynasty, the Emperor Haile Selassie, was overthrown and died in 1975. A distinctive Jewish community also remained in Ethiopia until the late twentieth century, when most of them immigrated to Israel.[25]

The exodus story has played an especially important role in the development of American identity. In 1630, on board the ship *Mayflower* on its way to Massachusetts Bay, the Puritan leader, John Winthrop, preached a sermon comparing the passengers to exodus Israel. He paraphrased Deuteronomy 30 to suggest that God was giving the Puritans a new land on condition that they keep God's commandments and covenant, or else they would lose the land again. The theme of America as a promised land and of its immigrant people as a new Israel was prominent in religious and political rhetoric through the seventeenth and eighteenth centuries. It climaxed in celebrations of the founding of the United States after 1776.[26]

However, the exodus story also held a very prominent place in the imagination of another group of Americans who had no reason to celebrate: Africans brought to America as slaves. After adopting Christianity in the evangelical revivals of the eighteenth century, they found the story of Israel's exodus from Egypt particularly poignant. Albert Raboteau observed:

> No single symbol captures more clearly the distinctiveness of Afro-American Christianity than the symbol of Exodus. From the earliest days of colonization, white Christians had represented their journey across the Atlantic to America as the exodus of a New Israel from the bondage of Egypt into the Promised Land of milk and honey. For black Christians, the imagery was reversed: the Middle Passage had

brought them to Egypt land, where they suffered bondage under a new Pharaoh. White Christians saw themselves as the New Israel; slaves identified themselves as the Old.... Identification with Israel, then, gave the slaves a communal identity as a special, divinely favored people. This identity stood in stark contrast with racist propaganda, which depicted them as inferior to whites, as destined by nature and providence to the status of slaves. Exodus, the Promised Land, and Canaan were inextricably linked in the slaves' minds with the idea of freedom. Canaan referred not only to the condition of freedom but also to the territory of freedom—the North or Canada.

Identification with Israel in the exodus became a prominent theme in African-American preaching and music. Black spirituals voiced the pain of bondage and echoed the command of Moses to "Let my people go!" (Box 6.15). The songs and sermons actualized the biblical story as a lens through which African Americans interpreted their experience of slavery.[27]

After the American Civil War, initial celebrations of being emancipated faded as African Americans experienced continuing discrimination, disenfranchisement, and violent oppression. They continued to identify with Israel in Egypt and in the wilderness through the Civil Rights Movement of the 1950s and 1960s. In the most poignant use of the Pentateuch in American rhetoric, Martin Luther King, Jr. evoked Moses' experience from Deuteronomy 34 in his last sermon on April 3, 1968, the day before he was assassinated:

I've been to the mountaintop. And I don't mind. Like anybody, I would like to live a long life. Longevity has its place. But I'm not concerned about that now. I just want to do God's will. And He's allowed me to go up to the mountain. And I've looked over. And I've seen the promised land. I may not get there with you. But I want you to know tonight that we, as a people, will get to the promised land.[28]

American history, then, shows that the evocative power of the exodus story continues to influence politics and religion. It also shows that it can fuel both the self-righteous pride of ruling classes as well as a spirit of resistance among oppressed people.

Other groups have also used the exodus story to resist colonialism and the cultural imperialism that brought the Bible to them in the first place. The Christian tendency to ignore the Pentateuch's purity and offering instructions presents an opportunity to claim ritual practices that are truer to the meaning of

## Box 6.15   "Go Down, Moses"

**African-American spiritual, from ca. 1850s Virginia**

When Israel was in Egypt's land,
let my people go;
oppressed so hard they could
not stand,
let my people go.

*Refrain:*
Go down, (go down)
Moses, (Moses)
way down in Egypt's land;
tell old Pharaoh
to let my people go!

"Thus saith the Lord," bold
Moses said,
let my people go;
"if not, I'll smite your first-born dead,"
let my people go. (*Refrain*)

No more shall they in
bondage toil,
let my people go;
let them come out with Egypt's spoil,
let my people go. (*Refrain*)

We need not always weep and
mourn,
let my people go;
and wear those slavery
chains forlorn,
let my people go. (*Refrain*)

Come, Moses, you will not get lost,
let my people go;
stretch out your rod and
come across,
let my people go. (*Refrain*)

As Israel stood by the water's side,
let my people go;
at God's command it did divide,
let my people go. (*Refrain*)

When they had reached the
other shore,
let my people go;
they sang a song of triumph o'er,
let my people go. (*Refrain*)

O Moses, the cloud shall
cleave the way,
let my people go;
a fire by night, a shade by day,
let my people go. (*Refrain*)

Your foes shall not before you stand,
let my people go;
and you'll possess fair
Canaan's land,
let my people go. (*Refrain*)

This world's a wilderness of woe,
let my people go;
O let us on to Canaan go,
let my people go. (*Refrain*)

O let us all from bondage flee,
let my people go;
and let us all in Christ be free,
let my people go. (*Refrain*)

the biblical text. In nineteenth-century south India, the Hindu Christian Church observed Jewish festivals and pentateuchal purity rules to cleanse Christianity of its Western decadence. In twentieth-century Jamaica, Rastafarians identified with exodus Israel by modeling their purity practices on those of the Nazarites in Numbers 6. Rastafarian preaching also identified the Messiah as the Ethiopian emperor Haile Selassie, who claimed descent from Solomon. African Zionist churches also advocate observance of the Pentateuch's purity regulations. In these communities, acceptance of the Pentateuch's rhetoric of identification with exodus Israel means observing its laws. Doing so allows them to criticize Western Christianity on the basis of the Bible and claim for themselves a more authentic Christian identity as the new Israel.[29]

Some victims of Western colonialism have instead rejected the biblical story of Israel's exodus and settlement in Canaan as a mythic justification for settler colonialism. They have identified with the story's Canaanites, the peoples subjected by conquest, rather than with Israel. At least, that is how scholars like Robert Warrior depicted the choice for Native Americans and how Edward Said described it for Palestinians.[30] Their religious expressions often take the form of rejecting the exodus story and the Bible altogether in favor of an alternative scripture or an indigenous tradition. Many people, such as Christian Palestinians and Christian Native Americans, find themselves identifying with both sides of the story simultaneously. In Israel and Palestine, conflicts over land have drawn attention to the contemporary political consequences of the Bible's stories as well as of historical and archeological research on ancient Israel.

The Pentateuch's rhetoric of identification with exodus Israel has proven to be very effective at shaping Jewish and Christian identities. It has preserved Jewish communities and traditions while fueling Christian persecution of Jews. It has legitimized colonial conquests and inspired resistance to them. Interpreting the Bible's semantic dimension is therefore deeply implicated in many religious and political struggles of both the past and the present.

## 6.7 THE PENTATEUCH BEFORE EZRA

Despite thousands of years of intensive interpretation, the Torah itself does not explicitly recommend ritualizing its semantic dimension. In contrast to its commands to ritualize its iconic and expressive dimensions, nowhere does it emphasize the need to interpret its laws carefully and diligently, much less its stories. Nevertheless, its detailed legal contents and urgent pleas to obey them imply that interpretation is necessary to comply properly. Furthermore, contradictions between key commands require sophisticated ritual and legal interpretation, as do contradictions within and between some of its stories. The need to interpret the Pentateuch, then, arises not just from its scriptural role in religious communities, but also from the nature of its contents.

## 6.7.1  Scribal Experts

Reading and, especially, writing require training. The invention of writing around 5000 years ago was therefore also the beginning of literacy education. Throughout ancient history, literacy skills were taught to only a small percentage of people, mostly boys who were being trained for careers as scribes. Scribes served as secretaries, accountants, and tax collectors. The best scribal jobs were in the bureaucracies of temples and royal courts (Figure 6.4).[31]

The Hebrew Bible features stories about four wise sages who epitomize this scribal ideal: Joseph in Genesis, Mordechai in Esther, and Daniel and Ezra in the books that bear their names. Within the Pentateuch, Joseph exemplifies the wise sage. He is a foreigner who rises from slavery and imprisonment to the top of the Egyptian bureaucracy because of his wise advice to the king. He then uses that position to save his Israelite relatives from famine

**FIGURE 6.4**  A scribe standing before Barrakib, the king of Samal. Relief from Samal/Zincirli, ca. 730 BCE. In the Vorderasiatisches Museum, Berlin.

(Gen. 36–50). Like Mordechai, Daniel, and Ezra, Joseph is so smart that he can serve the foreign king, his own people, and God all faithfully.

The other books of the Pentateuch, however, present a different scribal ideal. The Pentateuch does not say who can copy its text or read its contents. It does, however, specify its official interpreters. A divine oracle to Aaron grants his family the authority to teach Torah to the Israelites and to decide on correct ritual procedures (Lev. 10:10–11). The Pentateuch, then, designates its authoritative interpreters as a hereditary class, the <u>Aaronide priests</u>, rather than a scribal meritocracy. Unlike the stories about Joseph, Mordechai, Daniel, and even the priest-scribe Ezra, the Pentateuch presupposes scribal activity within a temple hierarchy rather than a royal court.

The Pentateuch's ideal scribe is <u>Moses</u>. It portrays Moses writing down the Torah at God's instruction (Exod. 24:4; Deut. 31:9) and repeating it to the Israelites (Exod. 24:7, and all of Deuteronomy). Moses also acts as a priest, making offerings (Exod. 24:4–6), directing the construction of the Tabernacle (Exod. 35–40), and inaugurating Aaron and his sons as priests (Lev. 8).

Interpreters often claim that the Pentateuch depicts the prophet, Moses, as superior to priests by doing their job as well as instructing them how to do it. This dichotomy between <u>priests</u> and <u>prophets</u> ignores the fact that priests, prophets, and scribes are in the Hebrew Bible often the same people. Both Jeremiah and Ezekiel, for example, were priests and prophets (Jer. 1:1; Ezek. 1:3), and Isaiah seems to have worked in the Jerusalem temple (Isa. 6:1). It is Aaron, not Moses, whom YHWH calls a prophet in the confrontation with Pharaoh (Exod. 7:1). The special privileges and responsibilities of Aaron's family include all these roles: the Pentateuch casts Moses as Aaron's younger brother (Exod. 4:14) and the prophet Miriam as their sister (Exod. 15:20). In the Pentateuch, legitimate religious leadership of all kinds is a family affair (Num. 12).

The Pentateuch's model scribe is therefore not Joseph, but Moses. Moses does not serve any human king: unlike Joseph, he humiliates and defeats the Egyptian Pharaoh. Unlike the Bible's other ideal scribes and wisdom literature generally, Moses is very concerned with the ritual practices of the sanctuary. Moses' speech in the book of Deuteronomy does employ wisdom rhetoric about learning and obedience (Deut. 4:1, 9; 5:1; 6:6–9). Near its end, it portrays Moses most fully as a scribe who writes down the Torah, ensures its preservation and publication, and teaches a song to the Israelites to warn them to obey it (Deut. 31:9–13, 22, 24–29).[32]

Exodus and Deuteronomy cast Moses as the model for all later readers, copyists, and interpreters of scripture. In the Hebrew Bible, nobody follows this model more than <u>Ezra</u>, who is presented as an expert scribe, "skilled in the Torah of Moses" (Ezra 7:6). This description links the two scribes through the text they both control, the Torah written down by Moses and read by Ezra. And it casts Moses and Ezra as models to be emulated by future scribes, teachers, and scholars.

## 6.7.2  The Sources of the Pentateuch

The Pentateuch's rhetoric of origins leads listeners and readers to think that what is most important is how it began, in God's revelation of the Torah to Moses at Mount Sinai in the middle of the second millennium BCE. Historians' efforts to establish the Pentateuch's real origins contradict the historical setting of this story, but their theories reproduce the story's emphasis that scripture's origins are important.

Historians in the nineteenth century developed a theory, the <u>Documentary Hypothesis</u>, that distinguished in the text of the Pentateuch four written sources, designated by the letters J, E, P, and D. They distinguished one source by its vocabulary and concern for ritual offerings, festivals, and calendars, so they called it the "priestly" source (P). They regarded Leviticus as completely from P, which also appears in Genesis, Exodus, and Numbers mixed with other material. The not-P material in Genesis divides between texts that refer to the deity by the personal name, *YHWH*, and others that use only *Elohim* "God." Historians therefore labeled them the "Yahwist" (J) and the "Elohist" (E) sources. They thought they had been combined together with P and then with Deuteronomy (D) by one or more editors, also called redactors (R).

According to the Documentary Hypothesis, J and P, and maybe E, originally told the Pentateuch's entire story from creation through Israel's wilderness wandering, reaching perhaps as far as the conquest of the land in the book of Joshua. The Pentateuch often preserves each source's account, sometimes separately and sometimes woven together. So, the P creation story (Gen. 1) precedes JE's story of the Garden of Eden (Gen. 2–3), but P's account of the covenant of Abraham (Gen. 17) follows J's (Gen. 15). The flood story in Genesis 6–8 weaves all three sources together, as indicated by the different counts of the animals – one pair of each species (6:19–20; 7:8–9, 15) or seven pairs of clean species (7:2–3) – and the different calculations for the duration of the flood (7:4, 11–12, 17, 24; 8:3–6, 12–13). Exodus usually mixes different versions of the same story together, such as in the plagues story (Exod. 7–12), but preserves two separate accounts of God revealing the divine name to Moses (J's in 3:13–15; P's in 6:2–8).

The Documentary Hypothesis dominated critical scholarship on the Pentateuch until the late twentieth century. Then increasing numbers of scholars questioned the existence of E and even J, at least as continuous stories stretching the length of the Pentateuch. They still agree that the stories and regulations of the Pentateuch show many signs of different sources and extensive editing. It remains clear that older material has been incorporated in multiple stages to create the Pentateuch as we have it. The major blocks of material, the priestly source (P) and Deuteronomy (D), can still be separated reliably by their literary styles and typical themes over the large scale of the five books. There is also other material that does not come from either P or D, so it is "not-P." The more one focuses on details in individual paragraphs or verses, however, the more subjective these distinctions become. On this smaller scale, it has proven impossible to find criteria by which different interpreters can consistently reconstruct the chronological development of sources and editions.

Many historical critics today think that the Pentateuch, though containing older independent traditions, was brought together only around the time of the exile or in the early Persian period, and continued to be amplified until the Hellenistic period. So, while the Documentary Hypothesis dated the Pentateuch's composition between the tenth and sixth centuries BCE, these models tend to date it later, between the seventh and third centuries. Where previously only P was dated to the Exile or later, now the Pentateuch and most of its component traditions seem to be products of the Babylonian Exile and the Second Temple period.[33]

## 6.7.3   The Pentateuch's Writers and Editors

What can we say with confidence about the Pentateuch's writers? The Pentateuch began to be ritualized as scripture in the time of Ezra in the fifth or fourth centuries BCE. Its largest pieces, P and Deuteronomy, seem to reflect conditions in the Babylonian Exile or early Second Temple period, that is, the sixth and fifth centuries BCE. However, their stories in Exodus, Leviticus, Numbers, and Deuteronomy tell of people, like Moses, Miriam, and Aaron, who lived almost 1000 years earlier. The stories in Genesis, about Abraham, Sarah, and their children and grandchildren, depict an even earlier time. One challenge in interpreting the Pentateuch, then, is whether we can reconstruct the historical development of its stories during that long period of time between the events and the documents that record them.

The influence of wisdom literature on Deuteronomy has led interpreters to contrast the Deuteronomic scribes with the priests of the P (Priestly) source in Exodus, Leviticus, and Numbers. The styles and interests of these two parts of the Pentateuch do diverge by emphasizing wisdom and ritual concerns respectively. But it is wrong to distinguish their writers as scribes and priests, and to describe these two groups as pursuing contrary agendas.

All ancient literature was produced by scribes. They composed some of it and wrote other texts from dictation, but they produced all of it. Competent scribes wrote and copied many different genres. Wisdom literature for scribal schools and ritual texts for temples were just two of the many kinds of texts that they produced. The distinction between wisdom and ritual texts points to the different institutions that used them rather than who wrote them.

Nevertheless, the differences between P and Deuteronomy do indicate that they were produced by two different groups of scribes. The evidence for this is that other biblical books resemble the style and ideas of one or the other pentateuchal source. 2 Kings and Jeremiah match the style of Deuteronomy very closely, while parts of Ezekiel resemble P. Chronicles, Ezra, and Nehemiah show the influence of both P and Deuteronomy. It is therefore very likely that two different groups of scribes produced much of the literature of the Pentateuch and the Prophets in the sixth or fifth centuries BCE. We can date their work by the fact that 2 Kings, Jeremiah, and Ezekiel all relate historical events up to the middle of the sixth century (2 Kgs. 25:22–30; Jer. 40–44; Ezek. 1:1; 40:1). Scribes in the later fifth and fourth centuries, when Ezra-Nehemiah is set, were using both collections. So it was likely in the sixth or fifth century that scribes wrote P and Deuteronomy and then juxtaposed them to create the Pentateuch.

Linguistics confirms this dating. The language of the Pentateuch is the same Hebrew used by the writers of these other books. Languages change over time. Vocabulary and grammar provide clues for dating texts to the time periods when their language was spoken and written. Many scholars currently distinguish classical biblical Hebrew from late biblical Hebrew. They disagree with each other over whether this distinction can be used to date P or not.[34] Be that as it may, biblical literature provides overwhelming evidence that biblical Hebrew, classical and late, was spoken and written in Judea between the eighth and fifth centuries BCE. Scribes in the fourth and third centuries could still compose in the older idiom. But the scribes who wrote the Dead Sea Scrolls after the third century use a later stage of Hebrew. The Hebrew language of the Pentateuch therefore provides solid evidence that it and any written sources and traditions it uses were written between the eighth and the third centuries BCE.

Scribal activities in other ancient cultures show that it is plausible that the Pentateuch was composed from multiple sources that were extensively edited. The different manuscripts of the Babylonian *Gilgamesh Epic* display its revisions and supplementations over more than 1000 years. The different editions of the book of Jeremiah preserved in Hebrew and Greek manuscripts show these processes at work in biblical books. The Dead Sea Scrolls demonstrate the variety of approaches taken by ancient scribes, from faithful reproduction of scriptural books to extensive rewriting of biblical traditions, including the Pentateuch, in works like *Jubilees* and the *Temple Scroll*. Though there is no direct manuscript evidence like this for the editing of the Pentateuch, the manuscripts of these other books provide empirical support for the methods and presuppositions of historical criticism.[35]

Comparative study of scribal practices therefore supports the conclusions of historical critics that the Pentateuch was frequently revised in antiquity. It warns, however, that the nature and extent of those changes become harder to determine as units of analysis become smaller. So, on the one hand, the empirical evidence for ancient scribal practices shows that source- and redaction-critical models of the composition of the Pentateuch are plausible. On the other hand, the lack of manuscript evidence and the pervasiveness of memory variants make it implausible to distinguish sources and editorial layers at the scale of phrases and individual verses, and perhaps even of paragraphs.

Many scholars reject these conclusions. Some continue to defend the outline of the Documentary Hypothesis, even if modifying some of its details. Others challenge the late dating of pentateuchal materials and argue that they were written, if not combined, in the Judean monarchy before the Babylonian Exile. And, of course, many religious conservatives continue to defend Moses' authorship of the whole Pentateuch.

## 6.7.4    External Evidence for Dating the Pentateuch

The search for external evidence to support the Pentateuch's stories has not been very successful. There was much travel and trade between Egypt and the eastern Mediterranean coast throughout the second and first millennia BCE, just as biblical stories indicate (e.g., Gen. 12:10; 47:27). However, archeologists have looked in vain for any signs of Israel's presence in Egypt. Only one second-millennium Egyptian text explicitly mentions Israel. The Merneptah stele from 1208 BCE lists Israel among the people Pharaoh Merneptah defeated:

> *Canaan is plundered, Ashkelon is carried off, and Gezer is captured. Yenoam is made into non-existence; Israel is wasted, its seed is not; and Hurru has become a widow because of Egypt.*[36]

Though historians dismiss Merneptah's claims as propaganda and some doubt that the name is really "Israel," this inscription provides the most plausible evidence outside the Hebrew Bible for the existence of a people calling themselves Israel in the late second millennium.[37]

Biblical interpreters have used details in the story of the exodus from Egypt to try to corroborate the Pentateuch's account. The name of the Egyptian city, "Raʿamses," in Exodus 1:11 echoes the throne names of 11 Egyptian kings from the thirteenth through the eleventh centuries. The names of Moses, Aaron, and Phineas are all Egyptian in origin, rather than Hebrew. These details indicate that Israel's traditions transmitted a genuine memory of Egyptian geography and culture. However, Egyptian trade, politics, and culture remained influential in Israel and Judah throughout the first millennium as well. The Pentateuch's familiarity with the land of Egypt and the Egyptian language does not help date its composition.

The stories of ancestors in Genesis portray a time and place very different from Israel's later history. Nevertheless, they sometimes project first-millennium conditions into stories that are supposed to have taken place in the preceding second millennium, such as the presence of Chaldeans in lower Mesopotamia (Gen. 11:31) and Philistines in Canaan (21:34; 26:1). It is difficult to decide if such anachronisms were produced by later editors of older stories or if the stories themselves come from the times reflected by these references.

Other books of the Hebrew Bible give mixed evidence that pentateuchal traditions were known in the kingdoms of Israel and Judah before the Babylonian Exile. Hosea 12 refers to many episodes in Jacob's life and alludes to the festival of *Sukkot*/Booths (12:9). It also alludes to the exodus from Egypt and to Moses, though without naming him:

*I am YHWH your God from the land of Egypt....*
*By a prophet YHWH brought Israel from Egypt,*
*and by a prophet he was guarded.* (Hos. 12:9, 13; also 11:1)

The books of Samuel and Micah name Moses and Aaron, and once Miriam, as the leaders of Israel's exodus from Egypt (1 Sam. 12:6, 8; Mic. 6:4). Micah also refers to Abraham (Mic. 7:20), the only reference to this ancestor in the pre-exilic prophets. These verses hint that the stories of Jacob and of the exodus were known to Israelites and Judeans prior to the Babylonian Exile. The exilic prophets, Jeremiah, Ezekiel, and Deutero-Isaiah, as well as the Deuteronomistic History, use themes from the exodus and ancestral stories much more often. So, these stories apparently increased in circulation in the sixth century.

The major pentateuchal theme of God giving the Torah to Israel on Mount Sinai, however, is missing from prophetic literature earlier than the sixth century. Some poetic texts depict YHWH as "from Sinai" (Judg. 5:4–5; Ps. 68:9, 18; Deut. 33:2). But the revelation of Torah there or in any other location appears only in texts that reflect the influence of Deuteronomy or P in or after the sixth century. The story of Moses receiving the Torah at Mount Sinai does not seem to have been widely known before the Babylonian Exile, if at all.

These observations suggest that the Pentateuch was composed by editing together independent blocks of tradition, rather than from four continuous sources as the Documentary Hypothesis maintained. Some of these independent traditions were probably known in Israel's monarchic period, such as the stories about Jacob and about Israel's exodus from Egypt. Others do not appear in older texts and were not widely known before the Exile. They may have been composed when the blocks of traditions began to be combined in the sixth and fifth centuries BCE. This later material includes the giving of Torah at Sinai, as well as Genesis' stories of world origins.

Influence from other Middle Eastern literary traditions provides another hint of the historical setting of the Pentateuch's writers. Neo-Assyrian treaties (Box 6.4) shaped the portrayal of the Sinai covenant and its contents (Exod. 19–24; Deuteronomy). The story of Noah's flood (Gen. 6–8) follows the plot of the Mesopotamian flood story closely but modifies it to match Israel's theology, as we can see by comparing it with *Atrahasis* and *Gilgamesh*. The story of the tower of Babel (Gen. 11) comments sarcastically on the characteristic architecture of Mesopotamian cities. P's story of world creation (Gen. 1) also seems to react against widespread stories of creation through reproduction and warfare, such as the Babylonian creation epic, *Enuma Elish*. So the portions of the pentateuchal story that are unparalleled in earlier biblical literature are more likely than others to reflect knowledge of foreign literature.

The beginning of Exodus also uses Mesopotamian literary traditions. The story of the baby Moses being cast adrift on a river and adopted by an Egyptian princess sounds similar to the birth legend of King Sargon of Akkad. Sargon ruled in the third millennium BCE. He was the first Akkadian king to conquer and unite the cities of Mesopotamia, so he was remembered as a model king in later Akkadian literature. An eighth-century Assyrian king even took the name Sargon as his own throne name. He sponsored the reproduction of the birth legend of the earlier Sargon in first-millennium Akkadian texts (Box 6.16). By adopting this storyline for Moses, the writers of Exodus 2:1–10 depict him as destined to defeat powerful enemies. They foreshadow his conflict with Egypt's king, Pharaoh.

Historians cite such parallels to date the composition of these pentateuchal stories to the sixth-century Babylonian Exile. In exile, Judean scribes would have been exposed to Mesopotamian culture and literature (see Figure 6.5). However, the exile lasted longer than the 70 years remembered

## Box 6.16  The birth legend of King Sargon

*My mother, the high priestess, conceived me, she bore me in secret.*
*She placed me in a reed basket, she sealed my hatch with pitch.*
*She left me to the river, whence I could not come up.*
*The river carried me off, it brought me to Aqqi, drawer of water.*
*Aqqi, drawer of water, brought me up as he dipped his bucket.*
*Aqqi, drawer of water, raised me as his adopted son.*
*Aqqi, drawer of water, set (me) to his orchard work.*
*During my orchard work, Ishtar loved me.*[38]

**FIGURE 6.5**    Cuneiform tablet cataloging 68 works of Sumerian literature, probably the collection of a temple library. From Nippur, ca. 2000 BCE. In the Louvre, Paris.

by biblical tradition. Northern Israelites were exiled already by the Assyrians in 701 BCE. For the next four centuries, Judah existed in dependence on Mesopotamian empires and, briefly, on Egypt. Judean scribes had many opportunities to learn about those traditions. Nevertheless, the Pentateuch's knowledge of other cultures and literatures is more noticeable in the creation and Sinai stories that are not reflected in older biblical literature. This observation reinforces the impression that they date from the sixth and fifth centuries BCE when Judea was ruled by the Babylonians and Persians.

### 6.7.5    The Composition of the Pentateuch

The way in which editors assembled the Pentateuch is evident from themes that structure the five books. One way that editors organized the Pentateuch, and especially Genesis, was with genealogies. Even world creation gets a genealogical summary:

> *These are the generations of the heavens and the earth when they were created.* (Gen. 2:4)

Each of the following cycles of stories begins with genealogies, called *toledot* in Hebrew (see Box 3.2). The genealogies of Genesis provide an editorial framework around material from diverse sources.[39] The Book of Exodus also begins by evoking this genealogical history (Exod. 1:1–6). Numbers carries it further by listing the generation of Israelite men who followed Moses out of Egypt (Num. 1, 3–4) and, later, the next generation born in the wilderness (Num. 26).[40] The Pentateuch's story of Israel's origin is thus arranged across four generations of ancestors in Genesis and two wilderness generations in Exodus, Leviticus, Numbers, and Deuteronomy.

Editors also used God's promises to the ancestors to unite the stories of Genesis with the rest of the Pentateuch. God swore to give the land to the descendants of Abraham, Isaac, and Jacob according to Genesis 50:24, Exodus 32:13, 33:1, Numbers 32:11, and Deuteronomy 34:4. Though this promise plays a major role in the structure of some chapters (e.g., Gen. 15, 17), in many other places it looks like an editorial addition that links materials together (e.g., Gen. 12:1–3; 26:2–5; 35:11–12). Exodus then cites the promise to the ancestors as motivating God's rescue of Israel from Egypt, thus linking stories about ancestors and exodus together (Exod. 2:24; 6:8; 32:13).

What is clear is that the combined Pentateuch emphasizes the origins of Torah in ancient tablets given by God to Moses and deposited in Israel's Ark of the Covenant. It also claims that Moses wrote a Torah scroll that Israel

> **Box 6.17   Ritualizing Decalogue and Torah in Pentateuchal sources**
>
> *From P*: Exod. 25, 31, 37
> *From not-P*: Exod. 24, 32, 34
> *From D*: Deut. 5, 10, 31

also kept beside the Ark. These claims are made by all three blocks of pentateuchal materials: P, not-P, and D (see Box 6.17). So though the story of Torah at Sinai is not found in other biblical books older than Deuteronomy and P, it forms a common foundation between the three blocks of pentateuchal traditions. Deuteronomy also requires the iconic and expressive ritualization of Torah explicitly, and the semantic dimension implicitly, in ways that later became characteristic of religious scriptures. As a result, the Pentateuch proclaims the supernatural origins of Torah by both modeling and requiring its iconic, expressive, and semantic ritualization.

So, in an important sense, scripture did begin with the story of Moses receiving the Torah on Mount Sinai. Though we cannot trace the events it narrates back to the time of Moses, we can trace the ritual practices it so vividly describes to the time of Ezra. By showing Moses enshrining Torah in the ark and reading it to the Israelites, receiving their unanimous agreement to its commandments, and demanding that they obey them, the story of Moses and Israel at Mount Sinai inscribed how to ritualize scripture into Jewish and Christian imaginations. This story has functioned ever since Ezra's time to ground their scriptural practices in ritual behavior that Deuteronomy also explicitly commands. In this story and these commandments lie the origins of Western scriptures.

## Summary of Part 1, The Torah

Religious communities distinguish books as scriptures by ritualizing them in all three dimensions (see Sections 1.1 and 1.2). Jewish tradition has focused its ritual attention mostly on the Torah, also called the Pentateuch, which contains the first five books of the Tanak/Old Testament.

In ritualizing scripture's iconic dimension, the Torah scroll gets paraded and displayed in synagogues. Its distinctive form as a manuscript scroll made of parchment, wrapped in cloth and stored in the arks of synagogues, distinguishes torahs and a few other biblical scrolls from all other books. The presence of a torah legitimizes a synagogue as Jewish sacred space. The Torah itself commands its iconic ritualization in amulets, inscriptions, and most dramatically by depositing the tablets of the law in the Ark of the Covenant, with the Torah scroll beside it.

In ritualizing scripture's expressive dimension, every year Jews read the whole Torah aloud in Hebrew in synagogue services. Other texts of scripture get read piece-meal to match the Torah reading. The sound of the chanted Torah reading and of the Hebrew and Aramaic prayers inspires feelings of devotion and marks the ritual as a Jewish worship service. Deuteronomy already requires ritualized reading of the Torah to all Israel every seven years.

In ritualizing scripture's semantic dimensions, the Torah is the subject of synagogue sermons, as well as of study groups, written commentaries, and legal interpretation. By these means, Jews and Samaritans, as well as many Christians, have internalized the Torah's rhetoric to identify themselves with Israel in covenant with God. Jews use other books of the Tanak to interpret the Torah, as well as the Mishnah and Talmud and other ancient rabbinic literature, medieval commentaries, and the interpretations of recent rabbis. The meaning of the Torah, then, gets expressed within the history of Jewish interpretation, which gains authority from its roots in the Torah. Historical criticism also studies these roots and wonders how old these stories really are. Many Jews have now incorporated modern historical debates about the Torah's origins into their tradition.

## CITED WORKS AND FURTHER READING


1   From the tomb of Intef, translated by Miriam Lichtheim, *Ancient Egyptian Literature* (Berkeley: University of California, 1973), 1: 197.

2   The Hebrew word, *hebel* "worthless," can also be translated "in vain" or "empty."

3   See further, Stuart Weeks, *An Introduction to the Study of Wisdom Literature* (London: T. & T. Clark, 2010); Athalya Brenner and Carole Fontaine, eds., *Wisdom and Psalms: A Feminist Companion to the Bible*, (Sheffield: Sheffield Academic Press, 1998); John Jarick, ed., *Perspectives on Israelite Wisdom* (London: T. & T. Clark, 2016).

4   On the Hasmonean influence on scripturalization, see especially David Carr, *Writing on the Tablet of the Heart: Origins of Scripture and Literature* (Oxford: Oxford University Press, 2005), 253–275.

5 For translations of Esarhaddon's Succession Treaty, see Jacob Lauinger, "Esarhaddon's Succession Treaty at Tell Tayinat: Text and Commentary," *Journal of Cuneiform Studies* 64 (2012), 112–113; and Simo Parpola and Kazuko Watanabe, eds., *Neo-Assyrian Treaties and Loyalty Oaths*, State Archives of Assyria, vol. 2 (Helsinki: Helsinki University Press, 1988), text 5, line 1; text 6, lines 1 and 283.

6 On ancient suzerainty treaties and the Pentateuch, see Bernard M. Levinson, "Esarhaddon's Succession Treaty as the Source for the Canon Formula in Deuteronomy 13:1," *Journal of the American Oriental Society* 130 (2010), 337–347.

7 For translation and discussion of the Weidner Chronicle, see Jean-Jacques Glassner, *Mesopotamian Chronicles* (Atlanta: SBL, 2004), 263–269. On ancient Near Eastern rhetoric of divine punishment of kings, see James W. Watts, "Ritual Rhetoric in Ancient Near Eastern Texts," in *Ancient Non-Greek Rhetorics* (ed. C. Lipson and R. Binckley; West Lafayette, IN: Parlor Press, 2009), 39–66.

8 For further readings about ancient apocalyptic thought and literature, see the essays in John J. Collins, ed., *The Oxford Handbook of Apocalyptic Literature* (Oxford: Oxford University Press, 2014).

9 For a convenient anthology of ancient Jewish and Christian apocalypses, see Mitchell Reddish, *Apocalyptic Literature: A Reader* (Peabody, MA: Hendrickson, 2015).

10 See David Charles Kraemer, *Responses to Suffering in Classical Rabbinic Literature* (Oxford: Oxford University Press, 1995), 56, 212–213.

11 On readers' assumptions when interpreting scriptures, see James L. Kugel, *The Bible as It Was* (Cambridge, MA: Belknap, 1997), 14–23.

12 On the rhetoric of lists, see J. D. O'Banion, *Reorienting Rhetoric: The Dialectic of List and Story* (University Park, PA: Pennsylvania State University Press, 1992), quotation from p. 12; Cornelia Vismann, *Files: Law and Media Technology* (tr. G. Winthrop-Young; Stanford: Stanford University Press, 2008; German 2000), quotation from p. 6; Jonathan Z. Smith, "Sacred Persistence: Toward a Redescription of Canon," in *Imagining Religion: From Babylon to Jonestown* (Chicago: University of Chicago Press, 1982), 36–52, quotation from p. 44; and Jack Goody, *The Logic of Writing and the Organization of Society* (Cambridge: Cambridge University Press, 1986), 42–121.

13 On the devotional shaping of the Psalter, see J. Clinton McCann, Jr., "The Shape and Shaping of the Psalter: Psalms in Their Literary Context," in *The Oxford Handbook of the Psalms* (ed. W. P. Brown; Oxford: Oxford University Press, 2014).

14 On inset psalms shaping narratives for use as scripture, see James W. Watts, *Psalm and Story: Inset Hymns in Hebrew Narrative,* JSOTSup 139 (Sheffield: Sheffield Academic Press, 1992).

15 On the figure of Ezra in history, in the Bible, and in later traditions, see Lisbeth S. Fried, *Ezra and the Law in History and Tradition* (Columbia, SC: University of South Carolina Press, 2014).

16 See James Kugel, "Levi's Elevation to the Priesthood in Second Temple Writings," *Harvard Theological Review* 86/1 (1993), 1–64; and Hindy Najman, "Interpretation as Primordial Writing: Jubilees and Its Authority Conferring Strategies," *Journal for the Study of Judaism* 30 (1999), 379–410.

17 For the translation of excerpts from *4QMMT,* see Florentino García Martínez, *The Dead Sea Scrolls Translated* (Leiden: Brill, 1994), 77–79; and Elisha Qimron and John Strugnell, *Qumran Cave 4: V, Miq at Maʿaśe ha-Torah* (Discoveries in the Judean Desert 10; Oxford: Clarendon, 1994), 45–63.

18 On Judah *ha-Nasi* and the Mishnah, see Stephen G. Wald, "Judah Ha-Nasi," *Encyclopaedia Judaica* (2 ed. 2007), 11:501–505; William Scott Green, *Persons and Institutions in Early Rabbinic Judaism* (Atlanta: Scholars Press, 1977); and Aharon Oppenheimer, *Rabbi Judah ha-Nasi* (Tübingen: Mohr Siebeck, 2017).

19 For the translation of Genesis Rabbah, see H. Freedman and Maurice Simon, *Midrash Rabbah Translated into English,* 10 vols. (London: Soncino, 1931).

20 On the rabbis in Late Antique synagogues, see Michael D. Swartz, "Sage, Priest, and Poet: Typologies of Religious Leadership in the Ancient Synagogue," in *Jews, Christians, and Polytheists in the Ancient Synagogue* (ed. Steven Fine; New York: Routledge, 1999), 101–117.

21 On medieval Jewish interpretation, see Barry D. Walfish, "An Introduction to Medieval Jewish Biblical Interpretation," in *With Reverence for the Word: Medieval Scriptural Exegesis in Judaism, Christianity, and Islam* (ed. J. D. McAuliffe; Oxford: Oxford University Press, 2003), 3–12.

22 On the standardization of ritual texts, see Russell Hobson, *Transforming Literature into Scripture: Texts as Cult Objects at Nineveh and Qumran* (Sheffield: Equinox, 2012).

23 On the Exodus story in Zionism, see Ariah Saposnik, "The Desert Comes to Zion: A Narrative Ends Its Wandering," in *Exodus in the Jewish Experience: Echoes and Reverberations* (ed. P. Barmash and W. David Nelson; Lanham, MD: Lexington, 2015), 213–246.

24 David W. Kling, *The Bible in History: How the Texts Have Shaped the Times* (Oxford: Oxford University Press, 2004), 193–229, quotation from pp. 195–196.

25 See John Binns, *The Orthodox Church of Ethiopia: A History,* (London: Bloomsbury, 2016); and Steven Kaplan, *The Beta Israel (Falasha) in Ethiopia: From Earliest Times to the Twentieth Century* (New York: New York University Press, 1995).

26 On the exodus story for Americans, see Conrad Cherry, *God's New Israel: Religious Interpretations of American Destiny* (Englewood Cliffs, NJ: Prentice-Hall, 1971); and John Winthrop, "A Modell of Christian Charity," in *Winthrop Papers* (Boston: Massachusetts Historical Society, 1931), 2: 282–284, 292–295.

27 On the exodus story for African Americans, see Albert Raboteau, "African-Americans, Exodus, and the American Israel," in *African-American Christianity* (ed. P. E. Johnson; Berkeley: University of California, 1994), 1–17, quotations from pp. 9 and 13–14; and Herbert Robinson Marbury, *Pillars of Cloud and Fire: The Politics of Exodus in African American Biblical Interpretation* (New York: NYU Press, 2015).

28 For the last speech of Martin Luther King, Jr., see Keith D. Miller, *Martin Luther King's Biblical Epic: His Final, Great Speech* (Jackson, MS: University Press of Mississippi, 2011), Appendix 1.

29 On colonial and post-colonial Christian identification with Israel, see R. S. Sugirtharajah, *The Bible and the Third World: Precolonial, Colonial and Postcolonial Encounters* (Cambridge: Cambridge University Press, 2001); R. S. Sugirtharajah, *The Bible and Empire: Postcolonial Explorations* (Cambridge: Cambridge University Press, 2005); and Philip Jenkins, *The New Faces of Christianity: Believing the Bible in the Global South* (Oxford: Oxford University Press, 2006).

30 On identifying with the Canaanites, see Edward W. Said, "Michael Walzer's *Exodus and Revolution*: A Canaanite Reading," in *Blaming the Victims: Spurious Scholarship and the Palestinian Question* (ed. E. W. Said and C. Hitchens; New York: Verso, 1988), 151–178; and Robert Warrior, "Canaanites, Cowboys, and Indians: Deliverance, Conquest, and Liberation Theology," *Christianity and Crisis* 29 (1989), 261–265.

31 On scribal expertise in the ancient world, see David M. Carr, *Writing on the Tablet of the Heart: Origins of Scripture and Literature* (Oxford: Oxford University Press, 2005).

32 On wisdom literature's influence on Deuteronomy, see Moshe Weinfeld, *Deuteronomy and the Deuteronomic School* (Winona Lake, IN: Eisenbrauns, 1972).

33 On late twentieth-century historical criticism, see David M. Carr, "Changes in Pentateuchal Criticism," in *Hebrew Bible/Old Testament: The History of Its Interpretation 3/2* (ed. M. Saebø; Berlin: Vandenhoeck & Ruprecht, 2015), 433–466.

34 On linguistic dating of biblical books, compare Avi Hurvitz, *A Concise Lexicon of Late Biblical Hebrew* (Leiden: Brill, 2014), with Ian Young, Robert Resetko, and Martin Ehrensvärd, *Linguistic Dating of Biblical Texts*, 2 vols. (London: Equinox, 2008).

35 On empirical evidence for historical criticism, see Jeffrey H. Tigay, *Empirical Models for Biblical Criticism* (Philadelphia: University of Pennsylvania, 1985).

36 The translation of the Merneptah Stele is by James K. Hoffmeier in *The Context of Scripture* (ed. W. Hallo; Leiden: Brill, 2003), 2.6.

37 On reconstructing the early history of Israel, see the essays in John Day, *In Search of Pre-Exilic Israel* (London: T. & T. Clark, 2004).

38 The birth legend of King Sargon was translated by Benjamin R. Foster in *The Context of Scripture* (ed. W. Hallo; Leiden: Brill, 2003), 1.133.

39 On the composition of Genesis and its connection to the Pentateuch, see Konrad Schmid, "Genesis in the Pentateuch," in *The Book of Genesis: Composition, Reception and Interpretation* (ed. C. A. Evans, J. N. Lohr, and D. L. Peterson; Leiden: Brill, 2012), 27–50; or Konrad Schmid, *Genesis and the Moses Story: Israel's Dual Origins in the Hebrew Bible* (Winona Lake, IN: Eisenbrauns, 2010).

40 On the genealogical structure of Numbers, see Dennis Olsen, *The Death of the Old and the Birth of the New: The Framework of the Book of Numbers and the Pentateuch* (Chico, CA: Scholars Press, 1985).

# PART 2

# THE GOSPELS AS A SCRIPTURE

This exploration of the Gospels as a scripture presupposes the ideas about ritualizing scriptures and about the scriptures and history of ancient Israel and Second Temple Judaism described in Part 1. It therefore begins immediately with the life and teachings of Jesus and Paul, and the rhetoric of the New Testament Gospels. This discussion sets the stage for describing the ritualization of the Gospels in the iconic, expressive, and semantic dimensions in later Christian traditions, and also their formation in early Christianity.

# CHAPTER 7

# Rhetoric About Jesus

Christianity focuses its religious attention especially on one person, Jesus Christ. Where Judaism emphasizes the Torah and how it mediates the relationship between God and Israel, Christianity teaches that Jesus mediates the divine–human relationship. Christian scriptures play a secondary role to Christ by testifying to Christ's mediation.

The comparative study of religions highlights this Christian tendency. Christians' focus on Jesus distinguishes their religion from its sibling religions, Judaism and Islam. Though Moses is very important to Jews and Mohammed even more important to Muslims, both prophets owe their status to the greater importance of the scriptures that they conveyed, the Torah and the Qur'an respectively. For Christians, it is Jesus who is most important. The Christian Bible is important because it testifies to Jesus Christ. Among Asian religions, Buddhism also stands out for the great importance it ascribes to one person, Siddhartha, the sixth-century BCE teacher whom it reveres as the Buddha. Like the Christian Bible, Buddhist scriptures gain their importance from the belief that they accurately convey the Buddha's teachings.

Because of the way in which Christians conceive of their scripture as testifying to Christ, we begin our discussion of Christian scripture by first focusing on the figure of Jesus.

## 7.1    JESUS IN THE GOSPELS

Christian bibles contain four books that narrate Jesus' life. They are called gospels, the Gospels of Matthew, Mark, Luke, and John. Later, we will study their structure and their differences from each other. But it is important to learn the basic story that they tell to understand Christianity. So here is a general summary of the story of Jesus in the four Gospels. (Most of this information appears in all four Gospels, but I will cite only one reference at a time, usually from Mark.)

The Gospels narrate events that they date during the time when Pontius Pilate was the Roman governor of Judea (Mark 15:1), which we know from other sources was from 26 to 36 CE. Jesus came from Nazareth in Galilee, which is in the northern part of Jewish territory (Mark 1:9). John the Baptist, an apocalyptic prophet, baptized him, that is, he immersed Jesus in water as a sign of purification (Mark 1:9). This act suggests that Jesus may have joined John's movement. But the Gospels insist instead that Jesus was already God's son at his baptism (Mark 1:11) and that John recognized this (John 1:19–42).

Jesus worked as an itinerant rabbi. In other words, he was a religious teacher who traveled from town to town. He may have done so for as long as three years, since John's Gospel mentions three Passovers (John 2:13; 6:4; 12:1). The narratives of Mark's Gospels could fit within just one year. Jesus frequently healed people and exorcized their demons. His reputation as a healer drew crowds of people to him (Mark 3 :7–10).

Jesus was followed around by a group of women and men who learned from him and supported his work. They are conventionally called disciples in English to translate the Greek word *mathetes*, which simply means "student." Jesus called on all his disciples to follow him, by which he meant for them to imitate him (Matt. 16:24). He singled out a core group of disciples consisting of 12 men (Mark 3:13–19). The number 12 probably symbolized the 12 tribes of Israel, thus showing that Jesus was calling all Israel to follow him.

The Gospels interpret Jesus' healings as signs of Jesus' compassion for everyone (Mark 1:41). Jesus himself interpreted them as signs of the kingdom of God, that is, as evidence that God's supernatural power is breaking into human history (Mark 1:15). The coming of the kingdom of God is the central theme of Jesus' public preaching in Matthew, Mark, and Luke. In John's Gospel, Jesus speaks more about himself as the mediator between God and humanity (John 5).

The Gospels apply a range of titles to Jesus. People in the story frequently call him "rabbi" (Mark 9:5), a common title of respect for Jewish religious teachers. Jesus most frequently refers to himself as "the human" (literally, "the son of man") in Matthew, Mark, and Luke. This title may simply be a common self-reference, but it may also evoke apocalyptic expectations (Dan. 7:13). The Gospels teach that Jesus is also (i) the Messiah or Christ and (ii) the son of God (Mark 1:1; see Boxes 7.1 and 7.2). John's Gospel also portrays Jesus as the embodiment of God's wisdom, the *logos* "word" (John 1:1), who is able to use God's divine name, the emphatic *ego eimi* "I (truly) am" (John 8:28, 58; cf. Exod. 3:14).

According to the Gospels, Jesus came into conflict with other Jewish religious teachers. His concern for morality rather than pollution gave him a reputation for being lax about maintaining purity rules (Mark 7). He challenged the oral torah of the Pharisees (see Box 7.3) and substituted his own tradition of interpretation (Matt. 5:21–48; 7:29). He predicted the destruction of the Temple in Jerusalem, which made the priests and Sadducees suspect his political goals (Mark 11:15–18). His preaching about the kingdom of God made supporters and opponents alike wonder if he was claiming to be the Messiah – a claim with political as well as religious implications.

Though Jesus was most critical of the Pharisees, it was the Temple's high priest who arrested him. The Roman governor then ordered his execution by Roman soldiers on a charge of treason against Rome (Mark 15:16–20). You may wonder why Jesus posed a threat to the Romans, since the Gospels insist that Jesus avoided criticizing Rome (Mark 12:13-17). The Gospels show the

## Box 7.1  Messiah/Christ

The Hebrew word *meshiach* is transliterated "messiah" in English. It means "the one who is anointed (with oil)." Greek translates this term with *christos*, which is transliterated into English as "christ." So, messiah and christ both mean "the anointed one."

Messiah is a royal title in the Hebrew Bible because the Israelites inaugurated new kings by anointing them with oil. The kings of Judah were called "the messiah" (1 Sam. 24:6) and so was the high priest (Lev. 4:3). But because Jews expected God to restore the kingdom of David in the future, "the Messiah" came to represent their apocalyptic hopes for a future king who would save Israel from its enemies and bring God's kingdom to earth. By calling him "the Messiah/Christ," the New Testament claims that Jesus will fulfill these expectations.

## Box 7.2   Son of God

The phrase <u>son of God</u> was a royal title in ancient Israel (Ps. 2:7) and in Hellenistic culture, where it was claimed by Greek kings and Roman emperors. Mark's application of the phrase to Jesus might use these political meanings (1:11; 9:7; 15:39). Hellenistic culture also celebrated superheroes like Hercules as sons of a god and a human mother. Matthew and Luke's description of Jesus' virgin birth resembles this idea (Matt. 1:20; Luke 1:34–35). The Hebrew Bible also uses "sons or children of God" to describe the supernatural beings around God in heaven (Job 1:6; Ps. 82:6). John's description of Jesus as existing before the world and assisting in its creation (John 1:1–3; cf. Prov. 8:22–31) evokes these supernatural beings and even surpasses them.

The Gospels do not explain clearly how this range of meanings of "son of God" applies to Jesus. This ambiguity stimulated the development of many theological explanations over the following centuries and millennia. In the fourth century, Catholic and Orthodox churches settled on the belief that Jesus is both fully human and fully divine. That remains the official teaching of most Christian denominations today, together with the doctrine of the <u>Trinity</u>, that the Father, the Son (Jesus Christ), and the Holy Spirit are "one God in three persons."

## Box 7.3   Religious parties in late Second Temple Judaism

In the Hasmonean and Roman periods, Jewish religious leaders were divided into at least three rival parties, according to Philo, Josephus, and the New Testament.[1]

Many priests identified as <u>Sadducees</u>, who emphasized literal interpretation of the Torah and the importance of temple rituals. High priests and other aristocrats were often Sadducees. This party lost its power base in the temple when it was destroyed by the Romans in 70 CE.

Many Torah teachers identified as <u>Pharisees</u>. They taught their own tradition for interpreting Torah to enable people to fulfill God's commandments in changing circumstances. After the wars against Rome in 70 and 135 CE, Jewish congregations increasingly looked to Pharisaic rabbis for religious leadership. The Pharisees' "oral torah" became the basis for the literature of Rabbinic Judaism in the following centuries (see Section 6.5.2).

Another group, the Essenes, emphasized very strict interpretations of the Torah, especially about rituals and purity practices. At least some of them seem to have segregated themselves from the rest of Jewish society. The Qumran community may have been an Essene community, and Essenes probably wrote many of the sectarian texts among the Dead Sea Scrolls.

The earliest Christians thought of themselves as one more Jewish religious party. They resembled the Pharisees. Jesus traveled around with his disciples, just like Pharisaic rabbis did. Paul explicitly identified himself as a Pharisee (Phil. 3:5). Yet the Gospels portray the Pharisees as Jesus' fiercest rivals, probably because these two similar movements competed for the same followers.

Roman governor, Pontius Pilate, finding no fault with Jesus but bowing to the wishes of the high priest and the Jerusalem crowds (Mark 15:1–15). This portrait of Pilate contrasts with his reputation in Jewish first-century texts by Philo and Josephus. They portray him as ruthlessly disregarding Jewish religious concerns.

The Romans crucified Jesus – that is, they hung him naked on a wooden crossbeam to die of exhaustion, exposure, and asphyxiation. Crucifixion was a method of public humiliation as well as execution. The Romans crucified their enemies as a warning against rebellion to everyone else. Pilate made that point explicit by placing a sarcastic sign on Jesus' cross that read in three languages "The King of the Jews" (Mark 15:26).

The New Testament Gospels, however, maintain that God wanted Jesus to die this way and that Jesus accepted his fate voluntarily (Mark 14:36). Jesus predicts his execution long in advance (Mark 10:33–34). He goes to Jerusalem for this purpose and resists his disciples' efforts to change his mind (8:31–33). The Gospels insist that Jesus had to die to bring God's forgiveness to humankind (Luke 24:45). Their stories therefore operate at two levels: they tell a story about a Galilean preacher executed by the Romans and interpret it as the story of the son of God who came to earth to die for the sake of others.

They also claim that God raised Jesus from the dead. The Gospels do not narrate how the resurrection took place. Instead they tell how some of his women disciples discovered his tomb empty (Mark 16:1–8) and that

Jesus then appeared to many of his disciples over a period of 40 days (Matt. 28; Luke 24; John 20–21). They end by proclaiming that Jesus is alive and present with his followers, either personally ("I am with you always" Matt. 28:20) or through the Holy Spirit (Luke 24:49).

## 7.2  PAUL'S TEACHINGS ABOUT JESUS CHRIST

The Gospels are not the oldest texts about Jesus. Our oldest sources are instead letters written by the apostle Paul.

We have more primary sources about the life of Paul than we do for Jesus. Most importantly, we have at least seven <u>letters</u> written by Paul himself. The letter to the Galatians narrates aspects of his own life, providing a kind of autobiography (Gal. 1–2), and other letters make occasional autobiographical references. In addition, half of the <u>book of Acts</u> narrates Paul's career as an apostle. It may have been written by a friend of his.

### 7.2.1  Paul's Career

<u>Paul</u> was a Jewish man who went by the Greek name *Paulos* "Paul" when speaking Greek and by the Hebrew name *Sha'ul* "Saul" when speaking Aramaic (Acts 13:9). He was born in Tarsus, a city in southern Asia Minor (now Turkey) whose residents benefited from Roman citizenship, a relatively rare privilege. Paul received a good rabbinic education which qualified him to identify as a Pharisee (Phil. 3:5–6; Acts 23:6). Acts 22:3 says his teacher was Gamaliel the Younger, a leading rabbi of the mid-first century CE. Paul's letters demonstrate that he also received a Greek education that taught him how to employ classical rhetoric and to quote some of the Greek poets (1 Cor. 15:33; Acts 17:28).

Paul, then, was a Hellenistic Jew, a Pharisee, and a Roman citizen. He held a relatively privileged position in both Hellenistic and Jewish society. And that is how Acts first portrays him, as a rising young Pharisee assisting in the lynching of early Christians in Jerusalem (Acts 7:58–8:1). Paul's autobiographical comments confirm his depiction in Acts as a persecutor of Christians (Gal. 1:13–14; Acts 9:1–2).

On a trip to Damascus, Paul had an experience that changed the direction of his life. Paul himself says simply that God "who had set me apart before I was born and called me through his grace, was pleased to reveal his son to me" (Gal. 1:15–16 NRSV; also 1 Cor. 15:8). Acts 9 tells a more elaborate story: a light from heaven blinded Paul so he fell off his horse. He heard Jesus' voice asking "Why do you persecute me?" (9:4). His companions took him to

Damascus where a Christian leader healed his eyesight. Paul then began to proclaim Jesus as the Messiah/Christ.

This account has echoed through Christian history as the paradigmatic *conversion* story. However, though Paul committed his life from this point forward to converting gentiles (non-Jews) to follow Jesus as Messiah/Christ, he never described himself as a convert. He instead described his experience as a calling to preach God's gospel about Jesus Christ (Rom. 1:1–6), like the Israelite prophets who were called to proclaim God's messages (Exod. 3; Isa. 6; Jer. 1). Paul thought Jesus had called him to be Christ's *apostolos* (transliterated in English as apostle), which means "messenger" and "ambassador." He introduced himself by this title in most of his letters. In his own mind, Paul remained a Jewish Pharisee who had been called by God to proclaim the gospel message of Jesus as the Messiah/Christ, and to do so especially to gentiles.

Paul traveled through Asia Minor, Macedonia, and Greece, preaching the gospel and founding house churches. He would usually start by preaching in local synagogues or in open markets. Once he had gathered a group of followers, meetings would take place in the homes of the wealthier members. Then Paul would move on to another town and start over again. In order to keep in touch with the churches that he founded, Paul wrote letters to his churches to explain aspects of Christian doctrine and to advise them about problems in their churches. That is why the New Testament writings of Paul consist of letters.

Letter writing in most cultures follows standard formats and styles. Paul's letters follow standard Greek letter style, consisting of (i) the names of the sender and recipients, (ii) greetings and thanksgiving for the recipients, (iii) the body of the letter that addresses the main subject, and (iv) concluding greetings and prayers on behalf of the recipients.

Paul often elaborated on each of these elements. For example, he attached the title "apostle" to his name and often described his calling from God. He addressed most of his letters to "all the saints," which meant all the Christians in a particular town. Paul also usually divided the main body of his letters into (i) discussions of beliefs or practices important to that congregation, and then (ii) exhortations to behave morally with each other and with outsiders.

Paul was a controversial figure both among Christians and with Jewish leaders. His preaching in local towns frequently created conflicts within synagogues (Acts 18:1–17) and with local business and civic leaders (Acts 19:23–41). Among Christians, he challenged the belief that gentiles must convert to Judaism to become Christians (see Section 14.1.2). This brought him into conflict with the apostle Peter and with James, who was the brother of Jesus and the leader of the church in Jerusalem. There, a meeting between these leaders reached a compromise solution (Acts 15; Gal. 2:1–10).

Some years later, Paul raised money from his churches to bring relief to those suffering from a famine in Judea (Rom. 15:25–28). When he brought the money to Jerusalem, he decided to undergo a week-long purification ritual in the Temple in order to prove that he was still an observant Jew. However, a rumor spread that Paul had brought a gentile into the inner Temple courts. This rumor caused a riot. Roman soldiers dispersed the rioters and arrested Paul (Acts 21:20–36). When the Temple priests asked for Paul to be turned over to them for trial, Paul exercised his right as a Roman citizen to appeal his case directly to the Roman emperor (Acts 25–26). The governor therefore sent him to Rome. The last scene of the book of Acts shows Paul in Rome under house arrest, preaching to all-comers while waiting for his case to be heard (Acts 28:16–31).[2]

## 7.2.2　Paul About Jesus

Paul's letters were written in the 50s of the first century CE, around 20 years after Jesus' crucifixion and before the stories and teachings of Jesus were written down in the Gospels. Paul's letters are therefore the earliest Christian documents and the oldest books in the New Testament. They interpret the semantic meaning of the oral tradition about Jesus, which had not yet been written down.

Paul called Jesus "the <u>Christ</u>," which is Greek for "the Messiah" (see Box 7.1). So he thought that Jesus fulfilled the Jewish hope for a coming king (Messiah) who would rescue the people. Paul also called Jesus *kurios* "<u>Lord</u>." This title replaces the divine name, YHWH, in the Greek translation of the Hebrew Bible, a translation that Paul often quoted. *Kurios* "Lord" was also a typical title of Greek and Roman kings. Paul used both the religious and political meanings of these terms when portraying Jesus as the liberating hope for all humankind. He expected Jesus to fulfill these apocalyptic expectations when Christ returns from heaven to earth to bring about the resurrection of the dead and the judgment of the dead (1 Thess. 4:13–5:11). Paul thought this might happen during his lifetime ("then we who are alive" 4:17).

For Paul, what was most important about Jesus was his death and resurrection. Paul quoted Jesus' words at his last supper with his disciples to identify him with the Passover sacrifice:

> *I received a tradition from the Lord, which I also handed on to you: on the night on which he was betrayed, the Lord Jesus took bread. After giving thanks, he broke it and said, "This is my body which is for you;*

*do this to remember me." He did the same thing with the cup, after they had eaten, saying, "This cup is the new covenant in my blood. Every time you drink it, do this to remember me." Every time you eat this bread and drink the cup, you broadcast the death of the Lord until he comes.* (1 Cor. 11:23–26 CEB)

This text shows that the earliest Christians were interpreting Jesus' life and, especially, his death by regularly celebrating together the ritual of Communion (also known as the Eucharist or the Lord's Supper).

Paul's letters provide our earliest interpretations of Jesus' role and significance (see further in Sections 11.1, 11.5, 14.1, 14.1.2). But they do not narrate Jesus' story. For that, we must read the Gospels.

## CITED WORKS AND FURTHER READING

1 For more about religious parties in the late Second Temple period, see Lawrence H. Schiffman, *From Text to Tradition: A History of Second Temple and Rabbinic Judaism* (Hoboken: KTAV, 1991), 98–119.

2 For more about Paul and his letters, see Morna Dorothy Hooker, *Paul: A Short Introduction* (Oxford: OneWorld, 2003); and David G. Horrell, *An Introduction to the Study of Paul* (London: Bloomsbury, 2015).

# CHAPTER 8

# The Rhetoric of the Gospels

Christian claims about Jesus are based mostly on the four Gospels in the New Testament. The word <u>gospel</u> translates the Greek word *euangelion*, which means "good news." English words like "evangelism" and "evangelical" come from this Greek word. The Gospel According to Mark starts by describing itself with this word:

> *The beginning of the euangelion (good news/gospel) of Jesus Christ, the Son of God.* (1:1)

Other ancient written accounts of Jesus are called gospels, too.

In Mark, "the gospel" refers to two related but different things. It refers to the message taught by Jesus (1:14) and also to the Christian message about Jesus, which is conveyed by the book as a whole.

## 8.1   THE GOSPEL ACCORDING TO MARK

Mark's Gospel gives no background about Jesus' family or where and how he grew up. It tells only about Jesus' work as an adult. The structure of the book falls into two unequal parts. After being <u>baptized</u> (immersed in water) by John the Baptist (1:4–11), Jesus works in the northern part of Jewish territory, the <u>Galilee</u> (chaps. 1–9). Then he travels south to Jerusalem where he comes into conflict with the priests, who arrest him. He is tried and executed by the Romans (chaps. 10–15). This entire story could fit within the time span of one year.

Mark ends with the announcement that Jesus rose from the dead (16:1–8). This abrupt conclusion leads many readers to think that the original ending is missing. That idea occurred to ancient scribes copying the Gospel. Most Greek manuscripts of Mark contain one of several different endings (16:9–20). They all reproduce or summarize the appearances of the resurrected Jesus as found in the other New Testament Gospels.

Mark presents Jesus as a <u>teacher</u> and <u>healer</u>. His teaching focuses on the message that the kingdom of God is about to come, or is even already here (1:15, 4:26–32).

> *Jesus said, "The time is fulfilled, and the kingdom of God has come near; repent and believe the good news."* (1:15 NRSV)

The <u>kingdom of God</u> reflects the apocalyptic hope that God will soon put an end to evil and bring about peace on earth. Such apocalyptic expectations (see Section 6.3) were popular in first-century Judea and fueled political resistance to the Roman Empire. But Mark insists that Jesus rejected political activity (12:17). Instead, he advised his followers to wait patiently for God to bring about the kingdom (13:14–23).

Jesus called on people to repent of their sins, that is, to stop doing wrong and follow Jesus' example. Mark emphasizes that Jesus' followers, called <u>disciples</u> or students, should imitate him by leaving behind jobs and families (1:16–20) in order to teach and heal others (6:7–12). Like him, Jesus' followers must also be willing to suffer and die for their faith:

> *If any want to become my followers, let them deny themselves and take up their cross and follow me. For those who want to save their life will lose it, and those who lose their life for my sake, and for the sake of the gospel, will save it.* (8:34 NRSV)

Jesus repeatedly predicts that his own life will end when he goes to Jerusalem (8:31; 9:31; 10:33–34).

Jesus' teachings frequently take the form of <u>parables</u> – short illustrations or stories to make his point vividly. Mark presents a collection of Jesus' parables in chapter 4. But Jesus' audience and even his disciples do not understand the parables (4:10–12, 33–34). Mark shows Jesus interpreting the parable of the sower (4:3–8) as an allegory (4:14–20). However, he does not interpret the other parables in this chapter, and they do not work easily as allegories. Many modern scholars have concluded that Jesus' parables communicate better as metaphors in the oral settings of his teaching than they do in writing. Recent literary studies, however, have challenged whether metaphors really allow scholars to distinguish clearly between parables and allegories.[1]

From its first verse, Mark's Gospel proclaims Jesus as both the Messiah/ Christ (see Box 7.1) and as the Son of God (see Box 7.2). But people are slow to catch on to Jesus' identity. His disciples eventually realize that Jesus is the Messiah/Christ, but Jesus warns them to tell no one (8:29–30). When Jesus exorcizes people, the demons recognize him as the Son of God, but Jesus refuses to let them say so (3:11–12). Aside from the demons, Jesus is proclaimed the Son of God three times in Mark's story line: God says so from heaven at the beginning when Jesus is baptized (1:11) and again in the middle at his transfiguration on the mountain (9:7). Only once does a human recognize him as the son of God and then only when he dies.

*When the centurion (a Roman officer), who stood facing Jesus, saw how he died, he said, "This man was certainly God's Son." (15:39* CEB)

In this way, Mark makes the point that only Jesus' death reveals what it means to be the Son of God.


## 8.2   THE GOSPEL ACCORDING TO MATTHEW

The Gospels of Matthew and Luke follow the same outline as Mark and repeat much of Mark's contents, so all three are often called the Synoptic Gospels. (For the argument that Matthew and Luke actually copied from Mark, see Section 11.4) As in Mark, Jesus first works in Galilee, then travels to Jerusalem, where he is crucified and then rises from the dead. Matthew, however, adds a great deal of additional material.

At the beginning, Matthew adds to this outline a genealogy that traces Jesus' ancestry from Abraham through David and the entire royal line of Judah down to Joseph, the husband of Mary, Jesus' mother (1:1–17). Matthew then tells of Jesus' miraculous birth to the virgin, Mary (1:18–25). This takes place at their home in Bethlehem, which was King David's home town (1 Sam. 17:12). Wise sages, or magi, from Mesopotamia read astrological omens to find the infant "king of the Jews" (2:1–6). This made the king of Judea, Herod, suspicious and he ordered the murder of all infant boys in Bethlehem. But Joseph, Mary, and Jesus escaped to Egypt until after Herod died (2:13–18). When they returned, they lived in Nazareth which they thought would be safer (2:22–23). Through this genealogy and story, Matthew emphasizes royal themes to foreshadow that Jesus will be the Messiah/Christ, which was the title of David and of Judah's other ancient kings.

Matthew inserts additional teachings by Jesus in five places in the Gospel (see Box 8.1). They have been organized topically, from advice on how to live morally in chapters 5–7 to parables added to Mark's predictions of the end of the world in chapters 24–25. Matthew emphasizes that Jesus has the authority to revise traditional norms radically, even the teachings of scripture. In the so-called "Sermon on the Mount" (5:1) – a location that calls for comparing Jesus to Moses – Jesus comments on some of the rules in the Ten Commandments:

> *You have heard that it was said to those of ancient times, "You shall not murder"; and "whoever murders shall be liable to judgement." But I say to you that if you are angry with a brother or sister, you will be liable to judgement; and if you insult a brother or sister, you will be liable to the council; and if you say, "You fool," you will be liable to the hell of fire. … You have heard that it was said, "You shall not commit adultery." But I say to you that everyone who looks at a woman with lust has already committed adultery with her in his heart.* (Matt. 5:21–22, 27–28 NRSV)

This rigorous ethic of inner accountability culminates in making the imitation of God's goodness the standard for human behavior:

> *Be perfect, therefore, as your heavenly Father is perfect.* (Matt. 5:48 NRSV)

## Box 8.1   Matthew's added teachings

| | |
|---|---|
| Chapters 5–7 | Moral teachings (the Sermon on the Mount) |
| Chapter 10 | Instructions for the disciples |
| Chapter 13 | Parables about the kingdom of God |
| Chapter 18 | Parables/instructions about community |
| Chapter 25 | Apocalyptic parables |

At the end of the Gospel, Matthew adds appearances of the resurrected Jesus to his women disciples in Jerusalem (28:10) and to his male disciples in Galilee (28:16–20). There he commissions them to

> *make disciples of all nations, baptizing them in the name of the Father and of the Son and of the Holy Spirit, and teaching them to obey everything that I have commanded you.* (Matt. 28:19–20 NRSV)

So Matthew's Gospel anticipates the universal mission of the Christian church. Jesus then promises to remain with his followers "always, to the end of the age" (28:20).

## 8.3    THE GOSPEL ACCORDING TO LUKE

Luke's Gospel begins by noting the existence of other gospels. It then announces the writer's intention to write his own account "so that you may know the truth" (1:1–4). Luke's Gospel nevertheless follows Mark's account and includes almost all of Mark's material, but adds other material just as Matthew does.

Luke adds to the beginning a story about Jesus' birth and his genealogy, but this story emphasizes other themes than Matthew's. While Luke and Matthew agree that Jesus was born to the virgin Mary in Bethlehem, they tell very different stories. Luke tells the birth stories of both John the Baptist and Jesus, who are described as first cousins. The stories emphasize the roles of their mothers, Elizabeth and Mary. (Throughout the book, Luke gives more attention to women and women's themes than the other New Testament Gospels do.) In this account, Nazareth is Joseph's and Mary's home from the start. They go to Bethlehem only because a Roman census requires it. There, Jesus is born in a stable and local shepherds, informed by angels, honor him. So where Matthew's birth story focused on kings, wise men, and royal themes, Luke emphasizes Jesus' humble origins and his significance for ordinary people. Luke's Gospel includes one story about Jesus' childhood (2:41–51) to show his precocious religious insight. In Luke, genealogy (3:23–38) links Jesus to all humans by going backwards from Joseph through David (but not Judah's other kings) and Abraham all the way to "Adam, the son of God."

Luke adds many teachings, many of them the same as Matthew's additions. But Luke places most of this additional material in the journey from Galilee to Jerusalem. Here that trip takes 10 chapters (9:51–19:57) because Jesus talks the whole way. Some of this material has become very famous: the parables about the good Samaritan (10:25–37) and about the prodigal son (15:11–32) can only be found in Luke. This Gospel shows Jesus especially concerned for poor and marginalized people, for whom the kingdom of God is coming:

> *Blessed are you who are poor, for yours is the kingdom of God.*
> (compare Matt. 5:3: *Blessed are the poor in spirit . . .*)
> *Blessed are you who are hungry now, for you will be filled.*
> *Blessed are you who weep now, for you will laugh. . . .*
> *But woe to you who are rich, for you have received your consolation.*
> *Woe to you who are full now, for you will be hungry.*
> *Woe to you who are laughing now, for you will mourn and weep.*
> (Luke 6:20–26 NRSV)

In Luke, Jesus often tells parables in pairs that feature a male and female character respectively (13:18–21; 15:3–10; 17:34–35). Luke in this way gives women a greater role in Jesus' teachings just as he does by highlighting Mary and Elizabeth in the birth stories. All the New Testament gospels agree that Jesus had many female disciples, and that women were the first to hear and report the news that Jesus rose from the dead (24:1–10).

Luke concludes with appearances of the resurrected Jesus in and around Jerusalem (24:13–53). Then Jesus rises to heaven out of sight of his disciples (24:51). In the Acts of the Apostles, a sequel to Luke's Gospel written by the same author (Acts 1:1), Jesus is replaced by the Holy Spirit, which soon descends on the disciples at Pentecost (Acts 2:1–4; Pentecost is the Greek name for the Jewish festival of *Shavuot*). Acts then illustrates how Jesus' followers are able to do everything that Jesus did through the power of the Holy Spirit.

## 8.4   THE GOSPEL ACCORDING TO JOHN

John's Gospel differs from the other New Testament gospels in its outline (see Box 8.2), style, theology, and much of its contents. Though it obviously tells about the life and death of the same character, Jesus of Nazareth, its writer does not seem to have known about the Synoptic Gospels, and they did not know about his work.

The Gospel of John depicts Jesus as more obviously divine than do the other gospels. It begins with a theological statement about the creation of the world:

> *In the beginning was the Word and the Word was with God and the Word was God. The Word was with God in the beginning. Everything*

*came into being through the Word, and without the Word nothing came into being.* (John 1:1–3 CEB)

The chapter goes on to say:

*The Word became flesh and made his home among us. We have seen his glory, glory like that of a father's only son. . . . As the Law was given through Moses, so grace and truth came into being through Jesus Christ.* (1:14, 17 CEB)

So John's Gospel begins by stating clearly that Jesus is the eternal Son of God since the creation of the world. That emphasis carries right through the narrative of Jesus' life and death. For example, in this Gospel, John the Baptist acknowledges Jesus as his superior instead of baptizing him (John 1:19–37; cf. Mark 1:13). Jesus does not suffer temptation and never doubts his mission (John 18:1; cf. Mark 14:33–36). His spoken word knocks down the soldiers sent to arrest him (18:6) and he tells the Roman governor, Pilate, that he has no power over him (19:11). Jesus' last words before dying, "It is finished!" (19:30 NRSV), claim success and victory. In John's Gospel, Jesus is the powerful and eternal Son of God who does exactly what God tells him to do.

Jesus moves back and forth several times between Galilee and Jerusalem in the Gospel of John. This story mentions three Passovers (John 2:13; 6:4; 11:55), which is why people think that Jesus' ministry lasted three years.

In John, Jesus performs only seven miracles, but they become the basis for his explanations of who he is and what his purpose is. For example, Jesus' miraculous feeding of a crowd (6:1–14) shows that Jesus himself is "the bread of life" (6:35). His healing of a blind man shows that Jesus is "the light of the world" (9:1–7), and also that his opponents are spiritually blind (9:40–41). Jesus does not tell parables in the Gospel of John. Instead, symbolic miracles

## Box 8.2   Outline of John's Gospel

| Chapter 1 | Prolog about the divine Word |
| --- | --- |
| Chapters 2–12 | Seven miracles and their symbolic interpretations |
| Chapters 13–17 | Jesus' farewell to his disciples |
| Chapters 18–20 | Jesus' arrest, crucifixion, resurrection |
| Chapter 21 | Epilogue about the disciples |

reinforce symbolic language to show that Jesus is the Messiah, the Son of God, and is in fact divine himself.

Jesus offers people salvation and <u>eternal life</u>. In John's Gospel, eternal life is not so much about what happens after death as it is about the present: those who believe in Jesus have eternal life now (3:16; 10:28). Where the other gospels emphasize what the disciples must do, the crucial issue in John's Gospel is <u>belief</u>:

> *Everyone who believes in [the Son of God] will not perish, but will have eternal life.... Whoever believes in him is not judged; whoever does not believe in him is already judged.* (John 3:16, 18 CEB)

Christians often recommend that people new to the Bible read the Gospel of John first, because of its explicit theology about Jesus Christ and its emphasis on believing in him.[2]

## CITED WORKS AND FURTHER READING

1 See the essays edited by Richard N. Longenecker, *The Challenge of Jesus' Parables* (Grand Rapids: Eerdmans, 2000).

2 For more extensive introductions to the New Testament Gospels, see Pheme Perkins, *Introduction to the Synoptic Gospels* (Grand Rapids: Eerdmans, 2007); and John T. Carroll, *Jesus and the Gospels: An Introduction* (Louisville: Westminster John Knox, 2016).

# CHAPTER 9

# The Gospels' Iconic Dimension

Christians ritualize the semantic, expressive, and iconic dimensions of the Gospels more than other parts of their New Testament. The comparative study of religions shows that Christians ritualize their scriptures similarly to many other religious traditions. In particular, Christians ritualize the iconic dimension of their bibles in ways that are somewhat similar, and also conspicuously different, from Jewish practices. Christians use codices instead of scrolls for almost all of their books, and especially for their scriptures (see Section 4.2.6). Today, Christian scriptures are usually published together in a single codex bound in distinctive ways to show it is the Bible. Earlier in history, however, Christian iconic ritualization of scripture focused mostly on the Gospels.

The arguments of Irenaeus provided a theological rationale for ritualizing the Gospels in place of the Torah. The role of the Pentateuch and other Old Testament books in Christian liturgy and interpretation is to support the New Testament, like the Prophets and Writings support the Torah in Jewish liturgy and interpretation.

*Understanding the Bible as a Scripture in History, Culture, and Religion*, First Edition. James W. Watts.
© 2021 John Wiley & Sons Ltd. Published 2021 by John Wiley & Sons Ltd.

## 9.1  IRENAEUS AND THE FOUR GOSPELS

At the same time that rabbis were reorganizing Judaism through their oral torah (see Section 6.5.2), Christians were forming their communities around traditions about Jesus and his apostles. In the late first century, these traditions took literary form as narratives about Jesus' life and teachings called "gospels," and as letters from first-generation apostles like Peter, Paul, James, and John. In the second century, Christian communities divided over which gospels and apostles to follow.

Irenaeus (ca. 140–201 CE) was the bishop of Lyon. His community of Christians included followers of Marcion, who advocated only Luke's Gospel and Paul's letters as the true teachings about Christ. Others followed Valentinius, who preached that Jesus taught mystical knowledge available only to those with spiritual insight. Valentinian ideas were popularized in second- and third-century gospels, such as the recently rediscovered Gospel of Thomas (see Section 11.2).

Irenaeus insisted on the importance of apostolic succession for deciding on Christian scripture as well as on church leaders. He argued that only gospels written by apostles (whom he limited to the 11 disciples of Jesus plus Paul) or associates of these apostles are trustworthy. On this criterion, Irenaeus identified four and only four legitimate gospels, even though none of these texts identifies its author. He thought that two were written by the apostles Matthew and John. He believed that two others were written by Mark on the basis of Peter's recollections and Luke on the basis of Paul's teachings (see further in Section 11.4.1).

Irenaeus insisted that God intended Christians to use only these four gospels and that all four were equally inspired (see Box 9.1). He found scriptural support for this idea in Ezekiel's vision of four supernatural winged sphinxes, called *cherubim* in Hebrew, that surround God's throne (Ezek. 1; see Figure 9.1 and Section 4.3.2). Irenaeus' application of Ezekiel's vision to the four gospels replaced the Jewish myth of a heavenly Torah with a myth of heavenly gospels. Ever since, artists have usually portrayed the writers of the four New Testament gospels together with one of the four cherubim who dictate the gospels to their human writers.[1]

Irenaeus defended the Old Testament as Christian scripture because New Testament books cite it as authoritative. However, following the lead of Luke 24:26–27, 44–47, he maintained that Jewish scriptures must be interpreted only through the Christian belief that Jesus is the Christ:

*If anyone, therefore, reads the Scriptures with attention, he will find in them an account of Christ . . . . When at this present time the*

## Box 9.1   Irenaeus on the necessity of four Gospels

*The Gospels could not possibly be either more or less in number than they are. Since there are four zones of the world in which we live, and four principal winds, while the Church is spread over all the earth, and the pillar and foundation of the Church is the gospel, and the Spirit of life, it fittingly has four pillars, everywhere breathing out incorruption and revivifying men. From this it is clear that the Word, the artificer of all things, being manifested to men gave us the gospel, fourfold in form but held together by one Spirit. As David said, when asking for his coming, "O sitter upon the cherubim, show yourself" [Ps 80:1]. For the cherubim have four faces, and their faces are images of the activity of the Son of God. For the first living creature, it says [Ezek 1:5,10; Rev 4:7–8], was like a lion, signifying his active and princely and royal character; the second was like an ox, showing his sacrificial and priestly order; the third had the face of a man, indicating very clearly his coming in human guise; and the fourth was like a flying eagle, making plain the giving of the Spirit who broods over the Church. Now the Gospels, in which Christ is enthroned, are like these....As is the activity of the Son of God, such is the form of the living creatures; and as is the form of the living creatures, such is also the character of the Gospel. For the living creatures were quadriform, and the gospel and the activity of the Lord is fourfold. Therefore four general covenants were given to mankind: one was that of Noah's deluge, by the [rain]bow; the second was Abraham's, by the sign of circumcision; the third was the giving of the Law by Moses; and the fourth is that of the Gospel, through our Lord Jesus Christ. (Irenaeus, Adversus Haereses, 3.11.8)[2]*

**FIGURE 9.1**   The four Gospels represented by a lion for Mark, a human-faced angel for Matthew, an eagle for John, and an ox for Luke. Mosaics from 817 to 824 CE in Santa Prassede Basilica, Rome.

*law is read to the Jews, it is like a fable; for they do not possess the explanation of all things pertaining to the advent of the Son of God, which took place in human nature; but when it is read by the Christians, it is a treasure, hid indeed in a field, but brought to light by the cross of Christ.* (Irenaeus, *Adversus Haereses,* 4.26.1)

Therefore, the Gospels and Paul – eventually, the New Testament as a whole – replaced the Pentateuch as the interpretive key to Christian scripture.

Irenaeus built his argument for the legitimacy of the four New Testament Gospels into his rationale for selecting church leaders. He thought that authority to interpret the Gospels and other scriptures rests only with legitimate successors to the apostles. That is, only bishops ordained by other bishops in a line of succession stretching back to the apostles (apostolic succession) can settle the meaning of scripture. So Irenaeus used arguments for the authority of the four New Testament Gospels to unify Christians organizationally around the bishops and to standardize Christian beliefs on the basis of a limited number of books.

The four Gospels established the claims of "orthodox" Catholic Christianity, which gathered influence and power over the centuries, especially after the Roman Emperor Constantine converted in 318 CE. Controversies over the exact list of books that comprise the Christian Bible continued, as they did over other matters of Christian belief. In fact, the nature of "true" Christianity remains contested today, as the diversity of twenty-first-century Christianities shows. But Irenaeus played a crucial role in setting the four Gospels and Paul's letters at the center of Christian worship and doctrine, where they have continued to be ritualized as scripture ever since.

## 9.2   ICONIC GOSPELS AND BIBLES

In the second century CE, the four Gospels and Paul's letters were already collected and bound together in books (codices) to be read aloud in churches. Soon gospels were being paraded in processions in church rituals. Wealthy people were buying expensive copies in elaborate bindings.

Unlike Jews and Samaritans, Christians do not ritualize the Pentateuch separately as the Torah, nor do they have anything that is comparable to a synagogue ark (see Section 4.2.4). Their belief that temple worship was superseded by Christ's death gave them no reason to reproduce something like Israel's ark in church architecture. Some Christians instead allegorized the ark as Mary, the mother of Jesus, who carried the "Word of God" in her womb. The equivalent in some church furnishings appears in chests called "tabernacles" that contain the Eucharistic elements, that is, the bread and wine that are believed to be the body of Christ.

The four Gospels of the New Testament were commonly bound together and made a focus of attention in church liturgies.[3] Sometimes Gospel books and other scriptures were enshrined in boxes and venerated as relics. Medieval Irish monks placed elaborate <u>illuminated manuscripts</u> like the Lindisfarne Gospels and the Book of Durrow in locked book shrines where they could not be seen, much less read. These books functioned purely as relics of the saints who copied and illuminated them, and as symbols of Christ's presence. These copies of scripture were much less accessible than synagogue Torah scrolls that get taken out of their arks and read publicly at least every week. Most Christian churches also display scriptures openly and make copies readily available for reading.

Gospel books are still a central focus in many worship services of Orthodox, Catholic, and Anglican churches. A Gospel book is held high and processed into the sanctuary before being laid on the altar. Some people reach out to touch it for a blessing as it passes them by. The deacon or priest kisses the book before and after reading it. The congregation stands for the reading of the Gospel. The covers of Gospel books display crosses and icons, often in precious materials befitting their prominent role in the worship service.

Ritualizing the Gospels in these ways began early in Christian history. Public reading of the four Gospels was characteristic of proto-Catholic services by the end of the second century. In the third century, Cyprian argued that, after being read, the Gospel book should be placed where it is "conspicuous to the multitude of the gentiles and be beheld by the brothers" (*Letters* 39,4). After the Roman Empire adopted Christianity in the fourth century, Gospel books grew larger and more expensive. Their covers became icons of Christ, so that displaying the Gospels simultaneously displayed the icon to the worshipful view of the congregation. The Gospel book represented the presence of Christ in the midst of the congregation. Gospels were enthroned in Church meetings of bishops and in Roman law courts to represent Christ presiding over the councils and trials.

Early Christians ritualized Gospel books in many of the same ways that ancient Jews ritualized the Torah. While Jews touched *mezuzahs* and manipulated *tefillin*, Christians carried amulets containing the names of God and Jesus in scriptural verses (see Section 4.2.3). While Jews processed and displayed torahs, Christians processed and displayed gospels (Figure 9.2). By ritualizing the Gospels, Christians distinguished themselves from Jews who ritualize the Torah. Gospel books became a symbol of Christian identity. The

**FIGURE 9.2**  Gospel procession in the Church of the Holy Sepulcher, Jerusalem.
Source: photo by Lyn Watts 2014; used by permission.

Roman persecution of Christians in the early fourth century targeted the
owners of Christian books. Many died rather than give up their gospels. The
codex of the Gospels or the Bible became a standard feature in Christian art,
where it appears in the hands of Jesus, Mary, saints, angels, scholars, priests,
and the pious dead. The Christian codex often appears juxtaposed to the tablets of the commandments, which in this context represent Jewish law in
contrast to the Christian gospel.

Since antiquity, the Bible's prestige has led to its reproduction in massive
and expensive forms intended for public display. Christian Roman emperors
commissioned the production of large bibles by imperial scribes. Medieval
monks labored for years on elaborately illuminated manuscripts as acts of
devotion. Their products became devotional objects in turn. These manuscripts distinguish the _nomina sacra_ ("sacred names") by abbreviating them
and, often, by distinctive illuminations to show that these texts are sacred.
When Johannes Gutenberg invented printing with movable type, one of his
first commercial products was a Latin bible. Gutenberg bibles remain among

the most prestigious and valuable objects in library and museum collections to this day. Nineteenth-century publishers sold massive bibles for use on church pulpits and home altars, as well as millions of inexpensive bibles for personal use.

Christian descriptions of their scripture's divine origins often draw on the Pentateuch's stories of Moses receiving the tablets and depositing them in the Ark of the Covenant. For example, a nineteenth-century hymn (Box 9.2) equates scripture with Christ as the "Word of God" come from heaven. It also compares scripture to Israel's ark ("the sacred casket") that stored the tablets of the Ten Commandments. In modern churches, the Pentateuch provides the foundational stories for understanding the nature of scripture and it continues to be venerated as part of the Christian Bible.

Most low-church Protestants spurn elaborate rituals that they associate with Catholicism. They emphasize the meaning of the Bible's contents alone. Yet their rejection of icons and relics leaves the Bible as their only sacred object. As a result, Protestant rituals tend to focus on the Bible even more than other Christian churches do. In traditional Scottish Presbyterian worship services, the "beadle" led the processional carrying the pulpit Bible,

---

**Box 9.2   Hymn, "O Word of God Incarnate," by William W. How, 1867**

O Word of God Incarnate,
  O Wisdom from on high,
O Truth unchanged, unchanging,
  O Light of our dark sky:
We praise thee for the radiance
  That from the hallowed page,
A Lantern to our footsteps,
  Shines on from age to age.
The church from thee, her Master,
  Received the gift divine,
And still that light she lifteth
  O'er all the earth to shine:
It is the sacred casket,
  Where gems of truth are stored;
It is the heav'n-drawn picture
  Of thee, the living Word.

followed by the minister. The Bible frequently sits on church altars and pulpits where the congregation can see it (Figure 9.3).

Many churches emphasize the value of everybody reading from their own bibles during the worship service. Preachers often model this behavior by holding a bible while they preach. The image of a group of people each carrying a black leather bible to church has become a stereotype of conservative and evangelical Christians. In modern culture, the black leather-bound codex has become just as recognizable as the cross as a symbol of Christianity.[4]

The practice of displaying a book of scripture in the position of greatest honor reaches beyond synagogues and churches into broader Western culture. For example, a Bible is placed on an altar in Masonic lodges and manipulated during initiation rituals.[5] Much more visible to the public are oath ceremonies using bibles. In the Middle Ages, people touched holy objects – relics, crosses, scriptures – when they swore oaths to guarantee their sincerity. After the Protestant Reformation, only the Bible remained available for such use in many countries. It therefore became conventional to take oaths in law courts and oaths of office on a bible. While secular states have now stopped requiring oaths on bibles in courts of law, they remain popular with politicians catering to their voters' religious sensibilities. As a result, scriptures of all sorts get manipulated in political oath ceremonies in countries around the world.

The Bible is the only material object that almost all Christians recognize as holy. They recognize the book of scripture as a common possession, even though the Orthodox, Catholic, and Protestant bibles differ somewhat (see Section 1.3). Their contents also overlap with Jewish scriptures, the Tanak,

**FIGURE 9.3**  Lectern Bible, Saint Andrews, Scotland.

which is therefore frequently called "the Jewish Bible." The differences in contents are often ignored to allow the Bible to function as a unifying symbol of the whole Christian religion, and of its family relationship with Judaism as well.

## CITED WORKS AND FURTHER READING

1  On Ireneaus and the Gospels, see Elaine Pagels, *Beyond Belief: The Secret Gospel of Thomas* (New York: Vintage, 2003).

2  For the translation of Ireneaus' *Adversus Haereses*, see Alexander Roberts and W. H. Rambaut, *The Writings of Irenaeus* (Edinburgh: T. & T. Clark, 1868).

3  On ancient Christian rituals with Gospel books, see the essays in William E. Klingshirn and Linda Safran, eds., *The Early Christian Book* (Washington, DC: Catholic University of America Press, 2007), especially John Lowden, "The Word Made Visible: The Exterior of the Early Christian Book as Visual Argument," 13–47, and Caroline Humfress, "Judging By the Book: Christian Codices and Late Antique Legal Culture," 141–158; also Dorina Miller Parmenter, "The Iconic Book: The Image of the Bible in Early Christian Rituals," in *Iconic Books and Texts* (ed. J. W. Watts; London: Equinox, 2013), 63–92, and Jason Larson, "The Gospels as Imperialized Sites of Memory in Late Ancient Christianity," in *Iconic Books and Texts*, 373–388.

4  On the iconic Bible in modern Protestantism, see Martin Marty, "America's Iconic Book," in *Humanizing America's Iconic Book: Society of Biblical Literature Centennial Addresses 1980* (ed. G. M. Tucker and D. A. Knight; Chico, CA: Scholars Press, 1982), 1–23; and Dorina Miller Parmenter, "A Fitting Ceremony: Christian Concerns for Bible Disposal," in *The Death of Sacred Texts: Ritual Disposal and Renovation of Texts in World Religions* (ed. Kristina Myrvold, London: Ashgate, 2010), 55–70.

5  On the Bible in Masonic rituals, see Cheryl Townsend Gilkes, "The Virtues of Brotherhood and Sisterhood: African American Fraternal Organizations and Their Bibles," in *African Americans and the Bible: Sacred Texts and Social Textures* (ed. Vincent L. Wimbush; New York: Continuum, 2003), 389–403.

# CHAPTER 10

# The Gospels' Expressive Dimension

Comparison of Jewish and Christian ways of ritualizing scripture's expressive dimension shows many common practices, but highlights the different texts upon which they focus. The four Gospels replaced the Torah as the scriptural focus of Christian worship services. This change is clearly reflected by how scripture gets read aloud in churches. Whereas synagogues read the Torah sequentially and match other scriptural passages to the Torah reading, most Christian calendars of scripture readings (called lectionaries) read one or more gospels sequentially for part of the year. They choose passages from other scriptural books based on thematic links to the gospel reading or to that day in the Christian calendar. Traditionally, the Gospel is read last, usually by a deacon or the presiding priest who recites blessings before and after the reading. After sitting through the other biblical readings, many congregations stand to hear the Gospel read.[1]

## 10.1 CHRISTIAN LECTIONARIES

Christian calendars of scripture readings (<u>lectionaries</u>) have varied over time and between Christian denominations. Twentieth-century efforts to create more consistency among Protestant and Catholic churches in North

*Understanding the Bible as a Scripture in History, Culture, and Religion*, First Edition. James W. Watts.
© 2021 John Wiley & Sons Ltd. Published 2021 by John Wiley & Sons Ltd.

> **Box 10.1 Reading scripture aloud in ancient Christianity**
>
> William Graham observed: "The (ancient) sources reflect the intensity of the preoccupation with the divine word: We find substantial references to memorization of scripture; to recitation/meditation as a major preoccupation in its own right; to liturgical recitation, including both communal worship and funeral rites; to the chanting of psalms and other scriptural passages while walking, weaving, baking, gathering rushes, and welcoming special visitors; and to scripture reading and recitation during the communal meals and as the basis of all teaching and preaching in the community."[2]

America led to a new lectionary for the Catholic Mass and a related "Common Lectionary" for many Protestant denominations. The four suggested scripture readings each day consist of readings from a Gospel and from a Psalm, another from the rest of the Old Testament, and one from another New Testament book. This contemporary Christian lectionary includes a larger percentage of the Bible than did many older lectionaries. It emphasizes sequential reading of part of one gospel over several months. It also enables semi-continuous readings of some Old Testament narratives over multiple Sundays. However, only a small part of the Old Testament ever gets read in Christian congregations that follow this lectionary. For example, they read only 5% of the Pentateuch, mostly from Genesis and Exodus.[3]

Many churches do not follow any prescribed lectionary. They leave the selection of scripture readings to the preacher. Most choose to preach on New Testament texts more often than readings from the Old Testament. Some preachers have been known to preach sequentially through the entire Bible, in which case the entire Old Testament gets read aloud over a period of many Sundays. Apart from this rare exception, however, Christians do not read much of it aloud in Sunday services. The portions that do get read emphasize the pentateuchal stories of creation, of the ancestors, and of the exodus from Egypt, and passages from the prophets that have traditionally been interpreted by Christians as predicting Jesus Christ. Christians do not reserve a special place for the Torah as Jews do, but ritualize the Pentateuch simply as the first part of their Old Testament.

Certain passages from the Hebrew Bible, however, play a larger role in Christian worship. The Ten Commandments were sometimes recited from memory by the congregation, especially in some Reformed Protestant churches. Christian priests and ministers frequently recite the Priestly

Blessing (Num. 6:24–26) at the conclusion of a service. The Psalms provide very many of the lyrics for chants, hymns, and anthems (see below).

Apart from formal worship services, scripture reading plays a large role in many Christians' devotional experience. Ancient Christian monks made the reading and recitation of scripture the central activity of their spiritual practice (see Box 10.1). This monastic *lectio divina* "divine reading" has shaped spiritual life for non-monks as well. For example, the American Catholic *Manual of Indulgences* promises benefits in the afterlife to "the Christian faithful who read sacred scripture with the veneration due God's word and as a form of spiritual reading."

Denominations that reject the monastic life have nevertheless emphasized spiritual reading as an ideal. The Protestant Reformers encouraged all Christians to read the Bible for themselves. Contemporary evangelical Christians distinguish themselves by individual and group "bible study" more than by any other religious practice.

In Christian devotional reading, the Gospels receive the most attention, followed by the rest of the New Testament, just as they do in Christian worship services. Of the Christian Old Testament, Christians read the Psalms and some parts of the Prophets more than most of the rest, except for many stories in Genesis and Exodus.

## 10.2  SINGING CHRISTIAN SCRIPTURES

Ancient Christians also sang their scriptures. The New Testament mentions Jesus and his disciples singing psalms (Matt. 26:30) and Paul recommends the practice (Eph. 5:19). Jennifer Knust and Tommy Wasserman observed:

> The sheer volume of surviving Psalters, psalm commentaries, allusions to psalms, and references to David and his songbook attest to the centrality of the psalms in emerging Christian liturgies, and from the earliest period.[4]

Christians soon chanted the reading of other scriptures just as Jews did. Some ancient churches employed Jewish cantors to teach the "proper" chanting of scripture. The sound of those ancient chants has been lost over time. However, surviving manuscripts from the tenth century and later contain notations to indicate how to chant scripture readings.[5]

Hymns and other kinds of religious songs often quote scripture. Songs allow composers and performers much greater melodic and musical creativity than liturgical scripture readings. Scripture texts feature in many of the most famous musical compositions in Western culture, ranging from medieval <u>Gregorian chants</u> through the hymns of Martin Luther, Isaac Watts, and Charles Wesley, to performance pieces such as George Frideric Händel's *Messiah* and Leonard Bernstein's *Chichester Psalms*. The Christian tendency to focus on New Testament texts, the Psalms, and the Prophets shapes much of this musical tradition. Some early Calvinist congregations sang the Ten Commandments. Some classical compositions, such as Franz Joseph Haydn's *Creation*, feature the beginning of Genesis. Christian music for the most part, however, alludes to pentateuchal stories but does not quote many pentateuchal texts.

A wide variety of people participate in oral and dramatic presentations of scriptures. This situation is very different from the scholarly expertise that dominates scriptural interpretation. It also contrasts with the Bible's own hierarchical depictions of Torah readings in Deuteronomy, Joshua, Kings, and Ezra. Performance <u>leadership</u> in congregations tends to be open to non-specialists and often to people otherwise excluded from religious leadership. Jews consider it a privilege to be "called to the Torah," and this experience plays the central role in a child's *bar* or *bat mitzvah*. Many Christian churches routinely ask members of the congregation to read scripture aloud, including women in traditions that exclude them from serving as priests or ministers. Even more people get involved in singing biblical texts as soloists, in choirs, and as members of congregations. Oral presentation practices in Muslim and Sikh communities are similarly inclusive, though they take different forms.

So religious communities regularly use oral presentation to expand the ranks of worship leaders, even as hierarchies of clergy and scholars often dominate authoritative interpretation. This expansion of religious leadership through readings, recitations, and dramatizations, together with their inspiring effects, explains much of the social power exerted by the Bible in many different cultures.

## 10.3   THE LANGUAGES OF CHRISTIAN SCRIPTURES

The comparative study of religions shows that scriptural religions take different approaches to questions of language and translation. Jewish tradition prioritizes the Hebrew text of the Torah and the Tanak in ritual and interpretation. Jews have also used translations since antiquity to make scripture's contents more understandable. Muslims and Hindus place even more emphasis on the original language of their scriptures. In their traditions, the oral expression of the Qur'an in Arabic or the Vedas in Sanskrit represents the highest form of revelation and inspiration (see Box 5.1). Christians and Buddhists, on the other hand, have ritualized their scriptures in vernacular translations since the origins of these religions.

The early Christians adopted the <u>Septuagint Greek translation</u> of the Hebrew Bible to serve as their scriptures. Almost from the beginning, many Christian worship services featured scripture readings in Greek. In the first generations of the movement, Christian missionaries received a more positive response from Greek-speaking Jews and converts to Judaism than from those who spoke Aramaic. Christianity soon established itself as a <u>Hellenistic</u> religion, that is, as Greek in language and culture.

The dominance of <u>Greek</u> in early Christianity finds its clearest expression in the books of the New Testament. The apostle Paul regarded himself as a Jew who followed the teachings of the Jewish messiah, Jesus (Phil. 3:3–7; Gal. 1:13–2:21). He spoke <u>Aramaic</u> and his Pharisaic education trained him in <u>Hebrew</u>. But because he spoke Greek to his Hellenistic congregations, his letters – which are the earliest New Testament books – were written in Greek. So were all the other New Testament books, including the four Gospels that convey the words and deeds of Jesus Christ. Though Jesus spoke Aramaic (Mark 7:11, 34; 15:34), the Gospels record his words already translated into Greek. As a result, Christianity has not preserved the words of its founder in the language in which he spoke them.

The New Testament book of the <u>Acts of the Apostles</u>, written by the author of Luke, narrates the early history of the Christian movement over several decades. Acts provided a justification for bible translations by relating a translation miracle as a model for Christian preaching. At the festival of Pentecost, 50 days after Jesus' crucifixion, his disciples

> *were filled with the Holy Spirit and began to speak in other languages, as the Spirit gave them ability. Now there were devout Jews from every nation under heaven living in Jerusalem. And at this sound the crowd gathered and was bewildered, because each one heard them speaking in the native language of each.* (Acts 2:4–6 NRSV)

This story depicts translation as an act of divine inspiration. The sermon that follows interprets the miracle as an act of prophecy (Acts 2:14–21). The Christian Bible thus models translation both with its Greek Old Testament and with this miraculous origin story for Christian translation activities. The book of Genesis accounts for linguistic diversity with the story of the tower of Babel (Gen. 11:1–9), in which God creates mutually incomprehensible languages to frustrate human unity. So, as many preachers have pointed out, the Christian Bible depicts different languages as a barrier to mutual understanding on the one hand, and translation as a divinely sanctioned means for overcoming that barrier on the other.

With such precedents for vernacular translation, Greek could not last long as the sole language of Christian scripture. It was soon rivaled by translations into Latin, Syriac, Coptic (Egyptian), and Armenian. Schisms then divided medieval Christianity along linguistic lines. This crystallization of religious identity around biblical translations continues among traditionalists today, especially in the churches of eastern Christianity. Greek Orthodox churches, however, read the New Testament in its original *koine* Greek, though they often attempt to overcome linguistic barriers by reading it in other languages as well.[6]

In Western Europe, the Renaissance revival of ancient cultures and languages breathed new life into the impulse to translate the scriptures. Protestant reformers championed vernacular translations in the sixteenth century. Then Catholic and Protestant missionaries translated the Bible into hundreds of new languages – thousands by the end of the twentieth century. Not coincidentally, Protestants have also become the most schismatic branch of Christianity, dividing into many independent denominations and churches. Today, it is often the case that different denominations using the same language nevertheless endorse different translations of the Bible.

Why did Christian attitudes toward the language of scripture tilt so decisively in favor of translations? Christianity emerged in a pluralistic cultural and linguistic environment in which Jewish communities already read their scriptures in multiple languages. Other reasons included the missionary desire to communicate widely and the possibility that Jesus himself may have spoken more than one language.

Another factor may have been cultural biases for and against certain languages and the people who spoke them. The dominant Hellenistic culture celebrated Greek as the language of philosophy and literature. Conversely, Aramaic may have been regarded in the Roman Empire as provincial. Christians quickly developed anti-Jewish prejudices and wished to establish a distinct identity for themselves. Embracing Greek and then other languages facilitated their separate group formation. John Sawyer summarized the results:

> The effect of translating Hebrew scripture into Greek was to construct a radically different text, one which, in the history of Christianity, virtually took the place of the Hebrew original as the Church's sacred text, and which the Jewish authorities soon rejected as alien.[7]

Christian translations of scripture have often unified a group of people around a vernacular language. Ancient translations consolidated the religious identities of Armenians, Egyptian Copts, and Syriac Christians. The Roman Church used the language of the Latin Bible and liturgy to create a single Catholic identity across the political divisions of medieval Europe. Two Protestant vernacular translations, the King James Version and the Luther Bible, encouraged nationalism in England and Germany by standardizing "the King's English" and "High German." European colonial empires, both Catholic and Protestant, wielded bible translations as a tool to dominate people in the Americas, Africa, and Asia. But translation into non-Western languages also inspired the rise of new ethnic churches, especially in Africa and Asia (see Figure 10.1).

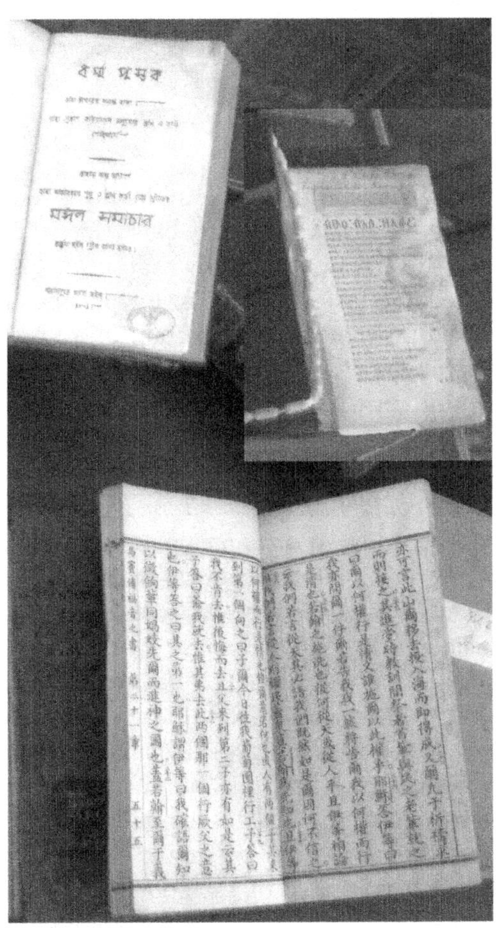

**FIGURE 10.1** Bible translations in Bengali, Coptic, and Chinese.

Bible translations have an iconic as well as expressive aspect, since they often bring new scripts to languages. Efforts to convert eastern Europeans to orthodoxy transcribed their languages into the Greek alphabet or modified it to produce Cyrillic. Colonial translations by Catholics and Protestants brought the Latin alphabet to indigenous languages in the Americas, whether they already had a writing system or not. These alphabets conformed many different languages to European culture by their visual script, even while reproducing the Bible orally in another language. The new bibles sounded native while looking European.[8]

Worship services thus establish the religious and ethnic identities of congregations by the sound of the language of their scripture. Bible translations, then, have played a major role in distinguishing Christians from Jews and in dividing Christians along ethnic, national, and denominational lines.

## 10.4   EXPERT TRANSLATORS

The Pentateuch was translated into <u>Greek</u> in the third century BCE, followed quickly by the rest of the Tanak. The very existence so early of a scholarly Greek translation of the Tanak shows how important the interpretation of written Torah had become to Jews living in Egypt. The *Letter of Aristeas* in the second century claims that the translation project was motivated by the goal of adding Jewish books to the comprehensive collection of the Alexandria library. *Aristeas* quotes the head librarian's letter to the king:

> *These (books) also must be in your library in an accurate version, because this legislation, as could be expected from its divine nature, is very philosophical and genuine. Writers therefore and poets and the whole army of historians have been reluctant to refer to the aforementioned books, and to the men past (and present) who featured largely in them, because the consideration of them is sacred and hallowed. (Aris. 31)*

The king then requested translators from Eleazar, the Jewish high priest in Jerusalem, who sent 72 scholars to Egypt. This translation is therefore called the <u>Septuagint</u>, from the Latin word for "seventy." Aristeas documents how the Egyptian Jews ritualized the Torah's iconic and expressive dimensions, but the letter lavishes the most attention on the semantic dimension. It presents a long speech by Eleazar praising the noble contents of the Torah (139–169), and devotes most of its space to celebrating the scholarship, piety, and wisdom of the 72 translators (121–127, 187–294, 305–306).

*Eleazar selected men of the highest merit and of excellent education due to the distinction of their parentage; they had not only mastered the Jewish literature, but had made a serious study of that of the Greeks as well. They were therefore well qualified for the embassy, and brought it to fruition as occasion demanded; they had a tremendous natural facility for the negotiations and questions arising from the Law, with the middle way as their commendable ideal; they forsook any uncouth and uncultured attitude of mind; in the same way, they rose above conceit and contempt of other people, and instead engaged in discourse and listening to and answering each and every one, as is meet and right. (Aris. 121–122)[9]*

The accuracy of their translation was affirmed by the Jewish community in Alexandria and guaranteed by reciting curses on anyone who might tamper with its text (310–311). The king, for his part, "marveled profoundly at the genius of the lawgiver" (*Aris.* 311). The reputations of the Septuagint translators grew over the centuries. <u>Philo of Alexandria</u>, a Jewish philosopher writing in the first century CE, claimed that the Septuagint's translators were divinely inspired and that their individual translations were miraculously identical with each other (Box 10.2). Christians quickly adopted the Septuagint as their Old Testament, and used Philo's story to validate the divine inspiration of their Greek scriptures.

## Box 10.2   Philo of Alexandria on the Septuagint as a miracle of translation

The translators of the Septuagint "*like men inspired, prophesied, not one saying one thing and another another, but every one of them employed the self-same nouns and verbs, as if some unseen prompter had suggested all their language to them.... in every case, exactly corresponding Greek words were employed to translate literally the appropriate Chaldaic words, being adapted with exceeding propriety to the matters which were to be explained.... considering these translators not mere interpreters but hierophants and prophets to whom it had been granted their honest and guileless minds to go along with the most pure spirit of Moses. On which account, even to this very day, there is every year a solemn assembly held and a festival celebrated in the island of Pharos, to which not only the Jews but a great number of persons of other nations sail across, reverencing the place in which the first light of interpretation shone forth, and thanking God for that ancient piece of beneficence which was always young and fresh.*" (Philo, *Vita Moses* 2.37–41)[10]

Christian churches, like Jewish synagogues, valued expertise in scripture interpretation. In Late Antiquity, churches increasingly granted leadership to bishops ordained by other bishops in a line that could be traced back to Christ's apostles, arguing that they are best placed to interpret scripture (see Section 9.1). Christians also depend on translations for at least their Old Testament in the Greek Orthodox churches, or for their entire Bible in all other churches. There was a tendency among early Christians to legitimize their translations through miracle stories, such as the Pentecost story (Acts 2) and Philo's description of the miracle of the Septuagint translators (Box 10.2). Slowly, however, linguistic expertise rather than miraculous inspiration or apostolic succession established itself as the benchmark of Christian biblical scholarship.

In the third century, Origen edited an Old Testament that presented different versions side by side. It was called the *Hexapla* for its six columns consisting of the Hebrew text, the Hebrew transliterated in Greek letters, and four different Greek translations. Origen's work was not widely reproduced, however, because he chose a losing side in the religious politics of his day.

The prototypical Christian biblical scholar is <u>Jerome</u>, the fourth-century hermit who produced the Latin <u>Vulgate</u> translation that became the official Bible of the Roman Catholic Church (Figure 10.2). Instead of working from the Septuagint Greek as many other church leaders preferred, he learned Hebrew and translated the Latin Old Testament directly from Jewish manuscripts. He also used Origen's *Hexapla*. His asceticism and orthodoxy made Jerome influential, and the superiority of his translation secured his reputation as a saint and "doctor" (teacher) of the Western Church.[11]

Jerome established two precedents for most subsequent Christian translations of scripture. The first is that bible translators should, whenever possible, produce vernacular translations directly from the original Hebrew and Greek languages. The second is the authority of philological expertise in the ancient languages for establishing the wording of Christian bibles.

Jerome's use of Hebrew as the basis for translating the Christian Old Testament undermined appeals to Greek as Christianity's "original" language by establishing a bilingual original scripture. This also reinforced the tendency to use vernacular scripture readings in the liturgy. Hebrew and, outside the Greek Orthodox churches, Greek were left to scholars who gained authority and prestige from their expertise in these languages. This effect was not widely felt in the Middle Ages when knowledge of Hebrew was rare even among Christian theologians. Since the Renaissance, however, expertise in the languages of scripture has become a hallmark of the Christian scholar.

Western Europe's rediscovery of classical and ancient languages in the fifteenth and sixteenth centuries led to widespread Christian study of

**FIGURE 10.2**  Jerome at his desk. Detail of stained glass window, ca. 1490. In the Stadtschloss Museum in Weimar, Germany.

the Bible's original languages. The invention of the printing press made it easier to produce and distribute multilingual publications in multiple fonts, such as the Complutensian Polyglot (Figure 12.4). Printing also increased concern for standardizing biblical texts that varied from one manuscript to another. The humanist scholar Desiderius Erasmus published a <u>composite text</u> of the Greek New Testament in 1516. He compared seven different manuscripts to determine where they diverged from each other, and then printed the readings he thought most likely original. This text became the basis for most vernacular translations of the New Testament until the nineteenth century.

The <u>Protestant Reformation</u> in the sixteenth century fueled efforts to translate the Christian Bible into vernacular languages. Protestants and Catholics increasingly considered it important to follow the example of Jerome, so they learned Hebrew (see Figure 10.3) as well as Greek. The German translation by Martin Luther and all the English bibles of the Reformation Era (Tyndale's, Geneva, Bishop's, King James, and also the Roman Catholic Rheims-Douay version) translated the Old Testament from Hebrew and the New Testament from Greek, which remains the standard practice today.[12]

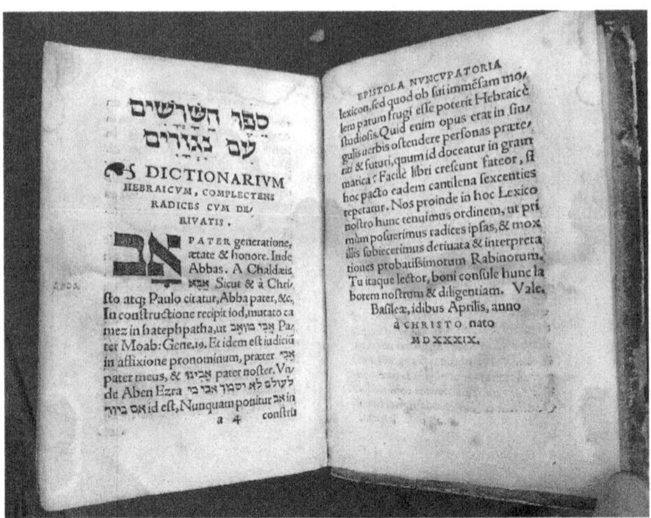

**FIGURE 10.3**   Sebastian Munster, *Dictionarium Hebraicum*, Basel, 1539. In a private collection.

Thus, despite the Pentecost story (Acts 2), Christian Bible translations have increasingly emphasized human linguistic expertise together with piety, rather than claiming divine inspiration for the translators. Inspired translation closes the gap between translation and original, giving the translation equal or even greater status than the scripture in the original language. That has happened several times in Christian history, but the more prominent accounts of Christian scripture translation have emphasized human expertise and piety. The letter of Aristeas in the second century BCE lavished attention on the Septuagint translators' scholarship and devotion. Jerome in the fourth century CE presented himself as both an ascetic and a philologist. Similarly, accounts of the sixteenth- and seventeenth-century translation work of Martin Luther and of the scholars who produced the King James Version emphasize their expertise in Hebrew and Greek as well as their religious piety.

Translation has been somewhat less important to Jewish tradition because of the dominance of the Hebrew language in ritual and in traditional Jewish education. Jewish scholars therefore tend to use Hebrew terms rather than worry about their translation, even when writing in vernacular languages. Nevertheless, important Jewish translations appeared in Greek, Aramaic, Arabic, and Yiddish. The political emancipation of European Jews in the nineteenth century and the emergence of the Reform movement led Jewish publishers to produce German and English translations of the Tanak that were fairly traditional in content. In the twentieth century, several prominent scholars created more distinctively Jewish translations. The philosophers Franz Rosenzweig and Martin Buber tried to reproduce the aesthetic and literary qualities of Hebrew in their German translation of 1925–1936. The reputation of the translators and their innovative methods immediately made their translation famous and controversial. Everett Fox reproduced their methods in English translation in 1995 and 2014, while the well-known literary critic, Robert Alter, finished a more idiomatic English translation in 2018.[13]

Celebration of translators' expertise calls attention to the ritualization of scripture's semantic dimension through scholarship. It uses the iconic legitimacy of the original text to authorize reading in the translated language. Celebration of scholarly translation thus allows the translated text to assume the original text's semantic authority while simultaneously preserving the iconic memory, if not knowledge, of the original language behind the translation. Celebration of particular translators can buttress veneration of one translation against others, as has sometimes been the case for the Latin Vulgate and the English King James Version. Nevertheless, vesting the translation's accuracy in human expertise leaves the door open for new translations based on better knowledge of ancient languages or due to changes in modern languages. As a result, the words of scripture expressed in Christian churches change whenever they start using new translations.

## 10.5   PORTRAYING JESUS IN VISUAL ART AND MEDIA

Christian cultures have not just relied on preachers and theologians to interpret Jesus. Since at least 200 CE, if not earlier, Christian artists have portrayed Jesus in scenes taken from the Gospels and the book of Revelation.[14] Early Christian artists especially showed Jesus healing people. They also portrayed him in popular Greco-Roman scenes and poses as a shepherd carrying a sheep, as a philosopher, and as God ruling in heaven surrounded by angels (Figure 10.4). Jesus appeared like a beardless Roman youth until the sixth century CE, when a long-haired, bearded Jesus began to appear. That stereotype was reinforced by popular relics, like the shroud of Turin, that were believed to be miraculous images of Jesus himself. Starting in the fourth century, artists frequently depicted the cross and scenes of the crucifixion, showing Jesus still alive. Crucifixes depicting a dead Jesus became common only around the beginning of the second millennium CE. Then they often appeared together with images of his resurrection or his descent into hell.

In the Middle Ages, the life of Jesus and the church's calendar of festivals dominated the art in churches. Many scenes featured Jesus' mother, Mary. The crucified Jesus could appear almost naked, as in the Gospels, but also dressed in a robe as a priest-king, as in Revelations 1:13. Later medieval European art increasingly emphasized the emotion and pain of the crucifixion and of other scenes in Jesus' life. This trend increased in Renaissance (fifteenth to sixteenth centuries) and Baroque art (seventeenth to eighteenth centuries). Artists have continued to illustrate Jesus' activities on earth, and also the resurrected Jesus of the apocalypse and Jesus as divine. You would never know from all this art that the Gospels say *nothing* about what Jesus looked like!

Art depicting Jesus has been controversial in several periods of Christian history. Many people objected that it contradicts the commandment against making and worshipping images (Exod. 20:4–5). In Eastern (Greek Orthodox) churches of the seventh to ninth centuries, this argument erupted into the <u>iconoclastic controversy</u>, in which the art in many churches was destroyed. The conflict was eventually resolved in favor of allowing two-dimensional art (icons) in churches, but not more realistic three-dimensional sculptures. Western (Roman Catholic) churches have allowed both kinds of art. During the Reformation in the sixteenth century, Protestants also objected to the religious attention and economic expense devoted to art. They destroyed or moved much of the art out of their churches. Most Protestant churches in the Reformed tradition remained bare of art up through the nineteenth century, and many remain so today.

In the Middle Ages, Greek theologians developed a theory of how religious <u>icons</u> work. The word *eikon* is simply Greek for "image," but they defined it more specifically to refer to a material object that shows us something invisible. So icons, while physical artifacts, reveal divine truth by portraying God, Christ, and the spiritual virtues exemplified by the saints.[15] In Eastern Orthodox Christian churches, icons most frequently depict Jesus Christ, Mary, Peter, Paul, and the four (supposed) writers of the New Testament Gospels: Matthew, Mark, Luke, and John. Icons depict many other Christian saints as well.

Despite the iconoclastic controversies, it is fair to say that Christian images, with Jesus most prominent among them, dominated European art from the early Middle Ages until the seventeenth or eighteenth century. That is because churches were the richest patrons of the arts. Many of them could afford to hire the best artists and sculptors, so the best art appeared in churches and featured Christian themes. Images of Christ became less prominent in Western nineteenth- and twentieth-century art, when secular museums and private citizens became more influential buyers of art.

Nevertheless, churches have continued to sponsor innovative religious art right up to today. One of the most widely reproduced images of Jesus in the twentieth century was Warner Sallman's "Head of Christ," painted in 1940, which epitomized the old stereotype of the bearded, long-haired, white Jesus. However, the world-wide spread of Christianity has produced more culturally and ethnically diverse portraits of Jesus. He appears in the artistic styles and dress of many different cultures, and resembles people of all kinds. Increasingly, Jesus no longer looks white (see Figure 10.5).

It is easy to criticize all artistic depictions of Jesus as unhistorical, since there is no information about his physical appearance in the Bible (only visionary descriptions in Rev. 1:13–16, 5:6–14, 19:11–16). However, artists who depict Jesus as looking like themselves or like their audience reflect the Christian belief that Jesus is the ideal human. The theological description of him as God in human form invites people to identify with him as "human like us." Artists who portray him with the ethnic appearance and artistic conventions of their own cultures do so on the basis of traditional Christian doctrine. It becomes problematic for both doctrine and morality, however, when one ethnic stereotype of Jesus dominates Christian imaginations in a multicultural society. The pluralism of contemporary images of Jesus counteracts such stereotypes.

Ethnic pluralism has not yet taken hold in the other major kind of expression of modern images of Jesus, namely, Hollywood movies. White

**FIGURE 10.4**  Christ in heaven supported by angels: ninth century ce mosaic in the dome of the San Zeno Chapel in the Basilica of Santa Prassada in Rome.

**FIGURE 10.5**  Crucifix (1997) by Juvenal Kaliki and Jeffrey Brosk in the Mother of Africa Chapel of the Roman Catholic National Shrine in Washington, DC.

actors continue to play the role of Jesus and most of the disciples.[16] Films have now become a decisive influence on how Christians and other people imagine Jesus. Cecile B. DeMille's *The King of Kings* (1927) exemplified the reverent treatment of him in early silent movies. Then, for 30 years, Hollywood producers avoided depicting Jesus frontally and at length for fear of the controversies that inevitably surround such movies. That moratorium was broken by liberalizing cultural and theological trends in the 1960s.

Jesus returned to the big screen first in movies such as Pier Paolo Pasolini's *The Gospel According to Saint Matthew* (1964) and George Stevens' *The Greatest Story Ever Told* (1965). They used the Gospels quite literally as screenplays. Movies have also tried to reproduce the look of Christian art: Franco Zeffirelli's *Jesus of Nazareth* (1977) cast an actor to play Jesus because he looked like Sallman's popular painting, "Head of Christ." Mel Gibson's *The Passion of the Christ* (2004) tried to reproduce the visual impact of Baroque art. Its plot reflected the visions of a nineteenth-century Catholic mystic, Sister Anne Emmerich, as well as the Gospels. Rock music was employed to present more radical re-imaginings of Jesus in Andrew Lloyd Webber and Tim Rice's *Jesus Christ Superstar* and Stephen Schwartz's *Godspell* (both stage musicals in 1971, films in 1973). Some films in the 1980s presented more speculative versions of Jesus' story based in literature, such as Martin Scorsese's *The Last Temptation of Christ* (1988), or based in modern theology, such as Denys Arcand's *Jesus of Montreal* (1989).

Meanwhile, Christian denominations and para-church organizations around the world increasingly produce their own films for theaters and for viewing in homes and churches. These productions then influence commercial productions as well. Films and television have now become as influential as religious art in shaping Christians' imaginations about Jesus – perhaps as influential as the printed Bible itself.

Visual art of all kinds ritualizes the expressive dimension of the Gospels' story. Just as reading aloud and singing bring alive the biblical words, art and movies resurrect Jesus again to inspire audiences. In this way, the inspiring power of video technology in modern culture has reinforced the already widespread belief in Jesus as a human ideal, as well as belief in the Bible's divine inspiration.

## CITED WORKS AND FURTHER READING


1 On scripture, especially Gospel, readings in Christian churches, see Adrian Fortescue, "Gospel in the Liturgy," *The Catholic Encyclopedia* (New York: Robert Appleton Company, 1909), vol. 6, online at http://www.newadvent.org/cathen/06659a.htm.

2 William Graham, *Beyond the Written Word: Oral Aspects of Scripture in the History of Religion* (Cambridge: Cambridge University Press, 1987), 131.

3 On Christian lectionaries, see *The Revised Common Lectionary* by the Consultation on Common Texts (Minneapolis: Augsburg Fortress, 2012), especially p. 4; Horace T. Allen, "Introduction: Preaching in a Christian Context," in *Handbook for the Revised Common Lectionary* (ed. P. C. Bower; Nashville: Abingdon, 1996), 1–24; and Felix Just, "Lectionary Statistics" on the Roman Catholic *Lectionary for Mass* (2009), online at http://catholic-resources.org/Lectionary/Statistics.htm.

4 Jennifer Knust and Tommy Wasserman, "The Biblical Odes and the Text of the Christian Bible: A Reconsideration of the Impact of Liturgical Singing on the Transmission of the Gospel of Luke," *Journal of Biblical Literature* 133 (2014): 341–365 (p. 344).

5 On chanting Christian scriptures, see Timothy Thibodeau, "Western Christendom," in *The Oxford History of Christian Worship* (ed. G. Wainwright; Oxford: Oxford University Press, 2006), 242–246; and William T. Flynn, "Liturgical Music," in *The Oxford History of Christian Worship*, 769–792.

6 On ancient Christian translations of scripture, see John F. A. Sawyer, *Sacred Languages and Sacred Texts* (London: Routledge, 1999), 83–89, 94–95; and Willard G. Oxtoby, "'Telling in Their Own Tongues': Old and Modern Bible Translations as Expressions of Ethnic Cultural Identity," in *The Bible as Cultural Heritage* (ed. W. Beuken and S. Freyne; London: SCM, 1995), 24–35 (pp. 29–30).

7 Sawyer, *Sacred Languages and Sacred Texts*, 93.

8 On the cultural effects of different scripts, see David Damrosch, "Scriptworlds: Writing Systems and the Formation of World Literature," *Modern Language Quarterly* 68/2 (2007), 195–219.

9 The *Letter of Aristeas* was translated by R. J. H. Shuttin in, *Old Testament Pseudepigrapha* (ed. J. H. Charlesworth; 2 vols.; New York: Doubleday, 1983), 7–34.

10 Translated by C. D. Yonge, *The Works of Philo Judaeus* (London, H. G. Bohn, 1854–1890), 2. 37–41.

11 On Jerome as translator of the Vulgate, see Megan Hale Williams, *The Monk and the Book: Jerome and the Making of Christian Scholarship* (Chicago: University of Chicago, 2006).

12 On the history of modern Bible translations, see Paul Ellingworth, "From Martin Luther to the English Revised Version," in *A History of Bible Translation* (ed. P. A. Noss; New York: American Bible Society, 2007), 105–139.

13 Martin Buber and Franz Rosenzweig, *Scripture and Translation* (tr. L. Rosenwald and E. Fox, Bloomington: Indiana University Press, 1994 [German 1936]); Everett Fox, *The Five Books of Moses*, Schocken Bible 1 (New York: Schocken, 1995); Everett Fox, *The Early Prophets*, Schocken Bible 2 (New York: Schocken, 2014); Robert Alter, *The Hebrew Bible: A Translation with Commentary* (New York: Norton, 2018); see further in Leonard Greenspoon, *Jewish Bible Translations: Personalities, Passions, Politics* (Philadelphia: Jewish Publication Society, 2020).

14 For surveys of Jesus in art, see Richard Harries, "Art," in *Jesus in History, Thought, and Culture: An Encyclopedia* (ed. L. Houlden; Santa Barbara: ABC CLIO, 2003), 1: 66–106; Hans J. Hillerbrand, "Jesus in the Visual Arts," *Encyclopedia Brittanica*, August 26, 2016. Available at: https://www.britannica.com/topic/Christology/Jesus-in-the-visual-arts (accessed: March 21, 2018); and Diane Apostolos-Cappadona, *A Guide to Christian Art* (London: T.&T. Clark, 2020), 11–66. For more attention to the relationship between art and

Christian thought, see Jaroslav Pelikan, *The Illustrated Jesus Through the Centuries* (New Haven, CT: Yale University Press, 1997).

15 On icons and theories of icons, see Annabel Wharton, "Icon, Idol, Totem and Fetish," in *Icon and Word: The Power of Images in Byzantium* (ed. A. Eastmond and L. James; Aldershot: Ashgate, 2003), 12–23; and John Stuart, *Ikons* (London: Faber & Faber, 1975).

16 For surveys of the depiction of Jesus in films and television, see Larry J. Krietzer, "Film," in *Jesus in History, Thought, and Culture: An Encyclopedia* (ed. L. Houlden; Santa Barbara: ABC CLIO, 2003), 1: 288–291; Peter Malone, *Screen Jesus: Portrayals of Christ in Television and Film* (London: Scarecrow, 2012); and W. Barnes Tatum, *Jesus at the Movies: A Guide to the First Hundred Years and Beyond* (Salem, OR: Polebridge Press, 2013).

# CHAPTER 11

# The Gospels' Semantic Dimension

The comparative study of religions illustrates the many ways in which religious scriptures can be ritualized in the semantic dimension (see Chapter 6). In the same way, Christians have ritualized the semantic dimension of the Gospels to create rich traditions of preaching, teaching, and commentary (see also Sections 6.4, 6.6, and Chapter 14).

Interpretation of the Gospels and of the rest of the New Testament has influenced Christian beliefs and practices decisively since the second century CE. The New Testament books emphasize the vital importance of Christ's death and resurrection, so I begin by reviewing how Christians across history have interpreted the significance of Jesus' death. However, other ancient gospels about Jesus show that not all early Christians focused on Jesus' death. Biblical and non-biblical gospels therefore lead us to discuss several historical questions: Did women play a larger role in the earliest Christian movement than the New Testament admits? How were the four New Testament Gospels written? Did Paul write all the letters attributed to him? And what can we know historically about Jesus?

## 11.1   INTERPRETING JESUS' DEATH

The letter to the Romans contains Paul's most extensive discussion of Jesus Christ's work. Here he describes Christ as the Son of God who intercedes for humans before God in heaven (Rom. 8:34). Paul argues that Adam's sin allowed death into human experience, but Christ's death provided "justification and life for all" (Rom 5:18). So, Jesus' crucifixion and resurrection bring about salvation for everyone, even the whole universe (Rom. 8:19–22). As a result, people who accept Christ are freed from the obligations of the law, that is, of Torah (Rom. 7–8). But their new freedom enables them to observe a strict moral code as they live in imitation of Jesus, even to the point of willingly becoming a "living sacrifice" as martyrs (Rom. 12:1).

Paul radically reinterpreted the Torah's laws and ritual instructions as applying first of all to Jesus Christ. Jesus completely fulfilled all the Torah's laws and offered himself as the required sin offering. As a result, later Christians felt free to ignore the Pentateuch's ritual rules, though Paul himself practiced some of them as an observant Jew (Acts 21:26). However, Paul and other New Testament writers retained the Hebrew Bible as Christian scripture because it authorized their interpretation of Jesus' life and death. The Pentateuch provides Paul's evidence for arguing that humans have been sinful since Adam (Rom. 5:14–21), and also his best example of faith and trust in God in the stories about Abraham (Rom. 4).[1] The Prophets and Psalms provide many texts that the New Testament interprets as predictions about Jesus and his mission (e.g., Rom. 3:10–12 on Pss. 14:1–2; 53:1–2; and Heb. 8:8–12 on Jer. 31:31–34).

The anonymous letter to the Hebrews uses the Pentateuch in even more detail to interpret Jesus. Like other New Testament books, Hebrews depicts Jesus' death as a sacrifice that mitigates human sin (Heb. 10:10). But it also portrays Jesus as the high priest who offers sacrifices to God (3:1; 4:14–5:10). Hebrews use Melchizedek, an obscure priest mentioned in Genesis 14:17–20 and Psalm 110:4, to argue for a priesthood superior to Aaron's (Heb. 6:13–10:25). Here, the innermost room of the Tabernacle or Temple that only the high priest may enter (Lev. 16) becomes a metaphor for reconciliation with God through Christ:

*We have this hope, a sure and steadfast anchor of the soul, a hope that enters the inner shrine behind the curtain, where Jesus, a forerunner on our behalf, has entered, having become a high priest forever according to the order of Melchizedek.* (Heb. 6:19–20 NRSV)

So Jesus' crucifixion replaces not only the ritual instructions for offerings in the Torah, but its authorization of the Aaronide priesthood as well. The Pentateuch's descriptions of Israel's priests and temple rituals become, in Hebrews, an interpretive lens for understanding who Jesus is and what his death accomplished. In this way, the early Christians used the Hebrew Bible not only to claim that the prophets predicted Jesus in advance (Heb. 11). They also used it to justify Christian innovations in religious beliefs and ritual practices.

Note that the goal of these early Christian writers was not the semantic interpretation of the Hebrew Bible. Instead, they used scripture to interpret Jesus, especially his death by crucifixion. The Hebrew Bible provided them with scriptural texts that they used to generate new ideas about the central figure of the Christian faith. Jesus is "the lamb of God who takes away the sin of the world" (John 1:29), because Jesus Christ's death is an offering that brings about forgiveness for human sin. Such interpretations reflect the description of sin offerings in Leviticus 4–5 that "mitigate" or "atone" so that offenders are forgiven their sins. Stories of Jesus' last supper base this interpretation in his own words: Paul quoted him as saying that the cup represents "the new covenant in my blood" (1 Cor. 11:25) to which Matthew 26:28 added the explanation, "for the forgiveness of sins" (similarly Col. 1:14; Eph. 1:7).

Many later Christian writers used this language about Christ's death for the <u>forgiveness of sin</u> without trying to explain its exact significance. A few tried to specify it more exactly. In the third century, Origen developed the <u>expiatory</u> view that Christ's sacrifice loosened the devil's hold on sinful humans. In the fourth century, Eusebius and John Chrysostom reflected the more popular <u>propitiatory</u> idea that Christ's crucifixion calmed God's anger at human sin through a kind of ransom payment. It was left to Athanasius to systematically reconcile these ideas by arguing that through Christ's crucifixion, God made an offering to death, but because of God's omnipotence, "that victory over evil becomes a divine self-reconciliation."[2]

Since then, Christian interpretations of Christ's atoning death have worried about the difference between calming (propitiating) an angry deity and cleaning (expiating) sin and its effects. Yet no specific doctrine of the <u>atonement</u> was ever endorsed in early Christian councils or crystallized in the ancient creeds. It was enough for ancient Christians to affirm that Christ's death was a sacrifice and that, through it, God defeated the power of death. This was often elaborated to portray Christ tricking Satan into accepting him into hell despite his innocence. This mistake cost Satan his claim on human sinners.

Many philosophical Christians have found this story of a divine ransom payment too amoral in its plot. They have looked for other explanations for the effectiveness of Christ's death. Their attempts led to replacing the analogy to Leviticus's temple offerings with comparisons to <u>laws</u>. On the basis of Roman private law, Anselm (1033–1109 CE) suggested that sin put humans in debt to God beyond their ability to pay, but Christ's death paid the debt. But this <u>satisfaction</u> theory of the atonement casts God as a rather cruel creditor who refuses to forgive the debt, though nothing in private law prevents creditors from doing so.

Hugo Grotius (1583–1645) revised the satisfaction theory on the basis of Roman criminal law, rather than private law. God as ruler has the responsibility to enforce the law. God could not forgive sins without reparations being paid, thus requiring Christ's death. Criminal law, however, does not usually allow substitution of an innocent person for the convicted criminal. This led Grotius to compare substitution of sacrificial victims in various cultures. He concluded that <u>substitution</u> was in fact permitted in the time of Jesus.[3]

Even further removed from Leviticus's depictions of sin offerings is the <u>moral influence</u> theory of the atonement associated with Peter Abelard (1079–1142) and Faustus Socinus (1539–1604). They maintained that Christ's death had only an exemplary effect on Christians who are moved to imitate his self-sacrifice. His death then did not affect God but only his human followers. Variations on this model have appeared repeatedly in theological and ethical treatises of the eighteenth through twentieth centuries, and were popularized again in recent decades by René Girard.[4]

## 11.2  OTHER ANCIENT GOSPELS

Not all early Christians agreed about the importance of Jesus' death. We know this because the four New Testament Gospels are not the only ancient gospels telling about the life and teachings of Jesus.

The <u>Nag Hammadi Codices</u> (Box 11.1) included a number of gospels credited to Jesus' disciples, such as the gospels of Philip, of Thomas, and of Mary Magdalene. Most of these books seem to rewrite and expand on material found in the New Testament. The Gospel of Thomas, however, presents many of the same sayings of Jesus as the Synoptic Gospels, but in shorter form. This has led many scholars to wonder if the Gospel of Thomas provides an independent witness to the early oral tradition about Jesus and his teachings.

The Gospel of Thomas presents *only* Jesus' teachings. It does not narrate the story of Jesus' ministry, arrest, crucifixion, and resurrection. That is because Thomas and many other Valentinian texts argue that what Jesus said is most important (see Box 11.1). They believed that Jesus came to teach his

### Box 11.1   The Nag Hammadi Codices

Thirteen volumes containing more than 50 works in Coptic (ancient Egyptian) were discovered in 1945 in Nag Hammadi, Egypt. These Christian works interpreted Jesus and his significance from a very different point of view than do the books of the New Testament. They express the views and beliefs of the followers of <u>Valentinius</u> and other Christian mystics of the second to fourth centuries CE.

The Valentinians and similar groups taught a dualistic theology. They emphasized opposition between mind and matter, spirit and the body, God and the world. The first elements of each dichotomy are aligned with each other in opposition to the second elements. As a result, it is not possible that God could become a physical human. They regarded such a mixture of spirit and body, of the immortal with the mortal, as impossible.

These mystics accepted that Jesus was the Son of God. Because of their dualistic beliefs, however, they could not accept that he was a real human, or that he really died. So many of them believed that Jesus came not to die, but to teach divine knowledge (Greek: *gnosis*) to his disciples. They are therefore often called <u>Gnostics</u>.[5]

disciples secret divine knowledge, in contrast to the New Testament books that argue that Jesus came to die for the sake of human sins.

The Nag Hammadi Codices show that early Christianity was quite diverse in its views about Jesus and about how Christians should follow him. While the New Testament preserves traditions that it credits to apostles like Peter, John, Matthew, Paul, and James, the Valentinians traced their traditions to other disciples, such as Thomas, Philip, and Mary Magdalene. The appearance here of texts credited to Mary hints that some early Christian groups were more open to women spiritual leaders than others.

The New Testament Gospels already show signs of struggling against gnostic views. John's Gospel, in particular, emphasizes that Jesus was really human: "the Word became flesh" (John 1:14; also 1 John 4:2). Its conclusion singles out Thomas as a doubter. He must touch the physical body of Jesus to believe that he rose from the dead (John 20:24–29). This story may be debunking claims like those in the Gospel of Thomas, which says that Jesus taught Thomas secret knowledge unknown to the other disciples:

*These are the secret sayings which the living Jesus spoke and which Didymos Judas Thomas wrote down.*

The four Gospels in the New Testament, then, aimed not only to preserve Jesus' words and the stories about him. They also meant to correct other written accounts (Luke 1:4). They were already responding to other traditions about Jesus, such as those that later circulated in Valentinian texts. They were written to convince readers and hearers of the truth of their interpretation of Jesus, "so that you will believe" (John 20:31).

## 11.3   WOMEN IN THE GOSPELS AND IN ANCIENT CULTURES

The New Testament Gospels all agree that three women – "Mary Magdalene, Mary the mother of James, and Salome" (Mark 16:1) – were the first to find Jesus' tomb empty. Women were therefore the first to proclaim the distinctively Christian message of Jesus' resurrection from the dead (Matt. 28:8). Yet the emerging Catholic church made no room for women in leadership defined by male apostolic succession. However, the prominence of women in the New Testament Gospels and, especially, in some of the Nag Hammadi gospels (see above) has led historians to wonder if women played a larger role in early Christianity.[6]

For the most part in ancient cultures, only free men had legal rights, that is, had the right to appear in court as plaintiffs or witnesses. Women had fewer rights, though these varied: women could own real estate in Egypt and in Rome, but not in pre-Hellenistic Greece. In all ancient cultures, a woman's economic and social status usually depended on a man – her father, brother, or son – who therefore controlled her to a greater or lesser extent. Biblical examples go so far as to show a man's control over whether a woman lives or dies in stories about Jephthah's daughter (Judg. 11:22–40) and the Levite's concubine (Judg. 19:22–30). A woman was defined by her status as daughter, wife, mother, or slave to such an extent that biblical texts often identify women only in relationship to their man, as in these stories, or by adding the man's name to hers, as in "Mary the mother of James" (Mark 16:1). Because status and wealth depended on a woman's place in a patriarchal family, the poorest and most vulnerable women were widows (Ruth) or unwed mothers (potentially Mary, Jesus' mother). Biblical laws stereotype widows, along with orphans and immigrants, as the people who are most vulnerable to abuse (Exod. 22:21–24; Deut. 24:17; 27:19).

In ancient village economies where men produced raw goods from which women made finished goods (e.g., food and clothing), women as a group controlled significant resources. Therefore, the matriarchs of such clans, such as Sarah (Gen. 16) and Abigail (1 Sam. 25), wielded significant influence over their households and even their husbands.[7] As economies became more stratified and urbanized, however, men increasingly earned wages as soldiers, scribes, and priests. They therefore became economically independent of the women in their households, and women's influence declined. Still, Proverbs 31 celebrated the "good wife" entirely in terms of her economic productivity, management, and trading skills.

Nevertheless, some exceptional women wielded their wealth independently. Lydia, a merchant of purple cloth (an expensive dye), provided Paul housing in Philippi (Acts 16:14–15). Three wealthy women bankrolled Jesus' ministry: "Mary Magdalene…, Joanna, the wife of Chuza, Herod's steward, and Susanna,…who supported him out of their resources" (Luke 8:2–3). Mary Magdalene, in particular, attracted the attention of later Christians. According to Luke, she was a wealthy woman healed by Jesus who funded his work. In the Gospels' lists of women disciples, her name always appears first. All the Gospels highlight her presence at the empty tomb. She is never identified by her family, only by her hometown, Magdala. Yet later Christian tradition has identified her with stories about unnamed women of bad reputation in Luke 7:37 and John 8:3. As a result, Mary Magdalene has been depicted in preaching and art as young, beautiful, and sexually promiscuous before meeting Jesus, rather than as a wealthy businesswoman.

Women could hold positions of religious authority in some ancient religious institutions. In some places, they could serve as temple priests (Figure 11.1). The Pentateuch, however, restricts Israel's priesthood to Aaron's male descendants (Exod. 28; Lev. 8). But several prominent Israelite prophets were women: Miriam who was a leader of the exodus (Exod. 15:20), Deborah who was also a judge (Judg. 4:4), and Huldah who certified King Josiah's Torah scroll (2 Kgs. 22:14).

Early Christians also recognized that women could prophesy (Acts 21:9). Paul even credited one woman in Rome, Junia, as "among the apostles" (Rom. 16:7). The non-canonical Gospels of Thomas and of Philip show that many early Christians regarded Mary Magdalene as one of Jesus' closest disciples. The Gospel of Mary depicts her transmitting teachings of Jesus unknown to the male disciples. The discovery of these texts (Box 11.1) has raised the suspicion that women played more prominent roles in Christianity's first generations than later Christian tradition has been willing to admit (see further in Section 14.2.6).

**FIGURE 11.1**  Priest at the Temple of Demeter at Pergamum. In the Bergama Museum. Suat Eracar/Shutterstock.com.

## 11.4  THE GOSPEL BEFORE THE GOSPELS

"The Gospel," i.e., the "good news about Jesus Christ" (Mark 1:1), was transmitted orally at first. For example, when Paul told the story of Jesus' last supper, he used an <u>oral transmission</u> formula:

> *I received from the Lord what I also handed on to you… (1 Cor. 11:23)*

The earliest Christians apparently saw no reason to record Jesus' words or the story of his life. There may be several reasons for that. Many believed, like Paul (1 Thess. 4:15), that Jesus would return within their lifetimes to bring about the end of the world. So there was no need to preserve written texts for posterity. It is also the case that many ancient people who could read and write nevertheless preferred to hear news from eyewitnesses. Papius, a Christian bishop who lived around 110 CE, looked for an eyewitness to tell him what Jesus said and did as he prepared his sermons. Failing that, he listened to people who had known eyewitnesses. Only when he failed to find such oral traditions did he turn to reading the written gospels that he had in his possession. Such reverence for "the living word" of oral tradition probably also inhibited the writing of gospels.

In the last three decades of the first century, however, the eyewitnesses to Jesus' life were dying out. The Christian message was also spreading far and wide, so many churches had no access to the few eyewitnesses still alive. Also, Jesus did not return to bring about the Last Judgment as many were expecting. Even the Roman attack on Jerusalem and destruction of the Temple in 70 CE, which seemed to fulfill Jesus' predictions in most other ways (Mark 13:1–2, 14–27), did not result in the Messiah's return. So the need to write down "a carefully ordered account" (Luke 1:3 CEB) became more pressing, especially in the face of increasing controversies over doctrine.

These conditions probably prompted Christians to start writing down the oral traditions about Jesus' teachings and actions and, especially, about his death and resurrection. It appears that the four gospels in the New Testament were all written between approximately 70 and 100 CE. That means they were based on oral traditions that had been circulating and developing for around 40 years since the crucifixion of Jesus. The written gospels therefore reflect several stages in the development of Christian ideas about Jesus.

## 11.4.1   Who Wrote the Gospels?

All four New Testament Gospels are technically <u>anonymous</u>: none of them names its author. The Gospel of John comes closest, crediting its traditions to Jesus' "favorite disciple" (John 21:24), but it does not name him. When the early Christians circulated these four gospels together in one volume, they needed to give them different names. So they assigned them to people mentioned in the Gospels or in Acts who they believed had written them. Two of the 12 disciples are credited with writing gospels: Matthew and John the son of Zebedee. The other two gospels were credited to known associates of leading apostles: Luke was a companion of Paul (Phil. 1:24), and Mark was associated with Barnabus (Acts 12:25). According to church tradition, Mark later joined Peter in Rome where he wrote the gospel at Peter's instruction.

The contents of the New Testament Gospels cause many modern scholars to doubt that they were written by these four people. As we have seen, the gospels according to Matthew, Mark, and Luke are called the <u>Synoptic Gospels</u> because their writers clearly depended on each other's work. John's Gospel, on the other hand, does not seem to know of the Synoptic Gospels, and they do not know of his work. The authorship of John's Gospel is therefore very difficult to determine. However, the fact that the Synoptic Gospels depend on each other provides clues about how they were written.

## 11.4.2   The Synoptic Problem

In some passages, all three gospels of Matthew, Mark, and Luke repeat each other verbatim. Obviously, they were copying each other. In other places, however, any two may duplicate each other while the third either omits the story or gives a different version of it. Yet again, there are places where all three go their own way.[8] Verbatim repetition proves that the writers copied from each other, but does not answer the question: who copied from whom?

The early Christians believed that Matthew wrote his Gospel first. That is one of the reasons it appears first in the New Testament. They believed that Mark and Luke, who were not eyewitnesses, copied from the eyewitness, Matthew, to compose their books. Luke adapted Matthew, according to this theory, and Mark abbreviated and combined both Matthew and Luke. This theory was championed by the nineteenth-century German scholar Johann Jakob Griesbach, and is therefore often called the Griesbach hypothesis. It is hard to understand, however, why the writer of Mark would omit so much if he had access to the accounts of Matthew and Luke. Though we can imagine the need for an abbreviated version, Mark leaves out much that became very popular among later Christians. Neither the stories of Jesus' birth, nor the Sermon on the Mount including the Beatitudes and the Lord's Prayer, nor the parables of the Good Samaritan and the Prodigal Son, nor most of the appearances of the resurrected Jesus, appear in Mark.

These omissions lead many scholars to think that Mark wrote first. Matthew and Luke then added all these materials and more to Mark's shorter account. If that is the case, then Matthew and Luke must have had another source in common, since they add many of the same materials. This hypothetical source is usually called Q, from the German word *Quelle* "source." This two-source hypothesis is more popular among modern historians because 90% of Mark reappears in Matthew and Luke, who also follow Mark's arrangement of the story. So, it is easy to see how they would have copied Mark and just added material from Q and other sources in various places. A few scholars think that Luke copied from Matthew as well as Mark. This Farrer hypothesis eliminates the need for Q.

However, if Mark was a source for Matthew, it is hard to believe that the gospel credited to Matthew was really written by an eyewitness, much less one of the 12 disciples. Why would someone who worked with Jesus himself copy a source written by someone who wasn't there? Mark contains many mistakes about Jewish customs and Palestinian geography, which suggest that he was unfamiliar with the local culture. Matthew corrects these problems. So it seems that none of the Synoptic Gospels was written by an eyewitness, though they no doubt depended on oral traditions from eyewitnesses.

Modern scholars think Mark's Gospel was written for non-Jewish Christians sometime around 70 CE. They usually date Matthew a decade later. This writer seems better informed about the local geography and culture in Palestine than his source, Mark's Gospel. So, Matthew may have been written by and intended for Jewish Christians. The writer of Luke and Acts uses very good Greek style and seems to write for a gentile audience. This writer shows the influence of Paul's letters, so perhaps he really was Luke the physician, writing in the last decades of the first century.[9] Most recent discussions of John's Gospel, however, do not try to name the author. At most, they suggest it may have originated in the Christian community at Ephesus, which was long associated with John the son of Zebedee.[10]

## 11.5  WRITING PAUL'S LETTERS

Christians traditionally count Paul as the author of 14 books in the New Testament. Of these, 13 letters explicitly mention Paul's name. The letter to the Hebrews does not, and its different ideas and style show that it was not written by the author(s) of the other letters.

Even the 13 letters that claim Paul explicitly as their author reveal differences in vocabulary and style, in their theology and ideas, and in their apparent dates and social settings. These differences can be explained in various ways. Paul sometimes wrote himself (Gal. 6:11), but he often used secretaries to write his letters (Rom. 16:22). If they sometimes drafted letters for his approval, that could account for stylistic and vocabulary differences while Paul remained their legitimate author. Paul's ideas probably changed over time, which could account for at least some of the differences in theology.

The differences in apparent date and setting are more difficult to accommodate to Paul's authorship. In particular, the letters to Timothy and Titus (called the Pastoral letters because they are addressed to the leaders, "pastors," of a church instead of to the church as a whole) reflect a more developed level of church organization with bishops, elders, and deacons. These letters, then, seem to reflect a later period than do Paul's other letters. In that case, they are pseudonymous, that is, they were written by somebody else in Paul's name.

Pseudonymity was a common literary device in antiquity. Sometimes pseudonymous writings tried to deceive readers as to their author, and so can legitimately be labeled forgeries. In other cases, pseudonymous authorship was used to continue the tradition of an important writer and apply that person's ideas to present circumstances. Pseudonymity was a way of saying, "this is what Paul would say if he were here now." Some New Testament

**Box 11.2   "Pauline" letters in the NT**

| Letter | Likely author |
| --- | --- |
| Romans | Paul |
| 1 Corinthians | Paul |
| 2 Corinthians | Paul |
| Galatians | Paul |
| Ephesians | Probably not Paul |
| Philippians | Paul |
| Colossians | Probably not Paul |
| 1 Thessalonians | Paul |
| 2 Thessalonians | Maybe Paul |
| 1 Timothy | Not Paul |
| 2 Timothy | Not Paul |
| Titus | Not Paul |
| Philemon | Paul |

letters seem to have been written a generation after Paul's time and attributed to him to adapt his teachings to the new situations that Christians found themselves in.

Modern historians agree that seven New Testament letters were almost certainly written by Paul himself. Many argue that the Pastoral Letters were not written by him.[11] There is considerable disagreement about the authorship of three other letters (see Box 11.2).

## 11.6   THE SEARCH FOR THE HISTORICAL JESUS

The New Testament Gospels leave out a great deal of information about Jesus. For example, they do not tell us what he looked like. They do not tell us much about his family, except for the names of his mother, Mary, and her husband, Joseph, and that they had other children (Mark 3:31–34). They say nothing about his education. Only the story of his baptism by John the Baptist provides any hint of his religious affiliations or background within Judaism.

Furthermore, the information provided by the Gospels is not always consistent. Matthew and Luke both provide Jesus' genealogy, but not the same one (compare Matt 1:2–27 with Luke 3:23–38). The events during his adult ministry in Galilee, and especially the situations in which he said certain things, appear in various sequences in the different Gospels.

This is not surprising. The Gospels are not modern histories or biographies. They are religious tracts aimed at educating people about Christ's teachings and his example in order to convert them to Christianity. As John 20:31 says explicitly, "All this is written so that you may believe." The Gospel writers, then, did not write and arrange their material as a chronological record. They instead tried to make it as persuasive as possible to their audiences in the first century CE.

There is very little information about Jesus from first-century sources apart from the New Testament Gospels. The Jewish historian Josephus knew that the early church in Jerusalem was led by "James, the brother of Jesus, the alleged Christ."[12] Other references to Jesus in Josephus's writings reflect Christian beliefs. Since there is no evidence that Josephus was a Christian, these passages must have been added by later Christian scribes. The Roman historian Tacitus confirmed that Jesus was executed by Pontius Pilate during the reign of the Emperor Tiberius.[13] But that is all we learn from non-Christian sources.

Since the early nineteenth century, historians have been trying to fill in these gaps and confirm the Gospels' account of Jesus' life. This effort has proven to be very difficult in the case of Jesus, much more so than for some other first-century figures. For example, the life of the apostle Paul is much easier to investigate historically. Historians like to find primary sources – written texts by eyewitnesses – about people and events. The New Testament provides us with two kinds of primary sources about Paul: his own letters and also an account of his life in the book of Acts that was most likely written by one of his companions. But we have no primary sources about Jesus. He did not write any part of the New Testament, or any other documents that we know about. And the stories about him that we do have, gospels both inside and outside the New Testament, were not written during his ministry and probably not by eyewitnesses.

The stories about Jesus were told orally for a generation before they were written down 40–70 years after his crucifixion. They therefore reflect developments in the early church's thinking about Jesus. Historians have tried to figure out inductively which sayings by Jesus and stories about Jesus are more likely to be accurate. Their evaluations are necessarily subjective and tend to disagree about particular events and sayings. Nevertheless, most historians do tend to agree on a historically probable minimum – things about Jesus that are very likely to be true. They are that:

1. Jesus was <u>Jewish</u>. This may seem patently obvious, but it has nevertheless escaped the notice of many anti-Semitic Christians over the centuries. Jesus' Jewish identity is historically more certain than anything else we can say about him.[14]

2. Jesus came from <u>Nazareth</u> in Galilee. Historians feel confident about this because there was no special significance to Nazareth and therefore no reason to invent it. <u>Bethlehem</u>, on the other hand, was the hometown of King David. It is very easy to see why the Gospels of Matthew and Luke, whose genealogies turn David into Jesus' ancestor, would also like to connect Jesus with the hometown of Israel's most famous king.

3. For the same reason, historians are confident that Jesus was in fact baptized by <u>John the Baptist</u>. The Gospel writers seem embarrassed by this event that casts Jesus as John's disciple, which they emphasize was not the case (Matt. 3:14). It is hard to imagine a reason why they would invent this story.

4. Jesus was an <u>apocalyptic</u> preacher. This did not make him unusual: there were many Jewish preachers in the first century, including John the Baptist, who announced a coming catastrophe followed by God's rule on earth. It is hard to explain the thoroughly apocalyptic message of the early Christians unless Jesus promoted such ideas himself.

5. Jesus taught in <u>parables</u>, short illustrative stories with ambiguous meanings. The Gospels say that Jesus' disciples did not understand the parables, and Mark feels the need to clarify how they should be interpreted (Mark 4). This suggests that Jesus was well known for speaking in parables.

6. Jesus also seems to have been known for performing <u>miracles</u>, especially healings and exorcisms. The Gospels admit that his miracles made Jesus more popular than his teachings did (Mark 3:7–10), which again indicates an authentic memory.

7. Jesus' criticism of the <u>Jerusalem temple</u> and his conflicts with its priests provide the most plausible explanation for his arrest and execution. These conflicts are likely historical. By contrast, Jesus' fierce criticisms of the <u>Pharisees</u> (Matt. 23:14–36) do not affect the course of his story. They may instead reflect conflicts between Christians and rabbinic groups later in the first century CE.

8. The <u>Romans</u> executed Jesus by <u>crucifixion</u> for treason against Rome. Jesus' death by public crucifixion was so scandalous in first-century culture that his supporters were very unlikely to have invented this idea. The Gospel writers go to great efforts to show that Jesus was not a rebel against Rome, most obviously by claiming that <u>Pontius Pilate</u> found no fault with him. Yet their depiction of Pilate bowing to pressure from the priests and the crowds in Jerusalem seems implausible. That leaves historians wondering why the Romans killed Jesus, but there is little doubt that they did so.

Every historian would add more historically likely facts about Jesus, but beyond this list they tend to diverge from each other. No doubt the Gospels say many other true things about Jesus. Beyond this list, however, it becomes increasingly difficult to use historical methods to figure that out. The historical Jesus remains shrouded behind the many traditions about him.[15]

## Summary of Part 2, The Gospels

Religious communities distinguish books as scriptures by ritualizing them in all three dimensions (see Sections 1.1 and 1.2). In Christian rituals, the codex of the New Testament Gospels took on the roles and functions of the Torah scroll in Jewish rituals. Though the Pentateuch remained part of Christian scripture, Christians shifted their ritual focus to the New Testament, and to the four Gospels in particular, because all Christian scriptures serve as testimonies to Jesus Christ, who is himself called "the Word of God."

In ritualizing scripture's iconic dimension, the Gospels have been paraded and displayed in churches and court rooms, decorated with elaborate covers, and used for oath ceremonies. Early Christians' preference for copying their scriptures in codices led to the codex becoming the preferred shape of books in later cultures. A codex of the Gospels visually legitimized Christian priests, churches, and law courts. Irenaeus justified scripturalizing four, and only four, Gospels by identifying them with the four cherubim around God's throne in heaven.

In ritualizing scripture's expressive dimension, more of the Gospels were read in worship than most other parts of the Bible, though Christians also used the Psalms frequently in their liturgical and devotional readings. Christian preference for translating scripture into vernacular languages left the original Hebrew and Greek texts mostly to scholars. Readings and chants of translated Gospels inspired Christian devotion in many different languages and cultures. Religious art and movies have promoted stereotypes about Jesus' looks, though the Gospels never describe him.

In ritualizing scripture's semantic dimension, Christian attention focused on interpreting the meaning of Jesus' life, teachings, and especially his death. The rest of the Old and New Testaments were employed to explain the significance of Jesus Christ, which reemphasized the importance of the four Gospels that tell his story. Other ancient gospels focused on Jesus' teachings instead of his death. Both biblical and non-biblical gospels suggest that women played an important role in the earliest Christian movement. Modern debates over how the New Testament books were written and over the historical accuracy of the Gospels have not diminished Christians' focus on Jesus as the center of their faith.

## CITED WORKS AND FURTHER READING


1  On Paul's use of the Hebrew Bible, see Richard B. Hays, *Echoes of Scripture in the Letters of Paul* (New Haven, CT: Yale University Press, 1989).

2  Frances Young, *The Use of Sacrificial Ideas in Greek Christian Writers* (Cambridge: Patristic Foundation, 1979), 193.

3  For a more detailed survey of atonement ideas in biblical and post-biblical traditions, see Christian Eberhart, Daniel Stökl Ben Ezra, Yechiel Shalom Goldberg, and Michael Zank, "Atonement," in *The Encyclopedia of the Bible and Its Reception* (Berlin: De Gruyter, 2011), 3: 25–51.

4  For an introduction to René Girard's theories of mimetic desire and sacrifice, see *The Girard Reader* (ed. James G. Williams, New York: Crossroad, 1996).

5  For more on the Nag Hammadi gospels, see Elaine Pagels, *The Gnostic Gospels* (New York: Vintage Books, 1979). For translations of the gospels, see Marvin W. Meyer, ed., *The Nag Hammadi Scriptures: The Revised and Updated Translation of Sacred Gnostic Texts* (New York: Harper One, 2009).

6  This very preliminary discussion should be supplemented by readings in the rich literature of feminist biblical criticism, e.g., Peggy L. Day, ed., *Gender and Difference in Ancient Israel* (Minneapolis: Fortress, 1989); Carol A. Newsom and Sharon H. Ringe, eds., *Women's Bible Commentary*, expanded edition (Louisville: Westminster, 1998); Alice Bach, ed., *Women in the Hebrew Bible:*

*A Reader* (New York: Routledge, 2013); Jorunn Økland, "Feminist Readings of the Bible," in *The New Cambridge History of the Bible, Volume 4: From 1750 to the Present* (ed. J. Riches; Cambridge: Cambridge University Press, 2015), 261–272; Wilda C. Gafney, *Womanist Midrash: A Reintroduction to the Women of the Torah and the Throne* (Louisville: Westminster John Knox, 2017); Susanne Scholz, *Introducing the Women's Hebrew Bible: Feminism, Gender Justice, and the Study of the Old Testament*, 2nd ed. (London: T.&T. Clark, 2017); L. Juliana Claassens and Carolyn J. Sharp, eds., *Feminist Frameworks and the Bible: Power, Ambiguity, and Intersectionality* (London: T. & T. Clark, 2017); and the many volumes in the series *Feminist Companion* [to different biblical books], from T.&T. Clark.

7 Carol Meyers, *Rediscovering Eve: Ancient Israelite Women in Context* (Oxford: Oxford University Press, 2013).

8 To compare the Gospels in detail, see a Gospels parallel online, such as John Marshall's *Five Gospels Parallels*, hosted by the University of Toronto at http://sites.utoronto.ca/religion/synopsis/; or, in print, Arthur J. Dewey and Robert J. Miller, *The Complete Gospel Parallels* (Farmington, MN: Polebridge Press, 2012).

9 On the composition and authorship of the Synoptic Gospels, see Pheme Perkins, *Introduction to the Synoptic Gospels* (Grand Rapids: Eerdmans, 2009); Mark Goodacre, *The Synoptic Problem: A Way Through the Maze* (London: T.&T. Clark, 2001); and Stanley E. Porter and Bryan R. Dyer, eds., *The Synoptic Problem: Four Views* (Grand Rapids: Baker Academic, 2016).

10 On the composition and authorship of John's Gospel, see Raymond E. Brown, *An Introduction to the Gospel of John* (New York: Doubleday, 2003); and Paul N. Anderson, *The Riddles of the Fourth Gospel: An Introduction to John* (Lanham, MD: Fortress Press, 2011).

11 On the history of the Pastoral Letters' interpretation, see Jay Twomey, *The Pastoral Epistles Through the Centuries* (Chichester: Wiley Blackwell, 2009).

12  Josephus, *Antiquities* 230: 199–203.

13 Tacitus, *The Annals*, 15:44; in The Loeb Classical Library, tr. J. Jackson (Cambridge, MA: Harvard University Press, 1937), 283.

14 See the discussion and literature cited in Amy-Jill Levine, *The Misunderstood Jew: The Church and the Scandal of the Jewish Jesus* (San Francisco: Harper One, 2006).

15 On the search for the historical Jesus, see the anthology of classic essays in James D. G. Dunn and Scot McKnight, eds., *The Historical Jesus in Recent Research* (Winona Lake, IN: Eisenbrauns, 2005).

# THE BIBLE AS A SCRIPTURE

This discussion of the Bible as a unified whole begins with how medieval and modern Jews and Christians have ritualized their bibles' iconic and expressive dimensions. Then it turns to the Bible's semantic dimension. To illustrate how interpretation has changed, it describes one issue, the interpretation of biblical law, that developed in antiquity and continued to evolve in the medieval and modern periods. It concludes by describing how interpretation of the early chapters of Genesis has fueled nineteenth- and twentieth-century religious debates over race, gender, science, and history – debates that continue today.

# CHAPTER 12

# The Bible's Iconic Dimension

When printers began to market scriptures widely in the late fifteenth and sixteenth centuries, the biblical texts increasingly took the form of a single book, a pandect Bible. Marketing the different books of scripture as one codex volume has encouraged people to think of the Bible as a single book. Thus, the printing and mass marketing of bibles played a role, along with many other factors, in changing how people think about bibles, as well as how they own them, express the words that they find in them, and interpret their meaning. That is why the various Jewish and Christian bibles of the last five centuries, the "modern" period, deserve separate attention.

The comparative study of religions highlights the different ways in which printing has influenced the production and ritualization of scriptures. Already in the Middle Ages, Tibetan and Chinese Buddhists were using woodblock printing to produce scriptures. The printing of multiple copies was itself regarded as a meritorious ritual by many Buddhists. Woodblock printed bibles also appeared in late medieval Europe, such as the elaborately illustrated "pauper's bibles." Printing presses with movable metal type were invented in Korea several centuries before they appeared in Europe. The Korean kings, however, monopolized printing for government purposes. Most European printers were not government or religious institutions, but merchants aiming to produce books for sale. Commercial interests therefore drove the explosive growth in the number of printed books in the fifteenth and sixteenth centuries, which included Jewish and Christian scriptures and other religious texts. Muslims, however, found it difficult to reproduce the flowing appearance of Arabic script in metal type. Printed Qur'ans became popular only after the nineteenth-century invention of lithographic printing, which can better reproduce Arabic texts. Different ritual, political, commercial, and technological factors have therefore shaped how religious communities accepted and used printing technology.[1]

## 12.1  PUBLISHING TANAKS AND BIBLES

Creating books has always been complicated. Scrolls may look simple, but the labor of tanning animal skins to create parchment, of mixing inks and cutting reeds for pens, and of manually inscribing the text is time consuming and expensive. The construction of codex books requires additional steps both before and after copying the text. Ancient books were therefore luxury items. Modern books have become inexpensive due to mass production, yet they still depend on investments in paper mills, printing presses, binderies, and sales networks. Publishing a book requires the labor of editors, designers, printers, and salespersons, as well as authors.

The sanctity of scriptures draws attention to how they get produced. Religious communities can be particularly concerned with the accuracy of copies of scripture. They often take measures to regulate the production of scriptures in order to guarantee their accuracy. For example, King Fuad of Saudi Arabia commissioned a standardized edition of the Qur'an in 1923, which has become the authoritative version accepted by Muslims around the world today. Another example: the Sikh community in India has given one publishing company a monopoly on printing its scripture, the Guru Granth Sahib, in order to regulate its accuracy and purity.

### 12.1.1  Biblical Manuscripts

Similar concerns have shaped the form and contents of Jewish and Christian scriptures since antiquity. The Dead Sea Scrolls show that manuscripts of the same biblical books varied from one another in the late Second Temple period. The rabbis of the following centuries selected one Hebrew text as the standard for each book, and other text types fell out of use. Around the same time, Christian concern over inaccuracies in Latin translations of the

Bible led <u>Jerome</u> to create a new translation, the <u>Vulgate</u>, which became the official Bible of the Roman Catholic Church (see Figure 10.2).

In the Middle Ages, Jewish scholars called "Masoretes" developed new scholarly tools to guarantee the accuracy of their biblical manuscripts. They invented vowel points and marginal notes about rare words and possible misspellings. They counted and recorded the number of words and letters in each book. Their <u>Masoretic</u> bibles, especially the <u>Aleppo Codex</u> and the <u>Leningrad Codex</u>, are today the standard models for the Hebrew biblical text.

<u>Scribes</u> often regard manually copying scriptures as a spiritual act that is important quite apart from how the finished book gets used. Medieval Christian monks reproduced and illuminated biblical manuscripts as ascetic exercises to discipline their minds and bodies and to express their commitment to God. For example, monastic scriptoria in the British Isles produced stunningly beautiful manuscripts, such as the Codex Amiatinus. Others, such as the Lindisfarne Gospels, seem to have been the work of individual hermetic scribes working for years alone. Equally elaborate manuscripts originated from monasteries spread throughout Europe and beyond, from Iberia (Spain) in the west to Armenia in the east and Ethiopia in the south.

Fascination with Jewish and Christian scriptures has created a commercial market for them. Scribes and publishers have produced very many copies to meet that demand. They have often created deluxe editions to attract the interest of wealthy buyers. Already in the fourth century CE, John Chrysostom complained about Christians who placed more value on how their books of scripture looked than on studying their contents: "All their care is for the fineness of the parchments, and the beauty of the letters, not for reading them."[2]

Beautifully illuminated manuscripts became symbols of wealth and power in the Middle Ages, and some monasteries catered to this market.[3] For example, in the Ottonian Gospels (see Figure 12.1), the monk, Liuthar, pictured himself giving this book illuminated in gold leaf to Emperor Otto III, who appears on the facing page enthroned like Christ. Many later emperors of the Holy Roman Empire took their coronation oaths on this book. Here the high value of the scripture gets represented by its expensive reproduction, which explicitly legitimizes its producer, Liuthar, and its owner, Otto III and his successors. Now it is displayed in the treasury of Aachen Cathedral, where its beauty supports the religious prestige and tourist attraction of this 1200-year-old church.

**FIGURE 12.1**    Frontispiece of the Ottonian Gospels, ca. 1000 CE. In the treasury of the Cathedral in Aachen, Germany.

## 12.1.2    Printed Bibles

After Johannes Gutenberg introduced printing with movable metal type in 1458, print shops quickly appeared in many European cities. Printing reduced the cost of book production by being able to print many identical pages at once. Early print runs numbered only several hundred copies, but they grew larger as the technology improved. The invention of printing raised hopes of eliminating errors by identical reproduction. But it also increased the commercial market for scriptures and the risk that publishers would be motivated more by profit than by concerns for accuracy.

Jewish and Christian denominations therefore developed their own publishing businesses to print scriptures and other religious texts. They continue to sponsor new editions and translations, which they recommend to their congregations. They have also attempted to regulate the publication of scriptures. For example, English monarchs who also led the Church of England licensed publication of the "Authorized" Version, more popularly known as the King James Version, to only three publishers over 300 years. In the nineteenth century, bible societies printed and distributed millions of copies of bibles in Europe and America, and missionaries carried them around the world. By the end of the twentieth century, bibles were available to almost anyone who wanted one and in almost every language. The Bible had become the most widely distributed book in human history.

Though many Jewish and Christian religious groups continue active publishing programs, commercial and academic publishers now dominate the publication of bibles and bible-related books, which is a profitable part of the publishing business (see Figure 12.2).

Commercial interest in generating sales now drives many bible publishing decisions and has resulted in many different editions for every kind of reader. In addition to the old tradition of producing highly edited and illustrated bibles for children, there are now bibles designed specifically for women, for men, for teen boys and teen girls. Usually, these books reproduce a standard translation of the biblical text, and surround it with commentary and illustrations directed at the intended audience. Publishers have appropriated the formats of other popular print genres for bibles, including glossy magazines and comic books. Though some devout people find such commercial marketing offensive, many others find it compatible with a religious mandate to "spread the Word" to as many people as possible. Missionary ideals and profit motives often converge in the religious publishing business.[4]

Printing technology not only increased the number of books for sale, it also grew the market for deluxe editions. Wood cuts and copper plate engravings embellished many older printed bibles with illustrations of famous scenes. Printing also made it economically feasible to provide access

**FIGURE 12.2**  Some contemporary English bibles.

to commentaries on the same page as the biblical text. Such glossed bibles had appeared as manuscripts already by 1200 CE, but printing made them cheaper. For example, a Rabbinic Bible (*Mikraot Gedolot*) surrounds the text of all the books of the Tanak with commentary by influential medieval Jewish scholars, such as Rashi and Ramban. The Jewish scholar Jacob ben Hayyim ibn Adoniyahu, together with the Christian printer Daniel Bomberg, established this form in the early sixteenth century (Figure 12.3) and it has remained popular ever since.[5] Rabbinic bibles shaped the semantic

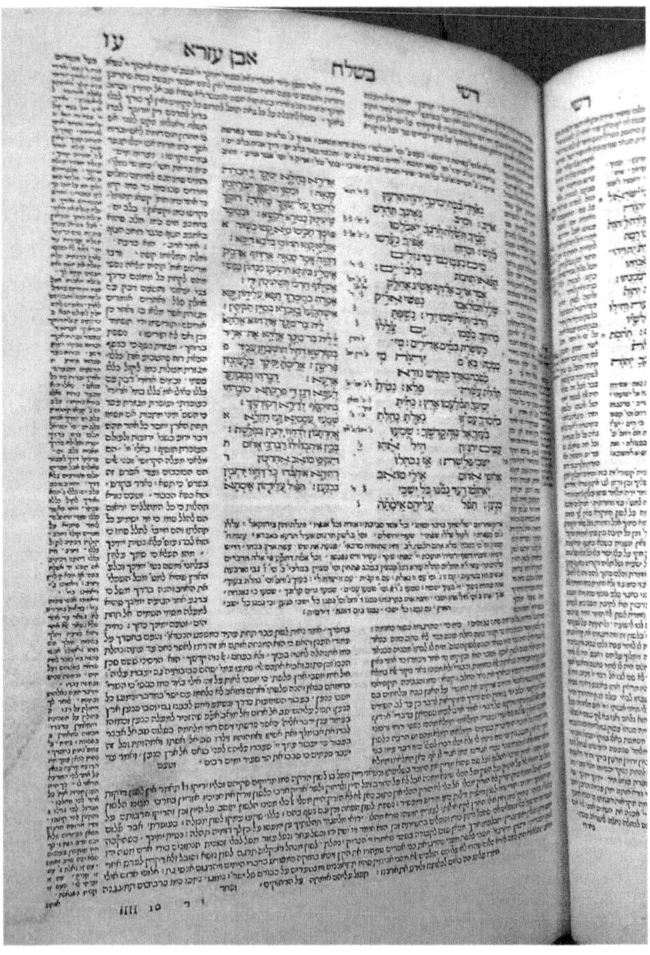

**FIGURE 12.3** Bomberg's Third Rabbinic Bible of 1547 open to Exodus 15 in Hebrew and the Aramaic Targum with commentaries by Rashi, Ibn Ezra, and others. In the Special Collections Research Center, Syracuse University Libraries.

dimension of Jewish scriptures by popularizing the medieval commentators, especially Rashi, as authorities for biblical interpretation. They shaped its iconic dimension by establishing the image of its pages – Hebrew biblical text surrounded by Aramaic targums and commentators – as a symbol of the Jewish combination of scripture and interpretive tradition. The typographical layout of such bibles encourages readers to understand the text in relationship to commentary and translation, as David Stern observed:

> The glossed format with the Biblical text and commentaries on the same page was obviously a more convenient text for a student. But more than being convenient, it was transformative. It changed the very nature of Bible-study. . . . He (or she) now read it verse by verse with the commentary intervening wherever it existed. The Biblical text was thus atomized into small lexical and semantic units that combined verse and exegesis.[6]

Early printers also produced glossed Christian bibles. The sixteenth-century Geneva Bible was famous for its interpretive notes. Christian scholars also seized on the new technology to produce <u>polyglot bibles</u> that placed the ancient sources in their different languages and type fonts side by side (Figure 12.4).

The marketing of <u>digital texts</u> since the 1990s has provided new ways to gloss biblical texts with multiple translations and commentaries. Indeed, digital hypertext seems ideal for this purpose. While free biblical texts quickly spread on the internet, established publishers and new companies marketed digitized bibles tagged with various kinds of "helps" and commentaries. The arrival of smartphones in the following decade led to the multiplication of digital bibles and commentaries as downloadable apps. Bible publishers have proven very eager to adopt the newest technology to market their ancient product.

As the printing industry matured, printers refined their <u>type fonts</u> to making reading easier and faster. Their goal has been to make the type practically invisible so that readers absorb the text's meaning without thinking consciously about the forms of the letters. This culminates a process begun already by medieval manuscripts that introduced spaces between words, lower-case lettering, verse divisions, and chapter headings. The goal has always been to make reading visually easier. It has steadily reinforced the efforts of individual readers to understand the meaning of scriptures for themselves. These incremental modifications to the look of a biblical page have joined rising literacy rates, the ever-growing commercial book market,

**FIGURE 12.4**    Complutensian Polyglot Bible of 1517 open to Genesis 1 in Hebrew, Latin, Greek, and Aramaic, with a Latin translation of the Aramaic. In the library of Saint Andrews University.

and religious reformations to emphasize individual interpretation and conviction. They encourage individualism and scripture-oriented devotion among Jews and Christians.[7]

A small but notable counter trend appears in the work of artists and craft printers who produce art bibles, a movement that began in the late nineteenth century and continues in the twenty-first.[8] For example, the illustrator and printmaker Barry Moser created engravings and modified type-faces to print the limited-edition Pennyroyal Caxton Bible, which he finished in 1999. An even more ambitious project was led by the calligrapher

Donald Jackson, who assembled a team to hand copy and illuminate the St. John's Bible. This vellum manuscript, finished in 2011 and bound in seven volumes, combines the qualities of original art, icon, and reproducible book. Images of its hand-written and hand-illuminated parchment pages draw visitors to see the unique original, and also generate interest in buying its reproductions in various formats and expense.

Unlike most other art bibles, however, the St. John's Bible retains a religious context through the monastery, St. John's Abbey in Minnesota, that sponsored its production. The monks of St. John's ritualize scripture in all three dimensions routinely in their worship services and devotions. The St. John's Bible functions as the Abbey's new relic text that reinforces the scriptural identity of the monks that sponsor it, display it, and market its reproductions. They consciously continue the tradition of medieval monks who illuminated books of the scripture to bring it fame and glory and, hopefully, to inspire readers as well.

So, for more than 2000 years, the iconic dimension of torahs, tanaks, gospels, and bibles has been ritualized regularly, often elaborately. Iconic ritualization of torahs and bibles shows no sign of diminishing in the twenty-first century.

## 12.2  RELIC BOOKS

Some books get treated like relics.[9] People value relics for being the specific objects that they are: the bone of a saint's body or a celebrity's personal possession. Relics are rare, if not one-of-a-kind, and are in theory not reproducible. Relics, as known from Christian and Buddhist traditions and many other religions, are believed to mediate the sacred, like icons. But icons are reproducible, while the value of relics lies precisely in the fact that they are unique. Of course, the demand for relics always outstrips the supply, so there are frequent scandals over the (re)production of relics. Relic texts, then, are particular books valued for their individual form or history.

Museums and libraries regularly display relic texts such as rare manuscripts and first editions. In fact, relic texts get ritualized only in their iconic dimension by collecting, preserving, and displaying them like works of art. They are rarely read or interpreted, because non-relic copies of the same texts are usually available for such activities. The iconic display of relic texts enhances the prestige of those who own them and legitimizes other copies of the same text.

## 12.2.1 Relic Torah Scrolls

Some Torah scrolls have become treasured relics because they survived the disasters of history. Jewish memory has been shaped by catastrophic experiences, from Egyptian servitude and Babylonian exile in the Bible through the Roman destruction of the Jerusalem Temple and medieval and modern pogroms, culminating in the twentieth-century Nazi gas chambers of the Shoah/Holocaust. Such experiences make survival feel miraculous. Torah scrolls that survived catastrophes represent the survival of the Jewish people against history's odds.

The biblical texts among the Dead Sea Scrolls quickly gained the status of relic texts after their discovery in the mid-twentieth century. Because they are 1000 years older than other manuscripts of the Hebrew Bible, for Jews and Christians they became symbols of the reliability and antiquity of biblical tradition. In 1965, the Israel Museum in Jerusalem built a special structure to house the scrolls and called it "the Shrine of the Book" (see Figure 12.5). Its monumental exterior and circular interior, which was designed to display the 24-feet-long Isaiah scroll at its center surrounded by other Qumran manuscripts, emphasize the manuscripts' uniqueness and importance. Its biblical manuscripts legitimize the antiquity of Jewish and Christian scriptures, and enhance the prestige of the State of Israel that owns

**FIGURE 12.5** The Shrine of the Book in the Israel Museum in Jerusalem.

them and enshrines them in this way. This exceptional building ritualizes the Dead Sea Scrolls visually and architecturally as relic texts.

Another famous Jewish relic text is the <u>Aleppo Codex</u>. This ninth-century manuscript of the whole Hebrew Bible was already celebrated by Maimonides in the twelfth century. Historians continue to regard it as the best testimony to the text of the Hebrew Bible. So it also serves to legitimize the accuracy of Jewish and Christian scriptures. A fire in the Aleppo synagogue in 1947 damaged the Codex, which lost almost all the pages of its Pentateuch. Israeli spies and politicians worked secretly to bring the rest of the manuscript from Aleppo to Jerusalem.[10] But some members of the Aleppo Jewish community kept fragments of the Codex for themselves as amulets (Box 12.1). Relic texts often create conflicts between the interests of individuals and of communities. Communities ranging from local congregations to nations gain legitimacy from owning and displaying relic texts, while individuals keep them for themselves because they offer prestige or a sense of protection.

The <u>Samaritans</u> of Nablus possess a Torah scroll with a colophon asserting very great antiquity: it claims to have been copied by Abisha, a grandson of Aaron, in the thirteenth year after Israel's conquest of Canaan. In Samaritan cultural memory, this relic from the time of the Pentateuch's wilderness generation provides some compensation for having lost so many books in Antiquity (see Box 12.2). Many historians, however, date the Abisha Scroll on the basis of its handwriting to the Middle Ages instead.

## Box 12.1  Fragment of the Aleppo Codex as an amulet

The Israeli newspaper *Haaretz* reported on November 6, 2007, that

> Sam Sabbagh salvaged the fragment from a burning synagogue in Aleppo, Syria in 1947....Sabbagh believed the small piece of parchment was his good luck charm for six decades. He was convinced that thanks to the parchment, which he kept with him always in a transparent plastic container, he had been saved from riots in his hometown of Aleppo during Israel's War of Independence, and he had managed to immigrate from Syria to the United States in 1968 and start a new life in Brooklyn and make a living.

Only after Sabbagh's death was the fragment donated to an Israeli museum to be reunited with the Aleppo Codex.

## Box 12.2   Lost Samaritan books

<u>Samaritan</u> traditions lament the loss of many of their religious books in the early second century CE:

*In those days the Book of Choice Selections was taken away, which had been in their hands since the days of Divine Favor; and there was also taken away the Songs and Praises, which they were accustomed to utter over the offerings, each offering according to its merits; and also the Hymns, which they used to sing in the days of Divine Favor. Now all these constituted a library which had been preserved with greatest care generation after generation, through the time of the prophets unto that day, by the hands of the chief imams. And there was also taken away the Book of the Imams, which they had, wherein their genealogy was traced back to Phineas; and there was also destroyed the Annals, wherein was recorded their birthdays and the years of their lives, and of these not one ancient book or chronicle was found except the Law and a book containing their lives.*[11]

Some Jewish communities have revered particular Torah scrolls as relics. Shalom Sabar tells of

La Ghriba, or the marvelous Torah scroll of Bône (now Annaba) in Algeria, and the Seghir, or the small Torah scroll of Darnah in Libya . . . they were believed to possess special protective powers or even perform miracles. . . . about the latter it is even told it was produced in the time of Ezra. Moreover these miraculous scrolls "traveled" by sea to Alexandria and from there, with no damage caused to them by the water, to the respective communities in North Africa. Many other stories are told about the miracles they performed, and that even Muslims recognized their sanctity.[12]

Stories circulate in many Jewish, Samaritan, and Christian communities about books of scripture that survived miraculously. When thrown into fire by enemies, they jumped out unscathed. Others were found intact in the ruins of burned buildings or vehicles, a story line still seen today in local news media. Such stories use the surviving copies to demonstrate the holiness of scripture.[2]

Modern Christians and Jews are often fascinated with influential ancient biblical texts like the <u>Dead Sea Scrolls</u> (see Section 4.2.2 and Box 6.9) and the <u>Nag Hammadi codices</u> (see Box 11.1). Some private collectors try to buy ancient biblical texts for themselves, which increases opportunities for unscrupulous dealers and forgers. This happened in the early twenty-first century when a wealthy evangelical Christian family bought thousands of texts. They planned to display them in the Museum of the Bible, which opened in Washington, DC in 2017. As a result, prices soared for scraps of ancient biblical manuscripts and related texts. The suspicion that many artifacts in the museum's collection were bought or imported illegally, or are outright forgeries, has now been confirmed (see Box 12.3). A federal lawsuit also required it to return more than 5000 texts to Iraq in 2017.[13]

Since the mid-twentieth century, Torah scrolls that survived destruction by the Nazis have gained relic status as "Holocaust scrolls." Many congregations are eager to buy them and preserve them in their synagogues. Many such scrolls did indeed survive in hiding during World War II, but the relic trade is famous for deceit, and the sale of relic texts is no different. A US dealer in Holocaust scrolls was convicted of fraud and imprisoned in 2012 (see Box 12.4). This scandal has drawn greater attention to trying to authenticate the twentieth-century history of Holocaust Torah scrolls.

## Box 12.3  Forged Dead Sea Scrolls at the Museum of the Bible in Washington, DC.

In 2020, Michael Greshko reported in *National Geographic* that

"Independent researchers funded by the Museum of the Bible announced that all 16 of the museum's Dead Sea Scroll fragments are modern forgeries that duped outside collectors, the museum's founder, and some of the world's leading biblical scholars.…While the pieces are probably made of ancient leather, they were inked in modern times and modified to resemble real Dead Sea Scrolls.…The report's findings raise grave questions about the 'post-2002' Dead Sea Scroll fragments, a group of some 70 snippets of biblical text that entered the antiquities market in the 2000s.…Careful microscopic analysis showed that the fragments' scripture was painted onto already ancient leather. On many of the pieces, suspiciously shiny ink pools in cracks and waterfalls off of torn edges that wouldn't have been present when the leather was new. On others, the forgers' brushstrokes clearly overlie the ancient leather's bumpy mineral crust.…The museum is also reevaluating the provenance of all the material in its collection, and it is prepared to return any stolen artifacts to their rightful owners."[14]

---

**Box 12.4   Fraudulent sales of Holocaust scrolls**

*The Washington Post* reported on October 11, 2012, that Rabbi Menachem Youlus pleaded guilty and was convicted of selling fake Holocaust scrolls and defrauding investors.

"Youlus, the self-proclaimed 'Jewish Indiana Jones'…spun cloak-and-dagger tales of 'rescuing' sacred Torah scrolls lost during the Holocaust, but those tales were lies.…Despite Youlus's claims that he found holy relics at concentration camps, in monasteries and in mass graves, passport records show he never traveled to Europe.…More than 50 of his purported Holocaust Torahs made their way to congregations in the Washington area and beyond. Synagogues held emotional ceremonies to rededicate the scrolls for worship—a symbolic show of Jewish triumph over Hitler."

Youlus was sentenced to 51 months in prison and ordered to pay almost one million dollars in restitution.

---

Relic texts are the exception that proves the rule about ritualizing scriptures in three dimensions. When copies of scriptures are readily available for semantic, expressive, and iconic ritualization, a few special copies can be set aside to serve purely iconic purposes as relic texts. Relic texts <u>legitimize</u> a story about a community's identity. People ritualize the possession and display of relic texts to identify with and place themselves in that story.

## 12.2.2   Desecrating Scriptures

Objects that can be ritually venerated can also be ritually <u>desecrated</u>. Their deliberate mutilation and destruction intend to cause anguish to those who treasure them. Because books represent the values of a culture or religion in condensed form, they have often been targeted by enemies of those traditions. Daniel Sarefield observed that

> To willfully destroy a text by placing it in a fire is to perform an ancient and persistent action that is in its essence a ritual of purification. Yet a book burning is more than a ceremonial act; it is a spectacle that transmits forceful social and religious messages to victims, witnesses, and participants alike.[15]

The Roman Senate, in periodic attempts to purify Rome's culture that began as early as the third century BCE, ordered books of magic and other unorthodox rituals publicly burned. In the early fourth century CE, persecution of Christianity in the Roman Empire targeted its books. Then Christian emperors rose to power, and the Roman state began to suppress the books of pagans and heretics instead. Burning one's own books became a symbol of conversion (already in the New Testament, Acts 19:18–19). The ancient book religion of Manichaeism died out in the Middle East and Europe by the end of the first millennium due to the destruction of its books and the suppression of its practices by Christian, Muslim, and Zoroastrian rulers. The Samaritans also remember losing many irreplaceable books due to persecutions in this period (see Box 12.2).

The Torah also attracted violent attention from enemies of the Jews. When the Seleucid Greek ruler Antiochus Epiphanes tried to suppress Jewish religious practices in the second century BCE, he ordered the destruction of Jewish altars, sanctuaries, and Torah scrolls. He equated those who obey scripture with those who own a copy of it. That is a typical result of ritualizing the iconic dimension of texts. Josephus claims that, in the first century BCE, the Roman emperor Augustus decreed that theft of a holy book from a synagogue should be punished as an act of desecration. He reports that, in the following century, a Roman governor beheaded a soldier for desecrating a Torah scroll (*Ant.* 16:164; 20:115–116). These incidents show that before the beginning of the Common Era, Torah scrolls had already become symbols of Jewish identity to Jews and non-Jews alike (see Box 12.5).

The rise to power of Christian emperors of Rome starting in the fourth century CE changed which books were burned by imperial forces, but did not stem the practice itself. Now anti-Christian books were burned, as were the ritual texts of non-Christian religions and of Christian sects that the empire classified as heretical. The laws of Justinian (sixth century CE) tolerated Jewish Torah scrolls while insisting that they be translated, but banned the Mishnah. Christians often destroyed torahs and talmuds in medieval and modern pogroms (riots) against Jewish communities in Europe.

As a result of this long history of attacks on scriptures, preserving Torah scrolls became an important religious ideal for Jews and Samaritans. The Mishnah requires that, even on the Sabbath, scrolls of scripture must be rescued from a fire (*m. Shab.* 16). Many stories from antiquity to today tell of Jews risking their lives to rescue torahs from burning buildings.

> **Box 12.5   Desecrating Torah scrolls**
>
> *The books of the law that they found they tore to pieces and burned with fire. Anyone found possessing the book of the covenant, or anyone who adhered to the law, was condemned to death by decree of the king.* (1 Macc. 1:56–57 NRSV)
>
> *One of the soldiers who had found a copy of the laws of Moses that was kept in one of the villages, fetched it out where all could see and tore it in two while he uttered blasphemies and railed violently. The Jews, on learning of this, collected in large numbers, went down to Caesarea, where Cumanus happened to be, and besought him to avenge not them but God, whose laws had been subjected to outrage. For, they said, they could not endure to live, since their ancestral code was thus wantonly insulted. Cumanus, alarmed at the thought of a fresh revolution of the masses, after taking counsel with his friends, beheaded the soldier who had outraged the laws.* (Josephus, *Antiquities* 20:115–116)[16]

## 12.3   DECALOGUE TABLETS

One part of the Bible often gets singled out for separate iconic ritualization. The Ten Commandments, also called the Decalogue, appears as two tablets on Torah arks and on the facades of synagogues. The text is usually abbreviated, sometimes represented only by numerals, or missing altogether. The image of two tablets is enough to refer to the commandments or to all the laws of God, and by extension to Judaism as a whole. The image of the two tablets plays the same role in Christian art, where it frequently represents Judaism as "the Old Covenant."

Christians have also used displays of the Decalogue to represent the essence of divine law as a guide to human morality. While Christians reject or ignore most of the ritual and legal instructions of the Pentateuch, they usually revere the Ten Commandments as eternal moral and religious obligations (see Section 14.1). During the Reformation in the sixteenth century, Protestants often replaced pictorial art with Decalogue boards to emphasize the text of scripture over visual art.

In Christian politics, the tablets of the commandments carry associations with the laws of nations. In England, displays of the Ten Commandments represented the enforcement of national law, especially in the churches. Similarly, the pediment of the US Supreme Court building shows Moses holding the tablets as the central and largest figure among three ancient lawgivers (Figure 12.6). Decalogue boards and plaques that display the full text of the commandments continue to hang in many churches and homes.

In contrast to older Jewish and Christian art that used the tablets to depict Jewish distinctiveness, associating the tablets with national law uses the Ten Commandments to represent common Judeo-Christian values. The popularity of the Hollywood film *The Ten Commandments* led to stone Decalogue monuments being placed in and around US courthouses in the 1950s and later (see Figure 12.7). In recent decades, lawsuits against this government endorsement of religion have removed many of them. Christian evangelicals, supported by some Jews, have responded by erecting even more. Placing the monuments on government property, especially in courthouses, makes a political claim that the United States is a <u>Judeo-Christian</u> country. Many Jews complain, however, that Jewish and Christian heritage cannot be so easily conflated. Some Christian and Jewish groups believe that government support for this religious icon undermines their religious freedom. They have joined lawsuits to remove the monuments from government properties. Decalogue monuments and plaques have therefore become divisive symbols in US politics and religion.[17]

**FIGURE 12.6**  Moses, Solon, and Confucius on the east pediment of the US Supreme Court in Washington, DC, built in 1935.

**FIGURE 12.7**    Ten Commandments on a monument at the Austin State Capitol. Image "TenCommandmentsAustinStateCapitol" licensed under Public domain via Wikimedia Commons.

## CITED WORKS AND FURTHER READING

1  On printing in Buddhist and Muslim traditions, see Will Tuludhar-Douglas, "Writing and the Rise of Mahayana Buddhism," in *Die Textualisierung der Religion* (ed. Joachim Schaper; Tubingen: Mohr Siebeck, 2009), 250–272 [264–68]; Natalia K. Suit, "*Muṣḥaf* and the Material Boundaries of the Qur'an," in *Iconic Books and Texts* (ed. J. W. Watts, Sheffield: Equinox, 2013), 189–206 [197–201].

2  John Chrysostom, *Homily on John 32.3*, in *Nicene and Post-Nicene Fathers*, ser. 1, vol. 14, 114 and in Parmenter, "Iconic Book," 80.

3  Michelle Brown, "Images to Be Read and Words to Be Seen: The Iconic Role of the Early Medieval Book," in *Iconic Books and Texts* (ed. J. W. Watts; London: Equinox, 2013), 93–118.

4  On the history of Bible production and publishing, see *The New Cambridge History of the Bible*, 4 vol. (Cambridge: Cambridge University Press, 2012–2016); also Paul C. Gutjahr, *An American Bible: A History of the Good Book in the United States, 1777–1880* (Stanford: Stanford University Press, 1999); Jeremy Stolow, *Orthodox by Design: Judaism, Print Politics, and the ArtScroll Revolution* (Berkeley: University of California Press, 2010); and Timothy K.

Beal, *The Rise and Fall of the Bible: The Unexpected History of an Accidental Book* (Boston: Houghton Mifflin Harcourt, 2011).

5 David M. Stern, *The Jewish Bible: A Material History* (Seattle: University of Washington Press, 2017).

6 David M. Stern, "The Hebrew Bible in Europe in the Middle Ages: A Preliminary Typology," *Jewish Studies* 11 (2012), 235–322 [310].

7 On the evolution of scripts and publishing fonts, see the summary in S. Brent Plate, "Looking at Words," in *Iconic Books and Texts*, 119–133.

8 See Ronald Patkus, *The Privately Printed Bible: Private and Fine Press Editions of Biblical Texts in the British Isles and North America, 1982–2000* (New Castle, DE: Oak Knoll Press, 2017).

9 James W. Watts, "Relic Texts," in *How and Why Books Matter* (Sheffield: Equinox, 2019), 55–69.

10 Matti Friedman, *The Aleppo Codex: In Pursuit of One of the World's Most Coveted, Sacred, and Mysterious Books* (Chapel Hill: Algonquin Books, 2013).

11 Quotation from *Samaritan Joshua* 47, a thirteenth–fifteenth-century Arabic manuscript translated by Oliver Crane in Robert T. Anderson and Terry Giles, *Tradition Kept: The Literature of the Samaritans* (Peabody, MA: Hendrickson, 2005), 137–138.

12 On relic torahs, see Shalom Sabar, "Torah and Magic: The Torah Scroll and Its Appurtenances as Magical Objects in Traditional Jewish Culture," *European Journal of Jewish Studies* 3 (2009), 167, 169; and James W. Watts, "Relic Texts," in *How and Why Books Matter*, 55–69.

13 Alan Feuer, "Hobby Lobby Agrees to Forfeit 5,500 Artifacts Smuggled Out of Iraq," *New York Times*, July 5, 2017; for a deeper analysis, see Candida R. Moss and Joel S. Baden, *Bible Nation: The United States of Hobby Lobby* (Princeton: Princeton University Press, 2017), 22–98, 188–189.

14 Michael Greshko, "'Dead Sea Scrolls' at the Museum of the Bible Are All Forgeries," *National Geographic*, March 13, 2020.

15 Daniel Sarefield, "The Symbolics of Book Burning: The Establishment of a Christian Ritual of Persecution," in *The Early Christian Book* (ed. W. E. Klingshirn and L. Safran; Washington, DC: Catholic University of America, 2007), 159–173, quotation from p. 159.

16 For Josephus's account of a desecrated Torah, see Louis H. Feldman, *Josephus: Jewish Antiquities, Book XX* (Loeb Classics; Cambridge, MA: Harvard University Press, 1965), quotation from pp. 61–63.

17 On Decalogue monuments, see James W. Watts, "Rival Iconic Texts: The Ten Commandments and the U.S. Constitution," in *How and Why Books Matter*, 117–134.

# CHAPTER 13

# The Bible's Expressive Dimension

Even a little knowledge of the comparative study of religions reveals the important role of art and theater in expressing the scriptures of many different traditions. For example, illustrations of scenes from the Buddha's life decorate Buddhist temples and stupas. Famous scenes from the Hindu epics appear on temples and on posters in people's homes, and the epics themselves get enacted in weeks-long performances. These religions that emphasize expressing scriptural words through recitation also express the contents of scriptures in art and theater. Similarly, Jewish synagogues and Christian churches have expressed their scriptures in art and theater, even if they have sometimes struggled over whether this is appropriate or not.

Like the Bible's iconic dimension, changes in ritualizing its expressive dimension have been stimulated by developments in art, architecture, and theater due to social changes and to technological innovations. While the public reading of scriptures (see above on torahs and gospels) has continued in synagogues and churches, visual expressions of biblical contents have evolved dramatically over the last two millennia.

## 13.1  THE BIBLE IN ART

Artists have found ample material in the Bible's narratives. For example, the Pentateuch's stories of creation, Adam and Eve, the tower of Babel, Abraham's near sacrifice of Isaac, the plagues on the Egyptians, the crossing of the Reed Sea, Moses receiving the tablets of commandments, and the Israelites worshipping the golden calf have repeatedly been depicted in art throughout Jewish and Christian history.

Many ancient Jewish synagogues were covered in art. Surviving floor mosaics typically depict a Torah ark flanked by lamp stands (*menorahs*), synagogue furniture that was inspired by pentateuchal prototypes. The floors often depict the story of Abraham and Isaac from Genesis 22 as well (see Figure 13.1). Their wall art has not survived except in one place: the synagogue of Dura Europos in Syria contains frescos from the third century CE showing scenes from Genesis, Exodus, Leviticus, Numbers, Samuel, Kings, Ezekiel, and Esther.

Stories from many of these books also appear frequently in Christian art. Icons and sculptures regularly depict portraits of some key characters. Abraham is usually shown with the boy Isaac. Aaron is dressed in priestly vestments and holds a censor. The prophets and the Gospel writers appear with pages or books in their hands. Moses appears very often in church art holding the tablets of the commandments (see Figure 13.2). The tablets,

**FIGURE 13.1**  Floor mosaic (sixth century CE) of Abraham sacrificing Isaac (Gen. 22:1–11). In the ruins of the Bet Alpha synagogue, Israel.

**FIGURE 13.2** Moses receiving the Ten Commandments. Woodcut from an early sixteenth-century design by Hans Holbein. From *Icones Veteris Testamenti: Illustrations of the Old Testament, Engraved on Wood, From Designs by Hans Holbein*. London: William Pickering, 1830 (first published 1538).

whether in Moses' hands or by themselves, became a common symbol for Judaism. Christian art regularly uses them to contrast the "old covenant" with the new, which is depicted by codex and chalice. Jews have embraced the tablets to visually represent the Torah. They commonly appear on synagogue buildings and on Torah arks.

In addition to New Testament stories about Jesus (see Section 10.5), Christian artists have frequently illustrated stories in the Hebrew Bible that theologians have interpreted as foreshadowing Jesus Christ. Such typologies focused especially on Adam's sin which brought about human death (for which Christ died) and Abraham's near sacrifice of his son, Isaac (foreshadowing the death of the son of God, Jesus). Typology led to some obscure stories becoming familiar through their artistic reproduction. For example, the parallel with viewing Jesus on the cross led many artists to the story of Moses putting a snake on a pole whose sight saved the Israelites from poisonous snake bites (Num. 21:4–9).

Art has sometimes amplified minor interpretations of the biblical text into widespread beliefs. An infamous example appears in most Christian art depicting Moses. Exodus 34:35 describes Moses' face "shining" after his encounter with God, but the Latin Vulgate translated the word as a noun, "horns." Jerome used the word to depict Moses positively as strong and powerful, but medieval Christian imagination associated his horns with the devil. Artistic portrayals of the horned Moses (see Figure 13.3) came to typify all Jews, leading to the anti-Semitic slur that Jews have horns like the devil. Both the image and the belief continue to circulate in many Christians' imaginations.[1]

Modern photography and mass media have made some biblical art famous world-wide. For example, mention of the biblical creation story often brings

**FIGURE 13.3**   A horned Moses, ca. 1894, on Alexander Hall, Princeton University.

to mind Michelangelo's sixteenth-century fresco on the ceiling of the Vatican's Sistine Chapel or William Blake's nineteenth-century painted etchings, as much as the text of Genesis 1–2. Mass tourism to view artistic masterpieces can draw attention to obscure biblical texts. Thus the stained glass windows that Mark Chagall made in 1962 for Hadassah Hospital in Jerusalem draw more attention than do the texts that they illustrate from Genesis 49 and Deuteronomy 33, which are poems blessing each Israelite tribe.

Art extends the oral presentation of biblical texts into visual media. It is too simplistic to think that old religious art aimed primarily at illiterate audiences. Its persistence in modern society shows a much more dynamic interaction between written story, oral retellings, and artistic representation. Usually, though not always, you must already know a story in order to recognize that art refers to it. Art, on the other hand, often emphasizes different things than semantic interpretation and leads you to notice different elements. Artists must interpret the text to depict it. We have seen how artists frequently follow the dominant interpretations in their culture, such as typological readings of Isaac as representing Christ. But artists can also deviate from the standardized views of clergy and scholars. That is because their work does not usually aim to support or challenge the authority of semantic interpretation, but rather to <u>inspire</u> viewers. The art of churches and synagogues therefore extends the ritualization of the Bible's <u>expressive dimension</u>, which aims to inspire. Much biblical art, from the most common icons to the most famous masterpieces, has clearly inspired millions of viewers.

## 13.2   ILLUSTRATED BIBLES

It is more difficult to distinguish the semantic, expressive, and iconic dimensions in <u>biblical illustrations</u> than in any other aspect of scripture ritualization. Decorated and illustrated bibles clearly ritualize scripture's iconic dimension by enhancing its value and beauty. They also interpret the semantic meaning of the text. However, their use to fascinate the religious imagination and inspire their viewers justifies discussing them together with other biblically inspired art as examples of ritualizing the expressive dimension of scriptures.

The earliest manuscripts of the Hebrew and Greek Pentateuch were not illustrated or decorated. After official recognition of Christianity in the fourth century CE, Christians began to produce prestige copies of their scriptures in expensive materials and decorations. By the early Middle Ages, monasteries from Egypt to Ireland competed with each other to produce the most magnificent manuscripts possible. Their <u>illuminations</u> used bright colors, frequently including gold leaf, for elaborate calligraphy, decorations, and illustrations of biblical scenes (see Figure 13.4).[2]

**FIGURE 13.4**   Moses receiving the law and giving it to the Israelites: an illuminated page from the Moutier-Grandval Bible created in Tours, France in 835 CE. Public domain image via Wikimedia Commons.

Manuscript illustrations usually feature the same biblical stories as Jewish and Christian art generally, often in almost exactly the same way. The codex format, however, permitted longer sequences of images, which occasionally led to picture-book bibles. In Paris in the twelfth century, scribes created expensive abridgements of the Old Testament called *Bible Moralisée*. Each page consists of eight pictures that interpret stories typologically by matching Old Testament scenes with their New Testament parallels. Fourteenth-century "pauper's bibles" featured much cruder art that could be reproduced inexpensively by block printing. Picture-book bibles have more recently been marketed primarily to children. In the decades around the turn of the twenty-first century, however, abridged bibles again took pictorial form as graphic novels, manga bibles, and art bibles.

Illustrations in bibles usually focus on stories, but not always. The Bible's descriptions of the Tabernacle (Exod. 25–40) and of Solomon's temple (1 Kgs. 6) have stimulated interest in visualizing them. The architecture and furnishings of the Tabernacle dominate late-medieval Jewish illuminations of the Torah's instructions. Some Jewish codices such as the Perpignan Bible of 1299 and the Farhi Bible of 1366–1383 devote several pages to illustrating the furnishings described in Exodus. The Kennicott Bible of 1476 and some others interleave full-page illustrations of the Tabernacle furnishings with abstract carpet pages that separate the Torah from the Prophets. With the development of printing, illustrated bibles included detailed renderings of the Tabernacle, its contents, and priests (Figure 13.5). These scenes sometimes contain a burning altar, but they focus on objects, not ritual practices.

## 13.3  BIBLE MAPS

Maps of the biblical "Holy Land" have also been used since antiquity to imagine the travels of biblical characters, and to reenact them through pilgrimages. Eusebius and Jerome in the fourth century CE may have included schematic maps to illustrate their lists of biblical place names. In the sixth century, the Church of Saint George in Madaba, Jordan, commissioned a large floor mosaic map of the Holy Land, which can still be seen today. In his eleventh-century commentary, Rabbi Shlomo Yitzchaki, better known by the acronym Rashi, drew schematic maps of the Israelites' route from Egypt to Canaan (Exodus, Numbers) and the territories of the Israelite tribes in the land (Joshua). His influence led to such maps appearing prominently in Protestant bibles in the sixteenth century, where they were usually joined by maps of Palestine in the time of Jesus and of Paul's journeys. These four

**FIGURE 13.5**   Illustration of Tabernacle furniture and high priest (Exodus 25, 28). From Henry Davenport Northrop, *Treasures of the Bible* (Philadelphia: International Publishing, 1894). In the public domain.

subjects appeared regularly in Christian bibles of the following centuries, often supplemented by maps of the location of Eden (Gen. 2), the peoples of the world (Gen. 10), the kingdoms of Israel and Judah (1 Kings), and the city of Jerusalem in various periods of biblical history.

Bible maps tend to illustrate texts from the Hebrew Bible to a much greater degree than other Christian art. That is because maps provide a visual means of reducing complicated and apparently contradictory literature – such as the Pentateuch's confusing itinerary of Israel's wandering in the wilderness – to a single, clear image. Maps summarize itineraries or boundaries detailed in complicated lists, often scattered across multiple chapters or books of the Bible. Nicolas Barbier, the sixteenth-century publisher of the popular English Geneva Bible, explained in the Bible's preface that maps are useful aids for reading: "Their purpose ... is to present clearly to the reader's eye what is otherwise difficult to grasp from the text alone." But bible maps do more than that. By illustrating trips and political boundaries directed by God's commandments, they fix a geographic ideal in readers' visual imagination. Like the illustrations of tabernacle furniture, the maps enable readers to imaginatively accompany the Israelites on their wanderings in the wilderness. They help readers visualize the prototypical journeys that inspire Jewish and Christian pilgrimages: Israel's travels to Sinai, to "the promised land," and to Jerusalem.

Early Protestant publishers were especially likely to include maps in their bibles. Elizabeth M. Ingram explained the interpretive principles at work in bible maps:

> The map functions not only as an aide for clarifying a specific text, but also as silent witness to a basic principle of Calvin's hermeneutics: that scripture is everywhere comprehensible and internally consistent. Consequently, its geographical dimensions must remain equally knowable, externally consistent, and therefore capable of being mapped.

Catherine Delano Smith argued that the early Protestants also wanted to direct how their readers understood the Old Testament:

> Reading, whether voiced or silent, bestows power on the reader. The reader is free to interpret the meaning of the message on the page as he or she likes (or is able)....Maps, as art and not just like art, became a mechanism for appropriating the (sacred) world by categorizing it in the manner approved by the religious authorities.

Even when Puritans increasingly banned pictures from their bibles (the 1611 Authorized King James Version was published without any illustrations in its text), maps and chronological charts could be bought separately and added as front or back matter, which is where they still appear in many bibles published today.[3]

Artistic illustrations in bibles, and even more their maps, help readers interpret the biblical text. They therefore help ritualize the Bible's semantic dimension. The physical sight and intricacy of illustrations and maps also make the bibles that contain them more attractive, thus ritualizing their iconic dimension. I have discussed them in this chapter, however, because biblical maps and illustrations inspire the visual imagination. They make the biblical stories seem more real to readers (see Box 13.1). In fact, many readers are far more likely to study Israel's journey through the wilderness on a map and the details of the Tabernacle's design in an illustration than they are to read the details in Exodus and Numbers. The illustrations and maps, along with other biblically inspired art, music, and films, have become presentations

### Box 13.1   Maps and religious imagination

Minnie Bruce Platt, in an essay titled "The Maps in My Bible," described her childhood fascination with bible maps. She recalled how they obscured one kind of geography and social reality while strengthening another: "Looking at these maps, I felt secure yet adventurous. Their details proved what I was learning in my religion, that there was a place whose terrain, cities, buildings corresponded to the words of a Bible that was to be believed literally and absolutely....I wished I could travel to this Land I felt so connected to, unaware that my maps were a hundred years out-of-date, unaware of my enmeshment in a history that had drawn and re-drawn them....There was no map to show me that I was living in a place and a time, Alabama in the deep South of the 1950s and 60s, marked by the convergence of racial and anti-Semitic theories developed in Europe and a specific racism practiced by white people in the United States against African-Americans. Buttressed by the Christian myth of Ham's eternal servitude, the white folks around me admitted no possibility of purification of the Black people living among us, almost all of them raised Christian....All of us caught on a map marked off by race, by color, by blood."[4]

of the biblical text that shape many people's religious imagination more than reading or hearing the text itself.

## 13.4   THE BIBLE IN THEATER AND FILM

Religious street <u>theater</u> developed in Europe during the Middle Ages and brought with it theatrical reenactments of biblical stories. One variety, called "mystery plays," presented narratives from the Christian Bible in vernacular poetry. Pentateuchal stories were featured in plays about "the Creation and Fall of Man," Cain and Abel, Noah's flood, Abraham and Isaac, and Moses. "Passion plays" portrayed the story of Jesus' life, death, and resurrection. Many towns would sponsor performances of cycles of mystery plays during annual festivals.[5]

The advent of the <u>Protestant Reformation</u> led to religious plays becoming instruments of intra-Christian polemic. Though Protestants criticized Catholic <u>art</u>, sometimes to the point of destroying it, they embraced religious theater as a means of spreading their message. For example, an English Reformer, John Bale, wrote and directed 24 plays with a traveling troupe of actors in the 1530s. In his repertoire was *Three Laws*, which dramatized biblical history in three parts as "the law of nature" from Adam to the exodus, the "law of Moses" for the rest of the Old Testament, and the New Testament as "the law of Christ." This play is unusual for emphasizing the theme of law, even while subordinating it to the New Testament's Christ. After the last decades of the sixteenth century, however, biblical plots disappeared from English plays. This was probably due to the popularity of the secular plays of William Shakespeare and Christopher Marlowe and also to the Puritans' disapproval of all theater. Antagonism between theater and church remained a feature of English Christianity to the end of the nineteenth century.[6]

Biblically inspired tableaus were more acceptable to conservative religious sensibilities. Bible illustrations of the Tabernacle and its furnishings as described in Exodus 25–40 fueled popular interest in scale models of the Tabernacle. In seventeenth-century Holland, Rabbi Jacob Judah Leon became known as "Templo" for displaying scale models of the Jerusalem Temple and Tabernacle. In the same city 200 years later, Rev. Leendert Schouten also attracted visitors with a model of the Tabernacle. In the late nineteenth-century United States, you could visit a full-size model of the Tabernacle in Chautaqua, New York. Replicas of the Tabernacle appear today at Holy Land Experience in Orlando, Florida, at the Mennonite Information Center in Lancaster, Pennsylvania, at New Holy Land in Eureka Springs, Arkansas, and at Timna Park near Eilat, Israel (Figure 13.6). Several manufacturers sell kits for constructing scale models of the Tabernacle, which appear on display

**FIGURE 13.6** Full-size reconstruction of the Tabernacle (Exod. 25–40) in Timna Park, Israel. Photo by J. W. Watts, 2014.

in the educational rooms of many congregations.[7] Other biblical scenes have also been the basis for public tableaus. For example, the Saint Louis World's Fair of 1904 featured a walk-through exhibit of the six days of creation. In 2016, creationists in Kentucky unveiled a 510-foot replica of Noah's ark.

Modern fascination with the details of the sanctuary, furnishings, and vestments in Exodus does not extend to reenacting the Pentateuch's ritual instructions. They are usually left to verbal explanation or artistic depiction, though Holy Land Experience does stage reenactments of the Day of Atonement ritual (Lev. 16) with a live actor but stuffed animals. Scale models, even those populated by a costumed cast, allow visitors to experience what it was like to be in ancient towns and temples. Christian reenactments usually reproduce traditional typologies of the Tabernacle and Temple rituals as foreshadowing and being superseded by Christ's atoning sacrifice. That is not always the case, however. Some African churches show greater interest in performing purity and offering rituals, to the point that the Mosama Disco Christo Church of West Africa has an Ark of the Covenant inside a Holy of Holies, which a high priest accesses once a year (Lev. 16). Jewish reconstructions, by contrast, recall the destruction of the ancient temples and, for some, anticipate their reconstruction. The Temple Institute in Jerusalem takes this expectation one step further: it is currently building furniture and making vestments in the expressed hope that they will be used in a rebuilt Jerusalem Temple.

Religious antagonism to professional theater waned in the twentieth century. Churches and professional companies increasingly staged biblical plays. In the early 1970s, two stage musicals featured Jesus as the main character: *Jesus Christ Superstar* and *Godspell.* Though pentateuchal stories have rarely reached the stages of Broadway or London (one exception is *Joseph's Amazing Technicolor Dreamcoat* by Tim Rice and Andrew Lloyd Webber), stories about Moses, Abraham, and the Creation feature prominently in the theatrical productions of religious organizations. For example, Sight and Sound Theaters operates theaters in Lancaster, Pennsylvania and in Branson, Missouri that stage only biblically based plays.

Biblical stories appear more prominently in films and television shows. Religious producers in many countries have produced devotional films. They distribute them through denominational networks of churches as well as secular media outlets. The Bible has also provided material for commercial Hollywood producers. The dominance of Christian culture in the United States guaranteed that Jesus movies based on the Gospels would be most prominent (see Section 10.5). But the story of Moses in the book of Exodus has provided the themes of several Hollywood blockbusters: Cecil

B. DeMille's *The Ten Commandments* (1956), Jeffrey Katzenberg's animated *Prince of Egypt* (1998), and Ridley Scott's *Exodus: Gods and Kings* (2014). As a result, films today dominate people's imagination of the Bible more than any other artistic medium, and often more than the written text itself.

The visual medium and the conventions of mass-market films lead to significant modifications of the biblical account. As is typical of Christian presentations of the Pentateuch, laws and instructions get little attention. Films of the exodus story focus on Moses more than on God or the Israelites in order to tell a story that conforms to modern heroic expectations. Brian Britt summarized the overall effect:

> Moses films eclipse biblical tradition more emphatically than any other medium. . . . The biblical Moses is a figure of writing rather than a figure of speech and action. Nevertheless, . . . each of the films brings writing into the story – not the writing of Moses, but the writing of Egypt . . . and in the case of The Ten Commandments, the fiery writing of God on the tablets of the law. . . . Forced by the medium and conventions of film to show Moses in heroic action, the movies nevertheless gesture . . . to a more biblical Moses, a Moses of tradition and writing.[8]

The interest of artists, actors, and film directors in biblical stories has reinforced the Christian tendency to ignore the Pentateuch's laws and instructions. Western cultural influence has spread that tendency around the world.

Bible films reach large and varied audiences, but that is true of biblically inspired art and music too. Of all the ritualized dimensions of scriptures, the <u>expressive dimension</u> crosses religious boundaries most easily. Music and art have the power to move anyone's emotions. People who do not regard themselves as Jews or Christians often find oral and visual presentations of scriptures <u>inspiring</u>. The Bible's expressive dimension often gets ritualized outside religious communities in concert halls and museums as well as cinemas. Classical choral masterpieces such as Händel's oratorio *The Messiah* and Mozart's *Requiem Mass* present words drawn mostly or entirely from the Christian Bible to concert hall audiences. Though much of their material comes from prophetic and New Testament books, they also draw on the Pentateuch. Some, like Haydn's *Creation*, focus there.

In the same way, many paintings and sculptures of biblical scenes appear in museum art collections. Some famous works draw sightseers from around the world and across religions and cultures. The crowds that view Michelangelo's ceiling of the Sistine Chapel, for example, do not need to know the biblical story line before traveling to Rome to see it. But they are nevertheless treated to a visual summary of the Christian Bible from creation to apocalypse, that is, from Genesis to Revelation. Some pictorial motifs, such as Eve posed naked with the snake, have become cultural clichés readily recognized by many people who have never read Genesis 3.[9]

Synagogues and churches use music and art to draw people's attention and interest. But it is also the case that much biblically inspired music and art escapes their control. In state museums, cinemas, and concert halls, biblical texts are viewed and presented apart from the ritual contexts of Jewish and Christian worship. Here the Bible's expressive dimension gets ritualized without the accompanying ritualization of its iconic and semantic dimensions. In these secular contexts, the Bible continues to inspire, but no longer as scripture.

## CITED WORKS AND FURTHER READING

1 See Ruth Mellinkoff, *The Horned Moses in Medieval Art and Thought* (Berkeley: University of California Press, 1970).

2 On illuminated manuscripts, see Michelle P. Brown, *The Lindisfarne Gospels: Society, Spirituality and the Scribe* (London: British Library, 2003).

3 On maps in bibles, see Catherine Delano Smith, "Maps as Art and Science: Maps in Sixteenth Century Bibles," *Imago Mundi* 42 (1990), 65–83; E. Wajntraub and G. Wajntraub, "Medieval Hebrew Manuscript Maps," *Imago Mundi* 44 (1992), 99–105; Elizabeth M. Ingram, "Maps as Readers' Aids: Maps and Plans in Geneva Bibles," *Imago Mundi* 45 (1993), 29–44, quotation from p. 35, and who provides the French quotation from Barbier and translates it on p. 30.

4 Minnie Bruce Platt, "The Maps in My Bible," *Bridges*, 2/1 (1991), 93–116, quotations from pp. 94, 103, 104.

5 On scripture in medieval mystery plays, see Peter Happe, *English Mystery Plays* (London: Penguin, 1975); and Timothy Thibodeau, "Western Christendom," in *The Oxford History of Christian Worship* (ed. G. Wainwright; Oxford: Oxford University Press, 2006), 246–247.

6 On the Bible in theater, see Paul Whitfield White, "The Bible as Play in Reformation England," in *The Cambridge History of British Theatre, Volume 1: Origins to 1660* (ed. J. Milling and P. Thomson; Cambridge: Cambridge University Press, 2004), 87–115. For an analysis of the performance of a twenty-first-century church passion play, see Anna Haapalainen, "Humanizing the Bible: Limits of Materiality in a Passion Play," in *Christianity and the Limits of Materiality* (ed. Minna Opas and Anna Haapalainen; London: Bloomsbury, 2017), 141–162.

7 On modern reconstructions of the Tabernacle and other biblical scenes, see the displays in Amsterdam's Jewish Museum and Bible Museum, and Burke O. Long, *Imagining the Holy Land: Maps, Models, and Fantasy Travels* (Bloomington, IN: Indiana University Press, 2003); Timothy Beal, *Roadside Religion: In Search of the Sacred, the Strange, and the Substance of Faith* (Boston: Beacon, 2006); and James S. Bielo, "Performing the Bible," in The Oxford Handbook of the Bible in America (ed. Paul C. Gutjahr; New York: Oxford, 2018). On building Noah's Ark Encounter in Tennessee, see James S. Bielo, "The Plausibility of Immersion: Limits and Creativity in Materializing the Bible," in *Christianity and the Limits of Materiality* (ed. Minna Opas and Anna Haapalainen; London: Bloomsbury, 2017), 122–140. On the Mosama Disco Christo Church, see Philip Jenkins, *The New Faces of Christianity: Believing the Bible in the Global South* (Oxford: Oxford University Press, 2006), 50. On the Temple Institute in Jerusalem, see its website: http://www.templeinstitute. org. (accessed August 3, 2020)

8 On films about Moses, see Brian Britt, *Rewriting Moses: The Narrative Eclipse of the Text* (London: T. & T. Clark, 2004), 40–58, quotation from p. 58; and Adele Reinhartz, *Bible and Cinema: An Introduction* (London: Routledge, 2013), 17–56.

9 On religious art in secular society, see Sally M. Promey, "Religion, Sensation, and Materiality," in *Sensational Religion: Sensory Cultures in Material Practice* (New Haven, CT: Yale University Press, 2014), 1–21; and Katie Edwards, *Admen and Eve: The Bible in Contemporary Advertising* (Sheffield: Sheffield Phoenix, 2012).

# CHAPTER 14

# The Bible's Semantic Dimension

Ritualizing the semantic dimension of scriptures depends on <u>literacy</u> in the scripts and languages of those scriptures. Comparative study of religions in the modern period shows the impact of rising literacy rates on how people read scriptures. The more people can read scriptures for themselves, the more they have wanted expert commentaries to explain to them what they are reading.

Mechanical <u>printing</u> produced many more copies of bibles than ever before, and made them less expensive. Changing technology also made it easier to bind biblical literature in one volume. Together with rising literacy rates and religious reformations, these developments encouraged Jewish and Christian readers to read more of the Bible for themselves. As a result, interpreting the Bible's semantic dimension increasingly influenced public debates about many different issues.

Biblical interpreters have therefore addressed a wide variety of issues for many different audiences. We can only focus on a few of them here. This survey of ritualizing the semantic dimension of Jewish and Christian bibles begins with an issue that has traditionally divided the two religions, the interpretation and application of biblical law. Then we turn to continuing public controversies over Genesis 1–10. They involve the Bible's teachings about race and gender, and also the fact that many readers think the origin stories in Genesis conflict with the findings of modern history and science.

## 14.1   BIBLICAL LAW AND AUTHORITY

There is no ancient evidence that <u>written laws</u> directed legal practice until the third or second century BCE. That is surprising, given how much the Pentateuch and other ancient texts talk about law. However, close examination shows that this rhetoric does not apply written law to legal practice. For example, the fourth-century Chronicler claims that King Jehoshaphat appointed a court of appeal in Jerusalem and instructed all judges to decide cases "for YHWH, who is with you in matters of justice" (2 Chr. 19:6; the story does not appear in the older book of 2 Kings). Since Chronicles also tells of Jehoshaphat's officers teaching Torah in the villages (2 Chr. 17:7–9), the two stories together could imply that Torah should guide the administration of justice in Judah's law courts. However, the Chronicler does not connect written Torah to legal practice explicitly.

### 14.1.1   Law in Ancient Judaism

It was the Pentateuch's <u>ritual rules</u> that first became <u>normative</u> for ritual practices, especially in the temples in Jerusalem and Samaria. Like other ancient cultures, Judean concern for following written instructions first focused on performing rituals by the book.[1] So Ezra's Torah reading led listeners to wonder how to celebrate *Sukkot* properly (Neh. 8:13–18). It also led the people to recommit themselves to

> *following God's Torah which was given through God's servant Moses, and to observe and do all the commandments and regulations and mandates of our Lord YHWH.* (Neh. 10:29)

The following verses tell us that "all" the Torah's obligations consist of giving tithes and other offerings to the temple, resting on the <u>Sabbath</u>, observing sabbatical years, and keeping separate from neighboring peoples, especially by avoiding <u>intermarriage</u> (Neh. 10:30–39). The offerings and Sabbath observances are obviously ritual concerns, but so is the commitment not to intermarry with other peoples. Ezra and Nehemiah are most concerned with the priests' marriages (Ezra 10:18–23; Neh. 13:1–9, 28–30). Priests must maintain their purity so that they can minister in the temple. Leviticus therefore restricts whom they can marry (Lev. 21:7–15), though it limits only the high priest to marrying "among his people" (21:14). The books of Ezra and Nehemiah think the community's holiness requires extending these rules to everybody. The people's ritual concern to preserve the purity of the community should motivate them to obey written Torah when marrying.

In the following centuries, the authority of written laws in Judea continued to direct <u>purity</u> practices and offerings, but began to be extended to <u>legal</u> procedures as well. Stories that mention marriage contracts and charges of illicit sex evoke the regulations and punishments written in the Pentateuch (Tob. 1:8; 7:12–13; Sus. 62; John 8:5). The histories of Judea in the second-century BCE depict the Maccabees following written Torah to purify the temple and make offerings (1 Macc. 2:19–22, 27, 48; 4:47, 53), and also when recruiting soldiers (1 Macc. 3:56). This Jewish development paralleled the increasing tendency to invoke written law in Hellenistic cultures at this time.

The Torah's spreading <u>authority</u> beyond the temple did not change its primary application to ritual. Instead, it had the effect of ritualizing more and more aspects of daily life. Like Ezra and Nehemiah, the <u>Dead Sea Scrolls</u> (see Section 4.2.2) redefined the temple community to cover the whole city of Jerusalem and bring all its inhabitants under the rules of the temple. The *Temple Scroll* (*11QT*) is primarily concerned with temple offerings, purity requirements, and festivals. The Qumran community's interest in civil law seems limited to repeating the Pentateuch's provisions with little amplification, except when it comes to regulating its internal life. Then the *Community Rule* (*1QS*) and the *Damascus Document* (*CD*) add many rules of behavior and discipline to extend the Torah's application to their own community. This line of interpretation seems to be based on the idea that the Torah, as the law book of the Temple, applies to whoever is in the temple community.

As interest spread in obeying the provisions of written Torah, concern to explain its rules also grew, especially around the <u>diet rules</u> that served as markers of Jewish identity. Already in the second century BCE, the *Letter of Aristeas* explained the distinction between clean and unclean animals (Lev. 11; Deut. 14) as a moral object lesson: herbivores are classified as clean and predators as unclean to teach people to avoid violence (see Box 14.1). Two centuries later, Philo of Alexandria described observing the biblical diet rules as an ascetic exercise aimed at teaching moderation (*Spec.* 4.100–118). Moral interpretations of the diet rules were elaborated in subsequent Jewish and Christian interpretation, and continue to find scholarly support today.[2]

<u>Rabbinic Judaism</u> (see Section 6.5.2) frequently interpreted biblical laws more flexibly than the strict interpretations in the Dead Sea Scrolls. The rabbis were therefore able to adjust for the catastrophic loss of temple and land at the end of the first century CE by focusing Jewish religious practice on prayer, good works, and Torah study. For example, they taught that you can gain the same merit by studying the laws of offerings as by making those

> ## Box 14.1  The *Letter of Aristeas* on food laws
>
> *Do not take the contemptible view that Moses enacted this legislation because of an excessive preoccupation with mice and weasels or suchlike creatures. The fact is that everything has been solemnly set in order for unblemished investigation and amendment of life for the sake of righteousness. The birds which we use are all domesticated and of exceptional cleanliness, their food consisting of wheat and pulse – such birds as pigeons, turtledoves, locusts, partridges, and, in addition, geese and others of the same kind. As for the birds which are forbidden, you will find wild and carnivorous kinds, and the rest which dominate by their own strength, and who find their food at the expense of the aforementioned domesticated birds – which is an injustice; and not only that, they also seize lambs and kids and outrage human beings dead or alive. By calling them impure, he has thereby indicated that it is the solemn binding duty of those for whom the legislation has been established to practice righteousness and not to lord it over anyone in reliance upon their own strength, nor to deprive him of anything but to govern their lives righteously, in the manner of the gentle creatures among the aforementioned birds which feed on those plants which grow on the ground and do not exercise a domination leading to the destruction of their fellow creatures. (Aris. 142–148)[3]*

offerings (Box 14.2). Such rulings make it possible to keep the covenant and to obey the Torah even when it is impossible to perform many commandments literally.

In fact, the rabbis tried to make Torah observance more important to Jewish everyday life than it had ever been before. They elaborated the Pentateuch's laws in order to "build a fence around the Torah" (*m. 'Avot* 1.1). That is, they established additional rules around the Pentateuch's regulations to ensure that the Torah's laws will not be broken. This led to greater attention to ritual <u>purity</u> in Jewish homes. For example, where Exod. 23:19 prohibits "boiling a kid in its mother's milk," the rabbis prohibited ever mixing meat with dairy foods (*b. Ḥul.* 108a–b).

The rabbis also required more scrupulous adherence to procedural safeguards when rabbinic courts heard <u>legal cases</u>. For example, Deuteronomy 17:6 requires the evidence of at least two witnesses to impose the death penalty. The rabbis required witnesses to also warn the accused in advance about the death penalty for doing this act. The accused must also verbally acknowledge this fact before doing the deed in order for the death penalty to apply (*m. Mak.* 1:10; *y. Sanh.* 22c). So, though the rabbis acknowledged that the Pentateuch mandates death as the punishment for many crimes, rabbinic procedures made the death penalty very difficult to carry out. In these and many other ways, Rabbinic Judaism made it possible in almost any circumstances for Jews to fulfill all 613 separate laws that the rabbis found in the Pentateuch (*b. Mak.* 23b).

## 14.1.2   Law in Ancient Christianity

While the ancient rabbis were emphasizing obedience to all the laws of Torah, most early Christians substituted <u>faith</u> in Christ for Torah observance. This new emphasis appeared first in the letters of the apostle <u>Paul</u> (see Section 7.2). Paul realized that some Jewish practices, especially <u>circumcision</u> and <u>diet rules</u>, limited Christianity's appeal among gentiles (non-Jews). He therefore argued that gentiles should be allowed to become Christians without observing these laws (Acts 15). To justify these exceptions, Paul developed a far-reaching argument (see Box 14.3) that contrasted obeying the law, that is, the Torah, with faith in Christ (Rom. 7). The law became a temporary custodian that convicts people of their sins under the Sinai covenant, but faith in Christ liberates people from the law's control (Gal. 3). Paul believed that

### Box 14.3   The Apostle Paul on the Law

*Christ is the goal of the Law, which leads to righteousness for all who have faith in God.* (Rom. 10:4 CEB)

*All those who rely on the works of the Law are under a curse, because it is written, "Everyone is cursed who does not keep on doing all the things that have been written in the Law scroll." But since no one is made righteous by the Law as far as God is concerned, it is clear that "the righteous one will live on the basis of faith."* (Gal. 3:10–11 CEB, quoting Deut. 27:26 and Hab. 2:4)

*Before faith came, we were guarded under the Law, locked up until faith that was coming would be revealed, so that the Law became our custodian until Christ so that we might be made righteous by faith. But now that faith has come, we are no longer under a custodian.* (Gal. 3:23–25 CEB)

*Christ canceled the detailed rules of the Law so that he could create one new person out of the two groups, making peace.* (Eph. 2:15 CEB)

Christians must still behave morally because they have been changed into moral people by Christ's salvation, not because of the Torah's rules.

The Gospels show Jesus voicing paradoxical views of pentateuchal law. Some texts quote his support for the Ten Commandments (Matt. 19:18–19) and the rest of scripture:

> *Do not think that I have come to abolish the law or the prophets; I have come not to abolish but to fulfil. . . . Therefore, whoever breaks one of the least of these commandments, and teaches others to do the same, will be called least in the kingdom of heaven; but whoever does them and teaches them will be called great in the kingdom of heaven.* (Matt. 5:17–19 NRSV)

In some cases, he interprets the laws strictly and even makes them harsher:

> *You have heard that it was said, "You shall not commit adultery." But I say to you that everyone who looks at a woman with lust has already committed adultery with her in his heart.* (Matt. 5:27–28 NRSV quoting Exod. 20:14)

On the other hand, the Gospels show Jesus ignoring purity rules that would restrict whom he can meet or touch (Mark 5:25–34; Matt. 9:11), and he seems to moralize food laws away:

*There is nothing outside a person that by going in can defile, but the things that come out are what defile.* (Mark 7:15 NRSV)

Jesus advocates interpreting the law based on underlying principles, such as the so-called "golden rule":

*Do to others as you would have them do to you; for this is the law and the prophets.* (Matt. 7:12 NRSV)

The Gospels denounce other traditions of legal interpretation, especially those of the Pharisees (Mark 7:1–13; Matt. 23). They depict Jesus teaching with great personal authority instead of quoting older traditions (Matt. 7:28–29). The Gospels, then, which were written in the late first century CE, already distinguished between early rabbinic traditions of the oral torah and Christian teachings based on Jesus' prophetic and messianic <u>authority</u>.

So the New Testament portrays Jesus making ambiguous statements about Mosaic law and Paul deploying a systematic argument for its replacement. However, it quotes some pentateuchal laws repeatedly and approvingly, especially the commands to love God (Deut. 6:5) and the neighbor and immigrant (Lev. 19:18, 34). These verses are notable for the number of times the New Testament repeats them:

*"Teacher, which commandment in the law is the greatest?" He said to him, "'You shall love the Lord your God with all your heart, and with all your soul, and with all your mind.' This is the greatest and first commandment. And a second is like it: 'You shall love your neighbor as yourself.' On these two commandments hang all the law and the prophets."* (Matt. 22:36–40 NRSV; see also Matt. 5:43–48; 19:19; Mark 12:28–34; Luke 10:25–37; Rom. 13:9; Gal. 5:14; Jam. 2:8)

As a result, Christians have read the New Testament as urging them to observe some pentateuchal laws, but not others. Their problem has been to figure out which are which.

Paul seems to have wanted a two-track Christianity in which Jews would observe circumcision and diet laws while gentiles would not, while both groups would be saved by Christ (Rom. 11). Instead, over the course of several centuries, Jews and Christians evolved into two separate religions, distinguished especially by their contrasting attitudes toward the laws of the Pentateuch. Already by 110 CE, some bishops threatened to excommunicate Christians who continued to observe <u>Passover</u>, as mandated in Exodus 12–13.

They argued that the Christian celebration of the <u>Lord's Supper</u>, also called <u>Communion</u> or the <u>Eucharist</u> (Luke 22:7–23; 1 Cor. 11:17–27), completely replaces the Passover meal. Later Christian churches frequently persecuted people who performed Jewish rituals, labeling them heretics.

### 14.1.3    Biblical Law in Medieval and Modern Times

Nevertheless, the continuing presence of rules for offerings and purity in the Christian Old Testament has proven attractive to dissident Christians throughout history. In various times and places during the Middle Ages, popular lay movements were reputed to practice Jewish rituals. It is hard to evaluate the accuracy of these claims, because anti-Semitic prejudices and charges of "Judaizing" were very common in Christian polemics.

The attraction to some pentateuchal rituals among modern Christian groups is better documented. Christians have been especially drawn to <u>Sabbath</u> laws. Many reject the Christian tradition of worshipping on Sundays, the day of Jesus' resurrection (Mark 16:2). They instead observe the seventh day, Saturday, as a day of rest and worship following pentateuchal law (Exod. 20:8–11; Deut. 5:12–15). Today, the Seventh-Day Adventists are the most familiar Christian "Sabbatarian" movement.

In the nineteenth and twentieth centuries, anti-colonial Christian movements in India, Africa, and Jamaica criticized Western Christianity for failing to follow the laws in its own Bible (see Section 6.6). In North America, some evangelicals created communities of Jewish Christians who observe Torah and also follow Christ. These "Messianic Jews" imitate the first Christian movement, which the New Testament depicts as consisting of Jewish followers of Jesus (Acts 6:1–7). Jewish organizations, however, do not usually recognize them as Jewish.

Christians generally believe that Jesus' crucifixion constitutes the ultimate and final <u>sacrifice</u> (Heb. 3–10). They therefore have almost never tried to make animal offerings to God. They accept the <u>Ten Commandments</u> and laws regarding love of God and neighbors because Jesus himself quoted them approvingly. However, interpreters have labored to determine which other laws apply to Christians and which do not. Christian arguments about pentateuchal laws have mostly revolved around its rules about the Sabbath, food, false religion, idolatry, slavery, and sex.

The books of the New Testament do not foresee Christians becoming politically powerful. They offer no advice about how to rule nations. Christian rulers have therefore frequently looked to their Old Testament for models of how to be "godly" rulers and for how to draft laws. The Christian emperors of Rome and of later European kingdoms inherited traditional legal procedures ("common law"), so in no case did they use only the Bible to draft their law codes. However, the Pentateuch provided a model of an authoritative written law in a single collection. That probably explains why it was Christian emperors, Theodosius and Justinian, who collected and edited Roman laws for the first time in the fifth and sixth centuries CE. Other early medieval kings followed suit. Thus, in the ninth century, the Anglo-Saxon laws of Alfred began with Exodus 20:1–23:13 and validated them for Christians by quoting Matthew 5:17, 7:12 and Acts 15:23–29 to justify creating further Christian laws that were collected by Alfred. For medieval Christian rulers, biblical law served as example and precedent for their own legislation.

In the twelfth century, the theologian Thomas Aquinas divided biblical laws into three categories: moral, judicial, and ritual. He argued that moral rules like the Ten Commandments apply to all Christians, while judicial rules may or may not apply depending on local circumstances. But Christians must not follow the Pentateuch's ritual laws. Aquinas's three categories of biblical law shape Catholic and Protestant thinking about biblical law up to the present day. Debates continue, however, over which laws belong in the mandatory moral category.

The codification of the Roman Catholic Church's rules as canon law in the twelfth century influenced the subsequent development of national law throughout Europe. However, the Protestant Reformation in the sixteenth century rejected canon law in the parts of northern Europe under Lutheran and Calvinist control. Political thinkers then discussed the proper sources of law and of legitimate government and increasingly cited the Pentateuch's example. Its description of Israel governed by written law but no king, or at least no royal legislation, led many to think of it as the "Mosaic constitution" of a "Hebrew Republic." Some based their calls to redistribute land on the biblical model of dividing land among the Israelite tribes and families. They also seized on the fact that God agrees to a written covenant with Israel to argue that kings should be subject to national constitutions. After all, if even God agrees to be constrained by written covenant, how can human kings claim the freedom of absolute sovereignty?[5]

In the eighteenth century, Enlightenment rationalism led political philosophers to dismiss religious precedents and argue for laws based on reason and experience alone. Their influence created the secular legal systems of the US Constitution (1789) and the French Code of Napoleon (1804). These laws guaranteed freedom of religion and prohibited government support for specific churches. Many other nations have followed their examples. Enlightenment though also shaped religious denominations (Box 14.4).

## Box 14.4   Jewish denominations and legal interpretation

Enlightenment philosophy influenced Jewish legal interpretation. In the eighteenth and nineteenth centuries, political emancipation allowed Jews to become citizens of European and American countries. Many philosophers then argued that Jewish law should be updated to reflect modern conditions. By the early twentieth century, these arguments led to the formation of three different Jewish denominations: (i) the Reform movement that emphasizes the importance of the Torah's ethics while leaving ritual practices to individual choice; (ii) the Conservative movement that regards all of the Torah's laws as obligatory but updates many of them to, for example allow women to participate equally in prayer and worship; and (iii) the Orthodox movement that preserves traditional rabbinic ways of observing Torah. Jewish denominations continue to evolve more varieties, especially in the United States. However, most American and Israeli Jews are not observant at all, which means they do not consider the Torah's laws obligatory or participate very often in religious services.

Nevertheless, some of the Bible's regulations continued to exert considerable influence over later laws. Its prohibitions on magic (Exod. 22:18; Lev. 20:6; Deut. 18:9–12) were frequently used to justify witch hunts in Christian communities. The Pentateuch's slave laws (Exod. 21:1–6; Lev. 25:39–55; Deut. 15:12–18) were cited to defend the African slave trade and its perpetuation in the United States. Abolitionists also cited the Pentateuch's more humane rules to try to end slavery (see Sections 14.2.7-8 below). The lists of prohibited sex acts (Lev. 18, 20) informed legal definitions of incest and are now commonly cited in arguments over sexual behavior and identity. All these debates have turned the old problem of distinguishing which biblical laws still apply into contemporary political conflicts. Arguments on both sides of these debates often invoke the medieval distinction between binding moral law and superseded ritual law, but disagree over which is which.

Thus, the law codes of the Pentateuch have rarely functioned with legal authority by themselves. Rabbinic literature molded and amplified Torah to direct the actions of rabbinic courts as well as other aspects of Jewish religion and life. The New Testament set aside many aspects of pentateuchal law while validating others. The Bible's law codes have, however, been imitated by many later legal developments: as a model of a collected written law for Roman Emperors, as a model of written religious law for the codifiers of medieval canon law, and as a model of constitutional law, even of republican values, for early modern political theorists. In the same way, many of its specific regulations still function as precedents. The Bible's rhetoric about law thus remains part of modern legal rhetoric, even though the Bible itself is rarely recognized as having legal authority in modern nations.

The heritage of biblical law has often been expressed by attention to the figure of <u>Moses</u> (see Section 3.2.3). Already in late Second Temple literature and the New Testament, the Pentateuch and especially its laws were called simply "Moses," as in the phrase "Moses and the Prophets" (*1QS 1.2–3; 4QMMT C 17*; Luke 16:29; 24:27). Just as Moses embodies the law in Western art (see Figure 12.6), the story of Moses has personified the idea of law in intellectual traditions. Moses has repeatedly been cast as a great law-giver and compared to the law-givers of other cultures, such as Hammurabi, Solon, and Muhammed. In antiquity, Philo and Josephus also depicted him as a solitary hero who rescued his people. Nineteenth-century historians, even while casting doubts on the accuracy of the pentateuchal story, nevertheless celebrated this depiction of Moses, as Brian Britt noted:

> *As the pivotal figure between Genesis and the history books, Moses combines myth and history to epitomize the German idealist hero. Moses is the lynchpin of biblical tradition, a liminal figure par excellence. For biblical scholars, Moses embodies legend itself. Whatever their status vis-à-vis history, legends of Moses present him as the central figure in a specific, heroic narrative.*[6]

For many modern thinkers, Moses' uniqueness involves especially <u>monotheism</u>, the belief in the existence of only one God, and laws that enforce this belief in religious practice. Sigmund Freud and Jan Assmann, for example, described Moses as a precedent and figurehead for monotheism and religious intolerance in Judaism, Christianity, and Islam.[7]

The Bible's rhetoric about law, then, has influenced cultures by shaping some specific laws. More often it has shaped their ideas about broader topics, such as the nature and function of law, of government, and of religion itself.

## 14.2   MODERN CONTROVERSIES ABOUT GENESIS

The Pentateuch's rhetoric of origins (see Section 3.1) explains where Israel and its religious institutions came from by telling stories about ancestors, about Israel's exodus from Egypt, and about the covenant with God at Mount

Sinai. It also reaches further back in time to tell of the origins of the nations, of civilization, and of the whole world. Through most of history, Jews and Christians believed these stories to be true accounts of past events. They were, in fact, the oldest accounts of human and world origins available to them.

Social reforms and intellectual advances over the last 500 years have challenged that belief. Developments in astronomy, biology, political theory, history, and archeology have undermined the Pentateuch's account of the distant past. History and archeology have also revealed older cultures and literatures in the ancient Middle East from which the Pentateuch drew many of its ideas about origins. Changing moral standards for social interactions, partly based on the Bible itself, have pointed out biases in biblical texts. As a result, the Pentateuch is no longer regarded as the oldest literature in the world. Its stories of origins compete with those of other cultures and are evaluated against the reconstructions of scientists, philosophers, and historians.

## 14.2.1   Genesis and Science

In Genesis, the stories of world creation and world flood reflect the same conception of the universe (<u>cosmology</u>).

> *When God started to create the heavens and the earth, the earth was formless and void. Darkness covered the deep, and God's spirit moved over the water.* (Gen. 1:1–2)

God creates the world by separating a cosmic ocean. The created world is a bubble floating in water: water surrounds the land while the dome of the sky holds back the water above (1:6–10). The sun, moon, and stars move underneath the sky's dome (1:14–18). The story of God destroying the world in Genesis 6–8 uses the same cosmology. The bubble begins to burst and the water floods in from below and above (7:11):

> *The fountains of the deep split and the windows of heaven opened.*

So, Genesis depicts the universe as a bubble of air and dry land in a cosmic ocean – a world view similar to maps drawn in ancient Egypt and Mesopotamia. It makes sense of what we see around us: an apparently flat earth and a blue sky that frequently leaks water.

Ancient Greek philosophers suggested that the earth is not flat but a sphere. They proposed a model of the universe in which the sun, moon, planets, and stars revolve around a spherical earth. This model is usually called the <u>Ptolemaic</u> universe after the mathematician who perfected it in the second century CE. Most Christian theologians in Late Antiquity and the Middle Ages accepted the Ptolemaic model, despite the fact that it contradicted Genesis's picture of a flat earth. To them, what mattered is not the shape of the earth but that it is at the center of the universe, which puts humans at the center of God's creation.[8]

The Ptolemaic model was challenged in the sixteenth and seventeenth centuries by the mathematical calculations of Nicolaus Copernicus and the observations of Galileo Galilei, who used the newly invented telescope. They demonstrated that the earth orbits the sun. Some Roman Catholic bishops rejected this conclusion and forced Galileo to recant his observations. He became famous as a scientific martyr of religious persecution. This did not stop most European scientists from quickly accepting the <u>Copernican</u> model of the universe. The credibility of religious beliefs as providing accurate insights into the nature of the physical universe suffered a severe blow.

However, early modern interaction between science and the stories of Genesis was not just conflictual. Peter Harrison has shown that, in the seventeenth century, a common interpretation of the story of Adam and Eve's "fall" in Genesis 3 encouraged <u>experimental science</u> (see Box 14.5). Many people had long believed that, before being expelled from Eden, humans reasoned clearly and had access to all knowledge. Human sin led to losing that knowledge and confusing their reasoning. But some philosophers concluded from this story that through rigorous effort humans can reason more clearly and improve their knowledge. The idea that accurate knowledge requires trial-and-error and painstaking effort motivated the work of early empirical scientists, such as Francis Bacon, and the empiricist philosophy of John Locke.

The popular perception that scientific discoveries were falsifying the Bible increased in the nineteenth century. Jews and Christians had traditionally thought the world was less than 6000 years old based on biblical genealogies. Observations of sedimentary rock layers led <u>geologists</u> to estimate the Earth's age at nearly four billion years. Then fossils in sedimentary rocks, together with observations of diverse living species, led Charles Darwin to conclude that life on earth evolved from simple to complex creatures over more than one billion years. He argued that <u>biological evolution</u> is driven by competition between species ("survival of the fittest"), rather than by a divine design.

Biologists quickly accepted and extended Darwin's conclusions. Many other people, however, think biological evolution undermines not just details of the biblical account of creation, but its fundamental premise: that God created the world and everything in it by an intentional plan. Though many theologians found ways to accommodate biological evolution within their

## Box 14.5  Adam's sin, reason, and empirical science

Peter Harrison concluded: "During the seventeenth century,…the bible came to occupy a position of unparalleled authority, informing discussions about the nature of the state, the rights of the individual, private property, education, international sovereignty, the status of indigenous peoples, work and leisure, agriculture and gardening, anthropology and moral psychology. In each of these spheres, the story of Adam had a significant place.…Advocates of 'rationalism' and 'empiricism' largely fall out along lines related to an underlying theological anthropology. Descartes' confident assertion that the 'natural light' of reason could provide the basis of a complete and certain science presupposed the persistence of the natural light and the divine image even in fallen human beings. This was strongly contested by those who believed that the Fall had effaced the divine image and all but extinguished the natural light. On this latter view, if knowledge were possible at all, it would be painstakingly accumulated through much labour, through trials and the testing of nature, and would rise to a modest knowledge that did not penetrate to the essences of things and was at best probable rather than certain. Such mitigated skepticism characterized the experimental approach commonly associated with such figures as Francis Bacon and Robert Boyle."[9]

religious beliefs, popular movements opposing the teaching of evolution have gained strength over the past century. In the early twentieth century, Christian fundamentalists began opposing the conclusions of historians and also rejected biological evolution. Fundamentalists influenced some US states to ban the teaching of evolution in their schools. This led to the highly publicized "monkey trial" of school teacher John Scopes in Tennessee in 1925. Attempts to counter evolution marshaled various kinds of evidence into theories of theistic creationism or "intelligent design," which could be taught to school children instead of, or at least in addition to, evolution. Advocacy of creationism has increased with the world-wide growth of evangelical Christianity since the 1950s. Creationism has also found a receptive audience among some Orthodox Jews and, increasingly, among conservative Muslims.[10]

These conflicts over the relationship between Genesis and science have become sharper in modern centuries. That is not just because of new scientific discoveries. It is also because modern people tend to read the Bible differently than their predecessors in ancient and medieval times.

## 14.2.2  Modern Reading Practices

For many centuries, Jewish and Christian interpretation of the Bible used mostly symbolic methods of interpretation, such as <u>midrash</u>, <u>typology</u>, and <u>allegory</u>. Interpreters assumed that its stories are true accounts of past events, but they were less interested in past history than in the text's religious meaning for themselves in the present (see Section 6.4).

By contrast, modern readers of the Bible, whether religious or secular, tend to read it "like any other book" even when they regard it as the most important book. Like any other book, their interpretations of particular passages pay attention first to the immediate <u>literary context</u>.

When biblical texts were commonly interpreted as symbolic expressions of religious truth, conflicts between the Bible and cosmological beliefs could easily be explained away. Modern reading practices, however, have increasingly focused on the <u>plain meaning</u> of the text, often called its "<u>literal</u>" meaning. This practice has caused many defenders of traditional religion to abandon symbolic interpretation and stake their cause on what they consider the literal meaning of Genesis 1–3. Modern conflicts between religion and science, then, are due to changes in Bible reading practices as well as to scientific discoveries. At the root of these modern debates lies a change in how many people read Jewish and Christian scriptures.

This change in reading practices has religious roots. Jewish medieval interpreters focused on the "plain meaning" (*pschat*) of the biblical text. The Protestant Reformers believed that the Bible's message would be plainly evident to every sincere reader.[11] It also has roots in philosophical efforts in the seventeenth and eighteenth centuries to analyze the Bible critically like any other ancient book. These tendencies joined, in the nineteenth century, with new methods of historical analysis to create <u>historical criticism</u> of the Bible. Historical research on the Pentateuch and on the Gospels has proven to be one of the most controversial aspects of biblical studies ever since.

We have already reviewed historical analysis of the origins of the Gospels and the search for the historical Jesus (Sections 11.4 and 11.6). What is left is to return to the Pentateuch and long-standing debates about how it was written, and when.

## 14.2.3  The Pentateuch and History

Already in 1670, the Jewish philosopher Baruch Spinoza argued that Moses could not have written the Pentateuch, which is "faulty, mutilated, tampered with, and inconsistent." The French philosopher Voltaire mocked the

Pentateuch and historical books of the Bible as violent, superstitious, and full of unbelievable stories. Criticisms like these prompted ardent defenses of biblical truth from Jews and Christians, who condemned Spinoza and Voltaire as heretics. Some scholars also tried to reconcile their religious faith with human reason by investigating biblical books more systematically using historical methods of research.[12]

Such approaches found a home especially in nineteenth-century German universities. Protestant German scholars developed a "higher criticism" that went beyond the lower criticism of philology and manuscript criticism. They investigated ancient religious history and the history of the biblical books themselves. Their methods and results spread to Britain and the United States in the late nineteenth century, and this historical criticism dominated biblical studies in the twentieth century. Its results transformed modern understandings of the origins and development of the Pentateuch.[13]

Doubts that Moses wrote the Pentateuch led historians to search for its origins in other periods of Israel's history. In 1805, Wilhelm De Wette pointed out that the religious reforms of King Josiah, who destroyed divine images and shrines to other gods and centralized worship of YHWH in one temple (2 Kgs. 22–23), reflect the themes of the book of Deuteronomy. De Wette argued that Deuteronomy was probably written in Josiah's time, the seventh century BCE, to motivate and justify these reforms (see Section 4.4). Later scholars have found this dating convincing because Josiah's reforms seem to reflect some of Deuteronomy's themes. Deuteronomy's Hebrew language is also very similar to that of 2 Kings and the book of Jeremiah, both of which narrate events up to the sixth century BCE. Dating Deuteronomy to the seventh century became the basis for dating other parts of the Pentateuch before or after this book.

Historical critics also tried to explain the strange literary form of the Pentateuch. Many readers notice that the Pentateuch does not read very smoothly. Its books contain contradictions in their plots and in their laws, they tell two or three versions of the same story, and they are inconsistent in how they characterize God and even how they name God. Eighteenth- and nineteenth-century historians concluded that several different sources were combined to create the Pentateuch. This division into four sources in the chronological sequence J-E-D-P became known as "the Documentary Hypothesis" (see Section 6.7). It was popularized by Julius Wellhausen in 1876 and, for the next century, most critical historians presupposed the Documentary Hypothesis. Many still defend it today.

The Documentary Hypothesis dated all the sources hundreds of years after Moses. It undermined the traditional belief that Moses wrote the whole

Pentateuch and the text's explicit claim that Moses wrote down the laws (Exod. 24:3–4; Deut. 31:9, 24). Conservative Protestant, Catholic, and Jewish scholars disputed the conclusions of historical critics, and their arguments remain influential in more conservative churches and synagogues.

Religious groups reacted with alarm when historical critics denied that God revealed the Torah to Moses at Mount Sinai. Pope Leo XIII in 1893 declared that the Bible is completely inspired and contains no mistakes, a belief commonly called inerrancy. Though sponsoring scholarship on the Bible, the Vatican prohibited Roman Catholic scholars from participating in historical criticism of the Bible until the middle of the twentieth century. Among Protestants, opposition to critical scholarship on the Bible coalesced in the early twentieth-century Fundamentalist movement, named for a series of 90 essays titled *The Fundamentals* that were published between 1910 and 1915. Many Protestant denominations in the United States divided between conservatives and liberals. While liberals adapted their beliefs to the findings of historical research, conservative fundamentalists claimed that belief in the inerrancy and infallibility of the Bible is essential for Christian faith. Jews of all denominations rejected higher criticism until the middle of the twentieth century, when Reform and Conservative movements (Box 14.4) adapted themselves to some of its ideas. Then their seminaries and the new Israeli universities began to support critical study of the Pentateuch. Historical criticism of the Pentateuch has therefore shaped the denominational history of many traditions.

## 14.2.4   The Discovery of Older Ancient Literature

Nineteenth-century historical research also challenged traditional ideas about the Bible in a completely different way. Europeans exploring ancient ruins in the Middle East brought home written texts in forgotten languages. After Egyptian hieroglyphics and Akkadian cuneiform were deciphered in the early nineteenth century, scholars translated and published many of these texts (see Box 14.6). The discoveries included Egyptian and Sumerian texts dating from the third millennium BCE and Akkadian texts from the early second millennium – not only older than biblical texts, but even older than characters like Abraham and Moses featured in biblical texts. The Hebrew Bible was no longer the oldest literature in the world.

Furthermore, some of these ancient texts contained stories that resembled parts of the Hebrew Bible in one way or another. Perhaps most shocking were the flood stories written in Akkadian cuneiform, which George Smith published in English translation in 1871. These accounts of a prehistoric

### Box 14.6    Publications of significant ancient Middle Eastern texts

| Language & contents | Text & century BCE | Scholar | Date of translation |
| --- | --- | --- | --- |
| Egyptian hieroglyphics deciphered | Rosetta Stone (second century) | Jean-François Champollion | 1822 |
| Akkadian cuneiform deciphered | Behistun Inscription (fifth century) | Henry Rawlinson | 1846–1851 |
| Akkadian flood stories | *Gilgamesh* (seventh century) & *Atrahasis* (seventeenth-century copy from older original) | George Smith | 1871 |
| Akkadian creation myth | *Enuma Elish* (seventh century from older original) | George Smith | 1871 |
| Egyptian tomb inscriptions | Pyramid Texts (twenty-fourth century) | Kurt Sethe | 1908 |
| Ugaritic myths | *Baal Cycle* (fourteenth century) | Charles Virollaud | 1931–1935 |
| Hebrew Dead Sea Scrolls | *Temple Scroll* (second century) | Yigael Yadin | 1977–1983 |

world flood resemble Genesis 6–8 in their plot and details as well as overall theme. Yet the oldest of these stories is older than any possible date for the Hebrew story of Noah's flood. The Akkadian texts also tell the flood story using the polytheistic theology of ancient Babylon. Their publication showed that the biblical writers sometimes used older, non-Israelite stories and adapted them to their own theological perspective.

Many other ancient texts were published in the course of the nineteenth and twentieth centuries that deepened our understanding of the historical, literary, and religious contexts in which Israel's theology and literature developed. The Babylonian creation epic, *Enuma Elish*, provides a vivid example of a violent cosmogony, against which Genesis 1 describes creation as deliberate and uncontested. Egyptian tomb inscriptions show that belief in an afterlife judgment was common in Egyptian culture, which contrasts with the Hebrew Bible's almost total lack of afterlife ideas. The Ugaritic myths provide a glimpse into the religious thought of Ba'al devotees, whom the books of Kings attack as idol worshippers. Finally, the Dead Sea Scrolls, though written later than the books of the Hebrew Bible, show how quickly the Hebrew Bible's ideas were developed and changed by its interpreters in the last few centuries BCE.

## 14.2.5   The Changing Face of Biblical Studies

By the middle of the twentieth century, then, the realization had sunk in that the Pentateuch is no longer the oldest literature in Western civilization, just as it is no longer widely regarded as a model for national laws or a credible account of world or human origins (see below). It is nevertheless still part of Jewish and Christian scripture, and therefore still vital to the religious identities of many Jews and Christians. Denominations and individual scholars engaged this new understanding of the Pentateuch in a variety of ways.

Jewish settlement in Palestine and the founding of the state of Israel in 1948 created strong support for archeological excavations to discover Israel's biblical past. Jewish scholars also began to engage in historical criticism of the Pentateuch.[14] In the 1950s and 1960s, the Roman Catholic Church stopped opposing scientific and historical research, and Catholic biblical scholars have played prominent roles ever since. Historical research on the Bible has therefore become an ecumenical and interreligious enterprise. The largest academic association of biblical scholars, the Society of Biblical Literature, counts adherents to a wide variety of religious denominations as well as to none among its more than 8000 members. At its meetings, it is usually impossible to determine the speakers' religious affiliations from the contents of their papers alone.

The spread of Christianity around the world has generated increasing research on the Bible by Asian, African, and South American scholars, though Europeans, Israelis, and North Americans still dominate the field. Non-Western scholars have brought new energy to investigating historical issues as well as post-colonial perspectives on the Bible and on ancient religious history (see Sections 6.6 and 14.1.3).

The last 50 years have also witnessed several profound challenges to the dominance of historical criticism within the academic study of the Bible. The first of these applied literary methods of analyzing modern stories and poetry to biblical literature. Literary criticism in biblical studies emphasized interpretation of the final, received form of the text instead of reconstructing earlier sources and stages of editing. It is therefore frequently called "synchronic" analysis in contrast to "diachronic" historical study. Its focus on plot, characterization, themes, and structural devices took difficulties that historical critics take as evidence of editing and explained them as intentional literary effects instead. For 20 years starting in the 1970s, literary analysis threatened to displace historical criticism as the dominant method for studying biblical texts.

Literary scholars criticized historical critics for the speculative nature of their reconstructed sources and editions, as demonstrated by lack of agreement between different scholars. The literary focus on the existing text seemed to offer a firmer basis for interpretation. The allusions, word plays, and elaborate structures uncovered by literary analysis, however, also turned out to be very speculative. Different scholars produced different literary interpretations just as often as different historical reconstructions. When these observations led scholars of modern literature to take a "post-modern" turn that focused on how texts deconstruct their own interpretation, biblical scholars followed suit by showing the indeterminacy of many biblical texts. However, because ancient biblical texts have always been ambiguous and difficult to interpret, deconstruction proved less innovative for biblical studies than it did for the study of modern literature.

Research on the cultural history of the Bible, often called biblical <u>reception history</u>, has recently become a prominent part of the field of biblical studies. Many books are published every year on the Bible's interpretation in one or another culture or time period, and many more focus on its influence on art, literature, and film. Major collections of essays bring together and summarize this research, such as the four volumes of the *New Cambridge History of the Bible* and of *Hebrew Bible/Old Testament: The History of Its Interpretation*, and the 18 volumes (so far) of the *Encyclopedia of the Bible and Its Reception*. In addition, anthropologists have started examining how communities ritualize the interpretation of the Bible in many different contemporary contexts.[15]

<u>Historical criticism</u> continues to try to trace the origins of biblical literature. The Bible's cultural history leads me to observe, however, that Israel's origin traditions only became important after the Torah began to be ritualized in the iconic, expressive, and semantic dimension by Jewish and Samaritan priests in the Second Temple period. Rabbinic literature increased the Torah's importance for Jews by codifying its place in ritual practice and interpretation. The Tanak's incorporation into Christian scripture as the Old Testament, even if secondary to the importance of the Gospels, guaranteed its influence in Christian thought and Western culture. Modern

revolutions in printing technology and book marketing have led to the Bible's reproduction worldwide in more copies and languages than any other literature. It is as Jewish and Christian scripture that the Bible became religiously and culturally important, and never for more people than now in the twenty-first century.

## 14.2.6  The Bible and Gender

Genesis does not just tell about the origins of the physical world and the origins of Israel's ancestors. It also narrates the origins of differences between human beings, especially between men and women and between ethnic groups. These texts have frequently been used in Jewish and Christian history to justify discrimination against women and prejudice against particular races, even to the point of violence. The same texts have also been interpreted to counteract sexism and racism.

The first story of creation describes women and men as created equally in the image of God (Gen. 1:27). However, the Garden of Eden story says the man was created first, then God created a woman out of his rib to be his "helper" (2:20). The snake convinced the woman to eat the forbidden fruit and then she gave it to the man (3:1–6). God punished the woman for this sin by saying that the man "will rule over you" (3:16).

Traditional interpreters therefore blamed the first woman and, by extension, women generally for human sin and its consequences, which they understood to include death (3:19). Already in the second century BCE, ben Sira concluded,

> *From a woman sin had its beginning, and because of her we all die.*
> (Sir. 25:24)

The New Testament repeats this interpretation (2 Cor. 11:3) and concludes from it that women should "not teach or have authority over a man" (1 Tim. 2:11–15).[16]

Women in significant numbers entered the ranks of professional biblical scholars only in the decades following 1970. Many of them introduced <u>feminist</u> perspectives that revolutionized the interpretation of some biblical texts. For example, Phyllis Trible pointed out that Genesis 3:16 describes patriarchy negatively (see Box 14.7). The first woman is not created subordinate to the man, but is punished for disobeying God by being subjected to the man's rule. She noted that the word *'ezer* "helper" used to describe Eve in Gen. 2:20 appears most commonly in the Hebrew Bible to describe God (e.g., Ps. 115:9–11). So

**Box 14.7   Phyllis Trible on Genesis 3:16**

"We misread if we assume that these judgments are mandates. They describe; they do not prescribe. They protest; they do not condone. Of special concern are the words telling the woman that her husband shall rule over her (3:16). This statement is not license for male supremacy, but rather it is condemnation of that very pattern. Subjugation and supremacy are perversions of creation. Through disobedience the woman has become slave. Her initiative and her freedom vanish. The man is corrupted also, for he has become master, ruling over the one who is his God given equal. The subordination of female to male signifies their shared sin."[17]

it implies no subordination to the man. Trible's observations simply read the story as written, but it required a woman interpreter to expose the male biases in the story's usual interpretation.

Feminist theories also highlighted the pervasive patriarchialism of biblical stories about male heroes and of laws that privilege the legal rights of free, male Israelites. Feminists uncovered the neglected stories of matriarchs like Sarah, Hagar, and Rebekah (see Section 3.1.1), and the crucial roles of professional women like the Hebrew midwives in Exodus 1, the prophets Miriam and Huldah (see Box 4.7), the judge Deborah, and Mary Magdalene (Section 11.3). Today, their analysis has expanded to embrace a wider range of sexualities and gender identities.[18] The work of feminists and gender critics has fueled debates about how the Pentateuch can remain authoritative for contemporary people who embrace different cultural values, such as gender equality, as well as modern scientific, political, and historical perspectives.

## 14.2.7   The Bible and Race

Slave owners used the Bible to justify owning people as property by quoting biblical laws allowing slavery (Exod 21:1–6; Lev. 25:39–55; Deut. 15:12–18; also in the New Testament: Eph. 6:5–8; Col. 3:22–25; Titus 2:9–1; Philemon). But no biblical text has been cited more often to justify enslaving Africans than the so-called "curse of Ham." Genesis 9 tells the story of Noah getting drunk and falling asleep, when

*Ham, the father of Canaan, saw the nakedness of his father (Noah) and told his brothers. (9:22)*

After waking up, Noah cursed Ham's son, Canaan, to be a slave (9:25). The list of nations descending from Noah's sons then records Ham's descendants (Gen. 10:6) as Canaan and the African nations of Egypt, Cush (Ethiopia), and Put (Libya). Later generations include Babylonia and Assyria in Mesopotamia as well (10:10–11). The Psalms also locate Egypt "in the land of Ham" (Pss. 78:51; 105:27; 106:22). The story, then, seems to blame the ancestor of African peoples for some kind of sexual offense against Noah, though Noah's curse falls on his grandson, Canaan.

Why Noah curses Canaan instead of Ham is not clear. An ancient line of interpretation held that Noah actually cursed Ham. Some rabbinic texts speculated that Ham's skin was also blackened because he had sex with his wife inside the ark, which apparently was not allowed. These ideas were combined into "the curse of Ham" to justify the African slave trade when it spread into Europe and the Americas in the sixteenth century. It became routine to regard Africans as "blackened" by Ham's sin and cursed to slavery. Few people noticed that Genesis 9 says no such thing. Their interpretations obscured the biblical text and condemned generations of African descent, often Christians themselves, to violent enslavement.[19]

From at least the nineteenth century on, many African and African-American preachers, scholars, and writers tried to counter the effects of this tradition by pointing out that Noah cursed Canaan, not Ham. They claimed Ham's identity with Africans and celebrated the cultural achievements of Ham's descendants in Egypt, Ethiopia, and Babylon. Descent from Ham became a point of pride. Zora Neale Hurston, for example, retold the Genesis 9 story in her 1922 play, *The First One*, which ends with Ham and his wife leaving the family for "where the sun shines forever, to the end of the Earth." Ham tells his father and brothers: "Oh, remain with your flocks and fields and vineyards, to covet, to sweat, to die and know no peace. I go to the sun."[20]

## 14.2.8   The Bible and Social Reform

People who have struggled against these biblical legacies of patriarchy and racism have found broader principles in the Bible to support their causes. To justify arguments for equal rights for all people, they have pointed to the fact that God rescued not just the descendants of Jacob but also a "mixed multitude" (Exod. 12:38) who came along with Israel out of Egypt and were included in the covenant at Mount Sinai. Moses requires that "men, women, children, and immigrants" must all hear the Torah read aloud and commit themselves to keeping it (Deut. 31:12). This inclusive tendency in covenant making continues in the New Testament, where Paul declares that there is "neither Jew nor Greek, neither slave nor free, neither male nor female" in Christ (Gal. 3:28).

Even more pervasive in biblical rhetoric are calls to care for poor people and to condemn all forms of economic oppression. For example, Leviticus prohibits maximizing profits. It requires landowners instead to provide free food to the poor and to immigrants:

> *When you reap the harvest of your land, don't reap to the very edges of your field, or gather the gleanings of your harvest; you must leave them for the poor and for the immigrant.* (Lev. 23:22)

The biblical prophets fiercely condemn oppression and injustice, and especially fraudulent business deals:

> *The voice of the Lord cries to the city . . ..: Hear, O tribe and assembly of the city! Can I forget the wealth of wickedness in the house of the wicked, and the fraudulent measure that is accursed?* (Mic. 6:9–10)

Jesus' voice, especially in Luke's Gospel, echoes the Hebrew prophets on this point to such an extent that many twentieth-century theologians proclaimed God's "preferential option for the poor":

> *Jesus looked up at his disciples and said: "Blessed are you who are poor, for yours is the kingdom of God. . . . But woe to you who are rich, for you have received your consolation."* (Luke 6:20, 24)

All these efforts at social reform get reinforced by the love commandment that echoes from the Pentateuch to the New Testament:

> *Love your neighbor/the immigrant/your enemy like yourself.* (Lev 19:18, 36; Matt 5:44)

I cite these examples together because they are some of the texts that Jews and Christians have used repeatedly to reform their communities and the larger society. The Bible in all its different forms is a large collection of documents that say many different things, and it has been interpreted in even more varied ways. It has provided resources both to defend the status quo and to motivate social reforms. It has also inspired scientific and historical research, while giving people reasons to resist some scientific and historical conclusions.

## CITED WORKS AND FURTHER READING

1  On normative written ritual rules, see James W. Watts, "Ritual Legitimacy and Scriptural Authority," *Journal of Biblical Literature* 124/3 (2005), 401–417.

2  On Philo's interpretation of diet laws, see Hans Svebakken, *Philo of Alexandria's Exposition of the Tenth Commandment* (Atlanta: SBL, 2012). For contemporary interpretations of diet laws as moral examples, see Jacob Milgrom, "Ethics and Ritual: The Foundations of the Biblical Dietary Laws," in *Religion and Law: Biblical, Jewish, and Islamic Perspectives* (ed. E. B. Firmage; Winona Lake, IN: Eisenbrauns, 1989), 159–191; and Mary Douglas, *Leviticus as Literature* (Oxford: Oxford University Press, 1999), 134–151, 232.

3  For the translation of the Letter of Aristeas, see *The Letter of Aristeas*, tr. by R. J. H. Shutt in *Old Testament Pseudepigrapha* (ed. J. H. Charlesworth; 2 vols.; New York: Doubleday, 1983), 7–34.

4  For the translation of *b. Menaḥ.* 110a, see Isidore Epstein, ed., *Menachos*, vol. 4, *The Soncino Babylonian Talmud* (London: Soncino, 1989).

5  On the Pentateuch in early modern political thought, see Daniel Elazar, *The Covenant Tradition in Politics*, 4 vols. (New Brunswick, NJ: Transaction Publishers, 1995–1998); Eric Nelson, *The Hebrew Republic: Jewish Sources and the Transformation of European Political Thought* (Cambridge, MA: Harvard University Press, 2010); and Graham Hammill, *The Mosaic Constitution: Political Theology and Imagination from Machiavelli to Milton* (Chicago: Chicago University Press, 2012).

6  On Moses as embodying Torah and monotheism, see Brian Britt, *Rewriting Moses: The Narrative Eclipse of the Text* (London: T. & T. Clark, 2004), quotation from p. 80.

7  Sigmund Freud, *Moses and Monotheism* (New York: Vintage, 1939); Jan Assmann, *Moses The Egyptian: The Memory of Egypt in Western Monotheism* (Cambridge, MA: Harvard University Press, 1998).

8  On Genesis and cosmology, see Kyle Greenwood, *Scripture and Cosmology: Reading the Bible Between the Ancient World and Modern Science* (Downers Grove, IL: IVP Academic, 2015).

9  Peter Harrison, *The Fall of Man and the Foundations of Science* (Oxford: Oxford University Press, 2007), quotations from pp. 2–3 and 6.

10  On Genesis, evolution, and creationism, see Ronald L. Numbers, "Scientific Creationism and Intelligent Design," in *The Cambridge Companion to Science and Religion* (ed. P. Harrison; Cambridge: Cambridge University Press, 2010), 127–147.

11 For the growth in Jewish and Christian attention to *pshat* and the "literal sense" of scripture in the Middle Ages and Early Modern periods, see essays in *Interpreting Scriptures in Judaism, Christianity and Islam: Overlapping Inquiries* (ed. M. Z. Cohen and A. Berlin; Cambridge: Cambridge University Press, 2016), especially Jon Whitman, "The Literal Sense of Christian Scripture: Redefinition and Revolution," 133–158, and Mordechai Z. Cohen, "Emergence of the Rule of *Peshat* in Medieval Jewish Bible Exegesis," pp. 204–223.

12 On the rhetoric of origins in early modern biblical criticism, see Jean-Louis Ska, "The Study of the Book of Genesis: the Beginning of Critical Reading," in *The Book of Genesis: Composition, Reception and Interpretation* (ed. C. A. Evans, J. N. Lohr, and D. L. Peterson; Leiden: Brill, 2012), 3–26.

13 On nineteenth-century historical criticism, see Thomas Römer, "'Higher Criticism: The Historical and Literary-Critical Approach," in *Hebrew Bible/ Old Testament: The History of Its Interpretation 3/1* (ed. M. Saebø; Berlin: Vandenhoeck & Ruprecht, 2013), 393–423.

14 On twentieth-century Jewish scholarship on the Pentateuch, see S. David Sperling, "Major Developments in Jewish Biblical Scholarship," in *Hebrew Bible/Old Testament: The History of Its Interpretation 3/2* (ed. M. Saebø; Berlin: Vandenhoeck & Ruprecht, 2015), 371–388.

15 For anthropological studies of "biblicism" among communities as diverse as North American Evangelicals, Central American Pentacostals, Jamaican Rastafarians, and South Asian Christians, see Brian Malley, *How the Bible Works: An Anthropological Study of Evangelical Biblicism* (Walnut Creek, CA: AltaMira, 2004); and James S. Bielo, ed., *The Social Life of Scriptures: Cross-Cultural Perspectives in Biblicism* (New Brunswick, NJ: Rutgers University Press, 2009).

16 On the interpretation of Eve in Genesis 1–3, see Hermann Spieckermann, Stefan Krauter, Benjamin G. Wright III, Tamar Kadari, Elyse Goldstein, Brian K. Reynolds, Gordon Nickel, Elizabeth J. Harris, Anthony Swindell, Anne Lapidus Lerner, Ori Z. Soltes, Linda Maria Koldau, and Alice Ogden Bellis, "Eve," in the *Encyclopedia of the Bible and Its Reception* (ed. D. C. Allison, Jr., et al.; Berlin: De Gruyter, 2015), 8: 285–316.

17 Phyllis Trible, "Depatriarchalizing in Biblical Interpretation," *Journal of the American Academy of Religion* 41 (1973), 30–48, quotation from p. 41.

18 On feminist biblical criticism, see the bibliography in notes 6 and 7 in Chapter 11.

19 There is debate about how old the association is between racism, slavery, and the "curse of Ham": compare David M. Whitford, *The Curse of Ham in the*

*Early Modern Era: The Bible and the Justifications for Slavery* (Farnham, UK: Ashgate, 2009) with David M. Goldenberg, *Black and Slave: The Origins and History of the Curse of Ham* (Berlin: De Gruyter, 2017).

20 Zora Neale Hurston, "The First One: A Play in One Act," in *Ebony and Topaz: A Collectanea* (ed. C. S. Johnson, 1927; reprinted Freeport, NY: Books for Libraries Press, 1971), quoted by Stephen R. Haynes, *Noah's Curse: The Biblical Justification of American Slavery* (Oxford: Oxford University Press, 2002), 193–194.

# CHAPTER 15

# The History of the Bible as a Scripture

The comparative study of scriptures shows that religions take different approaches to defining the scope and limits of their scriptures. Mahayana Buddhists acknowledge thousands of different sutras as scripture, even if in practice they focus on just a few. On the other hand, Muslims regard only revelations to the prophet Mohammed as scripture, and delimited them as the Qur'an shortly after his death. Jewish, Samaritan, and Christian scriptures have also been clearly defined since antiquity (see Section 1.3), but earlier they evolved from more diffuse collections.

## 15.1 SCRIPTURALIZATION AND CANONIZATION

Biblical scholars usually describe the development of scripture as a process of canonization. The word "canon" has been used since the fourth century CE to refer to the list of books in Christian scripture. Discussions of canonization focus on the contents of scripture and the criteria by which books were selected or rejected. Current studies also discuss the evolution of concepts about scripture and canons.[1] However, ancient lists of canonical books are after-the-fact rationalizations for using some books and not others. They reflect the fact that some books have already been scripturalized, rather than how scripturalization began.

This book had instead sifted the evidence for the origins and growth of Jewish and Christian scriptures by focusing on how religious communities ritualize texts. As we have seen, the Pentateuch commands and models its own ritualization. To the best of our knowledge, the story of Ezra's reading first imitated that model in all three textual dimensions, and began a scripturalizing trend that has continued ever since.

It is hard to say whether Ezra himself brought about this development. Our information about the Persian period in Judea is very limited. There are also many questions about the composition of the books of Ezra and Nehemiah. So we cannot say whether Ezra scripturalized the Torah or whether his story simply reflects prevailing practices at the time.

What is clear is that Ezra's actions exemplify what the Pentateuch itself commands and models in Moses' behavior. After Nehemiah 8's portrayal of Ezra in the fifth or fourth centuries BCE, ritualization of the Torah's three dimensions gradually grew more common in Second Temple Judaism. Then Ezra's story became a model of how to embody Moses' ideal for religious leaders of later millennia.

Jewish and Christian scripturalization, however, changed direction at least three other times in antiquity. Each time is associated with the actions of a particular individual. Like Ezra, we cannot know whether these people actually caused the changes or just exemplify developments around them. Associating stages of scripturalization with these individuals highlights how human choices have shaped the history of scripture.

Thus scripturalization was not just a gradual development. Biblical scripturalizing changed direction four ways at three different times in ancient history. Besides the time of Ezra in the fifth century BCE, it changed in the time of Judah Maccabee in the second century BCE and in the time of Rabbi Judah *ha-Nasi* and Bishop Irenaeus at the end of the second century CE. Each change in the scriptures was accompanied by changes in religious leadership. A New Testament writer already observed this connection:

*When there is a change in the priesthood, there is necessarily a change in the law as well.* (Heb. 7:12 NRSV)

## 15.2   UNDERSTANDING THE BIBLE AS A SCRIPTURE

The Bible known to us today changed several more times in subsequent history. It was shaped especially by the religious reformations and counter-reformations of the sixteenth century and by revolutions in printing

## Box 15.1  When Jewish and Christian scriptures changed

| | | |
|---|---|---|
| Torah/Pentateuch | Ezra | ca. 400 BCE |
| Prophets, histories, psalms | Judah Maccabee | ca. 150 BCE |
| Mishnah | Judah ha-Nasi | ca. 200 CE |
| Gospels | Irenaeus | ca. 200 CE |

technology in the fifteenth and nineteenth centuries. But the four ancient turning points in the times of Ezra, Judah Maccabee, Judah *ha-Nasi*, and Irenaeus established many of the enduring forms of Jewish and Christian scriptures and the practices that sustain them (see Box 15.1). For example, Christians ritualized the Gospels more than other New Testament books, just like Jews ritualize Torah more than the other books of the Tanak, until the printing revolution made pandect (one-volume) bibles the most common physical form of scripture. Then Christians increasingly focused iconic, expressive, and semantic ritualization on the whole scripture, which they reproduce and visualize now as one book.

The choices about scripture made in the times of Ezra, Judah Maccabee, Judah *ha-Nasi*, and Irenaeus could have been decided differently. We know this because other groups of people did make different choices. Most other religious groups in the Middle East and Mediterranean did not ritualize written texts in three dimensions as scripture. Those who did distinguished themselves in antiquity for resembling Jews and Christians. The prophet Mani in the second century CE scripturalized Manichean texts during his own lifetime. In the seventh century, the followers of the prophet Mohammed quickly ritualized the Qu'ran as Muslim scripture.

Within the traditions of Israel, the <u>Samaritans</u> did not expand their scripture beyond the Torah like the Hasmoneans did. They also maintained the religious authority of <u>Aaronide priests</u>, unlike Rabbinic Judaism and Christianity. Jews and Christians displaced the Aaronides with different lineages of leadership. The <u>rabbis</u> claimed an unbroken line of scholarly succession from teacher to student all the way back to Moses, while Christian <u>bishops</u> claimed an unbroken priestly succession through ordination back to Jesus. All three traditions retain the Pentateuch as scripture, but they use it differently. Comparing them shows clearly the connection between scripturalization and religious leadership, a connection first established by the Pentateuch's endorsement of Aaron's priesthood.[2]

As we have seen, Jewish, Samaritan, and Christian traditions ritualize their scriptures differently. In the <u>iconic dimension,</u> Christians ritualize the

Gospel codex or the entire Bible like Jews and Samaritans ritualize the Torah scroll: they display and process it prominently and they decorate or cover it distinctively so as to distinguish it from other books. Rabbinic rules for handling all scriptures demarcate other books of the Tanak that are not ritualized as much as the Torah. Now the unification of Jewish and Christian scriptures in a single codex, a Tanak or a Bible, demarcates all of its contents as sacred text. Nevertheless, the Jewish ritualization of Torah scrolls leads to different objects representing their respective religions in religious art and popular culture: tablets or a scroll symbolize Judaism while a codex stands for Christianity.

In the expressive dimension, Jews and Christians ritualize more of their scriptures but the Torah and the Gospels still get the most attention. They are read aloud more often and more sequentially than other scriptures. Congregational responses such as standing and blessings distinguish Torah or Gospel from other readings. Their contents appear more often in religious art.

It is, however, in ritualizing the semantic dimension of scriptures that the three religions differ the most. Aaronide high priests remain the religious leaders of Samaritan communities. Judah *ha-Nasi* and his rabbinic colleagues made the Mishnah and Talmuds authoritative for interpreting the Torah in most subsequent Jewish communities. The learned rabbi became the indispensable medium of scriptural tradition. Irenaeus and his Catholic colleagues established the New Testament as authoritative for Christian interpretation of the Hebrew Bible. The ordained bishop became the guarantor of correct doctrine and practice. Conflicts over religious leadership have challenged the primacy of priests, rabbis, and bishops and marked the history of all three religions. Now Jewish and Christian biblical scholars interact with each other and often present alternative interpretations to rabbinic and clerical teachings. But these developments have not undermined the Torah's priority in Judaism and the New Testament's precedence in Christianity.

Jewish Torah and Christian Gospels or New Testament overshadow the rest of their respective scriptures, though in ritualizing the semantic dimension of Jewish scripture, Mishnah and Talmud have traditionally overshadowed even the Torah. So despite the fact that the semantic contents of the Protestant Old Testament are the same as the Jewish Tanak, they function very differently.

The Pentateuch in particular has different roles in Jewish, Samaritan, and Christian traditions. It is venerated by Jews and Christians as part of their scriptures, and by Samaritans as their whole scripture. Yet how these traditions ritualize the Pentateuch's iconic dimension shows that their veneration is directed at very different *things*. A Samaritan Torah scroll in Samaritan script inside a three-part cylindrical case is not the same thing as a Jewish Torah scroll in Aramaic script wrapped in mantle and ornaments. Neither one resembles a Christian Bible much at all.

So how Jews, Samaritans, and Christians ritualize their scriptures in each of the three dimensions may lead us to wonder if these three religions really share a common scripture after all.

## Summary of Part 3, The Modern Bible

Religious communities distinguish books as scriptures by ritualizing them in all three dimensions (see Sections 1.1 and 1.2). Modern improvements in printing technology led to binding Jewish and Christian scriptures increasingly as one (pandect) codex volume. People then ritualized these one-volume bibles as scripture.

In ritualizing scripture's iconic dimension, bibles are usually distinguished from most other books by unusually thin pages, text set in two columns, and bindings or covers in distinctive materials or designs. Bibles get paraded and displayed in churches, carried by devout people, and used in oath ceremonies to claim religious and political legitimacy. Museums display relic texts whose ownership is often contested. Ten Commandments monuments make religious claims about law and politics.

In ritualizing scripture's expressive dimension, bibles get read in worship services and also devotionally by individuals and groups. Biblical verses infuse Jewish and Christian music. Illustrations and maps shape how people interpret the Bible in traditional ways, while biblical scripts for theatrical plays and Hollywood movies inspire both devotion and controversy.

In ritualizing scripture's semantic dimensions, the religious publishing industry markets vast numbers of study bibles, commentaries, and other interpretive aids, now also in the form of digital apps. The experience of ritualizing one-volume bibles as scripture have led people, especially Christians, to think of their scripture as a single book, and to interpret the Bible that way, too. The modern tendency to understand the Bible's plain or "literal" meaning as its religious meaning has made historical study of the Bible controversial and led to religious criticisms of some scientific theories. Conflicting claims of authority from biblical interpretation now divide Jewish and Christian denominations over religious doctrines and practices, and also over the Bible's significance for modern law, politics, gender roles, and race relations.

## CITED WORKS AND FURTHER READING

1 On the canonization of scripture, see Timothy H. Lim, *The Formation of the Jewish Canon* (New Haven, CT: Yale University Press, 2013); and Tomas Bokedal, *The Formation and Significance of the Christian Biblical Canon: A Study in Text, Ritual and Interpretation* (London: T. & T. Clark, 2014).

2 On comparing Jewish, Samaritan, and Christian scriptures, see James W. Watts, "The Pentateuch as 'Torah'," in *The Oxford Handbook of the Pentateuch* (ed. J. Baden; Oxford: Oxford University Press, 2021), 506–523. The power relationships mediated by scripturalization have recently become the basis for a broader program for analyzing and critiquing the "scripturalizing" of people and their identities: see Vincent L. Wimbush, *White Men's Magic: Scripturalization as Slavery* (Oxford: Oxford University Press, 2012); Vincent L. Wimbush, *Scripturalectics: The Management of Meaning* (Oxford: Oxford University Press, 2017).

# Index of Quotations and Citations of Biblical and Rabbinic Texts

(**bold-face** = quotations and Boxes, *italics* = Figures)

# Index of Authors

(**bold-face** = quotations and Boxes)

Allen, Horace T., 231
Alter, Robert, 227, 232
Anderson, Paul N., 250
Anderson, Robert T., 95, 271
Assmann, Jan, 297, 311

Bach, Alice, 249
Baden, Joel S., 271, 319
Barton, John, 95
Beal, Timothy K., 270–271, 286
Bell, Catherine, **3**, 14
Bellis, Alice Ogden, 312
Bielo, James S., 286, 312
Binns, John, 185
Bokedal, Tomas, 319
Brenner, Athalya, 129, 182
Britt, Brian, **284**, 286, **297**, 311
Brown, Michelle, 270, 285
Brown, Raymond E., 250
Brown, W. P., 182
Buber, Martin, 227, 232
Buc, Philippe, 14

Carr, David, **111**, 127, 128, 129,
    136, 182, 185
Champollion, Jean-François, **304**
Cherry, Conrad, 185
Childs, Brevard S., xv
Chrysostom, John, 96, 236, 255, 270

Claassens, L. Juliana, 250
Cohen, Mordechai Z., 312
Cohn, Yehudah B., 95
Collins, John J., 183
Cover, Robert, **28**, 58
Crawford, Timothy G., 59

Dalley, Stephanie, **82**, 96
Damrosch, David, 232
Day, John, 96, 186
Day, Peggy L., 249
deClaissé-Walford, Nancy L., 129
Dewey, Arthur J., 250
Douglas, Mary, 311
Dozeman, Thomas B., 130
Dunn, James D. G., 250
Dyer, Bryan R., 250

Eberhart, Christian, 249
Edwards, Katie, 286
Ehrensvärd, Martin, 186
Elazar, Daniel, 311
Ellingworth, Paul, 232
Epstein, Isidore, 311
Ezra, Daniel Stökl Ben, 249

Feldman, Louis H., 271
Feuer, Alan, 271
Flynn, William T., 232

# Index of Subjects

(**bold-face** = quotations and boxes, *italics* = figures)

Priestly Blessing, 49, 89–90, *90*, 97, 109, 123, 216–217
priestly families, 108
printing, 9, 12, *12*, *13*, 13, 79, *113*, 211, 255, 257, 261
  bibles, 12–13, 211–212, 231, 253, 256–261, 287, 207, 315–316, **318**
processions, 3–4, 6, 61–62, 76, 79, 209–210, *211*, 212
profit, 256, 257, 310
promised land, 33, 164, **166**, 167, **167–168**, 280
promises and threats, 48–51, 137–145
pronunciation, 6, 69, 78, **114**
prophecy, 148–149, 151–152
prophetic books and texts, xiii, 7, **10**, 39, 40, 58, **108**, 111, 118–120, 206, 284, **316**
  expressive dimension, **102**, 106, 109–111, 115–120, 217, 218, 278
  iconic dimension, **124**
  scripturalization, 145–152
  semantic dimension, 132, 135–137, 141, 142, 143, 145, 147, 148–149, 156, 158, 163, 175, 177
prophets, 7, 8, 18, 40, 46, 85, 92, 124, 135–136, 139, 147–148
  expressing the covenant, 118–120
  Jesus, 189–190, 216, 235–236, 293
  Mohammed, 155, 189, 297, 314, 316
  Moses, 34, 36, 46, 141, 172, 189, 297
  women, 240, 308
propitiatory idea, 236
prose, 115, 118, **134**
protagonist, 36, 44, 45
protection, 36, 69, 90, 142, 263
Protestant Reformation, 9, 13, 213, 216–217, 220, 225, 228, 268, 281, 295, 301

Protestants, 2, 9, 212–213, 215–216, 220–221, 225, 228, 268, 278, 280–281, 317
  canons, **10–11**
  history, 302–303
  laws, 295
psalms, 66, 109, 111, 115–117, 135–136, 143, 162–163, **164**, **316**
  Christianity, **216**, 216–218, 235, **248**
  scripturalization, 145, 147–151, 158
psalters, 140, 148, *150*, 150–151, **217**
pseudonymity, 244–245
Ptah-hotep, 30
Ptolemaic model, 65, 299
publication, 98
publishers, 5, 212, 227, 255–257, 259, 279–280, **318**
Puritans, **166**, 167, 280, 282
purity, 42, **157**, 168, 170, 191, 193, 283, 288, 289–290, 292, 294
  Sikh, 254
Pyramid Texts, **304**
pyramids at Gaza, 34

Q source, 240
Queen of Sheba, 167
Qumran, 65–66, 68, 106–107, 143, 149, 156, 163, **193**, 262, 289
quotations, 99
Qur'an, 22, *62*, 67, **82**, 99, **100**, 101, 189, 219, 254, 314, 316
Qur'anic verses, 67

Rabbinic Bible, *13*, 13, 258, *258*
Rabbinic courts, 290, 296
Rabbinic Judaism, xiii, 66–68, **100**, 108, 155, 158–161, 164, **193**, 289, 291, 316
  Pharisees, **158–159**, 159, 191, **192–193**, 247, 293

Made in the USA
Middletown, DE
24 January 2023